AF755096

INTRODUCTION TO DATA MINING

Dr. Bechoo Lal

Toronto Academic Press

INTRODUCTION TO DATA MINING

Dr. Bechoo Lal

Toronto Academic Press
4164 Lakeshore Road
Burlington ON L7L 1A4
Canada
www.tap-books.com

Email: orders@arclereducation.com

© 2025 Toronto Academic Press

ISBN: 978-1-77956-302-6

This book contains information obtained from highly regarded resources. Reprinted material sources are indicated and copyright remains with the original owners. Copyright for images and other graphics remains with the original owners as indicated. A Wide variety of references are listed. Reasonable efforts have been made to publish reliable data. Authors or Editors or Publishers are not responsible for the accuracy of the information in the published chapters or consequences of their use. The publisher assumes no responsibility for any damage or grievance to the persons or property arising out of the use of any materials, instructions, methods or thoughts in the book. The authors or editors and the publisher have attempted to trace the copyright holders of all material reproduced in this publication and apologize to copyright holders if permission has not been obtained. If any copyright holder has not been acknowledged, please write to us so we may rectify.

Notice: Registered trademark of products or corporate names are used only for explanation and identification without intent of infringement.

Toronto Academic Press publishes wide variety of books and eBooks. For more information about Toronto Academic Press and its products, visit our website at www.tap-books.com.

ABOUT THE AUTHOR

Bechoo Lal, PhD. became a Member (M) of IAENG: International Association of Engineers, USA with membership (108820) in 2010, a Senior Member (SM) in 2019. I am doctorate PhD in Computer Science, PhD- Information System from University of Mumbai, Master from Banaras Hindu University (BHU), PGP- Data Science from Purdue University, USA. Currently working as a Associate Professor in Department of Computer Science & Engineering, KLEF- KL University Vijayawada Campus Andhra Pradesh, India. His research areas are data science, big data analytics and Machine Learning.

Table of Contents

5 ALTERNATIVE TECHNIQUES 149

6 ASSOCIATION ANALYSIS: BASIC CONCEPTS AND ALGORITHMS 187

7 ASSOCIATION ANALYSIS: ADVANCED CONCEPTS 219

8 CLUSTER ANALYSIS: BASIC CONCEPTS AND ALGORITHMS 253

9 CLUSTER ANALYSIS: ADDITIONAL ISSUES AND ALGORITHMS 293

List of Figures

List of Tables

PREFACE

The rapid advancement of Information Technology has led to the creation of vast databases and enormous quantities of data across various fields. Research in databases and information technology has fostered new methods to store and manipulate this valuable data for decision-making purposes. One such method is data mining, which involves extracting useful information and patterns from large datasets. This process, also known as the knowledge discovery process, knowledge mining from data, knowledge extraction, or data/pattern analysis, is a logical procedure designed to sift through extensive amounts of data to uncover valuable insights.

The primary goal of data mining is to identify previously unknown patterns. Once these patterns are discovered, they can be utilized to make informed decisions that drive business development. For example, a credit card company might use data mining to gain insights into their members' purchasing habits. By analyzing the purchasing behavior of cardholders across different regions of the United States, the company can identify shopping trends among various demographics such as age, race, and location. This information can be instrumental in crafting targeted promotions for individual cardholders. Additionally, the analysis might reveal regional shopping patterns, which could benefit companies aiming to advertise or establish businesses in specific areas.

Online services like Google and Facebook extensively mine vast amounts of data to deliver targeted content and advertisements to their users. Google, for instance, analyzes search queries to identify popular searches in specific areas, which then influences the suggestions in the autocomplete list. Similarly, Facebook mines user activity data to uncover trending topics among different age groups, enabling them to provide targeted advertisements based on these insights.

While data mining is widely employed for marketing purposes, its applications extend far beyond this domain. Healthcare companies, for instance, use data mining to identify correlations between certain genes and diseases. Weather organizations mine data to discover patterns that can help predict future meteorological events. Traffic management authorities analyze automotive data to forecast future traffic conditions and develop appropriate plans for highways and streets. Retail stores can leverage data from shopping baskets at checkout to identify items frequently purchased together, which can inform promotional strategies and store displays. While some item pairings are intuitive, like bacon and eggs or cookies and milk, others might offer surprising and valuable insights.

Another common application of data mining is examining past customer behavior to rank customers based on their potential value. Banks, for example, may use this technique to predict whether a customer will respond to a campaign and assess their creditworthiness. Data mining can help companies across various industries identify their most valuable customers and streamline their operations, ultimately enhancing their overall efficiency and effectiveness.

This book is structured into 10 comprehensive chapters, each designed to guide readers through the various facets of data mining, from fundamental concepts to advanced techniques.

The opening Chapter 1 lays the groundwork for understanding data mining. It introduces the fundamental concepts and terminology, providing a historical context and explaining the importance of data mining in today's data-driven world. This chapter also covers the various stages of the data mining process and the broad range of applications in different industries.

Chapter 2 examines the nature and types of data that are commonly encountered in data mining. It explores different data formats, structures, and the importance of data quality. Topics such as data preprocessing, cleaning, and transformation are covered to prepare raw data for analysis. This chapter emphasizes the critical role of good quality data in producing accurate and meaningful mining results.

Chapter 3 focuses on techniques for exploring and visualizing data. It introduces methods for summarizing data, identifying patterns, and detecting anomalies. The use of statistical measures and graphical representations, such as histograms, scatter plots, and box plots, are discussed to help readers understand data distributions and relationships within datasets.

Chapter 4 introduces classification, one of the key tasks in data mining. It covers the basic concepts of classification, the construction and use of decision trees, and the process of model evaluation. The chapter explains how to train and test models, measure their performance using metrics such as accuracy, precision, recall, and the ROC curve, and the importance of cross-validation.

Building on the previous chapter, Chapter 5 explores alternative classification techniques beyond decision trees. It includes discussions on methods such as k-nearest neighbors, support vector machines, and neural networks. The chapter provides insights into the strengths and weaknesses of each technique, as well as practical advice on when and how to use them.

Chapter 6 introduces association analysis, which aims to find interesting relationships between variables in large datasets. It covers fundamental concepts such as support, confidence, and lift, and introduces algorithms like Apriori and FP-growth. These techniques are essential for tasks like market basket analysis, where the goal is to identify sets of items that frequently co-occur.

Chapter 7 presents the coverage of association analysis, exploring advanced concepts and techniques. It discusses issues such as handling large datasets, mining multilevel and multidimensional patterns, and discovering rare patterns. This chapter also covers the challenges of association analysis, including the evaluation and interpretation of discovered rules.

Cluster analysis, which groups similar data points into clusters, is introduced in Chapter 8. The chapter explains the basic concepts and objectives of clustering, along with common algorithms like k-means, hierarchical clustering, and DBSCAN. Practical applications and examples are provided to illustrate how clustering can be used to discover structure in data.

Building on the basics, Chapter 9 addresses more complex issues in cluster analysis. It explores topics such as cluster validation, the impact of different distance measures, and techniques for clustering high-dimensional data. The chapter also introduces advanced algorithms and approaches to improve clustering results.

The final Chapter 10 focuses on anomaly detection, the process of identifying unusual patterns that do not conform to expected behavior. It covers various techniques for detecting anomalies in different types of data, including statistical methods, proximity-based approaches, and machine learning algorithms. The chapter discusses practical applications of anomaly detection, such as fraud detection, network security, and fault detection in industrial systems. This book provides a thorough and practical guide to the field, equipping readers with the knowledge and tools needed to effectively mine and analyze data.

This book is particularly suitable for students, offering valuable insights for undergraduate and graduate students in computer science, information technology, data science, and related fields. The book serves as a comprehensive textbook for courses on data mining and knowledge discovery, covering fundamental concepts and advanced topics in the field.

Academics and researchers in data science, machine learning, and statistics will also find this book beneficial, as it presents detailed explanations and algorithms. It provides a solid foundation for conducting research and developing new data mining techniques.

Professionals working in data analysis, business intelligence, and data science roles will find practical insights and methodologies that they can directly apply to their projects. The book offers tools and techniques to extract meaningful patterns and insights from large datasets.

Furthermore, individuals in industries such as finance, healthcare, marketing, telecommunications, and e-commerce can leverage the knowledge gained from this book to solve real-world problems. The data mining techniques discussed can aid in decision-making, improving business processes, and gaining competitive advantages.

IT and software engineers involved in creating data-driven applications and systems will also benefit from understanding the principles and algorithms of data mining. This knowledge will help them design more effective and efficient systems for data processing and analysis.

The textbook includes various features to improve student comprehension. It outlines key topics with learning objectives at the start of each chapter, highlights important terms, and provides summary points at the end of chapters for quick review. Case studies, activities, and references are also included to enhance practical application and further exploration.

CHAPTER 1

Introduction to Data Mining

LEARNING OBJECTIVES

After studying this chapter, you will be able to:

- Give the overview of data mining
- Learn about data mining techniques
- List and discuss various data mining tools
- Narrate the key differences between the data mining and data warehousing
- Discuss various data mining applications
- Understand the problems in data mining

KEY TERMS FROM THIS CHAPTER

Association rules
Business intelligence
Data analytics
Data science
Deep learning
Neural network
Knowledge discovery in databases (KDD)
Big data
Cybersecurity
Data modeling
Data warehousing
Fraud detection
Predictive analytics
Risk management

INTRODUCTION

The process of "mining" or extracting knowledge from vast amounts of data is known as data mining. Knowledge mining is a fitting term for data mining. Numerous other terms, like Knowledge Mining from Databases, Knowledge Extraction, Data/Pattern Analysis, Data Archaeology, and Data Dredge, have somewhat different or similar meanings to data mining.

Applying clever techniques to extract patterns from data is a crucial process called data mining. Finding interesting information among the vast amounts of data kept in databases, data warehouses, or other information repositories is a process known as data mining.

1.1. OVERVIEW OF DATA MINING

The process of sifting through massive data sets to find relationships and patterns that can be used to solve business problems through data analysis is known as data mining. Businesses can forecast future trends and make more informed business decisions by utilizing data mining techniques and tools.

One of the fundamental subfields of data science, data mining employs sophisticated analytics methods to extract valuable insights from large data sets. More specifically, data mining is a phase in the data science methodology known as knowledge discovery in databases (KDD), which collects, processes, and analyzes data. Although KDD and data mining are sometimes used interchangeably, they are more frequently understood to be two different concepts.

Effective data collection, warehousing, and processing are prerequisites for the data mining process. Data mining can be used to identify bottlenecks and dependencies, describe a target data set, forecast outcomes, identify fraud or security problems, and learn more about a user base. Moreover, it can be carried out automatically or partially automatically.

Big data and data warehousing have grown in importance, making data mining more valuable today. To clean, process, and interpret data, data specialists who use data mining need to be proficient in statistical concepts as well as coding and programming languages.

1.1.1. Data Mining History and Origins

The late 1980s and early 1990s saw the emergence of data warehousing, business intelligence, and analytics technologies, which improved organizations' capacity to analyze the expanding volumes of data they were producing and gathering. When economist Michael Lovell coined the term "data mining" in 1983, it began to gain traction. In 1995, the First International Conference on Knowledge Discovery and Data Mining was held in Montreal, Canada.

The Association for the Advancement of Artificial Intelligence, which organized the conference every year for the following three years, provided sponsorship for the event. The ACM SIGKDD conference has been primarily organized by the Association for Computing Machinery's Special Interest Group for Knowledge Discovery and Data Mining since 1999.

Data Mining and Knowledge Discovery, a technical journal, released its inaugural issue in 1997. Peer-reviewed articles on data mining and knowledge discovery theories, techniques, and practices are published in this bimonthly publication. The American Journal of Data Mining and Knowledge Discovery, another peer-reviewed journal, was introduced in 2016.

1.1.2. Importance of Data Mining

A key element of an organization's successful analytics endeavor is data mining. Data scientists can use the information it produces for real-time analytics applications that look at streaming data as it is created or collected, as well as business intelligence (BI) and advanced analytics applications that analyze historical data.

A number of aspects of managing operations and developing business strategies are aided by effective data mining. This covers not only manufacturing, supply chain management (SCM), finance, and human resources (HR), but also customer-facing roles like marketing, advertising, sales, and customer support. Planning for cybersecurity, risk management, fraud detection, and many other crucial business use cases are all aided by data mining. It is also significant in other fields, such as government, science, mathematics, healthcare, and sports.

1.1.3. How Does Data Mining Works?

A tried-and-true method for directing your data mining efforts is the Cross-Industry Standard Process for Data Mining, or CRISP-DM. As a methodology, it comprises the tasks associated with each phase of a project, an explanation of the relationships between these tasks, and descriptions of the typical phases of a project. It offers a synopsis of the data mining life cycle as a process model.

The CRISP-DM model is adaptable and simple to modify. The six phases of the life cycle model are represented by arrows that show the most significant and common dependencies between them.

There is no set order for the phases. Actually, most projects alternate between phases as needed. Let's examine each stage of the CRISPDM in more detail, as depicted in Figure 1.1.

- **Business Understanding:** To get started, first ask these questions:
  - What is our objective?
  - What problem are we trying to solve?
  - What data do we need to solve it?

If the right data isn't understood clearly for mining, the project may result in mistakes, imprecise results, or results that don't address the right questions.

- **Data Understanding:** Proper data collection is required after determining the overall objective. The information must be pertinent to the topic at hand and is typically gathered from a range of sources, including customer surveys, sales records, and geolocation data. Making sure the data accurately includes all required data sets to address the objective is the aim of this phase.
- **Data Preparation:** Three steps make up the most time-consuming phase, called preparation, which is also known as extraction, transformation, and loading (ETL).

Data is first taken out of multiple sources and placed in a staging area. Subsequently, during the transformation phase, all of the data is assigned to tables, duplicate data is eliminated, null sets are filled in, and errors are fixed. The formatted data is loaded into the database for use in the last step, loading.

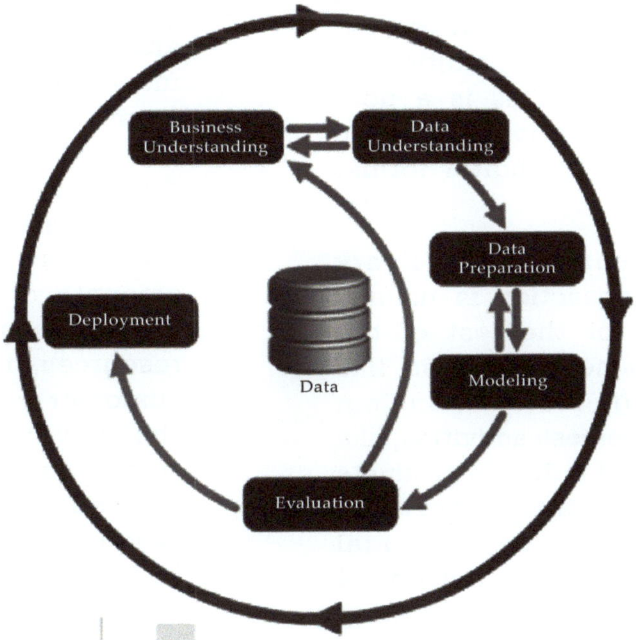

Figure 1.1. *Data mining life cycle.*

Source: https://egyankosh.ac.in/bitstream/123456789/89130/3/Unit-7.pdf.

- **Modeling:** When addressing the pertinent data set, data modeling takes into account the most effective statistical and mathematical strategy to address the objective question or questions. Numerous modeling techniques are available, including regression analysis, clustering, and classification. Additionally, applying various models to the same data in order to achieve particular goals is not unusual.
- **Evaluation:** It's time to assess the models' effectiveness in providing a response to the query that was identified during the business understanding phase after they have been constructed and tested. This is a human-driven phase where the project manager has to decide if the model's output adequately satisfies their goals. If not, alternative data can be prepared or a different model can be developed.
- **Deployment:** It's time to apply the data mining model after it has been determined to be accurate and successful in providing an answer to the objective question. A report with insights shared or a visual presentation can be used for deployment. It may also inspire action, like coming up with a fresh approach to sales or putting risk-reduction plans into place.

1.1.4. What Type of Data Are We Gathering

We've been gathering a wide range of information, from precise mathematical measures and text files to more sophisticated data including geographical data, multimedia channels, and web texts. This is a non-exhaustive list of information stored in databases and flat files in digital format (Nazib & Moh, 2021).

- **Business Transactions:** Every commercial transaction is usually "memorized" for the rest of the time. Inter-business activities, like swaps, buying, stocks, banking, etc., or intra-business activities, like administration of in-house products and resources, are examples of these transactions. Major departmental stores such as to retain millions of transactions every day, amounting to terabytes of data, owing to the extensive usage of bar codes (Novikov et al., 2019). Because the pricing of hard drives is constantly falling, storage capacity is not a big issue; however, the efficient usage of information in a realistic time frame for strategic decision making is the most critical challenge for firms struggling to survive in a fiercely competitive environment.
- **Scientific Data:** Our society is accumulating colossal amounts of scientific information that require to be analyzed, either in a Switzerland nuclear accelerator laboratory counting particles, in a Canadian woodland having studied measurements from a grizzly bear radio collar, on a South Pole ice field collecting data about oceanic activity, or in an American university probing human behavior. Regrettably, we may collect and store more fresh information quicker than we may evaluate the existing information.
- **Personal and Medical Data:** Large amounts of data on groups and individuals are collected regularly, from government censuses to customers and employees documents. Governments, businesses, and institutions like hospitals are collecting vast amounts of personal information to aid in the management of human resources, market research, and customer service. Irrespective of the private problems that this sort of data raises, it is collected, utilized, and even exchanged. When combined with the other information, this information may provide insight into customer behavior and other topics (Lacasse et al., 2012).
- **Observation of Images and Video:** Video cameras are more common because the price of video cameras continues to drop. Observation camera's videos and photos are frequently reprocessed, and the material is damaged as a result. Nowadays, although, there is a trend to retain and even digitize the recordings for future usage and study (Thurston, 2004).
- **Satellite Sensing:** Many satellites are circling the Earth, some of which are geostationary over an area and others are circling the Earth, however, all of which are constantly providing data to the surface. National Aeronautics and Space Administration (NASA), which is in charge of a huge number of satellites, receives

more data per second than all of the National Aeronautics and Space Administration engineers & researchers may handle. Several satellite images and information are available quickly as feasible with the aim of being analyzed by other scientists (Takaishi et al., 2014).

- **Games:** Our civilization accumulates a vast quantity of information and analytics about sports, athletes and players. All data is saved, including basketball passes, hockey scores, and car-racing gaps, as well as swimming timings, chess positions, and boxer's pushes. Such data is being used by journalists and commentators for coverage, although athletes and trainers will like to use it to enhance efficiency and gain a better understanding of their rivals (Mayer et al., 2014).
- **Digital Media:** One of the reasons for the growth of digital technology storage is the development of low-cost scanners, digital cameras, and portable cameras. Several radio stations, TV channels, and movie studios are also digitizing their sound and visual archives to effectively manage their multimedia resources. Organizations like the NBA & the NHL already have begun transferring their massive game records to digital formats (Webster & Ksiazek, 2012).
- **Software Engineering and Computer Assisted Design Data:** CAD (Computer Assisted Design) systems are used by designers to design buildings and engineers to design system circuits & components. Such systems generate a massive amount of information. Furthermore, software engineering generates a lot of comparable data, such as function libraries, objects, code, etc., that requires the use of maintenance and strong administration tools (Lethbridge et al., 2003).
- **Virtual Worlds:** The 3-D virtual locations are utilized for various uses. Specific languages, like VRML, are used to explain such areas and the things they include. Such virtual locations should ideally be specified in a way that allows them to exchange locations & objects. There are a lot of virtual reality items and location resources to choose from. Although the quantity of the archives continues to expand, administration of such sources, and also material search and retrieval from such collections, are ongoing research challenges.
- **Memoranda and Text Reports:** The majority of interactions inside and between corporations, research groups, and even private individuals are dependent on text documents and memoranda, which are frequently sent via electronic mail. Such communications are saved in digital format regularly for future usage and reference development in strong digital libraries.
- **The World Wide Web Repositories:** The files of various forms, descriptions, and content have been gathered and interlinked via hyperlinks as the World Wide Web's debut in 1993, making it the greatest storehouse of data ever constructed. Due to the wide range of topics encompassed and the limitless accomplishments of publishers and assets, the Www is a very essential collection of data routinely utilized for reference, notwithstanding its

vibrant and unorganized nature, non-homogenous characteristics, and frequent duplication and lack of consistency. Several people believe that the World Wide Web would eventually become a storehouse of human thought.

1.1.5. What Kind of Data Can Be Mined?

Data mining is, in theory, not limited to any one kind of media or data. It should be possible to use data mining on any type of information repository. Nevertheless, methods and algorithms may vary depending on the kind of data they are used with. The difficulties posed by various data kinds do, in fact, differ greatly. Databases such as relational, object-relational, and object-oriented databases, data warehouses, transactional databases, unstructured and semi-structured repositories like the World Wide Web, advanced databases like spatial, multimedia, time-series, and textual databases, and even flat files are all being studied and used with data mining. For more specific examples, see the following:

- **Flat Files:** The most popular data source for data mining algorithms is actually flat files, especially when it comes to research level data. Simple text or binary data files with a structure known only to the data mining algorithm to be used are called flat files. These files may contain transactional data, time-series data, measurements from science, etc.
- **Relational Databases:** In a nutshell, an entity relationship database is made up of a collection of tables that hold values from entity relationships or values from entity attributes. Tables consist of rows and columns, where rows are tuples and columns are attributes. In a relational database, a tuple is represented by a set of attribute values that together form a unique key and can be associated with an object or a relationship between objects. A fictional video store called Our Video Store is represented by the relations Customer, Items, and Borrow in Figure 1.2. These relations are only an example and represent a small portion of the potential database for the video store.

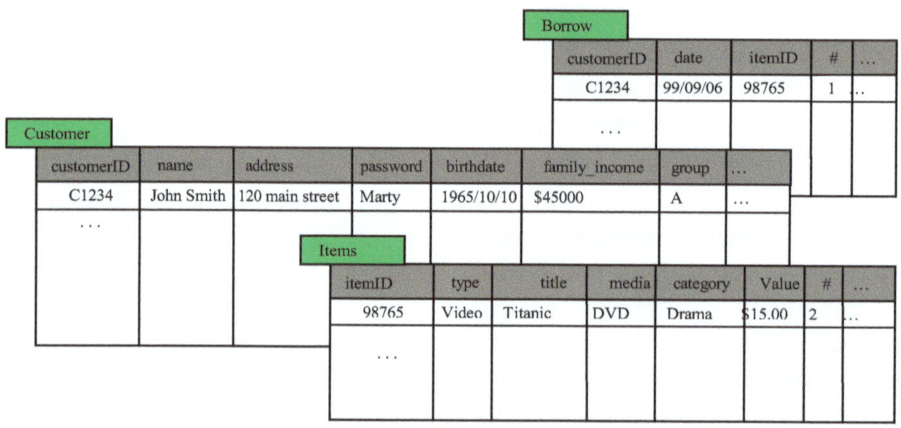

Figure 1.2. *Fragments of some relations from a relational database for OurVideoStore.*

Source: https://webdocs.cs.ualberta.ca/~zaiane/courses/cmput690/notes/Chapter1/ch1.pdf.

SQL is the most widely used query language for relational databases. It enables the computation of aggregate functions like average, sum, min, max, and count in addition to allowing for the retrieval and manipulation of the data contained in the tables. For instance, an SQL query to select the videos grouped by category would be:

SELECT count(*) FROM Items WHERE type=video GROUP BY category.

Because they can take advantage of the structure that relational databases have by default, data mining algorithms that use relational databases can be more flexible than those that are specifically designed for flat files. While SQL can help with data transformation, consolidation, and selection, data mining can do more, like comparison, prediction, and deviation detection.

- **Data Warehouses:** As a storehouse, a data warehouse is a collection of data gathered from various, frequently heterogeneous data sources that is meant to be utilized collectively under a single, common schema. The ability to analyze data from several sources under one roof is provided by a data warehouse. Assume for the moment that OurVideoStore opens up for franchising in North America. Several video stores under the ownership of OurVideoStore Company might have various databases and organizational setups. If a company executive needs to access data from all stores for marketing, future direction, strategic decision-making, etc., storing all the data in a single location with a uniform structure that enables interactive analysis would be more appropriate. Put differently, information from various sources would be combined, cleaned, and merged. Data warehouses are typically modeled by a multi-dimensional data structure to aid in decision-making and multi-dimensional views. An illustration of a three-dimensional subset of the data cube structure utilized in the Our Video Store data warehouse can be found in Figure 1.3.

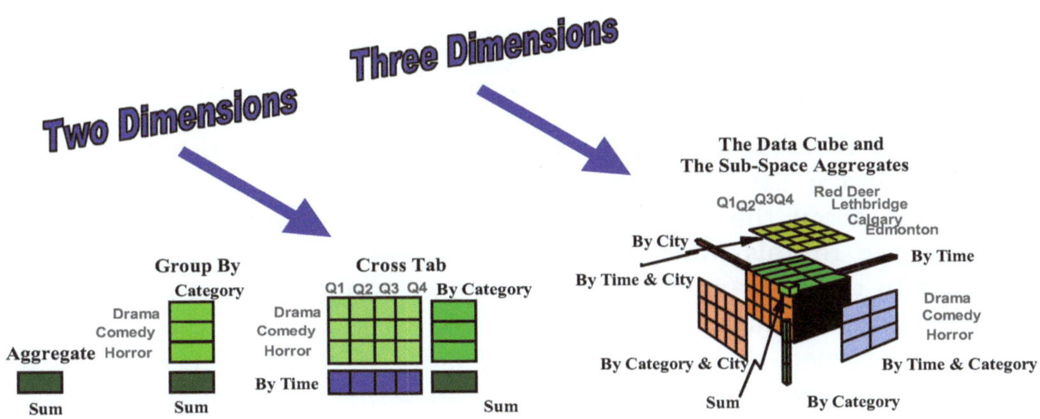

Figure 1.3. *A multi-dimensional data cube structure commonly used in data for data warehousing.*

Source: https://webdocs.cs.ualberta.ca/~zaiane/courses/cmput690/notes/Chapter1/ch1.pdf.

The Figure 1.3 displays summarized rentals categorized by film genres, followed by a cross-tabulation of summarized rentals by time (in quarters) and film genres. The category, time, and city summaries of the rentals are provided by the data cube. A cube has special cells that store summations along dimensions and cells that store values of some aggregate measures (rent counts in this case). A hierarchy of values for a single attribute can be found in each dimension of the data cube.

Due to their structure, pre-computed summarized data, and hierarchical attribute values of their dimensions, data cubes are a great fit for On-Line Analytical Processing (OLAP), which is a rapid interactive querying and analysis of data at various conceptual levels. Drill-down, roll-up, slice, dice, and other data navigation at various abstraction levels are made possible by OLAP operations. The drill-down (on the time dimension) and roll-up (on the location dimension) operations are shown in Figure 1.4.

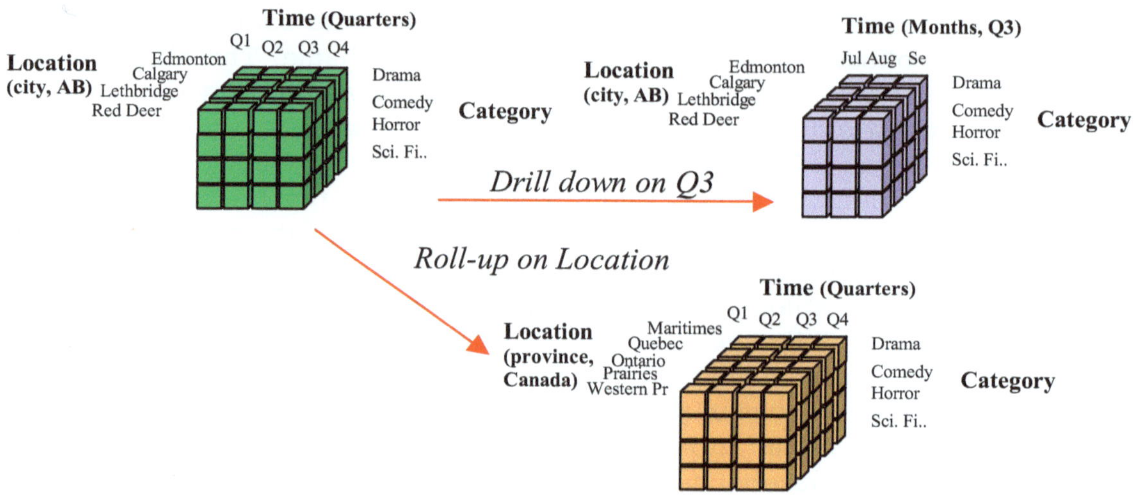

Figure 1.4. *Summarized data from OurVideoStore before and after drill-down and roll-up operations.*

Source: https://webdocs.cs.ualberta.ca/~zaiane/courses/cmput690/notes/Chapter1/ch1.pdf.

- **Transaction Databases:** A collection of records, each with a time stamp, an identifier, and a list of items, makes up a transaction database. Descriptive information about the items may also be attached to the transaction files. For instance, the rentals table, as seen in Figure 1.5, symbolizes the transaction database in the context of the video store. Every record is a rental agreement that includes the customer's ID, the date, and a list of the things that were rented (i.e., games, VCRs, video cassettes, etc.). Transactions are typically stored in flat files or two normalized transaction tables, one for the transaction and one for the transaction items, as relational databases do not support nested tables (i.e., a set as attribute value). The so-called market basket analysis, also known as association rules, is a common data mining analysis on such data that looks at associations between items that occur together or in sequence.

Rentals

transactionID	date	time	customerID	itemList
T12345	99/09/06	19:38	C1234	{I2, I6, I10, I45 …}
. . .				

Figure 1.5. *Fragment of a transaction database for the rentals at OurVideoStore.*

Source: https://webdocs.cs.ualberta.ca/~zaiane/courses/cmput690/notes/Chapter1/ch1.pdf.

- **Multimedia Databases:** Text, audio, image, and video media are all included in multimedia databases. They can be kept on a file system, in extended object-relational or object-oriented databases, or both. Due to the high dimensionality of multimedia, data mining is particularly difficult. Computer vision, computer graphics, image interpretation, and natural language processing techniques may be needed for data mining from multimedia repositories.
- **Spatial Databases:** Geographical data, such as maps and global or regional positioning, are stored in spatial databases in addition to regular data. Data mining algorithms face new challenges when dealing with such spatial databases (Figure 1.6).

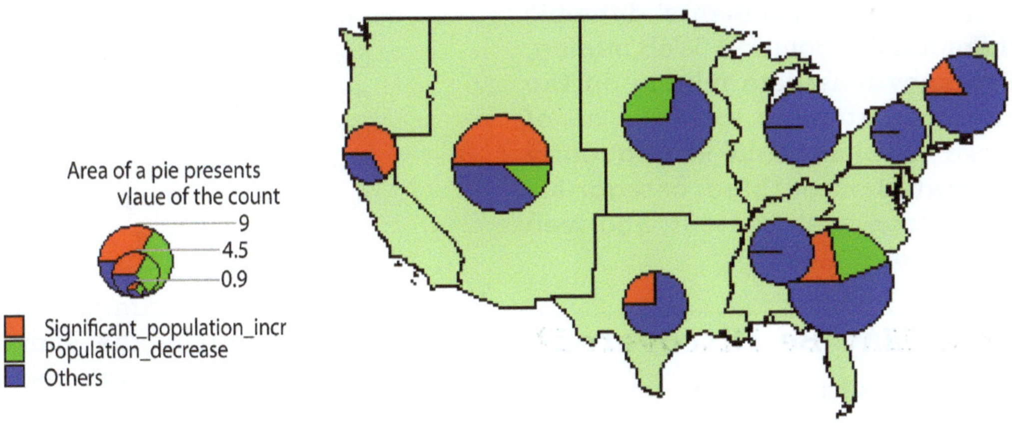

Figure 1.6. *Visualization of spatial OLAP.*

Source: https://webdocs.cs.ualberta.ca/~zaiane/courses/cmput690/notes/Chapter1/ch1.pdf.

- **Time-Series Databases:** Time-series databases hold information about events over time, such as stock market data or activity logs. These databases typically receive a steady stream of new data, which occasionally necessitates a difficult real-time analysis. In these kinds of databases, data mining typically entails forecasting future trends and movements of the variables as well as analyzing correlations and patterns between the evolutions of various variables.

- **World Wide Web:** The most dynamic and diverse repository that is currently accessible is the World Wide Web. Its growth and transformation are constantly aided by a huge number of writers and publishers, and a huge number of people use its resources on a daily basis. The World Wide Web organizes data into linked documents. Text, audio, video, raw data, and even applications can all be found in these documents. The World Wide Web can be conceptualized as having three main parts: the structure of the Web, which includes hyperlinks and relationships between documents; the content of the Web, which includes documents that are available; and the usage of the Web, which describes when and how resources are accessed. It is possible to include a fourth dimension that speaks to the documents' dynamic character or evolution. Web mining, also known as data mining on the Internet, attempts to tackle all of these problems and is frequently separated into three categories: web usage, web content, and web structure mining.

1.1.6. What May Be Discovered?

The types of trends that may be found are determined by the data mining activities performed. Generally, there have been 2 kinds of data mining techniques: predictive and descriptive. Predictive data mining jobs seek to make estimates depending upon judgment on existing data, whereas descriptive data mining activities explain the basic features of current data. The following is a quick overview of data mining capabilities and the types of information they investigate:

- **Categorization***:* Data categorization is the summary of fundamental characteristics of objects in a target class that results in feature rules. A database enquiry is used to obtain data related to a consumer-specified class, which is then processed via a summary module to retrieve the core of the data at multiple levels of analysis. Consumers that borrow more than 30 movies per year, for instance, can be described as OurVideoStore clients. The *attribute oriented induction* technique may be utilized to do the summary of data using idea hierarchy on the attributes explaining the target class (Lehmann et al., 2005). Basic On-Line Analytical Processing procedures meet the aim of data categorization with a data cube including the summary of data.
- **Discrimination:** Data discrimination is the association of generic characteristics of items among 2 classes known as the target class and the opposing class, resulting in discriminating criteria. For instance, one could wish to compare the basic features of consumers who leased over 30 movies in the previous year to those who leased below five. Data discrimination methods are essentially the same as data categorization methods, with the distinction that data discrimination findings contain comparable measurements (Ruggieri et al., 2010).
- **Association Analysis:** The identification of what are known as the rules of association is the goal of the analysis of association. It evaluates the frequency of items appearing together in transactional

databases and finds large items using a resource dependency. Another criterion utilized to localize association rules is a certainty, which is the conditional likelihood that an object will occur in a transaction when another object does. Market basket analysis frequently employs association analysis. For instance, knowing which films are frequently leased together or whether there is a correlation between renting a specific sort of film and purchasing snacks might be helpful information for the OurVideoStore management. P→Q [s,c], where Q and P are attributed value-pair conjunctions, s (used for support) is the probability that Q and P exist together in a transaction, and c (used for confidence) is the conditional probability that Q exists in a transaction if P is available. The hypothetic association rule, for instance (Tan et al., 2004):

Rent Type(X, "game") ∧ Age(X, "13–19") → Buys(X, "pop")[s=2%,c=55%] this means that 2 percent of the transactions examined are from consumers aged 13 to 19, who are leasing a game and purchasing snacks, and that certainty of 55% exists that young consumers who rent a game also purchase snacks.

- **Categorization:** The grouping of data into classes is referred to as categorization analysis. The categorization, also known as supervised categorization, employs supplied class labels to arrange the items in the collection of data. In most categorization techniques, all items are previously linked with predefined class labels in a training dataset. The categorization method develops a model by learning from the training dataset. Fresh items are classified using the model. For instance, after implementing payment terms, OurVideoStore management may examine client's responses concerning payment and classify clients who got rewards with one of 3 labels: "extremely risky," "dangerous," and "safe." The categorization study will result in a model that may be utilized in the future to approve or disapprove the requests for money.
- **Prediction:** Due to the possible consequences of effective forecasting in a commercial environment, the forecast has gotten a lot of attention. Forecasts may be of 2 kinds: first, may attempt to anticipate inaccessible data values or upcoming trends, or one may attempt to anticipate a class label for the certain dataset. The second is connected to categorization. The class label of an item may be predicted depending upon the attribute values of the item and the attribute values of the classes after a categorization model is created depending upon a training dataset. Forecasting is more commonly known as the forecasting of deficient numeric value or the decreased/increased patterns in a time-related dataset (Soni et al., 2011). The main concept is to evaluate a vast number of historical values to predict likely future values.
- **Clustering:** Clustering is the grouping of data into classes, comparable to categorization. In contrast to categorization, class labels are undefined in clustering,

and it is up to the clustering method to find appropriate classes. Since this categorization is not limited by supplied class labels, clustering is also known as *unsupervised categorization*. There are a variety of clustering techniques, all of which are dependent upon the idea of increasing intra-class resemblance and reducing resemblance among items of various classes (*inter-class resemblance*) (Bharara et al., 2018).

- **Outlier Analysis:** Data items that may not be classified into a single class or cluster are known as outliers. They're also referred to as surprises or outliers, and they're crucial to spot. Although outliers may be labeled noise in certain uses and disregarded, they may disclose crucial information in other areas, making them extremely relevant and its analysis is beneficial (Ilango et al., 2012).
- **Evolution and Deviation Analysis:** The examination of time-related information that varies through time is called evolution and deviation analysis. Evolution analysis is a type of data analysis that allows you to characterize, compare, categorize, or group time-related data. Deviation analysis looks at the discrepancies among predicted and measured values and tries to figure out what's causing the variances from the expected values.

Customers regularly lack a clear understanding of the types of trends they may or must find from the data available. As a result, having a dynamic and comprehensive data mining system that permits the finding of various types of knowledge at various levels of analysis is critical. Interactivity is thus a key feature of a data mining system (Chamatkar & Butey, 2014).

1.1.7. Is Everything You Discover Fascinating and Beneficial?

Data mining allows for the finding of previously unrecognized and possibly beneficial information. It is highly subjective to determine if the knowledge obtained is fresh, helpful, or entertaining, and it is dependent on the utilization and the client. Data mining has the capability of generating or discovering a huge amount of trends or rules. The number of regulations may be in the millions in certain situations. A meta-mining step may also be considered to analyze the larger data mining findings. To decrease the number of trends or rules identified with a high likelihood of being uninteresting, the patterns must be measured. This presents the issue of fullness. The client will like to learn all of the principles or trends, but only those that are important to them. The evaluation of how fascinating a finding is, known as interactiveness, may be dependent on measurable objective aspects like the patterns' validity when evaluated on fresh data with a high degree of certainty, or subjective descriptions like the patterns' novelty, utility, or understandability.

Patterns discovered may also be fascinating if they support or verify a theory that needs to be validated, or whether they suddenly challenge a well-held view. This raises the challenge of expressing what is interesting to find, like meta-rule guided discovery, which defines types of rules before the discovery phase, and interestingness modification languages, which interactively interrogate the results after the discovery stage for interesting trends. In most cases, user-defined criteria are used to determine how fascinating something is. The completeness of the patterns identified is defined by such criteria.

For the assessment of mined information and the knowledge discovery from data procedure as a whole, assessing and identifying the interestingness of rules and patterns identified, or still to be found, is critical. However, certain tangible metrics exist, determining the value of newly found information remains a major research challenge.

1.1.8. Classification of Data Mining Systems

Among the many classification criteria that can be used to group data mining systems are the following:

- **Classification According to the Type of Data Source Mined**: This classification divides data mining systems into groups based on the kinds of data they handle, including text, multimedia, spatial, time-series, and Web data.
- **Classification According to the Data Model Drawn on:** This classification divides data mining systems into groups according to the type of data model they use, including relational, object-oriented, data warehouse, transactional, and so forth.
- **Classification According to the King of Knowledge Discovered** Based on the types of knowledge found or data mining functionalities like characterization, discrimination, association, classification, clustering, etc., this classification divides data mining systems into different groups. Certain systems typically offer multiple data mining functionalities in one comprehensive package.
- **Classification According to Mining Techniques Used**: Different techniques are employed and provided by data mining systems. This classification divides data mining systems into groups based on the type of data analysis method applied, including genetic algorithms, machine learning, neural networks, statistics, visualization, database- or data warehouse-oriented, etc. The level of user interaction that occurs during the data mining process, such as in query-driven, interactive, or autonomous systems, can also be considered when classifying the systems. A comprehensive system would offer a wide range of data mining techniques to accommodate various options and circumstances, as well as provide varying levels of user interaction.

1.1.9. Benefits of Data Mining

In general, an organization's increased capacity to find hidden patterns, trends, correlations, and anomalies in data sets is what gives data mining its business benefits. They can combine traditional data analysis and predictive analytics with that information to enhance strategic planning and business decision-making.

Specific data mining benefits include the following:

- **More Effective Marketing and Sales:** By gaining a deeper understanding of consumer behavior and preferences through data mining, marketers are better able to develop targeted advertising and marketing campaigns. Similar to this, sales teams can increase lead conversion rates and close more business with current clients by utilizing data mining results.

- **Better Customer Service:** Data mining enables businesses to more quickly identify possible problems with customer service and provides contact center agents with the most recent information for use in customer calls and online chats.
- **Improved SCM:** Businesses are better equipped to identify market trends and project product demand, which helps them better manage their supply and product inventories. Additionally, supply chain managers can optimize distribution, warehousing, and other logistics operations by using information from data mining.
- **Increased Production Uptime:** By identifying possible issues before they arise, predictive maintenance applications can be supported by mining operational data from sensors on manufacturing machines and other industrial equipment, preventing unplanned downtime.
- **Stronger Risk Management:** Business executives and risk managers are better suited to evaluate and create plans for managing a company's financial, legal, cybersecurity, and other risks.
- **Lower Costs:** Data mining lowers waste and redundancy in corporate spending while increasing cost savings through operational efficiencies in business processes. In the end, data mining projects may result in increased earnings.

In the end, data mining projects can result in increased sales and earnings as well as competitive advantages that help businesses stand out from their competitors.

1.1.10. Industry Examples of Data Mining

Organizations in the following industries use data mining as part of their analytics applications:

- **Retail:** Online retailers use customer data and clickstream records to target specific customers with marketing campaigns, advertisements, and promotional offers. Along with inventory and supply chain management, recommendation engines that make recommendations to website visitors are also powered by data mining and predictive modeling.
- **Financial Services:** Data mining tools are used by banks and credit card companies to vet loan and credit applications, identify fraudulent transactions, and create financial risk models. Additionally, data mining is essential for marketing and locating chances for upselling to current clients.
- **Insurance:** Data mining is used by insurers for risk modeling, managing potential clients, and assistance with pricing insurance policies and determining whether to approve policy applications.
- **Manufacturing:** Manufacturers can use data mining to enhance supply chain performance, product safety, and production plant uptime and operational efficiency.
- **Entertainment:** Personalized recommendations are generated by

streaming services based on an analysis of the content that users are watching and listening to. People can also use data mining software to find out more information about it.

- **Healthcare:** Doctors can diagnose diseases, treat patients, and examine X-rays and other imaging results with the aid of data mining. Machine learning, data mining, and other analytics are also vital to medical research.
- **HR:** Typically, HR departments handle a lot of data. This contains information on salary, benefits, promotions, and retention. This data is compared through data mining to improve HR procedures.
- **Social Media:** Social media businesses collect a lot of information about users and their online activities through data mining. It is debatable whether or not this data is sold to outside parties or used for targeted advertising.

1.2. DATA MINING TECHNIQUES

Finding patterns in data and using those patterns to derive practical business insights are the main applications of data mining. Data miners employ a range of strategies to produce diverse outcomes in order to complete these tasks.

1.2.1. Types of Data Mining Techniques

Data mining can be done in a variety of ways for various data science applications. Anomaly detection, which aids in locating outlier values in data sets, and pattern recognition are frequent applications of data mining. The following categories of data mining techniques are popular:

- **Association Rule Mining:** Association rules are if-then statements used in data mining to determine the relationships between data elements. The relationships are evaluated using confidence and support criteria. Whereas confidence indicates the frequency with which an if-then statement is true, support quantifies how frequently the related elements occur in a data set.
- **Classification Analysis**: This method divides data points into classes or groups according to a particular issue that needs to be resolved. For example, to make the best possible decision when optimizing its coupon discount strategy for a particular product, a consumer packaged Goods Company may look at sales data, coupon redemption rates, inventory levels, and consumer behavior data.
- **Anomaly or Outlier Detection**: Data mining looks for unusual data within a set in addition to looking for patterns. The process of identifying data that deviates from the pattern is called anomaly detection. Retailers can discover instances of fraud and learn more about product sales spikes or declines by using this process.
- **Clustering Analysis**: By identifying patterns within a data set, clustering divides data points with similar characteristics into smaller groups. While clustering analysis groups data points similarly to classification analysis, it does so without assigning the data to pre-existing groups. When defining characteristics within a data set, such as customer segmentation based on purchase behavior, need state, life stage, or likely preferences in marketing communication, clustering can be helpful.
- **Regression Analysis**: Understanding which factors in a data set are crucial, which ones can be disregarded, and how these factors interact is the goal of regression analysis. Data miners can validate theories like "more bread and

milk will be sold before the storm when a lot of snow is predicted" with this technique. Although it might seem apparent, the store manager must confirm and measure a number of factors to ensure that there is adequate inventory on hand. Regression analysis can be used to recommend specific inventory levels of milk and bread (in units/cases) for specific levels of snow forecasted (inches), at specific points in time (days before the storm). For example, how much is "a lot" of snow? How much is "more milk and bread"? Which types of weather forecasts tend to cause consumer action and how many days before the storm will consumers start buying? Regression analysis is used in this way to optimize sales, reduce out-of-stock situations, and prevent overstocking, which leads to product spoilage following a storm.

- **Sequence and Path Analysis:** Additionally, patterns in which one set of events or values leads to another can be found by mining data.
- **Neural Networks:** A neural network is an algorithmic system that uses nodes to process data in a way that mimics the functioning of the human brain. Deep learning, a more sophisticated subset of machine learning, is used in complex pattern recognition applications where neural networks are especially helpful.
- **Decision Trees:** This procedure uses regression analysis or classification techniques to forecast or classify possible outcomes. The possible decision outcomes are represented by structures that resemble trees.
- **KNN:** Using this data mining technique, data is categorized according to how close it is to other data points. KNN is utilized to predict group features by making the assumption that data points close to one another are more similar than other data points.

1.3. DATA MINING TOOLS

Data mining techniques are derived from the application of domain knowledge from database systems, artificial intelligence, and statistical analysis to properly analyze data from various angles and viewpoints. Large data sets are collected, and data mining tools are used to turn the data into information that can be used to make decisions. Orange, SaS, Rattle, Rapidminer, DataMelt, Oracle BI, and other are some of the most widely used data mining tools.

1.3.1. Orange Data Mining

Orange is a suite of machine learning and data mining software developed at the bioinformatics laboratory at the faculty of computer and information science, Ljubljana University, Slovenia. It is a software that is built using Python-coded components and supports data visualization. Orange's constituent parts are referred to as "widgets." These widgets are used for predictive modeling and cover a wide range of tasks, including preprocessing, data visualization, and algorithm evaluation. Important functionalities like the following are provided by widgets.

- Displaying data table and allowing to select features
- Reading of data.
- Training predictors and comparison of learning algorithms
- Data element visualization, etc.

The widgets can be easily moved to any location at any time, and data arriving at Orange is formatted quickly to the desired pattern. Consumers find orange to be highly intriguing. Orange compares and analyzes data quickly, enabling its users to make more informed decisions more quickly. Python scripting or visual programming are two methods for carrying out data mining. Its drag-and-drop visual programming interface (connected with widgets) makes a lot of analyzes possible, and it typically supports a wide range of visual tools, including bar charts, scatterplots, trees, dendrograms, and heat maps. There are typically more than 100 supported widgets, which is a significant number.

The device is equipped with features for data analytics, machine learning components, and add-ons for text mining and bioinformatics. This serves as a Python library as well.

Orange includes a canvas interface that allows the user to arrange widgets and set up a workflow for data analysis. The widget suggests basic functions like reading data, displaying a data table, choosing features, training predictors, contrasting learning algorithms, and visualizing data elements, among other things. Orange includes algorithms for both classification and multiple regression.

Orange reads a variety of data formats in addition to native documents. Orange focuses on machine learning methods for supervised data mining and classification. Classifiers and learners are the two categories of objects used in classification. Students evaluate data that has been class-leveled and provide a classifier. Orange's regression techniques and Orange's classification techniques are highly similar in that they both need class-level data and are intended for supervised data mining. For precision gain, the learning of ensembles combines the predictions of individual models. The model may be derived from distinct training datasets or employ distinct learners on identical data sets.

1.3.2. SAS Data Mining

Statistical Analysis System is what SAS stands for. It is an SAS Institute product designed for data management and analytics. SAS is capable of managing data from multiple sources, altering it, mining it, and doing statistical analysis. Non-technical users can utilize its graphical user interface. With the use of SAS data mining, users can evaluate large amounts of data and produce precise insights for prompt decision-making. SAS boasts a highly scalable distributed memory processing architecture. It can be used for text mining, optimization, and data mining.

1.3.3. Rattle Data Mining

Popular R.-based graphical user interface (GUI) for data mining, Rattle shows statistical and visual summaries of data, transforms data to make it easily modelable, builds supervised and unsupervised machine learning models from the data, graphically displays model performance, and rates new datasets for production deployment. The software Rattle is open source and free. One important feature is that every action you take on the graphical user interface is recorded as an R script, which you can easily run in R without requiring the Rattle interface. Use it as a tool to hone your R skills and build your first models in Rattle, which can then be tuned in R, which offers much more robust options.

1.3.4. Rapid Miner

One of the most widely used programs for making predictions is called Rapid Miner. Java is the programming language used to write it. It provides an environment that is integrated for predictive analysis, deep learning, machine learning, and text mining.

Numerous uses for the instrument exist, such as business applications, commercial uses, research, teaching, training, application development, and machine learning.

The server is offered by Rapid Miner both locally and in private or public cloud infrastructure. Its foundation is a client/server architecture. Template-based frameworks that enable quick delivery with few errors (which are typically expected in the manual coding writing process) are included with a rapid miner.

1.3.5. Data Melt

A free tool for math, data analysis, visualization, and numeric computation is called Data Melt. With the power of hundreds of Java packages, this program gives you the simplicity of scripting languages like Python, Ruby, and Groovy.

Features

- Data Melt offers statistics, analysis of large data volumes, and scientific visualization.
- You can use it with different programming languages on different operating systems.
- It allows you to create high-quality vector-graphics images (EPS, SVG, PDF, etc.), which can be included in LaTeX and another text processor.
- Data Melt offers the usage of scripting languages, which are significantly faster than the standard Python implemented in C.

1.4. DATA MINING VS DATA WAREHOUSING

The process of gathering and organizing data from many sources to produce insightful business analysis is known as data warehousing. The combination of various components and technologies makes it possible to use data strategically. Large volumes of data are stored in data warehouses, which are intended for query and analysis purposes rather than transaction processing. It is the process of converting data into information so that users can examine it. However, data mining searches through enormous data sets for legitimate, hidden patterns that may be of use. Finding unexpected or previously unknown relationships in the data is the main goal of data mining. This multidisciplinary skill makes use of database technology, AI, statistics, and machine learning. Data mining can yield insights that are useful for a variety of purposes, including marketing, fraud detection, and scientific research (Table 1.1).

Table 1.1. Data Mining Vs. Data Warehouse

Data Mining	Data Warehouse
Data mining is the process of analyzing unknown patterns of data.	A data warehouse is database system which is designed for analytical instead of transactional work.
Data mining is a method of comparing large amounts of data to finding right patterns.	Data warehousing is a method of centralizing data from different sources into one common repository.
Data mining is usually done by business users with the assistance of engineers.	Data warehousing is a process which needs to occur before any data mining can take place.
Data mining is the considered as a process of extracting data from large data sets.	On the other hand, Data warehousing is the process of pooling all relevant data together.

One of the most important benefits of data mining techniques is the detection and identification of errors in the system.	One of the pros of Data Warehouse is its ability to update consistently. That's why it is ideal for the business owner who wants the best and latest features.
Data mining helps to create suggestive patterns of important factors. Like the buying habits of customers, products, sales. So that, companies can make the necessary adjustments in operation and production.	Data Warehouse adds an extra value to operational business systems like CRM systems when the warehouse is integrated.
The Data mining techniques are never 100% accurate and may cause serious consequences in certain conditions.	In the data warehouse, there is great chance that the data which was required for analysis by the organization may not be integrated into the warehouse. It can easily lead to loss of information.
The information gathered based on Data Mining by organizations can be misused against a group of people.	Data warehouses are created for a huge IT project. Therefore, it involves high maintenance system which can impact the revenue of medium to small-scale organizations.
After successful initial queries, users may ask more complicated queries which would increase the workload.	Data Warehouse is complicated to implement and maintain.
Organizations can benefit from this analytical tool by equipping pertinent and usable knowledge-based information.	Data warehouse stores a large amount of historical data which helps users to analyze different time periods and trends for making future predictions.

Organizations need to spend lots of their resources for training and Implementation purpose. Moreover, data mining tools work in different manners due to different algorithms employed in their design.	In Data warehouse, data is pooled from multiple sources. The data needs to be cleaned and transformed. This could be a challenge.
The data mining methods are cost-effective and efficient compares to other statistical data applications.	Data warehouse's responsibility is to simplify every type of business data. Most of the work that will be done on user's part is inputting the raw data.
Another critical benefit of data mining techniques is the identification of errors which can lead to losses. Generated data could be used to detect a drop-in sale.	Data warehouse allows users to access critical data from the number of sources in a single place. Therefore, it saves user's time of retrieving data from multiple sources.
Data mining helps to generate actionable strategies built on data insights.	Once you input any information into Data warehouse system, you will unlikely to lose track of this data again. You need to conduct a quick search, helps you to find the right statistic information.

Source: https://egyankosh.ac.in/bitstream/123456789/89130/3/Unit-7.pdf.

1.5. APPLICATIONS OF DATA MINING

These days, data mining is mostly employed by consumer-focused businesses, such as those in retail, finance, marketing, and communication. It allows these businesses to "drill down" into their transactional data to find out about pricing, customer preferences, and product positioning, as well as how these factors affect sales, customer satisfaction, and corporate profits. A retailer can use data mining to create products and promotions that target particular customer segments by using point-of-sale records of customer purchases. The following are a few uses for data mining.

1.5.1. Basket Analysis

Retailers use basket analysis, in its most basic form, to examine what customers purchase or place in their "baskets." This is an example of the association technique, which enables retailers to suggest additional products by providing them with information about consumer behavior. A less well-known use is in law enforcement, where enormous volumes of anonymous consumer data are analyzed in an effort to find product combinations that could be used to make bombs or produce methamphetamine.

1.5.2. Sales Forecasting

Businesses are allocating a larger portion of their budgets to predictive analysis techniques like sales forecasting. Businesses can use data mining to project sales and set targets by looking at historical data, including sales records, financial indicators (e.g., inflation markers, the consumer price index, etc.), spending patterns of customers, sales linked to particular seasons of the year, and trends that could affect widely held beliefs about the industry.

1.5.3. Bioinformatics

Given that bioinformatics is a data-rich field, data mining techniques seem to be a natural fit. Mining biological data facilitates the extraction of valuable information from the enormous datasets amassed in biology and other closely related life sciences fields like neuroscience and medicine. Gene discovery, protein function inference, disease diagnosis, prognosis, and treatment optimization, protein and gene interaction network reconstruction, data cleansing, and protein sub-cellular location prediction are a few bioinformatics applications of data mining.

1.5.4. Inventory Planning

Businesses can obtain current information about product inventory, delivery schedules, and production requirements through data mining. Additionally, data mining can assist in reducing some of the uncertainty associated with straightforward supply-and-demand problems in the supply chain. Businesses are able to manage their product stock more effectively and run more efficiently thanks to data mining's rapid ability to identify patterns and generate projections.

1.5.5. Customer Segmentation

While traditional market research might aid in customer segmentation, data mining enhances market effectiveness by delving deeper into the data. Data mining helps to group customers into specific segments and can customize needs based on the needs of the customers. The goal of the market is always to keep customers. Data mining makes it possible to identify a vulnerable customer segment so that a company can target them with offers that will increase customer satisfaction.

1.5.6. Customer Relationship Management

Customer relationship management is all about bringing in new business, keeping existing business, increasing customer loyalty, and putting customer-focused strategies into practice. In order to sustain a healthy customer relationship, a business must gather and evaluate data. Here's where data mining comes into play. The acquired data can be analyzed with the aid of data mining technologies. The solution seekers receive filtered results, saving them from being perplexed about where to concentrate in order to keep customers.

1.5.7. Healthcare

Predicting the number of patients in each category is possible with mining. In order to guarantee that patients receive the proper care at the appropriate time and location, procedures are developed. Healthcare insurance companies can identify fraud and abuse with the aid of data mining.

1.5.8. Education

The creation of techniques for extracting knowledge from data originating from educational environments is the focus of a recently-emerging field known as Educational Data Mining (EDM). EDM aims to advance scientific knowledge about learning, predict students' future learning behavior, and investigate the impact of educational support. An organization can use data mining to forecast student outcomes and make accurate decisions. The institution can concentrate on what to teach and how to teach it after seeing the results. The students' learning patterns can be recorded and utilized to create instructional strategies.

1.5.9. Intrusion Detection

An intrusion is any action that jeopardizes a resource's confidentiality and integrity. Information protection, avoiding programming errors, and user authentication are examples of defensive techniques to prevent an intrusion. By giving anomaly detection more attention, data mining can enhance intrusion detection. It facilitates the analyst's ability to differentiate an activity from regular, everyday network activity. Additionally, data mining aids in the extraction of more pertinent data for the issue.

1.5.10. Criminal Investigation

A process called criminology looks for traits that contribute to crime. Researching and identifying crimes as well as their connections to offenders are actually included in crime analysis. Applying data mining techniques to criminology is a suitable field due to the large volume of crime datasets and the intricate relationships among these types of data. Files for word processing can be created from text-based crime reports. To carry out the crime matching process, this data can be utilized.

1.5.11. Fraud Detection

While regularly occurring patterns in data can give teams insightful information, identifying anomalies in data can also be helpful in helping businesses identify fraudulent activity. Although banks and other financial institutions are well-known for using this technique, SaaS-based businesses have also begun implementing similar procedures to remove fictitious user accounts from their datasets.

1.5.12. Operational Optimization

Through the use of data mining techniques, process mining lowers costs associated with various operational functions, resulting in more efficient operations for organizations. Business executives' decision-making has improved and costly bottlenecks have been identified thanks to this practice.

1.6. PROBLEMS IN DATA MINING

Although data mining techniques have been around for a while, they have only recently been used as dependable and flexible tools that consistently outperform older statistical techniques. Even though data mining is still in its infancy, it is gaining popularity very quickly. Data mining has a few issues that need to be cleared up before it can be considered a reliable, established, and mature career. A few of these issues are covered in more detail below. It's important to remember that these issues aren't exclusive and aren't listed in any specific order (Yang & Wu, 2006).

1.6.1. Social and Security Challenges

Security must be taken into account in any data collection that is shared and intended to be used in making wise decisions. In addition, enormous amounts of private and sensitive data about individuals or organizations are obtained and retained when data is gathered for customer insights, client behavior analysis, merging personal data with other data, and other purposes. This information becomes controversial because parts of it are sensitive and there's a chance someone could access it without authorization. Additionally, data mining could unearth fresh information about individuals or groups, which could be illegal in terms of privacy, especially if the information is shared (Seifert, 2004). The appropriate use of data mining is another issue that arises from these worries. Owing to the enormous value of data, datasets covering a wide range of subjects are regularly sold. Additionally, because knowledge acquisition can provide a competitive advantage, some crucial data may be omitted while other data may be freely shared and used.

1.6.2. Problems with the User Interface

When data mining techniques yield interesting and, most importantly, client-comprehensible information, they can be useful. A strong visualization tool facilitates the analysis of data mining results and aids clients in better understanding their needs. For many data exploration and analysis tasks, the ability to view data in an appropriate visual manner is beneficial. Several visual concepts and recommendations are available for effective data graphical display (Alcalá-Fdez et al., 2009). Moreover, a great deal of work needs to be done to create suitable visualization tools for the massive database that could be used to display and alter mined data. The three main challenges in user interface design and visualization are screen real estate, data presentation, and data engagement. Interconnectivity between information and data mining results is crucial because it enables the client to focus and enhance mining operations as well as view the discovered knowledge from different conceptual angles.

1.6.3. Problems during Mining Methodology

These issues stem from the limitations of the data mining methods that are employed. Mining technique selections may be influenced by a number of factors, including the mining algorithms' adaptability, the range of data accessible, the dimensional domain, the wide analysis requirements (if defined), the assessment of the knowledge found, the manipulation of prior knowledge and metadata, the influence and management of information distortion, and other factors (Anand et al., 1998). For example, it's usually a good idea to have a variety of data mining techniques on hand because different methods can yield different results depending on the data. Furthermore, different strategies can suit and fulfill the client's needs in different ways.

Most methods work under the assumption that the data is noise-free. This is a bold assumption, to be sure. Exceptions, inaccurate or missing data, and other elements present in the majority of databases can complicate, if not completely obscure, the analysis process and, in certain cases, compromise the accuracy of the findings. Data preparation, including cleaning and modification, therefore gains significance. Even though data cleansing can be tedious and time-consuming, it is one of the most important steps in the knowledge discovery process and is often seen as a waste of time (Sinha, 2013). Both incomplete information and noise in the data must be handled by data mining techniques.

The size of the search area is even more crucial for data mining techniques than the size of the information. The size of the search area is often determined by the number of parameters in the domain space. The search area typically grows quickly as the number of parameters is increased. The dimensional problem is the name given to this. This issue has become one of the most urgent challenges to be solved because it negatively affects the effectiveness of different data mining techniques (Shahbaz et al., 2010).

1.6.4. Efficiency Problems

There are various artificial statistical and intelligence approaches available for information processing and explanation. However, many of these approaches were not originally designed to handle the massive data sets that data mining deals with today, where terabyte-sized data sets are common. This raises concerns about the sustainability and effectiveness of current data mining approaches for handling such large amounts of data. Data mining techniques with high complexity, such as exponentially or medium-order polynomial complexity, are not practical. Linear techniques are the most common method used. Sampling can be a useful alternative to mining the entire dataset, but it can present challenges such as specimen selection and completion issues. Parallel programming and progressive upgrading are performance-enhancing concepts that can help address the challenges posed by large datasets. Concurrent mining, where the database is segmented and findings are combined later, can help with handling large amounts of data. Progressive upgrading is also beneficial for incorporating new data without having to re-analyze the entire database.

1.6.5. Information Source Problems

Information resources present a number of challenges. Some are pragmatic, such as the diversity of data types, while others are philosophical, such as the problem of data glut. Because we already have more data than we could ever manage and because we are continuing to gather data even faster, researchers have an abundance of it. If the extensive use of dataset management setups has facilitated information gathering, then the advent of data mining is surely encouraging even more extensive data collection. The current strategy is to collect as much data as possible as soon as possible and analyze (or try to understand) it later. The questions are whether we will collect the right data in the right amounts, whether we will be able to identify what we're doing with it, and whether we will be able to distinguish between irrelevant and important data. Sustainable data resource concerns include the topic of heterogeneous datasets and the emphasis on various complex information types. Different types of data are kept in different repositories. It is impossible to predict how a data mining setup will work to get better mining results on all kinds of resources and information in an effective and efficient manner. For different kinds of information and resources, different strategies and methods may be required (Shin et al., 2000). While relational datasets and database systems receive most of the attention these days, new methods for handling other complex types of information still need to be developed. It might not be possible to use one data mining program for all kinds of information. Moreover, the development of heterogeneous data resources in terms of structure and semantics presents serious challenges to the dataset and data mining communities (Melli et al., 2006).

CASE STUDY

USAGE OF ASSOCIATION RULE MINING IN THE SYSTEMS OF RECOMMENDATION

Recommender systems gained immense popularity among various fields of the industry at the current time. Music, movies, books, search queries, research books, social tags, etc., are widely-known fields. These recommendation systems assist enterprises by combining ideas from intelligent systems, information retrieval, and machine learning to make assumptions regarding the customer's behavior. Recommender systems have two distinct approaches for their functioning;

- **Collaborative Filtering:** The method of collaborative filtering indulges in collecting and analyzing a huge chunk of information regarding the user's preferences, behavior, activities, etc., this will help them predict the like of a user in accordance with the other users. One of the approaches here is the usage of the Apriori algorithm.

Here you would know how the Apriori algorithm is used to squeeze out data concerning association rules from the user profiles. PVT is one of the prominent examples in this regard. PVT is one of those recommender systems that recommend various TV channels to the viewers, depending on their viewing experience. Channels with both positive and negative reviews work under the management of PVT. It treats TV viewers as transactions and the program ratings as itemsets.

One can use the Apriori algorithm to find out a set of rules and attached confidence levels between the programs. The confidence values resemble the similarity scores, and the system uses them to fill a program similarity matrix. There is an initiative to create a bridge between two TV shows. One who watches Splitsville or Roadies will not take an interest in shows like Kaun Banega Crorepati. However, if there is a line drawn between MTV Spitsvilla and Kaun Banega Crorepati, it will result in pattern watching.

CLASS ACTIVITY

Students identify and describe the features of some more open source/free data mining tools which were not discussed in this course content.

SUMMARY

- Data mining is the process of sorting through large data sets to identify patterns and relationships that can help solve business problems through data analysis. Data mining techniques and tools help enterprises to predict future trends and make more informed business decisions.
- Data mining techniques are derived that utilize the domain knowledge from statistical analysis, artificial intelligence, and database systems in order to analyze data in a proper manner in view of different dimensions and perspectives. Data mining tools discover patterns or trends from the collection of large sets of data and transforming data into useful information for making decisions. These are the most popular data mining tools are Orange, SaS, Rattle Data Mining, Rapidminer, DataMelt Data Mining, Oracle BI, etc.
- A data warehouse is a technique for collecting and managing data from varied sources to provide meaningful business insights. It is a blend of technologies and components which allows the strategic use of data. Data Warehouse is repository of a large amount of data, which is designed for query and analysis instead of transaction processing. It is a process of transforming data into information and making it available to users for analysis.
- Data Mining is primarily used today by companies with a strong consumer focus, in the areas like retail, financial, communication, and marketing organizations, to "drill down" into their transactional data and determine pricing, customer preferences and product positioning, impact on sales, customer satisfaction and corporate profits. With data mining, a retailer can use point-of-sale records of customer purchases to develop products and promotions to appeal to specific customer segments.
- Sales forecasting is a form of predictive analysis to which businesses are devoting more of their budgets. Data mining can help businesses project sales and set targets by examining historical data such as sales records, financial indicators (e.g., consumer price index, inflation markers etc.), consumer spending habits, sales attributed to a specific time of year, and trends which may impact standard assumptions about the business.
- Data Mining approaches seem ideally suited for Bioinformatics, since it is data-rich. Mining biological data helps to extract useful knowledge from massive datasets gathered in biology, and in other related life sciences areas such as medicine and neuroscience.

REVIEW QUESTIONS

1. What is data mining?
2. When was the first use of data mining?
3. Why is data mining important?

4. List the types of data mining techniques.
5. What is the difference between data mining and data warehousing?

REFERENCES

1. Alcalá-Fdez, J., Sanchez, L., Garcia, S., del Jesus, M. J., Ventura, S., Garrell, J. M., & Herrera, F. (2009). KEEL: A software tool to assess evolutionary algorithms for data mining problems. *Soft Computing, 13*(3), 307–318.
2. Anand, S. S., Patrick, A. R., Hughes, J. G., & Bell, D. A. (1998). A data mining methodology for cross-sales. *Knowledge-Based Systems, 10*(7), 449–461.
3. Bharara, S., Sabitha, S., & Bansal, A. (2018). Application of learning analytics using clustering data mining for students' disposition analysis. *Education and Information Technologies, 23*(2), 957–984.
4. Chamatkar, A. J., & Butey, P. K. (2014). Importance of data mining with different types of data applications and challenging areas. *Journal of Engineering Research and Applications, 4*(5), 38–41.
5. Ilango, V., Subramanian, R., & Vasudevan, V. (2012). A five-step procedure for outlier analysis in data mining. *European Journal of Scientific Research, 75*(3), 327–339.
6. Lacasse, M., Théorêt, J., Skalenda, P., & Lee, S. (2012). Challenging learning situations in medical education: Innovative and structured tools for assessment, educational diagnosis, and intervention. Part 1: History or data gathering. *Canadian Family Physician, 58*(4), 481–484.
7. Lehmann, T. M., Güld, M. O., Deselaers, T., Keysers, D., Schubert, H., Spitzer, K., & Wein, B. B. (2005). Automatic categorization of medical images for content-based retrieval and data mining. *Computerized Medical Imaging and Graphics, 29*(2–3), 143–155.
8. Lethbridge, T. C., Singer, J., & Forward, A. (2003). How software engineers use documentation: The state of the practice. *IEEE Software, 20*(6), 35–39.
9. Mayer, I., Bekebrede, G., Harteveld, C., Warmelink, H., Zhou, Q., Van Ruijven, T., & Wenzler, I. (2014). The research and evaluation of serious games: Toward a comprehensive methodology. *British Journal of Educational Technology, 45*(3), 502–527.
10. Mehenni, T., & Moussaoui, A. (2012). Data mining from multiple heterogeneous relational databases using decision tree classification. *Pattern Recognition Letters, 33*(13), 1768–1775.
11. Melli, G., Zaïane, O. R., & Kitts, B. (2006). Introduction to the special issue on successful real-world data mining applications. *ACM SIGKDD Explorations Newsletter, 8*(1), 1–2.
12. Nazib, R. A., & Moh, S. (2021). Sink-type-dependent data-gathering frameworks in wireless sensor networks: A comparative study. *Sensors, 21*(8), 2829.
13. Novikov, S., Kazakov, O., Kulagina, N., & Ivanov, M. (2019). Organization of data gathering and preparing on the basis of blockchain for the supporting system

of making decisions in the sphere of developing human capital of region. In *IOP Conference Series: Materials Science and Engineering, 497*(1), 012046.

14. Romero, C., & Ventura, S. (2013). Data mining in education. *Wiley Interdisciplinary Reviews: Data Mining and Knowledge Discovery, 3*(1), 12–27.
15. Ruggieri, S., Pedreschi, D., & Turini, F. (2010). Data mining for discrimination discovery. *ACM Transactions on Knowledge Discovery from Data (TKDD), 4*(2), 1–40.
16. Seifert, J. W. (2004). Data mining and the search for security: Challenges for connecting the dots and databases. *Government Information Quarterly, 21*(4), 461–480.
17. Shahbaz, M., Masood, S. A., Shaheen, M., & Khan, A. (2010). Data mining methodology in perspective of manufacturing databases. *Journal of American Science, 6*(11), 999–1012.
18. Shin, C. K., Yun, U. T., Kim, H. K., & Park, S. C. (2000). A hybrid approach of neural network and memory-based learning to data mining. *IEEE Transactions on Neural Networks, 11*(3), 637–646.
19. Sinha, P. (2013). Multivariate polynomial regression in data mining: Methodology, problems and solutions. *International Journal of Scientific and Engineering Research, 4*(12), 962–965.
20. Soni, J., Ansari, U., Sharma, D., & Soni, S. (2011). Predictive data mining for medical diagnosis: An overview of heart disease prediction. *International Journal of Computer Applications, 17*(8), 43–48.
21. Takaishi, D., Nishiyama, H., Kato, N., & Miura, R. (2014). Toward energy efficient big data gathering in densely distributed sensor networks. *IEEE Transactions on Emerging Topics in Computing, 2*(3), 388–397.
22. Tan, P. N., Kumar, V., & Srivastava, J. (2004). Selecting the right objective measure for association analysis. *Information Systems, 29*(4), 293–313.
23. Thurston, A. (2004). Promoting multicultural education in the primary classroom: Broadband videoconferencing facilities and digital video. *Computers & Education, 43*(1–2), 165–177.
24. Webster, J. G., & Ksiazek, T. B. (2012). The dynamics of audience fragmentation: Public attention in an age of digital media. *Journal of Communication, 62*(1), 39–56.
25. Witten, I. H., & Frank, E. (2002). Data mining: Practical machine learning tools and techniques with Java implementations. *ACM SIGMOD Record, 31*(1), 76–77.
26. Yang, Q., & Wu, X. (2006). 10 challenging problems in data mining research. *International Journal of Information Technology & Decision Making, 5*(04), 597–604.
27. Zaiane, O. R., Han, J., Li, Z. N., Chee, S. H., & Chiang, J. Y. (1998). Multimediaminer: A system prototype for multimedia data mining. *ACM SIGMOD Record, 27*(2), 581–583.

CHAPTER 2

Data

LEARNING OBJECTIVES

After studying this chapter, you will be able to:

- Explain the types of data
- Define the data quality
- Focus on data preprocessing

KEY TERMS FROM THIS CHAPTER

Asymmetric attributes
Data
Data Discretization
Data Normalization
Data set
Duplicate Data
Identification number (ID)
Record Data
Attribute
Data Cleaning
Data Integration
Data Reduction
Data Transformation
Grade point average (GPA)
Precision
Sequence data

INTRODUCTION

Transformed information into a format that is useful for processing or transportation is called data. Data is information that has been transformed into binary digital form for use with modern computers and transmission media. Data can be used as a single subject or as many subjects at once. Data in its most basic digital format is referred to as "raw data."

A collection of discrete or continuous values that describe quantity, quality, fact, statistics, and other fundamental units of meaning, or just a series of symbols that can be further formally interpreted, is commonly referred to as data. A single value in a set of data is called a datum. Typically, data is arranged into structures like tables, which can both be used as data in larger structures and offer extra context and meaning. Within a computational process, data can be utilized as variables. Concrete measurements or abstract concepts can be represented by data. Economics, science, and almost every other aspect of human organizational activity all make extensive use of data. Price indices (like the consumer price index), unemployment, literacy, and census data are a few examples of data sets. Here, "data" refers to the unprocessed facts and numbers that can be used to derive meaningful information.

Data is collected using techniques such as measurement, observation, query, or analysis, and is typically represented as numbers or characters which may be further processed. Field data is data that is collected in an uncontrolled in-situ environment. Experimental data is data that is generated in the course of a controlled scientific experiment. Data is analyzed using techniques such as calculation, reasoning, discussion, presentation, visualization, or other forms of post-analysis. Prior to analysis, raw data (or unprocessed data) is typically cleaned: Outliers are removed and obvious instrument or data entry errors are corrected.

The smallest units of factual information that can serve as a foundation for computation, reasoning, or discussion are called data. Abstract concepts and tangible measurements, such as statistics, are also examples of data. Data that is thematically related and presented in a pertinent context can be considered information. Then, contextually related information can be referred to as intelligence or data insights. Knowledge is then defined as the store of wisdom and intelligence that develops over time as a result of the synthesis of data into information. Data has been called the digital economy's new oil. In general, the term "data" refers to the fact that some knowledge or information already in existence is represented or coded in a way that makes it easier to use or process. Thanks to developments in computer technology, big data has emerged. Big data is a term used to describe extremely large amounts of data, typically measured in petabytes. Working with such massive (and expanding) datasets is challenging, if not impossible, to do with conventional data analysis techniques and computing. As a result, the relatively new discipline of data science makes use of machine learning and other forms of artificial intelligence (AI) to enable effective applications of analytical techniques to large data sets.

2.1. TYPES OF DATA

A grouping of data objects is frequently used to describe a data set. A data object can also be referred to as an entity, record, point, vector, pattern, event, case, sample, or observation. Conversely, a variety of attributes that capture an object's fundamental qualities, like an object's mass or the time of an event, are used to characterize data objects. A variable, characteristic, field, feature, or dimension are other terms for an attribute.

Example: (Student Information). A data set is frequently a file with records (or rows) as the objects and fields (or columns) as the corresponding attributes for each field. For instance, a data set containing student information is displayed in Table 2.1. A student is represented by each row, and an attribute—such as a grade point average (GPA) or identification number (ID)—defines each column.

Table 2.1. A Sample Data Set Containing Student Information

Student ID	Year	Grade Point Average (GPA)	...
	⋮		
1034262	Senior	3.24	...
1052663	Sophomore	3.51	...
1082246	Freshman	3.62	...
	⋮		

Source: https://www.ceom.ou.edu/media/docs/upload/Pang-Ning_Tan_Michael_Steinbach_Vipin_Kumar_-_Introduction_to_Data_Mining-Pe_NRDK4fi.pdf.

Although record-based data sets are common, either in flat files or relational database systems, there are other important types of data sets and systems for storing data. The types of data sets that are commonly encountered in data mining. However, we first consider attributes.

2.1.1. Attributes and Measurement

A property or characteristic of an object that can change over time or between objects is called an attribute. For instance, an object's temperature changes over time, but an individual's eye color varies. Keep in mind that there are only a few possible values for eye color—brown, black, blue, green, hazel, etc.,—making it a symbolic attribute. }, whereas temperature can have an infinite number of values as it is a numerical attribute.

At the most basic level, attributes are not about numbers or symbols. However, to discuss and more precisely analyze the characteristics of objects, we assign numbers or symbols to them. To do this in a well-defined way, we need a measurement scale.

A measurement scale is a rule (function) that relates an attribute of an object to a symbolic or numerical value. In formal terms, measurement is the process of applying a measurement scale to assign a value to a specific attribute of an object. Even though this might sound a little abstract, we constantly measure things. For example, we weigh ourselves on a bathroom scale, categorize people as male or female, or count the number of chairs in a room to make sure there are enough for everyone attending a meeting. The "physical value" of an object's attribute is mapped to a numerical or symbolic value in each of these instances.

2.1.1.1. The Type of an Attribute

The previous discussion should have made clear that an attribute's properties do not always have to match the properties of the values that are used to measure it. Put differently, attributes can have values that represent them that are not also properties of the attributes themselves, and vice versa. Two examples are provided to demonstrate this.

- **Example: (Employee Age and ID Number):** ID and age (in years) are two attributes that may be linked to an employee. It is possible to express these two qualities as integers. It is reasonable to discuss an employee's average age, but it is absurd to discuss an employee's average ID. Indeed, the uniqueness of each employee is the only quality we wish to record with the ID attribute. As a result, the only thing that can be done with employee IDs is to see if they are equal. However, when the employee ID attribute is represented by integers, there is no indication of this limitation. When it comes to the age attribute, the characteristics of the integers that are used to represent age closely mirror those of the attribute itself. Nevertheless, the correspondence is incomplete because integers do not have a maximum, whereas ages do.
- **Example: (Length of Line Segments):** Take a look at Figure 2.1, which displays some objects—line segments—and illustrates the two possible mappings of these objects' length attribute to numbers. From top to bottom, each line segment is formed by appending the line segment at the top to itself. As a result, the top line segment is appended to itself twice to form the second line segment from the top, three times to form the third line segment from the top, and so on. Every line segment is a physical multiple of the first in a very real sense. The measurements on the right side of the figure accurately reflect this fact, while the measurements on the left side do not. More precisely, the scale on the right captures both the ordering and additivity properties of the length attribute, whereas the scale on the left only records the ordering of the attribute. As a result, it is possible to measure an attribute without fully capturing all of its properties.

An attribute's type should indicate which of its characteristics are represented in the values that are used to measure it. Understanding an attribute's type is crucial because it helps us avoid making dumb decisions, like calculating the average employee ID, by indicating which properties of the measured values are consistent with the attribute's underlying properties. Keep in mind that the term "type of an attribute" often refers to the type of measurement scale.

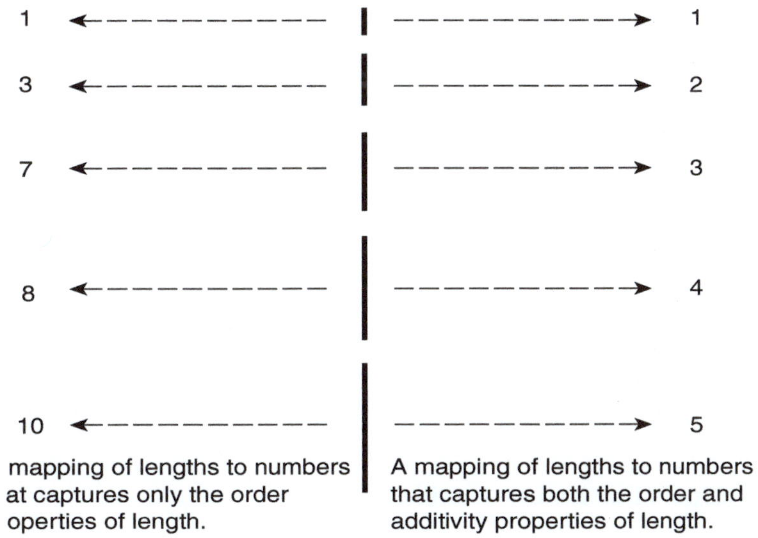

Figure 2.1. *The measurement of the length of line segments on two different scales of measurement.*

Source: https://www.ceom.ou.edu/media/docs/upload/Pang-Ning_Tan_Michael_Steinbach_Vipin_Kumar_-_Introduction_to_Data_Mining-Pe_NRDK4fi.pdf.

2.1.1.2. The Different Types of Attributes

Determine the characteristics of numbers that match the underlying properties of the attribute to provide a helpful (and straightforward) method of defining its type. Consider the numerous characteristics of numbers in an attribute like length. Speaking of length ratios and differences, as well as comparing and ordering objects based on their length, makes sense. Attributes are commonly described by the following operations or properties of numbers.

1. Distinctness = and =
2. Order <, ≤, >, and ≥
3. Addition + and −
4. Multiplication ∗ and /

We can categorize attributes into four categories based on these characteristics: nominal, ordinal, interval, and ratio. Every attribute type has all of the attributes and functions of the attribute types that come before it. As a result, any operation or property that holds true for interval, nominal, or ordinal attributes also holds true for ratio attributes. Stated differently, the attribute types are defined in a cumulative manner. This does not imply, however, that operations suitable for one attribute type are also suitable for attribute types above it.

Qualitative or category attributes are the combined terms for nominal and ordinal attributes. Qualitative attributes, like employee ID, don't have most of the characteristics of numerical data, as the name implies. It is better to treat them more like symbols even though they are represented by numbers, or integers. The terms "quantitative" or "numerical" refer to the two remaining categories of attributes: interval and ratio. Numbers are used to represent quantitative attributes, which share most of their characteristics. Be aware that continuous or integer-valued quantitative attributes are possible. The different attribute types can also be explained in terms of transformations that preserve the meaning of the original attribute. A length attribute, for instance, retains its meaning even if it is measured in meters as opposed to feet. For a given kind of attribute, the statistical operations that make sense are those that, when applied to the attribute, produce the same outcomes while maintaining the attribute's meaning. As an example, the average length of a collection of objects is different when expressed in meters as opposed to feet, even though the length is represented by both averages (Table 2.2).

Table 2.2. Transformations That Define Attribute Levels

Attribute Type		Description	Examples	Operations
Categorical (Qualitative)	Nominal	The values of a nominal attribute are just different names; i.e., nominal values provide only enough information to distinguish one object from another. ($=, \neq$)	zip codes, employee ID numbers, eye color, gender	mode, entropy, contingency correlation, χ^2 test
	Ordinal	The values of an ordinal attribute provide enough information to order objects. ($<, >$)	hardness of minerals, {*good, better, best*}, grades, street numbers	median, percentiles, rank correlation, run tests, sign tests
Numeric (Quantitative)	Interval	For interval attributes, the differences between values are meaningful, i.e., a unit of measurement exists. ($+, -$)	calendar dates, temperature in Celsius or Fahrenheit	mean, standard deviation, Pearson's correlation, t and F tests
	Ratio	For ratio variables, both differences and ratios are meaningful. (*, /)	temperature in Kelvin, monetary quantities, counts, age, mass, length, electrical current	geometric mean, harmonic mean, percent variation

Source: https://www.ceom.ou.edu/media/docs/upload/Pang-Ning_Tan_Michael_Steinbach_Vipin_Kumar_-_Introduction_to_Data_Mining-Pe_NRDK4fi.pdf.

- **Example: (Temperature Scales):** A good example of some of the ideas that have been discussed is temperature. First, depending on its measurement scale, temperature can be either an interval or a ratio attribute. Physically speaking, a temperature of 2° is twice that of a temperature of 1° when measured on the Kelvin scale. This is untrue whether using the Celsius or Fahrenheit scales to measure temperature because there isn't much of a physical difference between a 1° and a 2° Fahrenheit (Celsius). The issue is that the zero points on the Celsius and Fahrenheit scales are arbitrary in the physical sense, which means that the ratio of two temperatures in either Celsius or Fahrenheit has no physical significance.

2.1.1.3. Describing Attributes by the Number of Values

An independent way of distinguishing between attributes is by the number of values they can take.

- **Discrete:** There is a countably infinite or finite set of values for a discrete attribute. These characteristics can be numerical, like counts, or categorical, like zip codes or ID numbers. Integer variables are frequently used to represent discrete attributes. As a specific instance of discrete attributes, binary attributes only accept two values, for example.; 0/1, male/female, true/false, or yes/no. Boolean variables, or integer variables that can only take the values 0 or 1, are frequently used to represent binary attributes.
- **Continuous:** An attribute that takes real numbers as values is said to be continuous. Features like weight, height, and temperature are a few examples. Floating-point variables are commonly used to represent continuous attributes. Real values can only be accurately measured and represented in practice to a limited extent.

Theoretically, binary, discrete, and continuous attribute values could be combined with any of the measurement scale types—nominal, ordinal, interval, and ratio. That being said, some combinations are very uncommon or illogical. For example, a realistic data set containing a continuous binary attribute is hard to come up with. While interval and ratio attributes are typically continuous, nominal and ordinal attributes are typically binary or discrete. On the other hand, ratio attributes are also count attributes, which are discrete.

2.1.1.4. Asymmetric Attributes

Only presence—a non-zero attribute value—is considered significant for asymmetric attributes. Imagine a data set in which every object is a student and every attribute indicates whether or not the student completed a specific university course. An attribute for a particular student has a value of 1 if the student completed the course linked to that attribute, and 0 otherwise. Since only a small portion of all courses are taken by students, the majority of the values in such a data set would be 0. Therefore, concentrating on the non-zero values is more effective and meaningful. For example, most students would appear to be very similar if they were compared based only on the courses they do not take, especially if there are a lot of them. Asymmetric binary attributes are those in which only non-zero values are significant. This kind of attribute holds special significance in the context of association analysis. Moreover, asymmetric features can be continuous or discrete. For example, the resulting data set will have asymmetric discrete or continuous attributes if the number of credits associated with each course is recorded.

2.1.2. Types of Data Sets

There are many different kinds of data sets, and more and more of them are becoming available for analysis as data mining as a field grows and matures. Here, we go over a few of the most prevalent kinds. To make things easier, we have divided the different kinds of data sets into three categories: ordered data, graph-based data, and record data. Other groupings are undoubtedly possible, and these categories do not encompass all possibilities.

2.1.2.1. General Characteristics of Data Sets

Prior to going into specifics about different types of data sets, we talk about three properties: dimensionality, sparsity, and resolution, which are relevant to a wide range of data sets and greatly influence the data mining methods that are employed.

- **Dimensionality:** The number of attributes that the objects in a data set have is known as the data set's dimensionality. Small-dimensional data typically differs from moderate- or high-dimensional data in terms of quality. In fact, the term "curse of dimensionality" is occasionally used to describe the challenges involved in interpreting high-dimensional data. This is why dimensionality reduction is a key driver of preprocessing the data.
- **Sparsity:** In certain data sets—like those with asymmetric features—the majority of an object's attributes have values of 0; frequently, less than 1% of the entries have values that are not zero. Sparsity is advantageous in practice because it typically only requires the non-zero values to be stored and manipulated. This leads to considerable savings in terms of storage and computation time. Additionally, only sparse data can effectively utilize certain data mining algorithms.
- **Resolution:** Data can frequently be obtained at various resolutions, and the characteristics of the data often vary depending on the resolution. For example, at a resolution of a few meters, the Earth's surface appears very uneven, but at a resolution of tens of kilometers, it is relatively smooth. The degree of resolution affects the patterns in the data as well. A pattern could be obscured by noise or not visible at all if the resolution is too fine; it might even vanish if the resolution is too coarse. For instance, changes in atmospheric pressure over an hourly period show how storms and other weather systems move. These kinds of occurrences are undetectable on a monthly basis.

2.1.2.2. Record Data

A lot of data mining work is predicated on the idea that the data set is made up of records, or data objects, each of which has a fixed set of data fields, or attributes. See 2.2(a) in Figure 2.2. In the simplest type of record data, each record (object) has the same set of attributes, and there is no clear relationship between records or data fields. Relational databases or flat files are typically used to store record data. Relational databases are undoubtedly more than just a repository for records, but data mining frequently makes no use of the extra information found in relational databases. Instead, the database acts as a handy resource for finding records. The following describes various record data types, which are shown in Figure 2.2.

- **Transaction or Market Basket Data:** A unique kind of record data is transaction data, which comprises records (transactions) involving a collection of items. Think about a grocery store. A transaction is the collection of goods that a customer buys during a single shopping trip; the individual goods that were bought are the items. Because the products listed in each record are those that a person has in their "market basket," this type of data is also known as market basket data. Although transaction data is a collection of sets of items, it can also be thought of as a set of records with asymmetric attributes in their fields. In general, the attributes can be discrete or continuous, such as the number of items purchased or the amount spent on those items. Typically, the attributes are binary, indicating whether or not an item was purchased. A sample transaction data set is displayed in Figure 2.2(b). Every row shows a specific customer's purchases made at a specific point in time.

- **The Data Matrix:** The data objects in a collection of data can be conceptualized as points (vectors) in a multidimensional space, where each dimension represents a different attribute describing the object, if the data objects share a fixed set of numerical attributes. An m by n matrix with m rows for each object and n columns for each attribute can be used to represent a collection of these data objects. (It's acceptable to use a representation where attributes are rows and data objects are columns. This kind of matrix is known as a pattern matrix or data matrix. A data matrix is a type of record data that can be transformed and altered using standard matrix operations because it has numeric attributes. For the majority of statistical data, the data matrix is the accepted data format. A sample data matrix is displayed in Figure 2.2(c).

Tid	Refund	Marital Status	Taxable Income	Defaulted Borrower
1	Yes	Single	125K	**No**
2	No	Married	100K	**No**
3	No	Single	70K	**No**
4	Yes	Married	120K	**No**
5	No	Divorced	95K	**Yes**
6	No	Married	60K	**No**
7	Yes	Divorced	220K	**No**
8	No	Single	85K	**Yes**
9	No	Married	75K	**No**
10	No	Single	90K	**Yes**

(a) Record data.

TID	*ITEMS*
1	Bread, Soda, Milk
2	Beer, Bread
3	Beer, Soda, Diaper, Milk
4	Beer, Bread, Diaper, Milk
5	Soda, Diaper, Milk

(b) Transaction data.

Projection of x Load	Projection of y Load	Distance	Load	Thickness
10.23	5.27	15.22	27	1.2
12.65	6.25	16.22	22	1.1
13.54	7.23	17.34	23	1.2
14.27	8.43	18.45	25	0.9

(c) Data matrix.

	team	coach	play	ball	score	game	win	lost	timeout	season
Document 1	3	0	5	0	2	6	0	2	0	2
Document 2	0	7	0	2	1	0	0	3	0	0
Document 3	0	1	0	0	1	2	2	0	3	0

(d) Document-term matrix.

Figure 2.2. *Different variations of record data.*

Source: https://www.ceom.ou.edu/media/docs/upload/Pang-Ning_Tan_Michael_Steinbach_Vipin_Kumar_-_Introduction_to_Data_Mining-Pe_NRDK4fi.pdf.

- **The Sparse Data Matrix:** A data matrix that is asymmetric and has identical attributes—that is, where only values that are non-zero are significant—is known as a sparse data matrix. One type of sparse data matrix with only 0–1 entries is transaction data. Document data is another typical example. A document can specifically be represented as a term vector, where each term is an attribute of the vector and its value is the number of times the corresponding term occurs in the document, provided that the order of the terms (words) in the document is ignored. A document-term matrix is a common term for this depiction of a group of documents. A sample document-term matrix is displayed in Figure 2.2(d). In this matrix, the terms are the columns and the documents are the rows. In actuality, sparse data matrices are only stored with their non-zero entries.

2.1.2.3. Graph-Based Data

A graph can sometimes be a convenient and powerful representation for data. We consider two specific cases: (1) the graph captures relationships among data objects and (2) the data objects themselves are represented as graphs.

- **Data with Relationships Among Objects:** Important information is frequently conveyed by the relationships between objects. In these situations, a graph is frequently used to depict the data. Specifically, the data objects are mapped to the graph's nodes, and the links between objects—which include properties like weight and direction—capture the relationships between the objects. Think about World Wide Web pages, which have text and links to other pages. Web search engines gather and process Web pages to extract their contents in order to process search queries. However, it is commonly known that each page's links to and from other pages offer a wealth of information about how relevant a Web page is to a query; for this reason, they too need to be taken into account. A collection of linked Web pages is displayed in Figure 2.3(a).

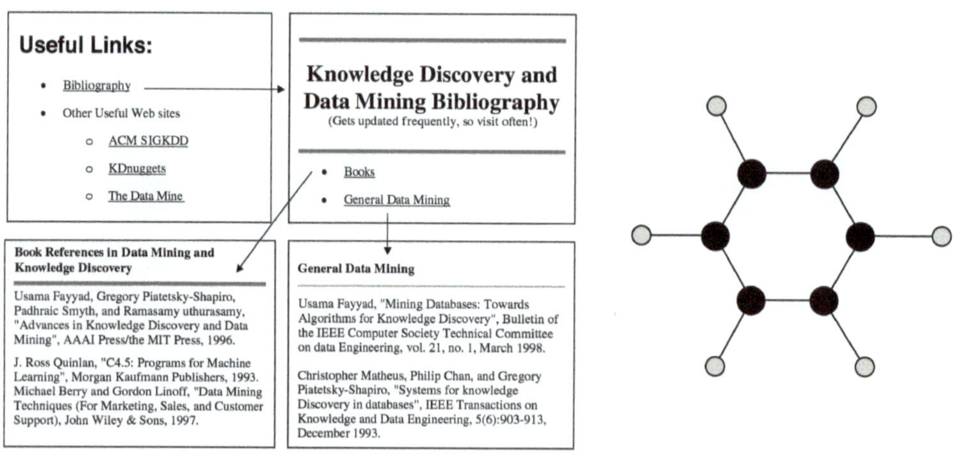

(a) Linked Web pages.

(b) Benzene molecule.

Figure 2.3. *Different variations of graph data.*

Source: https://www.ceom.ou.edu/media/docs/upload/Pang-Ning_Tan_Michael_Steinbach_Vipin_Kumar_-_Introduction_to_Data_Mining-Pe_NRDK4fi.pdf.

- **Data with Objects:** Those are graphs objects with structure, or those that comprise related sub-objects, are often depicted as graphs in computer programs. For instance, atoms can be the nodes in a graph, and chemical bonds can be the links connecting the nodes, to represent the structure of chemical compounds. A ball-and-stick diagram of the chemical compound benzene, which has hydrogen (gray) and carbon (black) atoms, is depicted in Figure 2.3(b). Finding which substructures recur frequently in a group of compounds and if any of these substructures are linked to the presence or lack of specific chemical properties, like melting point or heat of formation, can be done using a graph representation.

2.1.2.4. Ordered Data

There are relationships between the attributes for some types of data that involve order in space or time.

Sequential Data: Sequential data, which is also called temporal data, can be conceptualized as record data that has been extended to include times for each record. Examine a set of retail transaction data that includes the time the transaction was completed. Finding trends like "candy sales peak before Halloween" is made possible by this time information. Each attribute can also be linked to a time. A customer's purchase history, comprising a list of items purchased at various times, could be one example of each record. Patterns such as "people who buy DVD players tend to buy DVDs in the period immediately following the purchase" can be identified with the help of this data."

A sequential transaction data example is shown in Figure 2.4(a). There are three distinct customers (C1, C2, and C3), five distinct items (A, B, C, D, and E), and five distinct times (t1, t2, t3, t4, and t5). Every row in the top table represents the goods that each customer bought at a specific point in time. For example, at time t3, customer C2 bought items A and D. The same data is shown in the bottom table, but each row represents a different customer. Every row includes details on every transaction involving the customer; an item and the time it was purchased are considered to be part of a transaction. For instance, at time t2, customer C3 purchased items A and C.

Time	Customer	Items Purchased
t1	C1	A, B
t2	C3	A, C
t2	C1	C, D
t3	C2	A, D
t4	C2	E
t5	C1	A, E

Customer	Time and Items Purchased
C1	(t1: A,B) (t2:C,D) (t5:A,E)
C2	(t3: A, D) (t4: E)
C3	(t2: A, C)

(a) Sequential transaction data.

GGTTCCGCCTTCAGCCCCGCGCC
CGCAGGGCCCGCCCCGCGCCGTC
GAGAAGGGCCCGCCTGGCGGGCG
GGGGGAGGCGGGGCCGCCCGAGC
CCAACCGAGTCCGACCAGGTGCC
CCCTCTGCTCGGCCTAGACCTGA
GCTCATTAGGCGGCAGCGGACAG
GCCAAGTAGAACACGCGAAGCGC
TGGGCTGCCTGCTGCGACCAGGG

(b) Genomic sequence data.

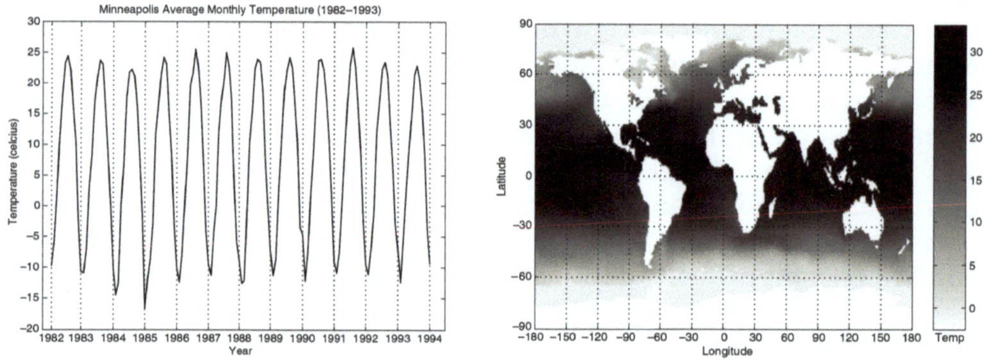

(c) Temperature time series.

(d) Spatial temperature data.

Figure 2.4. *Different variations of ordered data.*

Source: https://www.ceom.ou.edu/media/docs/upload/Pang-Ning_Tan_Michael_Steinbach_Vipin_Kumar_-_Introduction_to_Data_Mining-Pe_NRDK4fi.pdf.

- **Sequence Data:** A data set that is a series of distinct entities, like a series of words or letters, is known as sequence data. With the exception of the lack of time stamps and the presence of positions in an ordered sequence, it is fairly similar to sequential data. For instance, nucleotide sequences called genes can be used to represent the genetic information of plants and animals. Predicting similarities in nucleotide sequences from similarities in gene structure and function is a common problem when working with genetic sequence data. A portion of the human genetic code expressed using the four nucleotides—A, T, G, and C—from which all DNA is made is depicted in Figure 2.4(b).
- **Time Series Data:** A unique kind of sequential data is called time series data, where every record is a time series, that is to say a collection of measurements made throughout time. A financial data set, for instance, may include objects that are time series of different stocks' daily prices. Figure 2.4(c), which displays a time series of Minneapolis's average monthly temperature from 1982 to 1994, serves as another illustration. When working with temporal data, temporal autocorrelation should be taken into account. The values of two measurements are frequently very similar if they are taken at close intervals.
- **Spatial Data:** Some objects have spatial attributes, such as positions or areas, as well as other types of attributes. An example of spatial data is weather data (precipitation, temperature, pressure) that is collected for a variety of geographical locations. An important aspect of spatial data is spatial autocorrelation; i.e., objects that are physically close tend to be similar in other ways as well. Thus, two points on the Earth that are close to each other usually have similar values for temperature and rainfall.

Important examples of spatial data are the science and engineering data sets that are the result of measurements or model output taken at regularly or irregularly distributed points on a two- or three-dimensional grid or mesh. For instance, Earth science data sets record the temperature or pressure measured at points (grid cells) on latitude–longitude spherical grids of various resolutions, e.g., 1° by 1°. (See Figure 2.4(d).) As another example, in the simulation of the flow of a gas, the speed and direction of flow can be recorded for each grid point in the simulation.

2.1.2.5. Handling Non-Record Data

The majority of data mining algorithms are made for record data or its derivatives, like data matrices and transaction data. By taking features from data objects and using them to create a record for each object, record-oriented techniques can be used to handle non-record data. Think about the data on chemical structure that was previously discussed. Each compound can be represented as a record with binary attributes that indicate whether or not it contains a particular substructure given a set of common substructures. In reality, this kind of representation is a transaction data set, in which the items are the substructures and the transactions are the compounds.

While it can sometimes be simple to represent data in a record format, this kind of representation is not always effective in capturing all the information contained in the data. Think of time series data from every point on a spatial grid that makes up spatiotemporal data. This information is frequently kept in the form of a data matrix, in which each row denotes a place and each column a specific moment in time. Nevertheless, neither the spatial relationships among objects nor the time relationships among attributes are expressly captured by such a representation. This does not imply that such a representation is improper; rather, it means that the analysis must take these relationships into account. Applying a data mining technique, for instance, that makes the assumption that the attributes are statistically independent of one another, would not be a good idea.

2.2. DATA QUALITY

Applications for data mining are frequently used on data that was gathered for unidentified future uses or for another purpose. Because of this, data mining is typically unable to benefit from the substantial advantages of "addressing quality issues at the source." On the other hand, a large portion of statistics is concerned with creating surveys or experiments that produce data that meets predetermined standards of quality. Since it is usually not possible to prevent issues with data quality, data mining concentrates on two things: (1) identifying and fixing data quality issues; and (2) using algorithms that can handle low-quality data. Data cleaning is a common term for the first stage, which is detection and correction.

2.2.1. Measurement and Data Collection Issues

Data perfection is an unrealistic expectation. Human error, measurement device limitations, or flaws in the data collection procedure could all be contributing factors to the issues. Data objects may be missing whole or just certain values. Other scenarios could involve spurious or duplicate objects, which are data objects that are multiple copies of a single "real" object. A person who has recently resided at two different addresses, for instance, may have two distinct records. A person may have discrepancies even if all the information is there and "looks fine" for example, weighing only 2 kg but standing 2 meters tall.

Our focus is on data quality aspects pertaining to data measurement and collection. We start by defining measurement and data collection errors and then examine various problems related to measurement error including noise, artifacts, bias, precision, and accuracy. We end by addressing data quality issues that may stem from both measurement and data collection problems such as outliers, missing and inconsistent values, and duplicate data.

2.2.1.1. Measurement and Data Collection Errors

Any issue arising from the measurement procedure is referred to as a measurement error. A prevalent issue is when there is a partial discrepancy between the recorded and true values. The numerical difference between the true and measured values for continuous attributes is referred to as the error. Errors like missing data objects or attribute values, or incorrectly including a data object, are referred to as data collection errors. For instance, animals of a related species that resemble the target species in appearance may be included in a study on animals of that species. Errors in measurement and data collection can be random or systematic.

We will focus solely on general errors, as specific fields may have their own common data errors with established detection and correction methods. For instance, data entry programs often include tools to detect and correct keyboard errors frequently made during manual data entry.

2.2.1.2. Noise and Artifacts

Noise is the unpredictable element of an error in measurement. It can cause a value to become distorted or introduce false elements. In Figure 2.5, a time series is depicted both before and after it is affected by random noise. If more noise were to be introduced, the original shape of the time series would be lost. Figure 2.6 illustrates a group of data points before and after the inclusion of noise points (denoted by '+' symbols). Some of these noise points are mixed in with the non-noise points in the set. A lot of the time, data with a spatial or temporal component is referred to as noise. In these situations, noise reduction techniques from signal or image processing are often applicable to help find patterns (signals) that may be "lost in the noise." However, it can often be challenging to remove noise, so a lot of data mining research focuses on developing robust algorithms that yield satisfactory results even in the presence of noise. A more deterministic phenomenon, like a streak in the same spot across a series of photos, could be the cause of data errors. These kinds of deterministic data distortions are frequently called artifacts.

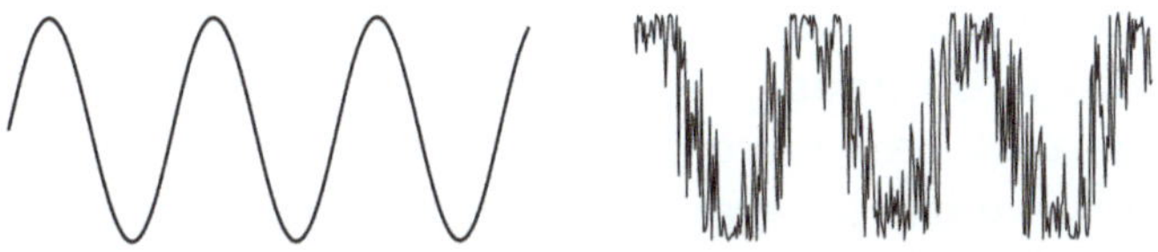

(a) Time series. (b) Time series with noise.

Figure 2.5. *Noise in a time series context.*

Source: https://www.ceom.ou.edu/media/docs/upload/Pang-Ning_Tan_Michael_Steinbach_Vipin_Kumar_-_Introduction_to_Data_Mining-Pe_NRDK4fi.pdf.

(a) Three groups of points. (b) With noise points (+) added.

Figure 2.6. *Noise in a spatial context.*

Source: https://www.ceom.ou.edu/media/docs/upload/Pang-Ning_Tan_Michael_Steinbach_Vipin_Kumar_-_Introduction_to_Data_Mining-Pe_NRDK4fi.pdf.

2.2.1.3. Precision, Bias, and Accuracy

Precision and bias are two metrics used in statistics and experimental science to evaluate the quality of the measurement procedure and the generated data.

- **Precision:** The closeness of repeated measurements (of the same quantity) to one another.
- **Bias:** A systematic variation of measurements from the quantity being measured.
- **Accuracy:** The closeness of measurements to the true value of the quantity being measured.

While bias is determined by calculating the difference between the set's mean and the known value of the quantity being measured, precision is frequently determined by calculating the standard deviation of a set of values. Only objects whose measured quantity is known through sources outside of the current circumstance can have bias determined. Let's say we wish to evaluate the accuracy and bias of our new laboratory scale using a standard laboratory weight of one gram. The following five values are obtained by weighing the mass five times: {1.015, 0.990, 1.013, 1.001, 0.986}. Since these values have a mean of 1 point001, the bias is 0 point001. The standard deviation indicates that the precision is 0.013. The degree of measurement error in data is commonly referred to by the more general term, accuracy. Since accuracy is a general concept, there is no precise formula for calculating accuracy in terms of precision and bias. When it comes to accuracy, using significant digits is crucial. The objective is to represent a measurement or calculation's result using the fewest number of digits necessary given the accuracy of the data. We should only record the length of data to the nearest millimeter, for instance, if the object's length is measured using a meter stick with millimeters as its smallest markings. A measurement with this level of precision would be within ± 0.5mm. Although they are sometimes disregarded, factors like significant digits, accuracy, bias, and precision are crucial for data mining as well as statistics and science. Data sets frequently lack information about the precision of the data, and the analysis programs that are used also return results devoid of this kind of information. However, an analyst bears the risk of making grave mistakes in data analysis if they lack a basic understanding of the accuracy of the data and the outcomes.

2.2.1.4. Outliers

Outliers can be defined as (1) data objects that differ from the majority of other data objects in the data set in some way, or (2) values of an attribute that are unusual when compared to the attribute's typical values. As an alternative, we could discuss anomalous values or objects. The statistics and data mining communities have put forth a wide range of definitions for what constitutes an outlier, and there is a great deal of flexibility in this regard. It's also critical to differentiate between the concepts of noise and outliers. Legitimate data objects or values can be considered outliers. Therefore, unlike noise, outliers can occasionally be interesting. For instance, the objective of fraud and network intrusion detection is to identify anomalous items or occurrences among a vast array of typical ones.

2.2.1.5. Missing Values

An object missing one or more attribute values is not unusual. Sometimes the data was not gathered; for example, some people choose not to disclose their age or weight. In other situations, certain attributes may not apply to every object; for example, conditional fields on forms are frequently filled out only in response to a particular question, but all fields are stored for simplicity's sake.

Nevertheless, when analyzing the data, it is important to consider any missing values. There are various approaches (and modifications on these approaches) for handling missing data, and each of them might be suitable in a given situation. The following is a list of these tactics along with a summary of their benefits and drawbacks.

- **Eliminate Data Objects or Attributes:** Eliminating objects with missing values is a straightforward and efficient tactic. But even a partially specified data object has some information, and if there are a lot of objects with missing values, it may be hard or impossible to do a reliable analysis. However, it might be more practical to exclude items with missing values if there aren't many in the data set. Eliminating attributes with missing values is a related tactic. But, care should be taken because it's possible that the attributes that were removed were crucial to the analysis.
- **Estimate Missing Values:** Missing data can occasionally be accurately estimated. Take a look at a time series that, while changing fairly smoothly overall, contains a few, widely dispersed missing values. In these situations, the remaining values can be used to estimate (interpolate) the missing values. Consider a data set with a large number of similar data points as an additional example. In this case, the missing value is typically estimated using the attribute values of the points that are closest to the point with the missing value. If the attribute is categorical, the most frequently occurring attribute value can be chosen; if the attribute is continuous, the average attribute value of the closest neighbors is used. Take measurements of precipitation that are taken by ground stations as a specific example. In places without a ground station, values from neighboring ground stations can be used to estimate the precipitation.
- **Ignore the Missing Value During Analysis:** Missing values can be ignored in many data mining techniques. Assume, for instance, that data objects are being clustered and that it is necessary to determine the similarity between pairs of data objects. If certain attributes are missing from one or both of the objects in a pair, the similarity can still be determined by utilizing the attributes that are complete. While it is true that the similarity will only be approximate, this degree of inaccuracy might not matter much unless there are a lot of missing values or the total number of attributes is small. Similarly, a lot of classification schemes are adaptable enough to handle missing values.

2.2.1.6. Inconsistent Values

Inconsistent values can be found in data. Take a look at an address field that has the city and zip code listed, but the zip code area that is being used is not part of that city. It is possible that the person entering this data entered two digits incorrectly, or that the data was scanned from a handwritten form and a digit was misread. Whatever the reason behind the inconsistent values, it's critical to identify them and, if at all feasible, fix them. Certain inconsistencies are simple to identify. One's height, for example, shouldn't be negative. In other situations, it might be essential to get information from a different source. For instance, an insurance company verifies the names and addresses on reimbursement forms against a customer database when processing claims for reimbursement.

Once an inconsistency has been detected, it is sometimes possible to correct the data. A product code may have "check" digits, or it may be possible to double-check a product code against a list of known product codes, and then correct the code if it is incorrect, but close to a known code. The correction of an inconsistency requires additional or redundant information.

- **Example: (Inconsistent Sea Surface Temperature):** The sea surface temperature (SST) at different locations throughout the ocean is measured using real time series data, which exhibits inconsistencies as demonstrated by this example. Originally, ship or buoy measurements taken in the ocean were used to compile SST data; however, more recently, satellite data collection has been employed. Both data sources must be used in order to produce a long-term data set. Nonetheless, the two components of the data are slightly different because they originate from various sources. Figure 2.7, which illustrates the correlation of SST values between years, provides a visual representation of this disparity. The location corresponding to a pair of years is colored white if there is a positive correlation between them, and black otherwise. Seasonal variations were eliminated from the data because they would have caused all of the years to have a strong correlation. When the data was combined in 1983, there was a noticeable shift in behavior. There is generally a positive correlation between years in the 1958–1982 and 1983–1999 groups, but a negative correlation with years in the other group. This does not imply that the data should not be used; rather, it means that the analyst needs to take into account how these discrepancies might affect the data mining analysis.

2.2.1.7. Duplicate Data

Data objects that are nearly or exactly duplicates of one another may be included in a data set. Many individuals receive duplicate mailings as a result of their repeated appearance in a database under slightly different names. In order to identify and remove these duplicates, two primary problems need to be resolved.

First, the values of corresponding attributes may differ between two objects that actually represent a single object; these inconsistent values need to be resolved. Second, caution must be exercised to prevent inadvertently merging data objects that are comparable but not identical, such as two different persons with the same name. One common term for the procedure used to address these problems is deduplication.

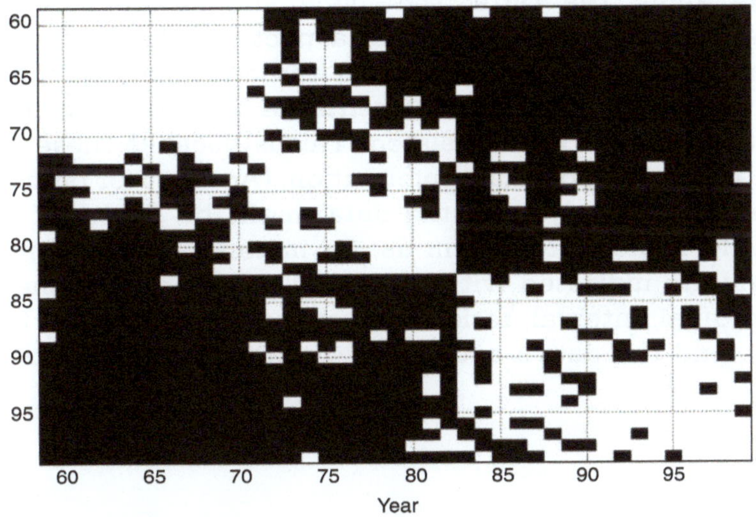

Figure 2.7. *Correlation of SST data between pairs of years. White areas indicate positive correlation.*

Source: https://www.ceom.ou.edu/media/docs/upload/Pang-Ning_Tan_Michael_Steinbach_Vipin_Kumar_-_Introduction_to_Data_Mining-Pe_NRDK4fi.pdf.

2.2.2. Issues Related to Applications

The adage "data is of high quality if it is suitable for its intended use" can also be used to examine data quality issues from an application perspective. This method of ensuring the quality of data has shown to be very beneficial, especially in business and industry. A similar perspective can be found in the experimental sciences and statistics, which place a strong focus on carefully planning experiments to gather information pertinent to a particular hypothesis. Similar to problems with quality at the level of measurement and data gathering, many problems are unique to certain fields and applications. Once more, we only look at a select few of the broad concerns.

- **Timeliness:** Certain data begins to lose value as soon as it is gathered. Specifically, if the data offers a moment in time of some ongoing phenomenon or process, like customer purchasing patterns or Web browsing habits, then this moment in time only accurately depicts reality. Models and patterns based on outdated data are also rendered obsolete.
- **Relevance:** The information required for the application must be present in the available data. Think about the challenge of developing a model that forecasts the frequency of car accidents. The model's accuracy is probably going to be restricted if the driver's age and gender are left out, unless other attributes make this information indirectly available. It can be difficult to ensure that the items in a data set are pertinent. Sampling bias is a prevalent issue that arises when a sample lacks a diversity of objects proportionate to their true presence in the population. For instance, survey data only includes information about survey respondents. Sampling bias usually leads to an incorrect analysis because the results of a data analysis can only reflect the data that is present.

- **Knowledge about the Data:** Data sets should ideally be accompanied by documentation that explains various aspects of the data; the effectiveness of this documentation can help or hinder the analysis that follows. For instance, we might choose to retain just one attribute if the documentation indicates that multiple attributes are highly related. This is because these attributes are likely to provide extremely redundant information. (Account for purchase price and sales tax. However, our analysis of the data might be flawed if the documentation is subpar and neglects to inform us, for instance, that the missing values for a specific field are indicated with a -9999. The accuracy of the data, the features (nominal, ordinal, interval, ratio), the scale of measurement (e.g., meters or feet for length), and the data's source are additional crucial attributes.

2.3. DATA PREPROCESSING

An essential phase in the data mining process is data preprocessing. It describes the steps taken to prepare data for analysis, such as cleaning, transforming, and integrating it. Enhancing the quality of the data and tailoring it to the particular data mining task are the objectives of data preprocessing.

Some common steps in data preprocessing include:

Data preprocessing is an important step in the data mining process that involves cleaning and transforming raw data to make it suitable for analysis. Some common steps in data preprocessing include:

- **Data Cleaning:** This involves identifying and correcting errors or inconsistencies in the data, such as missing values, outliers, and duplicates. Various techniques can be used for data cleaning, such as imputation, removal, and transformation.
- **Data Integration:** This involves combining data from multiple sources to create a unified dataset. Data integration can be challenging as it requires handling data with different formats, structures, and semantics. Techniques such as record linkage and data fusion can be used for data integration.
- **Data Transformation:** This involves converting the data into a suitable format for analysis. Common techniques used in data transformation include normalization, standardization, and discretization. Normalization is used to scale the data to a common range, while standardization is used to transform the data to have zero mean and unit variance. Discretization is used to convert continuous data into discrete categories.
- **Data Reduction:** This involves reducing the size of the dataset while preserving the important information. Data reduction can be achieved through techniques such as feature selection and feature extraction. Feature selection involves selecting a subset of relevant features from the dataset, while feature extraction involves transforming the data into a lower-dimensional space while preserving the important information.
- **Data Discretization:** This involves dividing continuous data into discrete categories or intervals. Discretization is often used in data mining and machine learning algorithms that require categorical data. Discretization can be achieved through techniques such as equal width binning, equal frequency binning, and clustering.

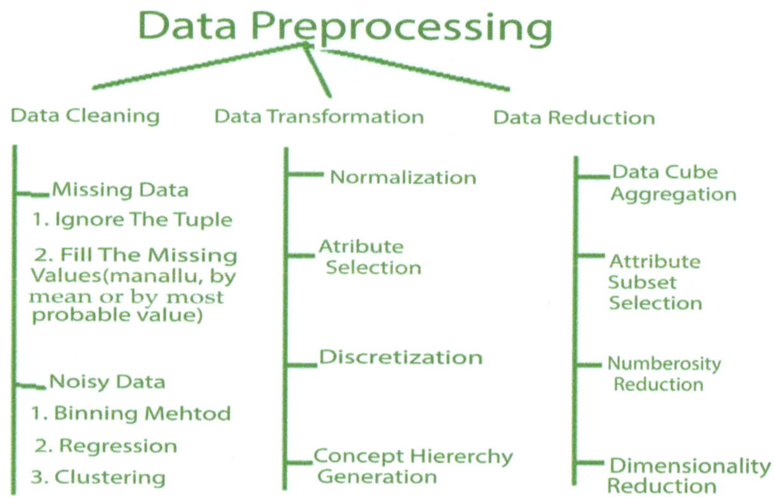

Figure 2.8. *Data-preprocessing-in-data-mining.*

Source: https://www.geeksforgeeks.org/data-preprocessing-in-data-mining/.

- **Data Normalization:** This involves scaling the data to a common range, such as between 0 and 1 or -1 and 1. Normalization is often used to handle data with different units and scales. Common normalization techniques include min-max normalization, z-score normalization, and decimal scaling.

In order to guarantee the accuracy of the analysis results and the quality of the data, data preprocessing is essential. The precise steps in data preprocessing can change based on the type of data and the objectives of the analysis. These actions improve the efficiency of the data mining process and increase the accuracy of the findings.

- **Preprocessing in Data Mining:** One data mining technique called "data preprocessing" is used to turn raw data into a format that is both efficient and useful (Figure 2.8).

2.3.1. Aggregation

Aggregation—the combining of two or more objects into a single object—is an example of when "less is more." Imagine a data collection made up of transactions (data objects) that document the daily sales of goods at different retail locations (e.g., Minneapolis, Chicago, Paris, etc.). on various days throughout the year. Replacing every transaction in a single store with a single storewide transaction is one method of aggregating transactions for this data set. This lowers the number of data objects to the number of stores and condenses the hundreds or thousands of transactions that happen every day at a particular store into a single daily transaction. It is evident that there is a problem with the process of creating an aggregate transaction in order to generate the aggregate transaction that represents the sales of a single store or date, the values of each attribute are added together across all the records that correspond to a specific location. A sum or an average are commonly used to aggregate quantitative attributes, like price. A qualitative attribute, like item, can be summed up as the collection of all the items sold at that location, or it can be left out entirely.

Another way to look at the data in Table 2.3 is as a multidimensional array, where each attribute represents a dimension. From this viewpoint, aggregation is the process of eliminating attributes, such as the type of item, or reducing the number of values for a particular attribute; e.g., so that the range of possible dates is reduced from 365 days to 12 months. Online analytical processing frequently makes use of this kind of aggregation (OLAP).

Aggregation is motivated by a number of factors. Aggregation may make it possible to employ more costly data mining algorithms because, in the first place, the smaller data sets obtained from data reduction require less memory and processing time. Second, by offering a high-level view of the data rather than a low-level view, aggregation can function as a change of scope or scale. Instead of a daily, per item view, the previous example's aggregation over store locations and months provides us with a monthly, per store view of the data.

Table 2.3. Data Set Containing Information About Customer Purchases

Transaction ID	Item	Store Location	Date	Price	...
⋮	⋮	⋮	⋮	⋮	
101123	Watch	Chicago	09/06/04	$25.99	...
101123	Battery	Chicago	09/06/04	$5.99	...
101124	Shoes	Minneapolis	09/06/04	$75.00	...
⋮	⋮	⋮	⋮	⋮	

Source: https://www.ceom.ou.edu/media/docs/upload/Pang-Ning_Tan_Michael_Steinbach_Vipin_Kumar_-_Introduction_to_Data_Mining-Pe_NRDK4fi.pdf.

Lastly, groups of objects or attributes tend to behave more consistently than individual objects or attributes. This claim is supported by statistics, which show that totals and averages have less variability than the individual items they are averaging. While the actual amount of variation for means is less than the actual amount for individual objects (on average), the actual amount of variation for totals is (on average) greater than that of individual objects but the percentage of variation is smaller. One drawback of aggregation is that valuable details may be lost. In the store example, the day of the week with the highest sales is lost when aggregating data over several months.

2.3.2. Sampling

A popular method for choosing a portion of the data objects to be examined is sampling. It has long been used in statistics for both the final data analysis and the initial data investigation. In data mining, sampling can also be very helpful. However, there are frequently differences between the reasons behind sampling in data mining and statistics. While data miners sample because processing all the data would be too costly or time-consuming, statisticians use sampling because obtaining the full set of relevant data is too expensive or time-consuming. A sampling algorithm may occasionally be able to reduce the amount of data to the point where a more effective but pricy algorithm can be applied.

The following is the fundamental idea of good sampling: if a sample is representative, it will perform nearly as well as using the complete data set. Conversely, a sample is considered representative if it nearly shares the same characteristic (of interest) as the original data set. A sample is considered representative if its mean is in close proximity to the original data, provided that the mean (average) of the data objects is the property of interest. The best we can do is select a sampling strategy that ensures a high probability of obtaining a representative sample, since sampling is a statistical process and any given sample's representativeness will vary. Selecting the right sample size and sampling methods are necessary for this.

2.3.2.1. Sampling Approaches

Though numerous sampling techniques exist, this article will focus on a handful of the most fundamental ones along with their variations. Simple random sampling is the most basic kind of sampling. Any specific item has an equal chance of being chosen in this kind of sampling. Random sampling comes in two flavors (as do other sampling methods): (1) sampling without replacement, in which each item chosen is taken out of the collection of all objects that together make up the population; and (2) sampling with replacement, in which objects remain in the population while being chosen for the sample. The same item may be chosen more than once when sampling with replacement. When samples are small in relation to the size of the data set, the samples generated by the two methods are similar; however, sampling with replacement is easier to analyze because the probability of selecting any object stays constant throughout the sampling process.

Simple random sampling may not be sufficient to accurately represent less common object types in a population that is made up of a variety of object types with significantly varying numbers of objects. When the analysis calls for accurate representation of every type of object, this could lead to issues. For example, it is crucial that the rare classes be sufficiently represented in the sample when developing classification models for rare classes. Therefore, a sampling plan that can take into account varying frequencies for the relevant items is required. One such method is stratified sampling, which begins with pre-specified groups of objects. In the most basic version, despite the fact that the groups are of varying sizes, the same number of objects are drawn from each group. In a variant, the quantity of objects selected from every group is directly related to the group's size.

2.3.2.2. Progressive Sampling

Adaptive or progressive sampling schemes are occasionally employed because it can be challenging to determine the ideal sample size. These methods begin with a small sample and gradually increase it until a sufficiently large sample is obtained. This method does away with the necessity to initially calculate the appropriate sample size, but it does necessitate the existence of an assessment method to determine whether the sample is sufficiently large. Let's say a predictive model is learned through progressive sampling. Predictive models become more accurate with increasing sample size, but eventually this increase in accuracy levels off. Here is the leveling-off point where we want to stop increasing the sample size. We can determine how near we are to this leveling-off point and stop sampling by monitoring the change in the model's accuracy as we take ever-larger samples and by taking additional samples that are roughly the same size as the current one.

2.3.3. Dimensionality Reduction

A vast array of features can be present in data sets. Take into consideration a collection of documents, each of which is represented by a vector made up of the frequencies at which each word appears in the document. In these situations, there are usually tens of thousands or even more attributes (components), one for every word in the lexicon. Another example would be to look at a set of time series that included the daily closing prices of different stocks for a 30-year period. Here, too, the attributes are in the thousands, and these are the prices on particular days.

The reduction of dimensionality has several advantages. One important advantage is that a lot of data mining algorithms perform better with less dimensionality, or attributes in the data. This is due in part to the curse of dimensionality, which is discussed below, as well as the ability of dimensionality reduction to remove superfluous features and reduce noise. Another advantage of dimensionality reduction is that it may result in a model with fewer attributes, making it easier to understand. Additionally, dimensionality reduction might make it easier to visualize the data. Data visualization typically involves examining pairs or triplets of attributes, and while dimensionality reduction may not completely reduce the amount of data, it does significantly decrease the number of possible combinations. Finally, a reduction in dimensionality results in a reduction in the time and memory needed by the data mining algorithm.

Techniques that reduce a data set's dimensionality by combining old attributes to create new ones are commonly referred to as "dimensionality reduction." Feature subset selection, also called feature selection, is the process of reducing the number of dimensions by choosing new attributes that are a subset of the old.

2.3.3.1. The Curse of Dimensionality

The phenomenon known as "curse of dimensionality" describes how many types of data analysis get noticeably more difficult as the data's dimensionality rises. More specifically, the data gets sparser in the space it occupies as dimensionality rises. When it comes to classification, this could indicate that not enough data objects are available to build a model that can accurately classify every potential object. Density and point-to-point distance definitions, which are crucial for clustering, lose some of their significance when discussing clustering. Because of this, a lot of clustering and classification algorithms (as well as other data analysis algorithms) struggle with high-dimensional data, leading to low-quality clusters and decreased classification accuracy.

2.3.3.2. Linear Algebra Techniques for Dimensionality Reduction

Some of the most popular methods for reducing dimensionality, especially when dealing with continuous data, involve projecting data from a high-dimensional space into a lower-dimensional space using methods from linear algebra. Principal Components Analysis (PCA) is a linear algebra method for continuous attributes that identifies new attributes (called principal components) that: (1) are orthogonal (perpendicular) to each other; (2) are linear combinations of the original attributes; and (3) capture the maximum variation in the data. For instance, using two orthogonal attributes that are linear combinations of the original attributes, the first two principal components capture the greatest amount of variation in the data. A linear algebraic method related to PCA, Singular Value Decomposition (SVD) is frequently employed for dimensionality reduction.

2.3.4. Feature Subset Selection

Reducing the number of dimensions by utilizing a subset of the features is an additional method. Although it might seem that this method would lose information, if superfluous and unimportant features are included, this is not the case. Features that are redundant replicate most or all of the data found in one or more other attributes. For instance, a lot of the same information can be found in the purchase price of a product and the sales tax paid. Almost no information is contained in irrelevant features that is relevant to the current data mining task. For example, predicting students' grade point averages does not depend on their ID numbers. The quality of the discovered clusters and the accuracy of classification can both be impacted by redundant and unnecessary features.

While some redundant and irrelevant attributes can be quickly removed using domain knowledge or common sense, choosing the optimal subset of features often necessitates a methodical approach. Trying every possible subset of features as input to the relevant data mining algorithm is the ideal method for selecting features; the subset that yields the best results should then be chosen. One benefit of this approach is that it can accurately represent the goal and prejudice of the data mining algorithm that will ultimately be employed. Unfortunately, in most cases, such an approach is impractical due to the fact that the number of subsets involving n attributes is 2^n. Instead, alternative strategies must be employed. Three common methods exist for selecting features: wrapper, filter, and embedded.

- **Embedded approaches:** Feature selection occurs naturally as part of the data mining algorithm. Specifically, during the operation of the data mining algorithm, the algorithm itself decides which attributes to use and which to ignore.
- **Filter approaches:** Features are selected before the data mining algorithm is run, using some approach that is independent of the data mining task. For example, we might select sets of attributes whose pairwise correlation is as low as possible.
- **Wrapper Approaches:** These methods use the target data mining algorithm as a black box to find the best subset of attributes, in a way similar to that of the ideal algorithm described above, but typically without enumerating all possible subsets.

2.3.4.1. An Architecture for Feature Subset Selection

Both the filter and the wrapper approaches can be included in a single architecture. Four components are thought to make up the feature selection process: a stopping criterion, a validation process, a search strategy that manages the creation of a new subset of features, and a measure for assessing a subset. The way that filter and wrapper methods assess a subset of features is the only distinction between them. The evaluation technique for a filter approach is different from the target data mining algorithm, whereas subset evaluation for a wrapper method uses the wrapper method's data mining algorithm. In theory, selecting a feature subset involves looking through all potential feature subsets. There are many different kinds of search strategies that can be employed; however, the search strategy should find sets of features that are either optimal or nearly optimal and should be computationally cheap. Since it is typically not feasible to meet both requirements, tradeoffs must be made.

An essential component of the search process involves evaluating the current subset of features in relation to other features that have been explored. This calls for an assessment metric that looks at how well a subset of attributes performs in relation to a specific data mining task, like clustering or classification. These kinds of measures, when applied to the filter approach, try to forecast the performance of the data mining algorithm itself on a given set of attributes. The subset evaluation function for the wrapper approach is just the standard criterion for gauging the outcome of data mining, since evaluation involves actually running the target application. An examination of every subset would be impractical due to their potential large number, so some kind of stopping criterion is required. This approach is typically predicated on one or more of the following: the quantity of iterations; whether the subset evaluation measure's value is optimal or surpasses a predetermined threshold; whether a subset of a specific size has been obtained; whether the simultaneous achievement of size and evaluation criteria has been attained; and whether any improvement can be realized by the search strategy's available options.

The outcomes of the target data mining algorithm on the chosen subset should then be validated after a subset of features has been chosen. Using the full set of features when running the algorithm and comparing the complete results to those derived from the subset of features is a simple evaluation strategy. With any lucky, the results from the subset of features will be either superior to or nearly as good as those from using all of the features. Another validation strategy is to create feature subsets using a variety of feature selection algorithms, and then compare the outcomes of applying the data mining algorithm to each subset.

2.3.4.2. Feature Weighting

An alternative to retaining or removing features is feature weighting. Features that are deemed more significant are given a higher weight than those that are deemed less significant. On the basis of domain knowledge regarding the relative importance of features, these weights are occasionally assigned. Or they could be ascertained automatically. Certain classification schemes, like support vector machines, generate models of classification where each feature is assigned a weight. Larger weighted features are more significant to the model. One may also think of the normalization of objects that occurs during the cosine similarity computation as a form of feature weighting.

2.3.5. Feature Creation

From the original attributes, it is often possible to derive a new set of attributes that much more effectively captures the important information in a given data set.

We can also benefit from all the dimensionality reduction advantages that have been previously mentioned when there are fewer new attributes added to the original set.

2.3.5.1. Feature Extraction

Feature extraction is the process of generating a new set of features from the original raw data. Think of a collection of images where each image must be categorized based on whether or not a human face is present. Since the raw data is just a collection of pixels, many different kinds of classification algorithms cannot be applied to it. However, a much wider range of classification techniques can be used to solve this problem if the data is processed to provide higher level features, such as the presence or absence of specific types of edges and areas that are highly correlated with the presence of human faces.

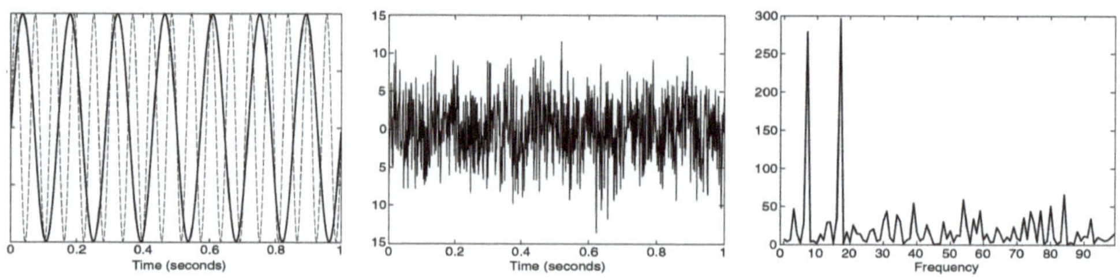

(a) Two time series. (b) Noisy time series. (c) Power spectrum

Figure 2.9. *Application of the Fourier transform to identify the underlying frequencies in time series data.*

Source: https://www.ceom.ou.edu/media/docs/upload/Pang-Ning_Tan_Michael_Steinbach_Vipin_Kumar_-_Introduction_to_Data_Mining-Pe_NRDK4fi.pdf.

Unfortunately, feature extraction is very domain-specific in the sense that it is most commonly used. Different features and methods for extracting them have been developed over time for a specific field, like image processing, and frequently these methods have limited applicability to other fields. Consequently, creating new features and feature extraction techniques is a crucial task whenever data mining is applied to a relatively unexplored field.

2.3.5.2. Mapping the Data to a New Space

Important and intriguing features can be seen by looking at the data from an entirely new perspective. Take time series data, for instance, which frequently exhibits periodic patterns. The pattern is simple to identify if there is only one periodic pattern and little noise. On the other hand, these patterns are difficult to identify if there are several periodic patterns and a large quantity of noise. However, by using a Fourier transform to convert the time series into a representation that makes frequency information explicit, such patterns are frequently detectable. It won't be important to understand the specifics of the Fourier transform for the example that follows. It suffices to understand that the Fourier transform creates a new data object with attributes connected to frequencies for every time series.

- **Example: (Fourier Analysis):** Three time series are combined to create the time series shown in Figure 2.9(b). Two of these time series, with frequencies of 7 and 17 cycles per second, respectively, are displayed in Figure 2.9(a). Random noise makes up the third time series. The power spectrum that can be calculated by transforming the original time series using a Fourier transform is displayed in Figure 2.9(c). Informally, the square of each frequency attribute corresponds to the power spectrum. Two peaks that match the periods of the two original, noise-free time series can be seen despite the noise. Again, the key takeaway is that enhanced features have the power to highlight significant data points. It is also possible to undergo many other kinds of transformations. The wavelet transform, in addition to the Fourier transform, has shown to be highly beneficial for time series and other kinds of data.

2.3.5.3. Feature Construction

The required information may occasionally be present in the original data sets' features, but it may not be in a format that the data mining algorithm can use. In this case, a feature or features that are created from the original features may end up being more beneficial than the original features.

- **Example: (Density):** To demonstrate this, take a look at a data set that includes details about historical artifacts and includes the mass and volume of each item in addition to other data. Assume for the sake of simplicity that these artifacts are composed of a limited range of materials (wood, clay, bronze, and gold), and that we wish to categorize the artifacts according to the materials they are composed of. In this instance, an accurate classification would most directly result from a density feature built from the mass and volume features, i.e., density = mass/volume. The most popular method is to construct features using domain expertise, though there have been some attempts to automatically perform feature construction by exploring simple mathematical combinations of existing attributes.

2.3.6. Discretization and Binarization

The data must take the form of categorical attributes for some data mining algorithms, particularly those that deal with classification. Binary attributes are the only format that is required for data in order for algorithms to identify association patterns. As a result, it is frequently required to discretize continuous attributes into categorical attributes and to binaryize both continuous and discrete attributes into one or more binary attributes. Additionally, it might be advantageous for some data mining tasks to combine some of the values in a categorical attribute in order to reduce the number of categories, particularly if the attribute has a large number of values (categories) or some values occur infrequently. The discretization and binarization technique that "produces the best result for the data mining algorithm that will be used to analyze the data" is the optimal one, much like with feature selection. Direct application of such a criterion is usually impractical. As a result, discretization or binarization is carried out in a way that meets a criterion that is assumed to be associated with successful completion of the data mining task at hand.

2.3.6.1. Binarization

If a categorical attribute has m values, then a straightforward method to binarize it is to assign each original value to an integer within the interval $[0, m^{-1}]$ in a unique way. An assignment that maintains order is required if the attribute is ordinal. (Note: This procedure is required if the integers are not in the interval $[0, m^{-1}]$, even if the attribute was originally represented using integers. Afterwards, output a binary number for each of these m integers. The representation of these integers in binary requires $n = [\log_2(m)]$ binary digits; thus, use n binary attributes to represent these numbers. For instance, three binary variables, x_1, x_2, and x_3, would be needed for a categorical variable with five values: {awful, poor, OK, good, and great}.

Complications from this kind of transformation could include the unintentional relationships that arise between the transformed attributes. Because both attributes are used to encode information about the good value, attributes x_2 and x_3 are correlated. Asymmetric binary attributes are also necessary for association analysis, where the presence of the attribute (value = 1) is the only factor that matters. It is therefore necessary to introduce one binary attribute for each categorical value in association problems. The methods listed below can be used to decrease the number of categorical values prior to binarization if the number of resultant attributes is excessive.

Similarly, it might be required to substitute two asymmetric binary attributes for a single binary attribute in association problems. Think of a binary characteristic that indicates a person's gender, either male or female. This data must be converted into two asymmetric binary attributes—one that is a 1 only in the case of a male person and another that is a 1 only in the case of a female person—for the purposes of conventional association rule algorithms.

2.3.6.2. Discretization of Continuous Attributes

Generally, discretization is done on attributes that are utilized in association or classification analysis. The optimal discretization generally relies on the other factors taken into account along with the algorithm being applied. Generally speaking, though, an attribute's discretization is taken into consideration separately. Determining how many categories to have and how to map the continuous attribute's values to them are the two subtasks involved in transforming a continuous attribute into a categorical attribute. Following sorting, the continuous attribute values are divided into n intervals in the first step by designating n – 1 split points. The values in a single interval are all mapped to the same categorical value in the second, relatively simple step. Consequently, selecting the number and location of split points is the discretization problem. The result can be represented either as a set of intervals $\{(x_0, x_1],(x_1, x_2],\ldots,(x_{n-1}, x_n)\}$, where x_0 and x_n may be $+\infty$ or $-\infty$, respectively, or equivalently, as a series of inequalities $x_0 < x \leq x_1,\ldots, x_{n-1} < x < x_n$.

- **Unsupervised Discretization:** Using supervised or unsupervised discretization techniques for classification depends on the use of class information. In the event that class information is not utilized, fairly straightforward methods are typical. For example, the equal width approach splits the attribute's range into a number of intervals that the user specifies, each with the same width. An equal frequency (equal depth) approach, which aims to place the same number of objects into each interval, is frequently chosen because such an approach can be severely impacted by outliers. Another example of unsupervised discretization is the application of a clustering algorithm like K-means. And last, there are instances when looking at the data visually can be a useful strategy.

- **Supervised Discretization:** While the above-discussed discretization techniques are generally preferable to none at all, applying class labels and keeping the end goal in mind frequently yields superior outcomes. This shouldn't come as a surprise because class labels are frequently mixed together in an interval that is created without any knowledge of class labels. Placing the splits to maximize the purity of the intervals is a conceptually simple approach. In actuality, though, this method necessitates making potentially arbitrary choices regarding the minimum size and purity of an interval. Some statistically based methods start with each attribute value as a separate interval and combine adjacent intervals that are similar based on a statistical test to create larger intervals in order to allay such worries. One of the most promising methods for discretization is entropy-based methods, and this article will outline a straightforward entropy-based method.

First, it is necessary to define entropy. Let k be the number of different class labels, mi be the number of values in the ith interval of a partition, and m_{ij} be the number of values of class j in interval i. Then the entropy e_i of the ith interval is given by the equation;

$$e_i = \sum_{i=1}^{k} p_{ij} \log_2 p_{ij},$$

where $p_{ij} = m_{ij}/m_i$ is the probability (fraction of values) of class j in the ith interval. The total entropy, e, of the partition is the weighted average of the individual interval entropies, i.e., where m is the number of values, $w_i = m_i/m$ is the fraction of values in the ith interval, and n is the number of intervals. Intuitively, the entropy of an interval is a measure of the purity of an interval.

If an interval contains only values of one class (is perfectly pure), then the entropy is 0 and it contributes nothing to the overall entropy. If the classes of values in an interval occur equally often (the interval is as impure as possible), then the entropy is a maximum. The first step in splitting a continuous attribute into two intervals with the least amount of entropy is to bisect the starting values. Because it is assumed that intervals contain ordered sets of values, this technique only needs to take each value into consideration as a potential split point. After that, the splitting process is repeated with a different interval, usually selecting the interval with the worst (highest) entropy, until a stopping criterion is satisfied or a user-specified number of intervals are reached.

2.3.6.3. Categorical Attributes with Too Many Values

There are situations when categorical attributes have too many values. Methods for reducing the number of categories can be applied to categorical attributes that are ordinal, just as they are to continuous attributes. Other strategies are necessary, though, if the categorical attribute is nominal. Think about an academic institution with numerous departments. As a result, the value of a department name attribute could be in the hundreds. In this case, we could merge departments into more expansive categories, like engineering, social sciences, or biological sciences, using our understanding of the connections between various departments. It is necessary to use a more empirical approach, such as grouping values together only if doing so improves classification accuracy or achieves another data mining goal, if domain knowledge is not a useful guide or if using this approach leads to poor classification performance.

2.3.7. Variable Transformation

A transformation applied to certain values of a variable is referred to as a variable transformation. Put another way, the revolution is applied to the value of the variable associated with each object. For example, if a variable's significance alone is what matters, then determining its absolute value will allow you to alter the variable's values. There are two types of variable transformations: simple functional transformations and normalization.

2.3.7.1. Simple Functions

Each value is calculated separately using a straightforward mathematical function. If r is a variable, then examples of such transformations include x^k,logx, e^x,$\sqrt{x}$,1/x,sinx, or |x|. Variable transformations, specifically sqrt, log, and 1/x, are utilized in statistics to convert data that lacks a Gaussian (normal) distribution into information that does. While important, there are other considerations that may come first in data mining.

The variable of interest pertains to the number of data bytes in a session, which can vary from one to one billion. Given the large range, it could be beneficial to use a log10 transformation to compress it. Session A which transferred 10^8 bytes and session B which transferred 10 bytes would be more similar to each other in this scenario (9–8 = 1 versus 3–1 = 2). Since variable transformations alter the nature of the data, they should be used carefully. If the transformation's feature is not fully respected, problems may arise. The transformation 1/x, for instance, increases the significance of values between 0 and 1 but decreases the significance of values that are 1 or higher.

2.3.7.2. Normalization or Standardization

Another common type of variable transformation is the standardization or normalization of a variable. The objective of standardization or normalization is to create a whole group of values that have a specific property. A common instance is that of "standardizing a variable" in statistics. If x' is the mean (average) of the attribute values and $s_{x'}$ is their standard deviation, then the transformation $x' = (x - \bar{x}) / s_x$) creates a new variable that has a mean of 0 and a standard deviation of 1.

Such a transformation is frequently required if different variables are to be combined in any way to prevent a variable with large values from dominating the calculation's results. Outliers have a significant impact on the mean and standard deviation, so the transformation mentioned above is frequently adjusted. Initially, the median is used in place of the mean, i.e., the midway figure. Secondly, the absolute standard deviation takes the place of the standard deviation. Specifically, if r is a variable, then the absolute standard deviation of r is given by $\sigma_A = \sum_{i=1}^{m} |x_i - \mu|$, here x_i is the ith value of the variable, m is the number of objects, and μ is either the mean or median.

CASE STUDY

NASDAQ USES AWS TO PIONEER STOCK EXCHANGE DATA STORAGE IN THE CLOUD

Nasdaq is a multinational financial services and technology corporation that owns and operates the Nasdaq Stock Exchange. Nasdaq operates a total of 27 markets, a central securities depository, and clearinghouse across a variety of asset classes in North America and Europe. It is home to nearly 4,000 listed companies globally across its markets and also provides its mission-critical technology to other market infrastructure operators located in 50 countries.

The Nasdaq Stock Exchange is the largest equities franchise globally by volume, and it manages the matching of buyers and sellers at high volume and velocity, while providing data feeding the price quote for stocks in electronically entered trades. Nasdaq relies on an internal application to capture and store all protected exchange data. "This data includes orders, quotes, trades, and cancelations," says Robert Hunt, vice president of software engineering for Nasdaq. Every night, Nasdaq receives billions of records that need to be loaded for billing and reporting processes before the markets open the following morning.

As automated trading platforms have entered the market, the pace and volume of transactions has grown. In 2014, to increase scale and performance and lower operational costs, Nasdaq moved from a legacy on-premises data warehouse to an Amazon Web Services (AWS) data warehouse powered by an Amazon Redshift cluster. Between 2014 and 2018, this Amazon Redshift cluster grew to 70 nodes as the company expanded the solution to support all its North American markets. By 2018, the solution ingested financial market data from thousands of sources nightly, ranging from 30 billion to 55 billion records and surpassing 4 terabytes. Over time, growth in data led to a change in approach for managing that data for analytics. The overnight batch processing that runs against the warehouse caused challenges in processing enormous volumes to meet stringent deadlines. Users rely on the data to complete billing, reporting, and surveillance. "When market volatility increased in early 2018, data volumes for the warehouse grew substantially, peaking at about 55 billion records per day in 2018," says Hunt.

More sophisticated trading practices lead to a massive growth in data and it was critical that Nasdaq started planning to evolve a new architecture to continue to achieve the performance standards and operational excellence that the ecosystem expects. "We have to both load and consume the 30 billion records in a time period between market close and the following morning. Data loading delayed the delivery of our reports," says

Hunt. "We needed to be able to write or load data into our data storage solution very quickly without interfering with the reading and querying of the data at the same time."

- **Using AWS Services for Flexibility, Scalability, and Performance**

In 2018, Nasdaq chose to build the foundation of a new data lake on Amazon Simple Storage Service (Amazon S3), which enables the company to separate compute and storage and to scale each function independently. In traditional data warehouse deployments, scaling storage capacity often requires companies to scale compute capacity at the same time because the application and storage are tightly linked, with onsite hardware modifications needed for any change to the ratio of the two. "In addition to the flexibility that comes with separation of compute and storage, Amazon S3 has better scaling properties in terms of writing and reading large datasets at the same time," Hunt says. "Amazon S3 gave us a solution that enables zero contention between data loading and querying processes."

By integrating AWS Identity and Access Management (AWS IAM) policies, Amazon S3 also provides comprehensive access control across multiple AWS accounts. Additionally, Nasdaq uses Amazon S3 to store critical financial data and move it to Amazon S3 Glacier, where it can be archived at a lower cost. The company relies on the Amazon S3 Object Lock feature to further enable compliance.

In January 2019, Nasdaq attended an AWS Data Lab, where it worked with AWS Solutions Architects and analytics service experts who provided prescriptive architectural guidance to rethink how Nasdaq implemented data warehousing. In the four-day lab, Nasdaq reinvented how it delivers analytics by using Amazon Redshift as a compute layer. As a result, Nasdaq began using Amazon Redshift Spectrum, a feature that powers a lake house architecture to query data both in the data warehouse and in the Amazon S3 data lake. "We're putting all the data that comes from our internally operated exchanges into Amazon S3 and Amazon Redshift Spectrum," says Hunt. "That includes orders, cancelations, quotes, and trades. Those are turned into messages and archived in Amazon S3, and those messages drive our downstream billing and reporting surveillance processes."

The new data lake contains 15 terabytes of data on Amazon S3, which Nasdaq can query in place without data loading immediately after writing data to Amazon S3. This provides minimal time-to-insight and enables the Nasdaq economic research team to conduct data analysis and run complex queries against the data. In addition, the company's surveillance business team queries the data lake after receiving inquiries from the U.S. Securities and Exchange Commission (SEC).

What began as a performance-focused solution has become a multi-use data lake shared between teams, creating additional benefit for the business.

- **Scaling to Support 70 Billion Records a Day:**

With compute and storage scaling independently, Nasdaq can now flex its compute layer to support the volume of transactions, with the data lake built on Amazon S3 storage easily supporting data that continues to grow in volume and complexity. For example, market volatility spiked in late February 2020, at the beginning of the COVID-19 pandemic, and the solution scaled to support an ingest of 70 billion records daily—with a peak volume of 113 billion. "We were able to easily support the jump from 30 billion records to 70 billion records a day because of the flexibility and scalability of Amazon S3 and Amazon Redshift," says Hunt. "We kept up with the spike in data volumes and provided the necessary billing, reporting, and surveillance processes to support our obligations to the market." Nasdaq can also easily and quickly scale its environment down to ensure there is no idle capacity when the market adjusts again.

- **Loading Market Data for Reporting 5 Hours Faster:**

Using its new lake house architecture based on Amazon S3 and Amazon Redshift, Nasdaq is reaching its 90 % mark for data load completion 5 hours sooner than before. In addition, by optimizing its data warehouse, the company was able to run Amazon Redshift queries 32 % faster. "These improvements helped us accelerate our billing and reporting processes," says Hunt. "For example, we're done ingesting data within an hour or two of the market closing, which gives us a head start on billing and reporting. This helps immensely when we're dealing with the volume spikes we've seen recently, and it also helps us meet or exceed our deadlines for our internal customers." Over time, the Amazon S3 and Amazon Redshift data lake has enabled transformation at Nasdaq. "We're free to focus on our expertise in our industry to innovate for Nasdaq while relying on AWS to provide cloud expertise," says Hunt. "Going forward, we will continue to take advantage of new AWS services and technologies as the market requires."

CLASS ACTIVITY

EXPLORING PATTERNS AND TRENDS THROUGH DATA MINING

- Objective: Students will gain hands-on experience with basic data mining techniques, learning how to extract meaningful patterns and trends from a given dataset. They will use a simplified dataset to perform tasks such as data cleaning, data transformation, and basic pattern analysis.
- **Materials:** Computers or tablets with internet access, Spreadsheet software, Sample dataset, Graph paper, Markers or colored pencils
- **Sample Dataset:** A small dataset related to student performance, which includes the following attributes:
    - Student ID
    - Age
    - Gender
    - Hours Studied per Week
    - Test Score
    - Participation in Extracurricular Activities (Yes/No)

SUMMARY

- A datum is an individual value in a collection of data. Data is usually organized into structures such as tables that provide additional context and meaning, and which may themselves be used as data in larger structures.
- A data set can often be viewed as a collection of data objects. Other names for a data object are record, point, vector, pattern, event, case, sample, observation, or entity.
- Most data mining algorithms are designed for record data or its variations, such as transaction data and data matrices. Record-oriented techniques can be applied to non-record data by extracting features from data objects and using these features to create a record corresponding to each object.
- Data quality issues can also be considered from an application viewpoint as expressed by the statement "data is of high quality if it is suitable for its intended use." This approach to data quality has proven quite useful, particularly in business and industry.
- Data preprocessing is an important step in the data mining process. It refers to the cleaning, transforming, and integrating of data in order to make it ready for analysis. The goal of data preprocessing is to improve the quality of the data and to make it more suitable for the specific data mining task.
- Data preprocessing allows for the removal of unwanted data with the use of data cleaning, this allows the user to have a dataset to contain more valuable information after the preprocessing stage for data manipulation later in the data mining process.
- Semantic data mining is a subset of data mining that specifically seeks to incorporate domain knowledge, such as formal semantics, into the data mining process. Domain knowledge is the knowledge of the environment the data was processed in. Domain knowledge can have a positive influence on many aspects of data mining, such as filtering out redundant or inconsistent data during the preprocessing phase.
- Sampling is a commonly used approach for selecting a subset of the data objects to be analyzed. In statistics, it has long been used for both the preliminary investigation of the data and the final data analysis. Sampling can also be very useful in data mining.

REVIEW QUESTIONS

1. What is an attribute in the context of data mining, and how is it different from a variable?
2. How does the type of attribute influence the choice of data mining technique?
3. What are some common characteristics of data sets that can affect data mining processes?

4. Describe graph-based data and give an example of a data mining application that uses graph-based data.
5. What are some common issues encountered during data measurement and collection?
6. Differentiate between systematic and random errors in data measurement.
7. Explain the concept of data aggregation and its importance in data preprocessing.
8. Why is sampling important in data mining, and what are the different sampling techniques?
9. Discuss the different types of variable transformations and their purposes.
10. How does the choice of attribute type impact the design and implementation of a data mining model?

REFERENCES

1. Bock, H. H., & Diday, E. (2000). *Analysis of Symbolic Data: Exploratory Methods for Extracting Statistical Information from Complex Data (Studies in Classification, Data Analysis, and Knowledge Organization)*. Springer-Verlag Telos.
2. Cochran, W. G. (1977). *Sampling Techniques* (3rd ed.). John Wiley & Sons.
3. Elomaa, T., & Rousu, J. (1999). General and efficient multisplitting of numerical attributes. *Machine Learning, 36*(3), 201–244.
4. Kaufman, L., & Rousseeuw, P. J. (1990). *Finding Groups in Data: An Introduction to Cluster Analysis*. Wiley Series in Probability and Statistics. John Wiley & Sons.
5. Liu, H., & Motoda, H. (1998). *Feature Selection for Knowledge Discovery and Data Mining*. Kluwer International Series in Engineering and Computer Science, 454. Kluwer Academic Publishers.
6. Liu, H., Motoda, H., & Yu, L. (2003). Feature extraction, selection, and construction. In N. Ye (Ed.), *The Handbook of Data Mining* (pp. 22–41). Lawrence Erlbaum Associates, Inc.
7. Olken, F., & Rotem, D. (1995). Random sampling from databases—A survey. *Statistics & Computing, 5*(1), 25–42.
8. Provost, F. J., Jensen, D., & Oates, T. (1999). Efficient progressive sampling. In *Proceedings of the 5th International Conference on Knowledge Discovery and Data Mining* (pp. 23–32).
9. Redman, T. C. (2001). *Data Quality: The Field Guide*. Digital Press.
10. Zaki, M. J., Parthasarathy, S., Li, W., & Ogihara, M. (1996). Evaluation of sampling for data mining of association rules. Technical Report TR617, Rensselaer Polytechnic Institute.

CHAPTER 3

Exploring Data

LEARNING OBJECTIVES

After studying this chapter, you will be able to:

- Explain the types of data
- Define the data quality
- Focus on data preprocessing

KEY TERMS FROM THIS CHAPTER

Absolute average deviation (AAD)
Categorical variable
Data exploration
Information visualization
Median absolute deviation (MAD)
Multidimensional structure
Raw data
Visual data mining
Box plots
Data analysis
Data matrix
Interquartile range (IQR)
Multidimensional data array
Principal components analysis
Summary statistics

INTRODUCTION

When choosing the right preprocessing and data analysis methods, data exploration can help. It can even answer some of the questions that data mining is usually used to answer. For instance, looking at the data visually can occasionally reveal patterns. Furthermore, comprehension and interpretation of data mining results can be achieved through the application of certain data exploration techniques, such as visualization.

Three main subjects are covered in this chapter: On-Line Analytical Processing (OLAP), visualization, and summary statistics. Standard procedures that are frequently used for data exploration include summary statistics, like the mean and standard deviation of a set of values, and visualization techniques, like histograms and scatter plots. A more recent development is OLAP, which is a collection of methods for working with multidimensional arrays of values. The analysis functions related to OLAP concentrate on different methods of generating summary data tables from a multidimensional data array. Data aggregation across different dimensions or attribute values is one of these techniques. For example, we can use OLAP techniques to create a summary that breaks down the sales activity at a specific location by month and product category if we are given sales information reported by product, location, and date.

3.1. DATA EXPLORATION

In order to better understand the nature of the data, data analysts use data visualization and statistical techniques to describe dataset characterizations, such as size, quantity, and accuracy. This process is known as data exploration.

In order to reveal patterns and points of interest and provide data analysts with a deeper understanding of the raw data, data exploration techniques include both manual analysis and automated data exploration software solutions. These tools visually explore and identify relationships between various data variables, the dataset's structure, the presence of outliers, and the distribution of data values.

Data analysts are often faced with the challenge of sifting through massive amounts of unstructured data collected from different sources. Before proceeding with further analysis techniques like univariate, bivariate, multivariate, and principal components analysis, it is crucial for analysts to first gain a thorough understanding and develop a comprehensive view of the data.

3.1.1. Data Exploration Tools

Manual data exploration techniques involve manually filtering data into spreadsheets or writing scripts to analyze raw data. Data scientists can more easily monitor data sources and conduct big data exploration on otherwise excessively large datasets with the aid of automated data exploration tools, such as data visualization software. Bar charts and scatter plots are two examples of graphical data displays that are useful tools for visual data exploration.

Microsoft Excel spreadsheets are a common tool for manual data exploration. They can be used to view raw data, create simple charts for data exploration, and determine the correlation between variables. Excel's CORREL() function can be used to determine the correlation between two continuous variables. The chi-square test, the stacked column chart method, and the two-way table method can all be used to determine the correlation between two categorical variables in Excel. (Gray, Chaudhuri, Bosworth, et al., 1997).

Business intelligence tools, data visualization programs, providers of data preparation software, and data exploration platforms are just a few examples of the many proprietary automated data exploration options available. Regression and visualization features are also available in open-source data exploration tools that can assist businesses in integrating disparate data sources for quicker data exploration. Data visualization tools are present in most data analytics software packages.

3.1.2. Importance of Data Exploration

It is extremely difficult for data scientists and analysts to assign meaning to thousands of rows and columns of data points and communicate that meaning without any visual components because humans process visual data better than numerical data.

In data exploration, data visualization makes use of well-known visual cues like angles, lines, points, colors, and shapes to help data analysts define and visualize metadata efficiently before performing data cleansing. When data analysts carry out the preliminary stage of data exploration, they are better equipped to comprehend and visually identify relationships and anomalies that they might miss otherwise.

3.1.3. Data Exploration Step by Step

Before beginning the data exploration process, it is essential to acknowledge the significance of having high-quality input data in order to achieve a successful output. This includes performing necessary data cleaning and normalization steps to ensure consistency and accuracy in the dataset. For example, if the data gathered includes sensor information from various locations but is in different units of measurement, it is important to standardize these values. These preparatory steps are fundamental in ensuring reliable and insightful business analysis results.

We must first determine the categories, variables, and types of input and output, all of which need to be precisely defined.

The investigation of each variable in detail will be the focus of the following stage of data exploration. The choice of methods for this kind of analysis can be made depending on whether the variables are continuous or categorical.

To comprehend each category distribution for categorical variables, one must utilize a frequency table that shows the percentage of values by count and count percent metrics.

We have to comprehend central tendency and spread when dealing with continuous variables. You can check for dispersion using metrics like variance, quartile, standard deviation, and range. On the other hand, we will primarily use min, max, mean, median, etc., for central tendency. Most of the time, visualization techniques like plots and histograms make it simple for us to take our observations. When conducting data exploration, data visualization tools can be helpful in identifying noteworthy relationships or anomalies within datasets.

Relationships between different variables have to be analyzed as well. Association and disassociation between predefined variables are considered in the following combinations:

- **Categorical and Continuous:** box plots for each categorical variable to be drawn.
- **Continuous and Continuous:** linear or nonlinear relationship will be defined by conducting analysis between two continuous variables with scatter plot of categorical variable.
- **Categorical and Categorical:** easiest way to achieve some insights will be using a two-way table or stacked column chart.

3.1.4. Data Exploration Techniques

Your data analysts employ a variety of data

exploration strategies to discover more about the datasets that your business has. Some of them may be more or less accurate to select, depending on the type of data. Before beginning the actual data exploration process, it is imperative to determine which technique will work best and be most beneficial for extracting important information from the dataset. These are a few illustrations that could aid in making the ultimate choice.

- **Unique Value Count**: It is the first thing that can be helpful in the exploration process; it displays the number of unique values that are present in each category column. This will help us understand the content of the data in general.
- **Frequent Value Count**: Determining the frequency with which a given value appears in a given column. This will provide information about each categorical variable's content.
- **Variance**: There are many simple ways to obtain basic information about numerical values, such as the variance, maximum, and minimum. Variance provides a useful indication of how values are distributed across a particular variable.
- **Pareto Analysis**: With the help of this data exploration technique, you can concentrate on what matters most. The 80–20 Pareto rule is a useful tool for determining the point at which a particular value begins to take on significant meaning.
- **Histogram**: The range of values falling in the majority sector is shown by the histogram. It shows the minimum and maximum values as well as any skew data.
- **Correlation Heat-map**: In essence, correlation is the association of two variables. Expressing the connections between various data columns is helpful. Heat maps are among the best tools for displaying correlation between numerical columns. On the other hand, correlation may be helpful for different kinds of data.
- **Pearson Correlation and Trends**: Searching for patterns and Pearson correlation is another fascinating method of data exploration. We can use a heat-map to view the correlation trend between two numerical columns once we have one.
- **Cramer-V Correlation**: A method for exploring data that offers correlation between all categorical variables is called Cramer-V. Heat maps can also be used to visualize the outcome.
- **Categorical Columns Pair Correlation**: Further investigation can concentrate on particular pairs of categorical columns after the correlation between categorical variables and the Cramer-V matrix has been verified. A bubble plot is just one of many visualization techniques available.
- **Cluster Size Analysis**: When examining vast amounts of data that have been divided into various groups or clusters prior to actual analysis, this type of analysis is frequently used for data exploration purposes. Verifying cluster size will be the first step in the segmentation process. This kind of analysis will demonstrate how data can be divided into various groups.
- **Clustering or Segmentation**: Data must be divided into a predetermined number of segments or clusters after the number of clusters has been verified.

- **Outlier Detection**: When doing data exploration, we should not be concerned if anomalies are discovered. They don't always have a bad connotation. This kind of analysis raises the standard of the entire exploratory process. Algorithms like Isolation Forest or the standard deviation can be used to identify numerical value outliers.
- **Outlier Analysis for Specific Numeric Column**: Once we have reviewed the minimum and maximum values for numeric columns, we can begin analyzing them individually.
- **Outlier Analysis for Multiple Columns**: Finding the outlier based on multiple columns is crucial (at row level). A helpful tool for this kind of investigation will be the scatter plot. Outliers will be displayed and colored differently.

3.2. SUMMARY STATISTICS

Summary statistics are measures like the mean and standard deviation that represent key aspects of a large set of values with just one number or a few numbers. This can include things like average household income or the percentage of college students who graduate in four years. For many, summary statistics are the most common way of understanding data. While our focus will be on summary statistics for individual values, we will also touch on some multivariate summary statistics.

We only take into account summary statistics' descriptive nature. In contrast, some of the summary statistics covered here can be seen as estimates of the statistical parameters of the underlying distribution that produced the data. This is because statistics sees data as the result of an underlying statistical process that is characterized by a number of parameters.

3.2.1. Frequencies and the Mode

There isn't much that can be done to further characterize a set of unordered categorical values other than calculating the frequency with which each value occurs for a specific set of data.

Given a categorical attribute x, which can take values $\{v_1,\ldots,v_i,\ldots v_k\}$ and a set of m objects, the frequency of a value vi is defined as:

$$frequency(v_i) = \frac{number\ of\ objects\ with\ attribute\ value\ v_i}{m} \quad (1)$$

The value with the highest frequency is the mode of a categorical attribute.

The mode and frequencies of the values that make up a categorical attribute can be informative and fascinating because they frequently, though not always, have a limited number of values. However, take note that the three flower types have the same frequency for the Iris data set and the class attribute, so the idea of a mode is not compelling.

The mode as it exists now is frequently useless for continuous data since a single value might not occur more than once. However, in certain instances, the mode might reveal crucial details regarding the type of values or the existence of missing values. When measuring the heights of twenty people to the nearest millimeter, for instance, the results usually do not repeat; however, if the measurements are made to the nearest tenth of a meter, some individuals may have the same height. Furthermore, a unique value will frequently appear as the mode if it is used to represent a missing value.

3.2.2. Percentiles

It is more helpful to think about a set of values' percentiles when dealing with ordered data. To be more precise, the pth percentile x_p of an ordinal or continuous attribute x and a number p between 0 and 100 is the value of x at which p percent of the observed values of x are less than x_p. The 50th percentile, for example, is the value $x_{50\%}$, meaning that half of all values of x are less than $x_{50\%}$.

3.2.3. Measures of Location: Mean and Median

For continuous data, two of the most widely used summary statistics are the mean and median, which are measures of the location of a set of values. Consider a set of m objects and an attribute x. Let $\{x_1,\ldots,x_m\}$ be the attribute values of x for these m objects. As a concrete example, these values might be the heights of m children. Let $\{x_{(1)},\ldots,x_{(m)}\}$ represent the values of x after they have been sorted in non-decreasing order. Thus, $x_{(1)} = \min(x)$ and $x_{(m)} = \max(x)$. Then, the mean and median are defined as follows:

$$\text{mean}(x) = \overline{x} = \frac{1}{m}\sum_{i=1}^{m} x_i \tag{2}$$

$$\text{median}(x) = \begin{cases} x_{(r+1)} & \text{if } m \text{ is odd, i.e., } m = 2r+1 \\ \frac{1}{2}(x_{(r)} + x_{(r+1)}) & \text{if } m \text{ is even, i.e., } m = 2r \end{cases} \tag{3}$$

To summarize, the median is the middle value if there are an odd number of values, and the average of the two middle values if the number of values is even. Thus, for seven values, the median is $x_{(4)}$, while for 10 values, the median is $\frac{1}{2}(x_{(5)} + x_{(6)})$.

The middle of a set of values is sometimes understood to be the mean, but this is only accurate when the values are distributed symmetrically. The median is a more accurate representation of the middle in a skewed value distribution. The mean is also susceptible to the existence of outliers. Once more, the median offers a more reliable approximation of the middle of a range of values for data containing outliers.

There are instances when the idea of a trimmed mean is employed to get around issues with the conventional definition of a mean. The top and bottom (p/2)% of the data are removed, a percentage p between 0 and 100 is given, and the mean is then computed as usual. The standard mean corresponds to p = 0%, while the median is a trimmed mean with p = 100%.

3.2.4. Measures of Spread: Range and Variance

The summary statistics that quantify the dispersion or spread of a set of values are another popular set for continuous data. These metrics show whether the attribute values are comparatively concentrated around a single point, like the mean, or if they are widely dispersed.

The simplest measure of spread is the range, which, given an attribute x with a set of m values $\{x_1,\ldots,x_m\}$, is defined as;

$$\text{range}(x) = \max(x) - \min(x) = x_{(m)} - x_{(1)}. \quad (4)$$

Even though the range shows the maximum spread, it can be deceptive if the majority of the values are concentrated in a small range and there are also a few, relatively extreme values. As a result, the variance is the favored spread measurement. The variance of an attribute x's (observed) values is defined below and is commonly expressed as s_2^x. The square root of the variance, or standard deviation, is represented by the symbol s_x and has the same units as x.

$$\text{variance}(x) = s_x^2 = \frac{1}{m-1}\sum_{i=1}^{m}(x_i - \overline{x})^2 \quad (5)$$

Outliers have the ability to distort the mean, and since the variance is calculated using the mean, outliers can also affect it. Since the variance is based on the squared difference between the mean and other values, it is susceptible to outliers more than other variables. Because of this, more accurate estimates of a set of values' spread are frequently employed. The definitions of these three metrics are as follows: interquartile range (IQR), median absolute deviation (MAD), and absolute average deviation (AAD).

$$\text{MAD}(x) = \textit{median}\Big(\{|x_1 - \overline{x}|, \ldots, |x_m - \overline{x}|\}\Big) \quad (6)$$

$$\text{AAD}(x) = \frac{1}{m}\sum_{i=1}^{m}|x_i - \overline{x}| \quad (7)$$

$$\text{interquartile range}(x) = x_{75\%} - x_{25\%} \quad (8)$$

By calculating the mean or median for each attribute independently, one can determine the location measures for data with multiple attributes (multivariate data).

Thus, given a data set the mean of the data objects, $\overline{\mathbf{x}}$, is given by:

$$\overline{\mathbf{x}} = (\overline{x_1}, \ldots, \overline{x_n}), \quad (9)$$

Where; $\overline{x_i}$ is the mean of the i th attribute x_i.

For multivariate data, the spread of each attribute can be computed independently of the other attributes using any of the approaches.

However, for data with continuous variables, the spread of the data is most commonly captured by the covariance matrix S, whose ijth entry s_{ij} is the covariance of the i th and j^{th} attributes of the data. Thus, if x_i and x_j are the i th and j^{th} attributes, then

$$s_{ij} = \text{covariance}(x_i, x_j). \tag{10}$$

In turn, covariance(x_i, x_j) is given by:

$$\text{covariance}(x_i, x_j) = \frac{1}{m-1}\sum_{k=1}^{m}(x_{ki} - \overline{x_i})(x_{kj} - \overline{x_j}), \tag{11}$$

Where; x_{ki} and x_{kj} are the values of the ith and j^{th} attributes for the kth object. Notice that covariance(x_i, x_i) = variance(x_i). Thus, the covariance matrix has the variances of the attributes along the diagonal.

The degree to which two attributes vary together is measured by their covariance, which is dependent on the magnitudes of the variables. The absence of a (linear) relationship between two attributes is indicated by a value close to 0, however the covariance value alone cannot be used to determine the strength of the relationship between two variables. Correlation is preferred over covariance for data exploration because it provides an instantaneous indication of how strongly two attributes are (linearly) related. The ij^{th} entry of the correlation matrix R, is the correlation between the ith and j^{th} attributes of the data. If x_i and x_j are the i th and j^{th} attributes, then

$$r_{ij} = \text{correlation}(x_i, x_j) = \frac{\text{covariance}(x_i, x_j)}{s_i s_j}, \tag{12}$$

where s_i and s_j are the variances of x_i and x_j, respectively. The diagonal entries of R are correlation(x_i, x_i) = 1, while the other entries are between −1 and 1. It is also useful to consider correlation matrices that contain the pairwise correlations of objects instead of attributes.

3.2.5. Other Ways to Summarize the Data

Of course, summary statistics come in other forms. For example, the degree to which a set of values is symmetrically distributed around the mean is measured by its skewness. Other aspects of the data, such as whether the value distribution is multimodal—that is, whether the data has multiple "bumps" where the majority of the values are concentrated—are also difficult to quantify. However, viewing the values graphically in the form of a histogram is frequently the most efficient way to comprehend the more intricate or subtle aspects of how the values of an attribute are distributed.

3.3. VISUALIZATION

The display of information in a tabular or graphic format is known as data visualization. For data visualization to be successful, the information must be transformed into a visual format. This allows for the analysis and reporting of the attributes and features of the data as well as their relationships. The purpose of visualization is to help someone understand the information they have seen and create a mental model of it (Sancho, Dominguez, & Ochoa, 2014). In everyday life, the preferred method for explaining the weather, the economy, and the outcomes of political elections is frequently the use of visual aids like graphs and tables. Similarly, although most technical disciplines—including data mining—tend to emphasize algorithmic or mathematical approaches, visual techniques can be very important in data analysis. In fact, the term "visual data mining" is occasionally used to describe the application of visualization techniques in data mining.

3.3.1. Motivations for Visualization

People's ability to swiftly process and discern patterns in vast amounts of visual information is the primary driving force behind the use of visualization. Take a look at Figure 3.1, which displays the July 1982 Sea surface temperature (SST) in degrees Celsius. This image can be easily understood in a matter of seconds and condenses the data from about 250,000 numbers. It is evident, for instance, that the ocean's temperature rises at the equator and falls at the poles.

The utilization of domain knowledge that is "locked up in people's heads" is a common incentive for visualization. Even though applying domain knowledge to data mining is crucial, using such knowledge to its full potential in statistical or algorithmic tools is frequently challenging or impossible. In some circumstances, an analysis can be carried out with non-visual tools, and the results can then be visually presented for the domain expert to assess. In other situations, it might be best to have a domain specialist look over data visualizations to identify interesting patterns. This is because domain knowledge can help one quickly identify and eliminate a lot of uninteresting patterns, focusing attention on the important ones.

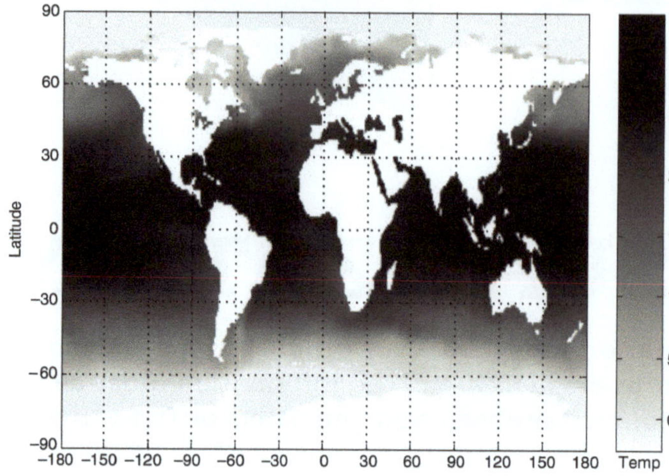

Figure 3.1. *Sea surface temperature (SST) for July, 1982.*

Source: Pang-Ning Tan, Michael Steinbach, and Vipin Kumar, Introduction to Data Mining, ISBN 13: 978–1-292–02615–2.

The utilization of domain knowledge that is "locked up in people's heads" is a common incentive for visualization. Even though applying domain knowledge to data mining is crucial, using such knowledge to its full potential in statistical or algorithmic tools is frequently challenging or impossible. In some circumstances, an analysis can be carried out with non-visual tools, and the results can then be visually presented for the domain expert to assess. In other situations, it might be best to have a domain specialist look over data visualizations to identify interesting patterns. This is because domain knowledge can help one quickly identify and eliminate a lot of uninteresting patterns, focusing attention on the important ones.

3.3.2. General Concepts

We examine a few broad ideas in the field of visualization, specifically generic methods for displaying the data and its characteristics. It is assumed that the reader is acquainted with scatter plots, bar charts, and line graphs.

3.3.2.1. Representation: Mapping Data to Graphical Elements

Mapping a set of information's objects, attributes, and relationships to visual representations of those same objects, attributes, and relationships is the first step in the visualization process. In other words, graphical elements like points, lines, shapes, and colors represent data objects, their characteristics, and the connections between them.

There are typically three ways to represent an object. First, if an object is only being evaluated for one categorical attribute, it is common practice to group objects into categories based on the attribute's value. These categories are then shown as entries in tables or sections on screens. Second, an object with several attributes can be shown as a line on a graph or as a row (or column) in a table. In conclusion, an object is frequently understood as a point in two or three dimensions. A geometric figure, such as a circle, cross, or box, may graphically represent the point.

Whether an attribute is nominal, ordinal, or continuous (interval or ratio) determines how it is represented. Continuous, ordered graphical features, such as location along the x, y, or z axes; intensity; color; or size (diameter, width, and height), can be mapped to ordinal and continuous attributes. Each category for categorical attributes can be mapped to a different column, embellishment, color, shape, orientation, or arrangement in a table. However, when using graphical features that have an inherent ordering associated with their values, like color and position, care should be taken with nominal attributes, whose values are unordered. Put differently, ordinal values lack order, but the graphical elements that represent them frequently do.

Relationships can be explicitly or implicitly represented through graphical elements. The standard graph representation for graph data is typically used, which consists of a set of nodes connected by links. Graphical representation is used when nodes (data objects) or links (relationships) have unique attributes or characteristics. For example, if the links are highways and the nodes are cities, the width of the links could represent the amount of traffic, and the diameter of the nodes could represent the population.

Generally speaking, however, when objects and attributes are mapped to graphical elements, the relationships in the data are implicitly mapped to relationships among graphical elements. For example, the relative positions of the graphical objects corresponding to the data objects tend to naturally preserve the actual relative positions of the objects if the data object represents a physical object with a location, such as a city. Similarly, when two or three continuous attributes are used as the coordinates of the data points, the resulting plot frequently provides a great deal of insight into the relationships between the attributes and the data points since visually similar data points have similar attribute values.

It is generally challenging to guarantee that a mapping of objects and attributes will map to relationships between graphical elements that are simple to observe. This is one of the trickiest parts of visualization, in fact. Since there are numerous implicit relationships in any given set of data, selecting a visualization technique that makes the relationships of interest easily observable is a major challenge.

3.3.2.2. Selection

Selection is an important aspect in visualization, involving the removal or downplaying of specific objects and attributes. Mapping data objects with few dimensions to a two- or three-dimensional visual representation is usually simple, but it becomes more difficult when dealing with data containing multiple attributes. Visualizing a large number of data objects can lead to a cluttered display, while handling numerous attributes and objects presents an even greater challenge.

The most popular method for managing a large number of attributes is to display a subset of the attributes—typically two. A matrix of bivariate (two-attribute) plots can be created for simultaneous viewing if the dimensionality is not too high. Alternatively, a visualization program may display a sequence of two-dimensional plots automatically; the user may choose to direct the sequence or it may follow a predetermined plan. It is hoped that putting a number of two-dimensional plots together visually will give a more comprehensive picture of the data.

Enough information about each object cannot be displayed when there are many data points (more than a few hundred) or if the data range is wide. Certain data points may make other data points difficult to see, or a data object may not take up enough pixels to properly display its features. For instance, if an object has only one pixel available for display, its shape cannot be used to encode that characteristic. In these cases, the ability to remove some of the objects—either by selecting a sample of the data points or by zooming in on a specific area of the data—is helpful.

3.3.3. Techniques

Techniques for visualizing data are frequently tailored to the kind of data being examined. In fact, new approaches and techniques for visualization are constantly being developed, along with specialized versions of already-existing approaches. These developments usually stem from the need to visualize increasingly complex data sets and tasks.

There are some general classification schemes for visualization techniques, despite this specialization and the ad hoc nature of visualization. One way to categorize data is to see how many attributes are involved (1, 2, 3, or many) or if the data has any unique features, like a graph or hierarchical structure. The kind of attributes involved can also be used to categorize visualization techniques. The type of application—scientific, statistical, or information visualization—is the basis for yet another classification. Three categories will be used in the discussion that follows: data visualization with few attributes, data visualization with spatial and/or temporal attributes, and data visualization with many attributes. The majority of the visualization methods covered here are found in many different statistical and mathematical packages, some of which are open source. Additionally, the World Wide Web has a number of data sets that are openly accessible.

3.3.3.1. Visualizing Small Numbers of Attributes

The methods for visualizing data in relation to a limited number of attributes are covered in this section. A few of these methods, like histograms, provide information about how the observed values for a particular attribute are distributed. Other methods, like scatter plots, are meant to show the connections between two attributes' values.

- **Stem and Leaf Plots:** Stem and leaf plots can reveal the distribution of integer or continuous data in one dimension. To create a basic stem and leaf plot, values are grouped based on their last digit. The groups are called stems, while the last digits are represented as leaves. Hence, if the values are two-digit integers, e.g., 35, 36, 42, and 51, then the stems will be the high-order digits, e.g., 3, 4, and 5, while the leaves are the low-order digits, e.g., 1, 2, 5, and 6. By plotting the stems vertically and leaves horizontally, we can provide a visual representation of the distribution of the data.
- **Histograms:** A particular kind of histogram that shows the distribution of values for attributes by grouping possible values into

bins and counting the number of objects that fit into each bin is called a stem and leaf plot. Every value in categorical data represents a bin. Values are combined in some way if this yields an excessive number of values. When dealing with continuous attributes, the range of values is separated into bins, which are usually counted and may or may not have equal widths.

Once the counts for each bin are known, a bar plot is created with one bar for each bin, and the area of each bar equal to the number of values (objects) falling into the relevant range. All bars have the same width if all intervals have the same width, and a bar's height is proportional to the number of values in the associated bin.

The histogram plot is not the only one. The relative frequency is used to replace the count in a relative (frequency) histogram. But the histogram's shape remains unchanged—this is merely a shift in the y axis' scale. The Pareto histogram is another popular variation that is particularly useful for unordered categorical data. It is similar to a standard histogram but has the categories sorted by count in a way that the count decreases from left to right.

- **Two-Dimensional Histograms:** Histograms in two dimensions are also feasible. Every attribute is separated into two sets of intervals, which together define two-dimensional value rectangles (Figure 3.2).

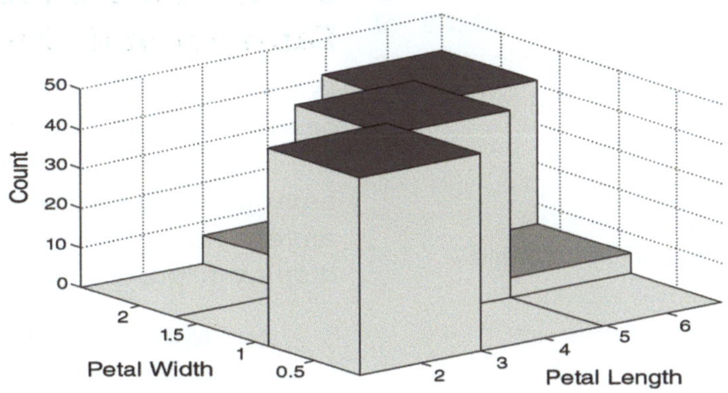

Figure 3.2. *Two-dimensional histogram of petal length and width in the Iris data set.*

Source: Pang-Ning Tan, Michael Steinbach, and Vipin Kumar, Introduction to Data Mining, ISBN 13: 978-1-292-02615-2.

Two-dimensional histograms are more visually complex, but they can be used to uncover fascinating facts about the co-occurrence of two attribute values. For example, it's simple to envision a scenario where some columns are obscured by others.

- **Box Plots:** Another technique for displaying the distribution of values for a single numerical attribute is a box plot. The labeled box plot for sepal length is displayed in Figure 3.3. The 50th percentile's value is indicated by the line inside the box, while the lower and upper ends of the box represent the 25th and 75th percentiles, respectively. The 10th and 90th percentiles are shown by the top and bottom lines of the tails. Outliers are indicated by a "+" symbol. Because box plots are comparatively small, multiple of them can be displayed on a single plot. You can also use more compact versions of the box plot that are simplified.

- **Pie Chart:** Comparable to a histogram, a pie chart is usually used for categorical attributes with a limited number of possible values. In a pie chart, relative area of a circle is used to indicate relative frequency rather than the area or height of a bar, as in a histogram, which shows the relative frequency of various values. Pie charts are common in popular articles but are less common in technical publications due to the difficulty in judging the relative sizes of the areas. It is preferable to use histograms for technical work.

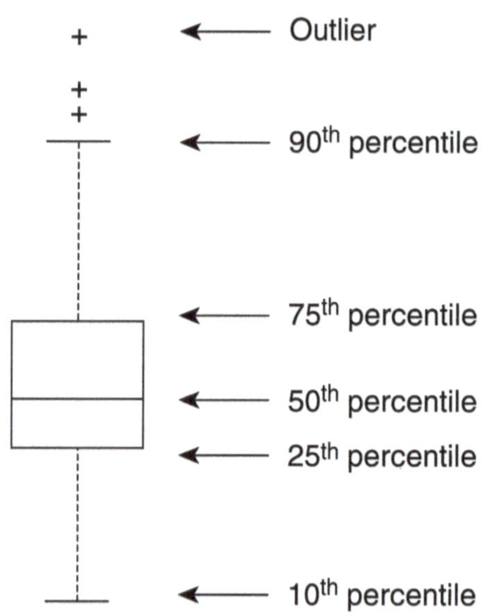

Figure 3.3. *Description of box plot for sepal length.*

Source: Pang-Ning Tan, Michael Steinbach, and Vipin Kumar, Introduction to Data Mining, ISBN 13: 978-1-292-02615-2.

3.3.3.2. Percentile Plots and Empirical Cumulative Distribution Functions

Plotting an empirical cumulative distribution function is one kind of diagram that provides a more quantitative depiction of the data distribution. Although the idea behind this kind of plot may seem complex, it is actually quite simple. A cumulative distribution function (or CDF) displays the probability that a point will be less than a given value for every value in a statistical distribution. An empirical cumulative distribution function (ECDF) displays the percentage of points that are less than each observed value. The empirical cumulative distribution function is a step function since the number of points is finite.

3.3.4. Visualizing Higher-Dimensional Data

We examine visualization methods that are capable of displaying more dimensions than the few that are visible with the methods we have just covered. Even so, these methods have some limitations because they only display a portion of the data.

- **Matrices:** A rectangular array of pixels, each with its own color and brightness, can be thought of as an image. A rectangular array of values is called a data matrix. As a result, by linking each data matrix entry to a pixel in the image, a data matrix can be shown as an image. The value of the matching entry in the matrix determines the pixel's brightness or color.

  When visualizing a data matrix, there are a few crucial practical factors to take into account. Rearranging the data matrix to group all objects of a class together is helpful if class labels are known. This facilitates tasks like determining whether all objects in a class have identical attribute values for a given attribute. The attributes are frequently standardized to have a mean of zero and a standard deviation of one if different attributes have different ranges. This stops the feature with the highest magnitude values from taking center stage in the plot.

- **Parallel Coordinates***:* Each attribute in parallel coordinates has its own coordinate axis, but unlike in traditional coordinates, the axes are parallel to each other rather than perpendicular. Moreover, a line rather than a point is used to represent an object. To be more precise, the coordinate axis for each attribute of an object is mapped to a point, and these points are connected to form the line that represents the object.

  One could worry that this would result in a significant mess. On the other hand, objects frequently belong to a small number of groups where the points have similar values for their respective attributes. In that case, if there aren't too many data objects, an intriguing pattern may emerge from the parallel coordinates plot that results.

3.3.4.1. Star Coordinates and Chernoff Faces

An additional method for presenting multidimensional data involves encoding objects as glyphs or icons, which are nonverbal symbols that convey information. To be more precise, every attribute of an object is mapped to a specific glyph feature, and the attribute value determines the precise feature type. As a result, we can quickly discern the differences between two objects. Coordinates for stars are one example of this method. Each attribute is represented by one axis in this method. Similar to a wheel's spokes, each of these axes radiates from a central point and is equally spaced. The range [0,1] is typically mapped to all attribute values.

The process of mapping an object onto a star-shaped set of axes involves converting each attribute value of the object into a fraction based on its position between the minimum and maximum values. These fractions are then used to plot points on the corresponding axes, which are connected by line segments to create a polygon. The size and shape of the polygon visually represent the attribute values of the object. To make interpretation easier, a separate set of axes is used for each individual object, resulting in each object being represented by its own polygon.

The values of features can also be mapped to those of more recognizable objects, like faces. In honor of its inventor, Herman Chernoff, this method is known as Chernoff faces. With this method, every attribute is linked to a distinct facial feature, and the expression of that feature is determined by the value of the attribute. As a result, when the value of the corresponding data feature rises, the face's shape may get longer.

The four features mentioned below are mapped to the features by the program we used to create this face. Default values are assigned to other facial features, like the distance between the eyes and the length of the mouth. These kinds of diagrams are visually appealing, but they don't scale well, which makes them unusable for a lot of data mining applications. However, they could still be useful for swiftly comparing small groups of objects that have been chosen using different methods.

3.4. ONLINE ANALYTICAL PROCESSING

One method for rapidly responding to multi-dimensional analytical (MDA) queries is online analytical processing, or OLAP. OLAP falls under the larger umbrella of business intelligence, which also includes data mining, report writing, and relational databases. Business reporting for sales, marketing, management reporting, business process management (BPM), budgeting and forecasting, financial reporting, and related fields are typical uses for OLAP. New applications, like those in agriculture, are also becoming more prevalent (Parseye, et al., 1998).

Online transaction processing (OLTP), a term from traditional databases, was slightly modified to become OLAP (Figure 3.4).

With the aid of OLAP tools, users can interactively examine multidimensional data from several angles. Drill-down, slicing and dicing, and consolidation (roll-up) are the three fundamental analytical operations that make up OLAP. The process of consolidation entails gathering data that can be totaled and processed in one or more dimensions. To anticipate sales trends, for instance, all sales offices are rolled up into the sales division or department. On the other hand, the drill-down method enables users to peruse the details. Users can see, for example, the sales of each product that goes into the sales of a particular region. Using the slicing and dicing feature, users can extract (slice) a particular set of data from the OLAP cube and observe (dicate) the slices from various angles. These perspectives—such as examining the same sales by salesperson, date, customer, product, or region—are sometimes referred to as dimensions.

OLAP-configured databases employ a multidimensional data model, which enables quick execution of intricate analytical and ad hoc queries. They incorporate elements of relational, hierarchical, and navigational databases.

Online transaction processing, or OLTP, is commonly used to compare OLAP and is typified by much simpler queries in higher volumes that are processed for transaction processing instead of business intelligence or reporting. While OLTP systems must handle all query types (read, insert, update, and delete), OLAP systems are primarily optimized for reading.

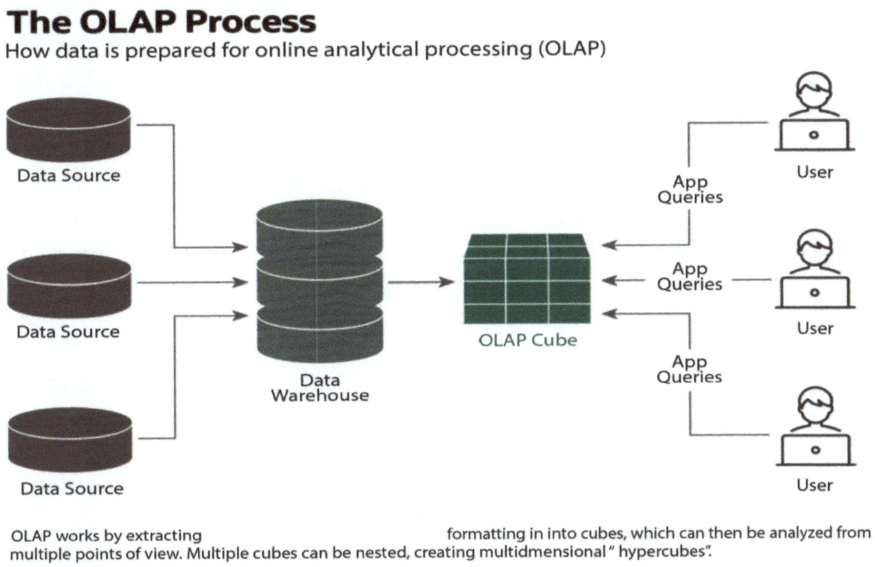

Figure 3.4. *The OLAP process.*

Source: https://www.netsuite.com/portal/resource/articles/erp/online-analytical-processing-olap.shtml.

3.4.1. Overview of OLAP systems

An OLAP cube, also known as a "multidimensional cube" or a "hypercube," is the central component of any OLAP system. It is made up of quantifiable facts grouped by dimensions called measures. The dimensions span a vector space called the hypercube, around which the measures are positioned at its intersections. An OLAP cube is typically manipulated using a matrix interface, which works along the dimensions to perform projection operations like aggregation and averaging. These interfaces are similar to pivot tables in spreadsheet programs.

Usually, a star schema, snowflake schema, or fact constellation of tables in a relational database is used to generate the cube metadata. Dimensions come from the dimension tables, and measures come from the records in the fact table. One way to conceptualize each measure is as a collection of labels, or meta-data, related to it. These labels are characterized by a dimension, which offers details regarding the measure.

A cube with the sales of a store as the measure and the date and time as the dimension would be a straightforward example. Every sale has a Date/Time label with additional information about the sale.

3.4.1.1. Multidimensional Databases

A multidimensional structure is a variant of the relational model that expresses the relationships between data and organizes data using multidimensional structures. The structure is divided into cubes, each of which has its own space for storing and accessing data. A multidimensional structure's cells each hold aggregated information about elements along each of its dimensions. Data is still accessible and maintains its compact database format even after it has been altered. The information is still connected. For analytical databases that make use of online analytical processing (OLAP) tools, multidimensional structure is highly common. These databases are used by analytical databases because they can provide complex business query answers (Williams, Garza, Tucker, et al., 1994).

3.4.1.2. Aggregations

According to some claims, OLAP cubes can respond to complex queries in about 0.1 percent of the time needed to respond to the same query on OLTP relational data. The use of aggregations is the primary OLAP mechanism that enables it to achieve such performance. By altering the granularity on particular dimensions and aggregating data along these dimensions using an aggregate function, aggregations are constructed from the fact table (or aggregation function). All possible combinations of dimension granularities determine the total number of possible aggregations.

All queries that can be answered by the data are contained in the combination of all conceivable aggregations and the base data.

Only a predetermined number of aggregations are frequently fully calculated because there are typically many that can be calculated; the remaining aggregations are solved on demand. The view selection problem is the process of choosing which aggregations (views) to compute. The size of the chosen set of aggregations as a whole, the amount of time it takes to update them in light of changes in the base data, or both may limit the choice of views. Though some studies also aim to minimize the update time, the general goal of view selection is to reduce the average response time to OLAP queries. The chosen view is NP-Complete. Numerous methods have been investigated for solving the issue, such as genetic algorithms, randomized search, greedy algorithms, and the A* search algorithm.

By pre-calculating values for each cell and then aggregating these aggregates, it is possible to compute some aggregation functions for the entire OLAP cube. Then, by applying a divide and conquer algorithm to the multidimensional problem, these aggregations can be efficiently computed for a roll-up of cells. A roll-up, for instance, has an overall sum that is equal to the sum of the sub-sums in each cell. Self-decomposable aggregation functions, such as COUNT, MAX, MIN, and SUM, can be computed for each cell and then aggregated directly. These functions are also referred to as decomposable aggregation functions.

In other situations, the aggregate function can be calculated as follows: AVERAGE (which tracks sum and count and divides at the end) and RANGE (which tracks max and min and subtracts at the end) are two examples of auxiliary numbers that can be computed for cells, aggregated, and then the overall number at the end. Other cases include DISTINCT COUNT, MEDIAN, and MODE; for instance, the median of a set is not the median of the medians of subsets. In these cases, the aggregate function cannot be computed without analyzing the entire set at once, though in some cases approximations can be computed. The latter are more challenging to implement effectively in OLAP since they necessitate calculating the aggregate function on the base data, which can be done in two ways: online (slow) or in advance for potential rollouts (large space).

3.4.2. Types

OLAP systems have been traditionally categorized using the following taxonomy.

3.4.2.1. Multidimensional OLAP (MOLAP)

The traditional version of OLAP, known as MOLAP (multi-dimensional online analytical processing), is also sometimes referred to as simply OLAP. Instead of storing this data in a relational database, MOLAP stores it in an optimized multi-dimensional array storage.

Processing is the process of pre-calculating and storing derived data, like consolidations, for some MOLAP tools. These MOLAP tools typically make use of a data cube, which is a pre-calculated data set. All of the potential responses to a specific set of questions are contained in the data cube. They respond to inquiries very quickly as a result. On the other hand, the level of pre-computation can affect how long updating takes. Another consequence of pre-computation is a phenomenon called "data explosion."

Other MOLAP tools, especially those that use the functional database model, compute all calculations on demand, save for those that were previously requested and cached. Instead of pre-compiling derived data.

1. Advantages of MOLAP
   - Fast query performance due to optimized storage, multidimensional indexing and caching.
   - Smaller on-disk size of data compared to data stored in relational database due to compression techniques.
   - Automated computation of higher level aggregates of the data.
   - It is very compact for low dimension data sets.
   - Array models provide natural indexing.
   - Effective data extraction achieved through the pre-structuring of aggregated data.
2. Disadvantages of MOLAP
   - Within some MOLAP systems the processing step (data load) can be quite lengthy, especially on large data volumes. This is usually remedied by doing only incremental processing, i.e., processing only the data which have changed (usually new data) instead of reprocessing the entire data set.
   - Some MOLAP methodologies introduce data redundancy.

3.4.2.2. Relational OLAP (ROLAP)

ROLAP does not require pre-computation and interacts directly with relational databases. To store the aggregated data, new tables are created and joined to the base data and dimension tables, which are stored as relational tables. It is dependent upon a unique schema design. This methodology is based on modifying the relational database's data to mimic the look and feel of traditional OLAP's slicing and dicing capabilities. Slicing and dicing is essentially the same as adding a "WHERE" clause to the SQL statement. Instead of utilizing pre-calculated data cubes, ROLAP tools query a typical relational database and its tables to retrieve the information needed to respond to the query. Because the methodology used in ROLAP tools is not restricted to cube contents, any question can be asked. Additionally, ROLAP can drill down to the database's most basic level of detail.

Even though ROLAP uses a relational database source, ROLAP typically requires careful database design. An OLTP-designed database will not perform well in a ROLAP environment. As a result, ROLAP still requires making a second copy of the information. But since it's a database, you can fill it with data from a range of technologies.

1. Advantages of ROLAP

- ROLAP is thought to be more scalable when managing massive amounts of data, particularly for models with extremely high cardinality dimensions (i.e., millions of participants).
- Compared to automated MOLAP loads, load times are typically substantially lower due to the availability of a wide range of data loading tools and the capacity to customize the extract, transform, and load (ETL) code to the specific data model.
- Any SQL reporting tool can access the data, which are kept in a typical relational database; an OLAP tool is not required.
- Textual descriptions are examples of non-aggregatable facts that are better handled by ROLAP tools. MOLAP tools typically perform poorly when attempting to query these elements.
- Data that would not otherwise fit into a strict dimensional model can be successfully modeled by separating the data storage from the multi-dimensional model.
- Utilizing database authorization controls like row-level security, which filters query results based on predetermined criteria applied, for instance, to a specific user or group of users, is possible with the ROLAP approach.

2. Disadvantages of ROLAP

- The industry as a whole agrees that MOLAP tools perform faster than ROLAP tools. But take a look at the discussion of ROLAP performance below.
- Custom ETL code is required to control the loading of aggregate tables. This task is not aided by the ROLAP tools. This implies more code to support and more time for development.
- The larger detailed tables must be queried, which negatively affects query performance if the step of creating aggregate tables is skipped. It is still impractical to create aggregate tables for every combination of dimensions and attributes, even though this can be somewhat fixed by adding more aggregate tables.
- Since ROLAP depends on the general purpose database for caching and querying, it is not able to use some of the specialized methods that MOLAP tools employ (like special hierarchical indexing). On the other hand, contemporary ROLAP tools leverage the most recent enhancements in the SQL language, including DB2 Cube Views, CUBE and ROLLUP operators, and additional SQL OLAP extensions. The advantages of the MOLAP tools may be offset by these SQL enhancements.

- ROLAP tools are not appropriate when the model contains a lot of calculations that don't convert well into SQL because they rely entirely on SQL for all of their calculations. These models include financial reporting, allocations, budgeting, and other scenarios.

3. Performance of ROLAP

Within the OLAP space, ROLAP is typically thought to be more scalable for larger data sets than MOLAP, but at the expense of slower query performance. Companies using ROLAP report slower performance than those using MOLAP, even when data volumes are taken into account, according to the OLAP Survey, the largest independent survey across all major OLAP products, which was conducted over six years (2001–2006). But, as with any survey, there are a few nuanced considerations that need to be made when analyzing the findings.

- According to the survey, within each company, ROLAP tools have seven times as many users as MOLAP tools. During periods of peak usage, systems with a higher user count are likely to experience more performance issues.
- Another concern is the model's complexity, which is determined by the number of dimensions as well as the depth of the computations. There isn't a reliable method in the survey to account for these differences in the data being examined.

4. Downside of Flexibility

Since relational database tables are often not optimally designed for OLAP use, some businesses choose ROLAP with the intention of reusing them. This subpar design can function because of the greater flexibility of ROLAP tools, but performance suffers. On the other hand, MOLAP tools would require that the data be loaded again into an ideal OLAP design.

3.4.2.3. Hybrid OLAP (HOLAP)

The majority of commercial OLAP tools today employ a Hybrid OLAP (HOLAP) approach, which gives the model designer the ability to select which portion of the data will be stored in ROLAP and which portion in MOLAP due to the unfavorable trade-off between slow query performance and additional ETL costs. The industry is divided on what exactly qualifies as Hybrid OLAP, other than the fact that a database will split data between relational and specialized storage. Relational tables, for instance, are used by some vendors in HOLAP databases to store the larger amounts of detailed data, while specialized storage is used for some or all of the smaller amounts of more-aggregate or less-detailed data. By combining the advantages of MOLAP and ROLAP, HOLAP overcomes their respective flaws. Relational data sources and pre-calculated cubes can both be used with HOLAP tools. (Kaser, Owen; Lemire, Daniel, 2006)

- **Vertical Partitioning:** In this mode, HOLAP optimizes cube processing time by storing detailed data in ROLAP and aggregates in MOLAP for quick query performance.
- **Horizontal partitioning:** In this mode, HOLAP saves a portion of the data in ROLAP for older data and typically stores the more recent data (i.e., sliced by Time dimension) in MOLAP for quick query performance. Furthermore, we can take advantage of the fact that a large cuboid will have both dense and sparse subregions by storing some dice in MOLAP and others in ROLAP.

3.5. OLAP VISUALIZATION OPERATOR FOR COMPLEX DATA

Online Analysis Processing (OLAP) and data warehouses are two well-known and practical tools for aiding in decision-making. Multiple-dimensional data display is made possible by operators in online analysis. This technology works best with simple data and fact analysis using both quantitative measurements and qualitative descriptors in multiple dimensions. The emergence of complex data has called into question the data warehousing and online analysis process, though.

Complex data often contain a document, an image, a video,..., and each of these elements can be described and observed by a set of low-level descriptors or by semantic descriptors. This set of elements can be seen not only as complex data but also as a complex object. A complex object is a heterogeneous set of data, which, when combined, form a semantic unit.

Complex objects require modifications to online analytical processes and warehousing procedures. Online analysis aims to: (1) compile a large amount of data to provide a summary of the information it contains; (2) present the data using various dimensions; and (3) search through the data to investigate them.

For traditional data, OLAP operators are well-defined. However, when dealing with complex data, they fall short. Using different methods, like data mining, could be beneficial. An intriguing way to improve OLAP's capacity to analyze complex objects is to integrate data mining techniques with the platform.

3.5.1. Positioning and Principle

A cube is typically represented by an OLAP interface as a table or cross-table. More sophisticated tools (interactive scatter plots, hierarchical visualizations, trees of decomposition multi-scale views) provide visual alternatives to represent the data contained in a cube and to interact with the cube in an effort to go beyond the limitations of standard interfaces. In order to improve information visualization, Sureau et al recommend rearranging a level's modalities using genetic algorithms, heuristics, or measurements of the distances between the elements in a dimension. Ordonez and Chen used a statistical test to look for adjacent cells with noticeably different measures inside a low-dimensional cube. Regarding OLAP and Web applications, Aouiche et al. utilize a tag cloud to depict a cube in which the size of each keyword is determined by the fact's measured value (cell), and each keyword is represented by a cell (Aouiche, Lemire & Godin, 2008).

We propose a visualization operator (1) in the context of online analysis (2) that considers the semantic content of the data (3) that is appropriate for complex objects (4) and does not require any assumptions about the data, in contrast to the other approaches that have been presented. Even though some may be modified for such data, OLAP visualization works do not handle complex objects or account for the semantic content—tag clouds appear to be the only ones that do this.

We suggest a technique that makes use of factor analysis, a well-known data mining technique, to visualize complex objects. It is possible to visualize complex objects and highlight interesting facts for analysis by using the factor method. There is frequently no measure in the traditional sense of multi-dimensional modeling when facts are complex objects. That being said, one can always count the facts. In this instance, a contingency table can be perceived in the multi-dimensional complex object cube with the COUNT function. It is possible to present the facts using correspondence analysis (CA). Factor axes, or "factor dimensions," are created by CA and can be utilized as new dimensions. These additional dimensions or axes create a new space where the facts, or complex objects, can be plotted. Since the objective of this approach is the same as that of OLAP navigation and exploration, using CA as the visualization operator is entirely justified.

3.5.2. Process

We offer OLAP users a procedure that consists of the following steps: (1) creating the contingency table, (2) building the complex object cube, (3) finishing the correspondence analysis, and (4) mapping complex objects on the factorial axes. Assume that the user wishes to research keywords to determine the main areas of study that researchers are engaged in. The user would also like to see which researchers are focusing on the same keywords.

- **Notation:** Let C be a cube with a non-empty set of d dimensions $D = \{D^1, .., D^i, .., D^d\}$ and m measures $M = \{M_1, .., M_q, .., M_m\}$. H_i is the set of hierarchical levels of dimension D_i . H_j^i is the j hierarchical level of dimension D_i . For example, the type of publication dimension D1 has two levels: the level Type denoted H_2^1. and the level Scope denoted H_2^1. $\mathcal{A}^{ij} = \{a_1^{ij}, ..., a_t^{ij}, ..., a_l^{ij}\}$ is the set of the l members or modalities a_t^{ij} of the hierarchical level H_j^i of the dimension D^i. The level Scope (H_2^1) has two members: International, denoted a_1^{12} and National, denoted a a_2^{12}.
- **Complex Object Cube:** Depending on what the user wants to analyze, a cube is defined. This constructed cube is a sub-cube from the initial cube C. Let D⊠ be a non-empty sub-set of D with p dimensions $\{D^1,$

.., D^p} ($D' \subseteq D$ and $p \leq d$). The p-tuple (Θ^1, .., Θ^p) is sub-cube if $\forall_i \in \{1, .., p\}$, $\Theta^i /= \emptyset$ and if there is an unique $j \geq 1$ such that $\Theta i \subseteq A^{ij}$. A sub-cube, noted C′, corresponds to a portion from the initial cube C. Of the d existing dimensions, only p are chosen. For each chosen dimension $Di \in D'$, a hierarchical level H_j^i is selected and a non-empty sub-set Θ^i of members is taken from all the member set A^{ij} of the level.

- **Contingency Table:** Classically, correspondence analysis takes as input a contingency table. Our idea is to use traditional OLAP operators to build this contingency table.

  In the sub-cube C ′, the user chooses two levels (one level for two different dimensions), on which he wants to visualize complex objects. Let Θ^i (respectively $\Theta^{i'}$) be the set of l (respectively l′) members chosen for the level of the dimension i (respectively i′). The contingency table T has l rows and l′ columns the titles of which are given by $\{a_1^{ij}, ..., a_t^{ij}, ..., a_l^{ij}\}$ and $\{a_1^{i'j'}, ..., a_{t'}^{i'j'}, ..., a_{l'}^{i'j'}\}$. At each intersection of row t and column t′, are counted the facts having the members a_t^{ij} and $a_{t'}^{i'j'}$.

- **Correspondence analysis:** Projecting data onto artificial axes allows a minimum number of axes to express a large amount of information, which is the process of processing a CA. The objective is to decrease the number of rows and columns in the representation space, thereby decreasing its size. The projections of rows and columns in the same plane can be seen simultaneously thanks to the CA. It is possible to interpret the distances between the rows and columns.

  In actual use, the process begins with computing the eigen values, from which the eigen vectors that specify the factor axes are inferred. The first factor plane is defined by the first two axes because they have the most information. Auxiliary statistics are presented after row and column points have been projected onto axes in order to assess the accuracy of the axes and their interpretation. The weight, the relative contribution of the point to the axis' inertia, and the quality of the representation on the axis (as determined by the $cosine^2$) are the most crucial statistics for each point. Only points that are well represented by the axis (whose $cosine^2$ is greater than 0.5) and that significantly contribute to the axis' inertia (whose contribution is three times the average contribution) are considered when interpreting an axis and analyzing the proximity between points on it.

CASE STUDY

ADVANCED VISUALIZATION FOR OLAP

In the last years, On-Line Analytical Processing (OLAP) and data warehousing have become major research areas in the database community. Although the modeling of data has been extensively dealt with, an equally important issue of the OLAP domain, the visualization of data, has not been adequately investigated. In the context of OLAP, data visualization deals with the techniques and tools used for presenting OLAP specific information to end-users and decision makers. The database

community expects visualization to be of significant importance in the area, during the next years, and although research has provided results dealing with the presentation of vast amounts of data, OLAP has not been part of advanced visualization techniques so far.

In this study, we start by adopting a newly introduced presentation model for OLAP called Cube Presentation Model – CPM and demonstrate how it can be combined with nontraditional visualization techniques. The CPM model distinguishes representation from data retrieval. It is separated in two layers: a logical that deals with data retrieval and representation and a presentational that provides a generic model for data representation. We present a quick informal overview of the main characteristics of CPM and accompany them with its respective UML modeling for ease of understanding.

- Initially, we present a mapping of the generic presentational scheme of CPM to the particularities of an advanced visualization technique coming from the field of Human Computer Interaction. The Table Lens technique is particularly tailored for cross-tab reports, which are most commonly used for OLAP purposes and it is accompanied by a set of handy features for the exploration of data sets which are presented in this way.
- Next, we provide algorithms for the automated proactive support of the user during his interaction with an OLAP screen, based on the particularities of Table Lens. Specifically, Table Lens employs a particular distortion of the presentation to highlight areas of increasing interest to the user. We provide a generic algorithm to support this task proactively.
- Finally, we discuss the necessity and the applicability of such visualization techniques in the presence of current technological developments.

1. **The Cube Presentation Model:** Although OLAP has been an active research area for the past few years, the efforts devoted to the visualization of OLAP screens are very scarce. To our knowledge, only two such efforts exist. The first is from the industrial field, where Microsoft has issued a commercial standard

for multidimensional databases and where the presentational issues form a major part. In this approach, a powerful query language is used to provide the user with complex reports, created from several cubes (or actually subsets of existing cubes). The second is an academic approach, the Tape Model, based on the notion of "Tapes," called so due to their look and feel. Tapes are infinite and can overlap (if they contain shared data dimensions), or intersect with each other. A two dimensional intersection is called a matrix and represents a kind of cross-tab between the corresponding dimensions. Each tape comprises of a variable number of tracks. The most important operations on tapes include: (a) insertion and deletion of tracks, (b) changing the sequence of tracks (i.e., sorting) and (c) scrolling on tracks. The Tape Model offers the possibility of defining hierarchical structures within a tape.

We have presented the Cube Presentation Model (CPM), a novel proposal towards a presentation model for OLAP screens. CPM is composed of two parts: (a) a logical layer which involves the formulation of cubes and (b) a presentational layer that involves the presentation of these cubes (normally, on a 2D screen). The main idea behind CPM lies in the separation of logical data retrieval (which we encapsulate in the logical layer of CPM) and data presentation (captured from the presentational layer of CPM). This duality provides the flexibility of possibly replacing one of the two layers with an alternative proposal smoothly. The logical layer that we propose is based on an extension of a previous proposal with additional functionality that allows us to incorporate more complex cubes. In a nutshell, the logical model involves (a) dimensions defined as lattices of dimension levels, (b) ancestor functions mapping values between related levels of a dimension, (c) detailed data sets, practically modeling fact tables at the lowest granule of information for all their dimensions and (d) cubes, defined as aggregations over detailed data sets. In this paper, we will not deal with the formal presentation of the underlying logical layer of CPM but focus on the mapping of our presentation layer to alternative visualization techniques from the area of Human Computer Interaction.

Following, we give an intuitive and informal description of the presentation layer of CPM that provides a formal model for OLAP screens.

The most important entities – as far as display aspects are concerned – of the presentation layer of CPM include:

- **Points:** A point over an axis resembles the classical notion of points over axes in mathematics. In the simple case, a point is characterized by an equality selection condition over a level (e.g., City=Seattle). Nevertheless, as we shall see, we can multiplex several logical dimensions to one presentational axis; therefore, a point will be formally defined to handle this kind of situations, too.
- **Axis:** An axis can be viewed as a set of points. We introduce two special purpose kinds of axes, Invisible and Content. An Invisible axis is a placeholder for the

levels of the data set which are to be presented to the user. The Content axis has a more elaborate role: it is a place holder for the content of the multicube, as computed over the detailed data

- **Multicubes:** A multicube is defined over (a) a multidimensional space, comprising a set of axes, (b) an underlying data set providing all the data which will be filtered and aggregated before presented to the user and (c) a mapping among the multidimensional space and the underlying data set that shows the computation of the multicube contents.
- **2D-slice:** A 2D slice is a 2D layer of data that can be presented on the screen. Consider a multicube MC, composed of K axes. A 2D-slice over MC can be sufficiently defined by a set of (K-2) points, each from a separate axis. Intuitively, a 2D-slice pins the axes of the multicube to specific points, except for 2 axes, which will be presented on the screen (or a printout).
- **Tape:** Intuitively, a tape is column or a row over a 2D-slice, i.e., a construct parallel to an axis. Again, if we consider a 2Dslice SL over a multicube MC, composed of K axes, a tape is sufficiently defined by a set of (K-1) points, where the (K-2) points are the points of SL. A tape is always parallel to a specific axis: out of the two "free" axis of the 2D-slice, we pin one of them to a specific point which distinguishes the tape from the 2D-slice.
- **Cross-join:** Intuitively, if we take one tape parallel to the horizontal axis and another parallel to the vertical axis, their intersection is a cell. In the most general case, as we shall see, it can be a set of cells. In both cases, the intersection of two non-parallel tapes is called a cross-join. Consider a 2D-slice SL over a multicube MC, composed of K axes and two tapes t_1 and t_2 which are not parallel to the same axis. A cross-join over t_1 and t_2 is defined by a set of K points, where the (K-2) points are the points of SL and each of the two remaining points is a point on a different axis of the remaining axes of the slice.
- **Content Function:** At the schema level, we assume a function assigning the computation of measures to the Content axis of the multicube, along with ordering and other restrictions. We also assume a function, mapping combinations of multicube coordinates, one from each of the coordinate axis of the multicube to the measure axis. Each such assignment is practically a row in the result set of one of the queries/expressions/... computing the multicube, which we call cell. For brevity, in the sequel, we simply tag the Content axis with this information.

```
SELECT CROSSJOIN({Venk,Netz},{USA_N.Children,USA_S,Japan}) ON COLUMNS
{Qtr1.CHILDREN,Qtr2,Qtr3,Qtr4.CHILDREN} ON ROWS
FROM SalesCube
WHERE (Sales,[1991],Products.ALL)
```

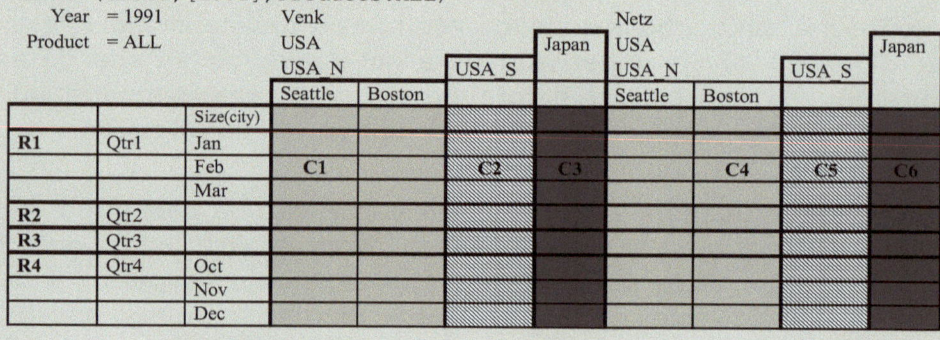

Figure 3.5. *Motivating example for the cube model.*

Interpreting our motivating example in terms of CPM, we assume a detailed data set, named SalesCube, under the schema:

S = [Quarter.Day, Salesman.Salesman,

Geography.City, Time.Day,

Product.Item, Sales, PercentChange,

BudgetedSales]

The following axis schemata can also be discerned in Figure 3.6:

Row_S = {[Quarter], [Month,Quarter, Quarter,

Month]}

Column_S = {[Salesman×Geography],

[Salesman]×[[City,Size(City)],

Region,Country]}

Section_S = {[Time],[Year]}

Invisible_S = {[Product],[Product.ALL]}

Content_S = {[Sales],[sum(Sales0

)]}

Along with their respective axes:

```
Rows =    {Row_S,[anc_day^month(Month)=Qtr1,
          Quarter=Qtr2, Quarter=Qtr3,
          anc_day^month(Month)=Qtr4]}
Columns = {Column_S, {[Salesman='Venk',
          Salesman='Netz'],
          [anc_city^region(City)='USA_N',
          Region='USA_S', Country='Japan']}
Sections = {Section_S,[Year=1991,Year=1992]}
Invisible = {Invisible_S,[ALL='all']}
Content = {Content_S}
```

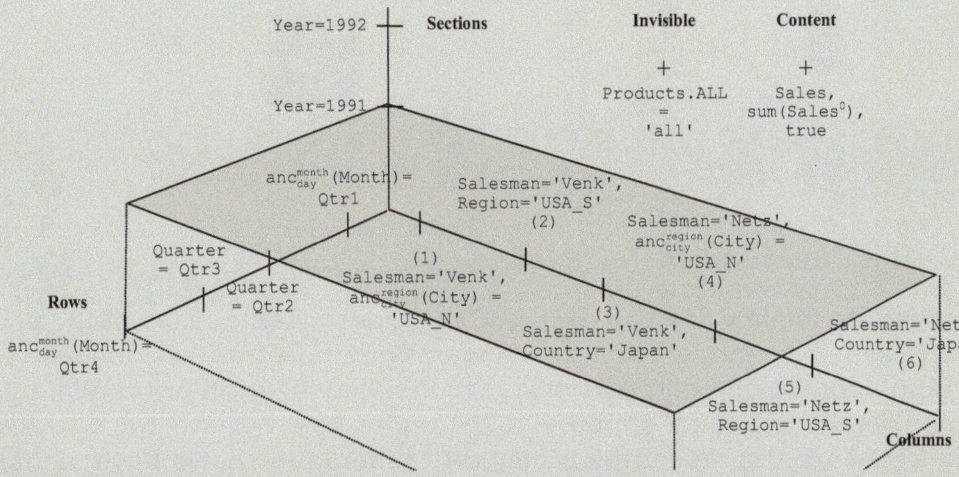

Figure 3.6. *The 2D-slice SL.*

In Figure 3.6, we can also observe an exemplary point over an axis, incorporating equality conditions for each of the involved dimensions of the axis:

$$p_1 = ([\text{Salesman}, [\underline{\text{City}}, \text{Size(City)}]], [\text{Salesman='Venk'}, \text{anc}_{\text{city}}^{\text{region}}(\text{City})=\text{'USA\_N'}])$$

Thus, a multicube MC can be defined as:

MC = {Rows, Columns, Sections, Invisible, Content}

Finally, in Figure 3.7, we present some more comprehensive visualization representations of multicubes, axes, points, 2D slices and cross-joins on a 3D and 2D layout.

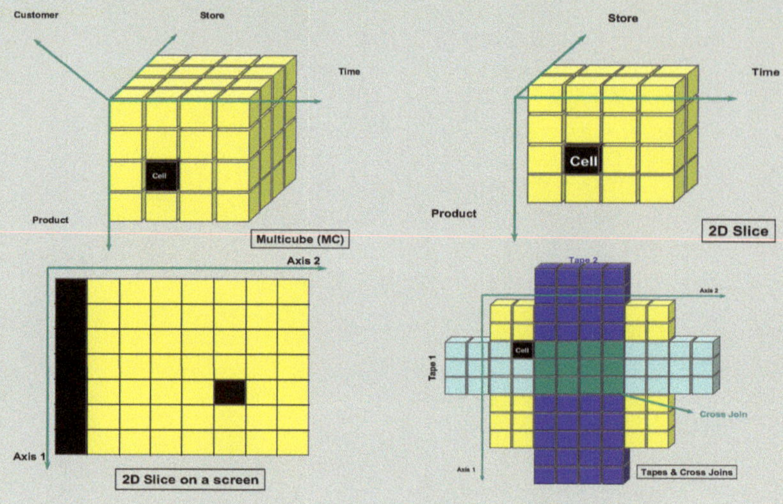

Figure 3.7. *Mapping CPM objects to 3D and 2D cross tabular layouts.*

2. Mapping CPM to Visualization Techniques

We will demonstrate how CPM can be combined with Table Lens (TL), a traditional cross-tabular presentation model from the Human Computer Interaction area. This model is widely used in applications and platforms for the visualization of tabular, multivariate and multidimensional data and appears to be quite appropriate for OLAP purposes. Table Lens is based on the "focus plus context" technique that allows visualizing and manipulating large 2-D tables. Using Table Lens, we can easily examine patterns and correlations in large tables and effectively zoom in without losing the global picture of our data. We have chosen Table Lens as an advanced visualization technique due to the fact that it is based on a cross tabular paradigm for the presentation of information; a paradigm quite popular in OLAP screens, too.

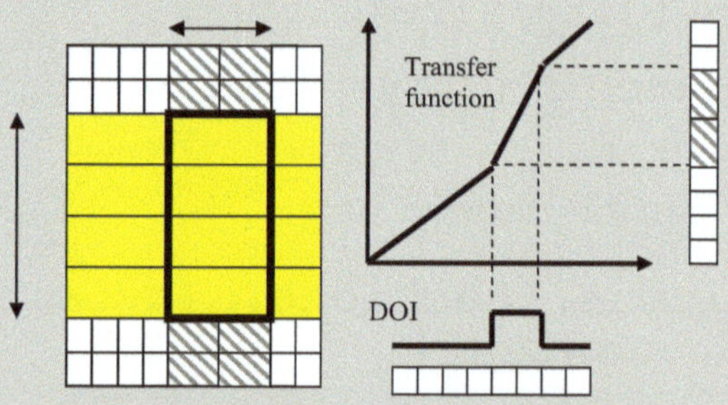

Figure 3.8. *A table lens example: (a) a 2x4 focus window is defined over a space of 8x8 points; (b) Table Lens distortion of the columns axis.*

Mapping CPM to Table Lens

We will present the main features of Table Lens, and then we will link it to the CPM model. The main constructs of the Table Lens technique involve:

- **Axes:** The Table Lens model assumes two axes. For clarity, we will use Rows and Columns to denote these two axes.
- **2D Space:** The 2D space is constructed from the Cartesian product of the two Table Lens axes. It is a (finite) matrix of cells.
- **Degree of Interest Function (DOI):** DOI is a function that maps each axis point to a value that indicates the level of interest for that point. For each axis a different DOI function is prescribed.
- **Transfer Function:** A transfer function maps each cell to its physical locations, indicating the level of zoom for each cell. Practically, the transfer function is the translation of the respective DOI function (operating at the "interest" space) to the "pixel" space.

Motivation and Assumptions

Before providing the generic algorithm, let us clarify our contribution through a specific example. Let us assume that when the user activates this OLAP screen, he would like to be informed on three particular cross-joins: one involving the maximum sales, another involving the lowest and a third involving the cross-join with behavior closest to the average of the whole screen. Practically, this involves three windows of focus, which we depict through a thick border around the involved cross-joins. In this particular case, the cross-join R1/C6 is the one with the lowest summary of values, the cross-join R4/C4 the one with the highest sum and the cross-join R2/C3 is the one closest to the average sales per cross-join (which amounts to 240.5 sales per cross-join).

A vanilla algorithm to compute the aforementioned quantities proceeds as follows: (a) summarizes all cells per cross-join; (b) sorts cross-joins and computes the average cross-join value and (c) pinpoints the three regions of interest. This algorithm has linear (precisely, one-pass) complexity on the number of cells and nlogn (due to sorting) complexity on the number of cross-joins. Actually, if we are simply to keep the max, min or closest-to-avg cross-join, a linear single pass from all the cells is sufficient, without any sorting. In the case of avg, each time that we summarize the cells from a cross-join we can compute the average of the individual cross-join summaries and compute the closest cross-join to the current value of this average.

A Generic Algorithm for Determining the Window of Focus

Naturally, we can do better than the aforementioned vanilla algorithm by adding extra criteria to the proactive selection of the starting window of focus. We propose a guided greedy generic algorithm, GenericFocusWindow, to deal with the issue. The simple idea underlying the algorithm is that there are certain conditions to be met for the focus window. For example, one could require that the focus window occupies at most/least a certain percentage of the screen size, or of a certain size of cells. Moreover, the selected window optimizes an objective function. The property Determining Quality of the algorithms captures exactly this requirement in the form of a certain function. Since our algorithm is greedy, we need an Original Pick routine to start the processing; in general this is closely related to the Determining Quality function and we require that it starts with a smallest value. Moreover, a Guard Condition checks for the satisfaction of the desired property (meaning that we can possibly allow a certain approximation error ⊠ to out obtained solution). Finally, a function Pick provides the necessary details for working from the original small-in-value solution towards the final result, practically picking the next cross-join to enlarge the current window of focus.

One implicit assumption that our algorithm makes is that the Original Pick fits inside the allowed window. This constraint can easily be relaxed by an extension of the algorithm picking subparts of a cross-join in a similar fashion with the proposed algorithm, if we consider that we pick subparts of a 2Dslice. For lack of space we do not incorporate this extension too.

Discussion

At this point, we would like to take the time to discuss the larger framework of the contribution of this paper. First, as the Lowell report mentions, visualization is one of the big issues of database research for the next years. To copy from the Lowell report, "The original Laguna-Beach report lamented that there was little research on user interfaces to DBMSs. ... There have not been comparable advances in the last 15 years. There is a crying need for better ideas in this area." We claim that of all fields of database research, decision support and OLAP are the ones to be affected most out of this phenomenon.

Someone could possibly question the need for a new model. For us it is clear that one of the main reasons for the research community not dealing with visualization issues so far, is the heritage of the computing paradigm of the past three decades. This paradigm silently made the assumption that the user sitting in front of a console makes one query and retrieves one answer (as would have happened in a UNIX terminal 30 years ago). This is not the case with modern user interfaces for datasets, especially in the context of OLAP. The user makes simultaneously many queries, combined in one or more screens; nevertheless, all our modeling techniques and languages so far (from the relational model, to SQL and the OLAP modeling efforts proposed in the academia) simply ignore this fact. Our effort tries to formalize the simultaneous presence of more than one queries and this is done in two layers. In the presentational layer we provide a uniform and generic model for the user interface, which hides the complexity of answer retrieval, detached in the logical layer. As a second interesting difference, note that the users work in sessions of queries, as opposed to sequences of unrelated queries. OLAP is a typical, but not the only, case for this behavior. As a first attempt towards the issue, we have carefully selected a visualization technique from the fields of Human-Computer Interaction and Information Visualization with the particularity of being crafted specifically for tabular data and we have customized it for OLAP. Naturally, we do not claim that this is the ultimate solution to the problem, but rather we wish to indicate that there is quite an interesting research field in this area and a supportive body of knowledge from other disciplines, such as Human Computer Interaction and Information Visualization.

At the same time, new hardware developments pose new requirements for our visualization techniques. One of our goals is to implement OLAP visualization techniques for particularly small devices such mobile phones and palmtops. Although the processing power of these gadgets is no more negligible (actually, the buzzword 'thin client' seems to disappear from the standard vocabulary of the area) their screen sizes shrink over time. To make OLAP screens presentable to such devices one can follow several paths, such as: (a) show only high level summaries which involve small 2D slices or (b) show simply pie- or bar-charts. We choose an alternative approach where (a) the contents of the screen do not have to be squeezed in size in order to fit in the screen, and most importantly (b) the report does not have to be rewritten neither do we have to check for the aggregation level of the presented data. On the contrary, a certain part of the report is presented depending on the particularities of the device. Here, we make the reasonable assumption that either the device has the computational power to determine the amount of cells that can be presented to the user or, if this is not an option, the device can at least piggy-back its characteristics to the OLAP server and let the server decide on the focus window.

Third, making the discussion a little broader, we bring up the Table Lens technique to highlight the possibility of making proactive user decision support in the presence of large datasets (in our case, the value axis is quite larger than the size that someone can handle efficiently). Clearly, as report screens are limited not only due to hardware constraints, but also due to the particularities of human nature (e.g., the classical discussion on the limited capacity of persons in processing information), it comes quite natural that automated proactive support to the users is thus one of the new requirements that decision support tools have to provide. Thus, this end of our contribution is related to a broader line of research.

Conclusions

In this study, we have demonstrated how the Cube Presentation Model, a novel presentation model for OLAP data can be naturally mapped into an advanced visualization technique, the Table Lens. Initially, we have defined the mapping scheme from the Cube Presentation Model to Table Lens entities and objects. Then, we have introduced suitable algorithms for proactive automated support of the user towards the highlighting of interesting areas of a report. Finally, we have discussed on the usefulness and applicability of the proposed techniques to modern technological developments.

CLASS ACTIVITY

Divide students into small groups and provide each group with the sample dataset. Assign each group to perform specific OLAP operations on the dataset using spreadsheet software or an OLAP tool.

Group 1: Perform a Roll-up operation.

Group 2: Perform a Drill-down operation.

Group 3: Perform a Slice operation.

Group 4: Perform a Dice operation.

Group 5: Perform a Pivot operation.

SUMMARY

- Data exploration refers to the initial step in data analysis in which data analysts use data visualization and statistical techniques to describe dataset characterizations, such as size, quantity, and accuracy, in order to better understand the nature of the data.
- Manual data exploration methods entail either writing scripts to analyze raw data or manually filtering data into spreadsheets.
- It is most important to understand that high quality of input data is crucial for achieving a good quality of output before getting to the actual data exploration process.
- Summary statistics are quantities, such as the mean and standard deviation, that capture various characteristics of a potentially large set of values with a single number or a small set of numbers.
- For continuous data, two of the most widely used summary statistics are the mean and median, which are measures of the location of a set of values.
- Data visualization is the display of information in a graphic or tabular format. Successful visualization requires that the data (information) be converted into a visual format so that the characteristics of the data and the relationships among data items or attributes can be analyzed or reported.
- The first step in visualization is the mapping of information to a visual format; i.e., mapping the objects, attributes, and relationships in a set of information to visual objects, attributes, and relationships.

- Another key concept in visualization is selection, which is the elimination or the de-emphasis of certain objects and attributes.
- Visualization techniques are often specialized to the type of data being analyzed. Indeed, new visualization techniques and approaches, as well as specialized variations of existing approaches, are being continuously created, typically in response to new kinds of data and visualization tasks.
- Stem and leaf plots are a type of histogram, a plot that displays the distribution of values for attributes by dividing the possible values into bins and showing the number of objects that fall into each bin.
- Box plots are another method for showing the distribution of the values of a single numerical attribute.
- A pie chart is similar to a histogram, but is typically used with categorical attributes that have a relatively small number of values.
- Online analytical processing, or OLAP, is an approach to quickly answer multi-dimensional analytical (MDA) queries. OLAP is part of the broader category of business intelligence, which also encompasses relational databases, report writing and data mining.

REVIEW QUESTIONS

1. What do you understand by data exploration? Also discuss its tools for data exploration.
2. What are data exploration techniques.
3. How might you extend the notion of multidimensional data analysis so that the target variable is a qualitative variable?
4. Discuss the ways to summarize the data.
5. How to map data to graphical elements.
6. Wha tare different types of OLAP systems.

REFERENCES

1. Ankerst, M., Ester, M., & Kriegel, H. (2000). Towards an effective cooperation of the computer and the user for classification. In *Proceedings of the SIGKDD International Conference on Knowledge Discovery and Data Mining* (pp. 179–188).
2. Ankerst, M., Ester, M., & Kriegel, H.-P. (2000). Towards an effective cooperation of the user and the computer for classification. In *Proceedings of the 6th ACM SIGKDD International Conference on Knowledge Discovery and Data Mining* (pp. 179–188). Boston, MA.
3. Aouiche, K., Lemire, D., & Godin, R. (2008). Web 2.0 OLAP: From data cubes to tag clouds. In *Proceedings of the 4th International Conference on Web Information Systems and Technologies (WEBIST 08)* (pp. 5–12).

4. Bornelöv, S., Enroth, S., & Komorowski, J. (2012). Visualization of rules in rule-based classifiers. In *Intelligent Decision Technologies, Smart Innovation, Systems and Technologies* (Vol. 15, pp. 329–338).
5. Chernoff, H. (1973). The use of faces to represent points in k-dimensional space graphically. *Journal of the American Statistical Association, 68*, 361–368.
6. Dilla, W. N., & Raschke, R. L. (2015). Data visualization for fraud detection: Practice implications and a call for future research. *International Journal of Accounting Information Systems, 16*, 1–22.
7. Fayyad, U. M., Piatetsky-Shapiro, G., & Smyth, P. (1996). From data mining to knowledge discovery: An overview. In *Advances in Knowledge Discovery and Data Mining* (pp. 1–34). AAAI Press and MIT Press.
8. Frawley, W., & Batheus, C. (1991). Knowledge discovery in databases: An overview. In G. Piatetsky-Shapiro & W. Frawley (Eds.), *Knowledge Discovery in Databases* (pp. 1–27). MIT Press.
9. Fua, Y., Ward, M., & Rundensteiner, E. A. (1999). Hierarchical parallel coordinates for exploration of large datasets. In *Proceedings of IEEE Visualization* (pp. 43–50).
10. Gordon, L., & Olshen, R. A. (1984). Almost sure consistent nonparametric regression from recursive partitioning schemes. *Journal of Multivariate Analysis, 15*, 147–163.
11. Grainger, S., Mao, F., & Buytaert, W. (2016). Environmental data visualization for non-scientific contexts: Literature review and design framework. *Environmental Modelling and Software, 85*, 299–318.
12. Gray, J., Chaudhuri, S., Bosworth, A., Layman, A., Reichart, D., Venkatrao, M., Pellow, F., & Pirahesh, H. (1997). Data cube: A relational aggregation operator generalizing group-by, cross-tab, and sub-totals. *Journal of Data Mining and Knowledge Discovery, 1*(1), 29–53.
13. Inselberg, A., & Dimsdale, B. (1990). Parallel coordinates: A tool for visualizing multi-dimensional geometry. In *Proceedings of Visualization 90* (pp. 361–370). San Francisco, CA.
14. Kaser, O., & Lemire, D. (2006). Attribute value reordering for efficient hybrid OLAP. *Information Sciences, 176*(16), 2304–2336.
15. Ling, C., & Li, C. (1998). Data mining for direct marketing: Problems and solutions. In *Association for the Advancement of Artificial Intelligence (AAAI), Knowledge Discovery and Data Mining* (98(11)).
16. Sancho, J. L. V., Dominguez, J. C., & Ochoa, B. E. M. (2014). An approach to the taxonomy of data visualization. *Revista Latina de Communicacion Social, 69*, 486–507.

CHAPTER 4

Classification: Basic Concepts, Decision Trees, and Model Evaluation

LEARNING OBJECTIVES

After studying this chapter, you will be able to:

- Explain the types of data
- Define the data quality
- Focus on data preprocessing

KEY TERMS FROM THIS CHAPTER

Algorithms	Boolean logic
Class	Classifier
Data	Dataset
Decision tree	K-nearest neighbor algorithm
Linear regression	Logistic regression
Machine learning	Multi-output Decision Tree Regression
Naive Bayes algorithm	Probability
Random forest classifier	Rudimentary classification algorithm

INTRODUCTION

The process of classifying objects into one of several predefined categories is a ubiquitous problem with a wide range of applications. Examples include classifying galaxies according to their shapes, identifying spam email messages based on their header and content, and classifying cells as benign or malignant based on the results of MRI scans. This chapter provides an overview of classification, discusses some of the major problems (like model overfitting), and offers techniques for assessing and contrasting classification methods.

4.1. GENERAL FRAMEWORK FOR CLASSIFICATION

One popular method used in data mining to divide data points into distinct classes is classification. It enables you to arrange datasets of all kinds, from small and straightforward datasets to large and complicated ones. To improve the quality of the data, it mainly uses easily modifiable algorithms. This is a major factor in the popularity of supervised learning in data mining techniques involving classification. Linking an interesting variable to the necessary variables is the main objective of classification. The relevant variable needs to be of the qualitative variety.

The prediction algorithm creates the connection between the variables. In data mining, the classification algorithm you use is referred to as the classifier, and the observations you make using it are referred to as instances. When working with qualitative variables in data mining, you employ classification techniques. Classification algorithms come in a variety of forms, each with special features and uses. Data extraction from a dataset is accomplished using each of those algorithms. The purpose of the task and the type of data you need to extract will determine which application you use for it.

4.1.1. Purpose of Data Classification

Analyzing data from customers, staff members, and market feedback can offer insightful information about how well a business is performing and even aid in future decision-making. Classification aims to present data in the best possible light, increasing the overall effectiveness of the data mining procedure.

4.1.2. Importance of Data Classification

Systems for classifying data are now commonplace in our daily lives. For example, the AI that manages your inbox's spam folder filters emails using data classification methods. Classification has become essential for keeping an organized and effective data environment.

4.1.3. Types of Classification Techniques in Data Mining

Let's first take a look at the different kinds of classification techniques that are available before talking about the different classification algorithms in data mining. First, the classification algorithms can be separated into two groups:

1. Generative; and
2. Discriminative.

Here's a brief explanation of these two categories:

1. **Generative:** A generative classification algorithm simulates how different classes are distributed. It makes an effort to understand the model that generates the data by estimating distributions and model assumptions. Generative algorithms can be used to forecast unknown data. Among generative algorithms, the Naive Bayes Classifier is well-known.
2. **Discriminative:** A simple classification algorithm is used to assign a class to each row of data. Instead of relying on the distributions of the data, it models using the observed data. One of the best kinds of discriminative classifiers is the logistic regression.

4.1.4. Classifiers in Machine Learning

Data mining is widely known for its classification capabilities, leading to the development of numerous classifiers in machine learning.

1. **Logistic Regression:** You can model the probability of a specific event or class using logistic regression. It models a binary dependent variable using a logistic. It provides you with the chances of a solitary attempt. Because it was designed for classification, logistic regression enables you to comprehend how several independent variables affect a single outcome variable. The problem with logistic regression is that it only functions when all of the predictors are independent and your predicted variable is binary. Furthermore, it makes the assumption that there are no missing values in the data, which can be problematic.
2. **Linear Regression:** Linear regression is a supervised learning technique used for regression analysis. It predicts a value based on independent variables and is commonly used to determine the relationship between variables. It predicts the value of a dependent variable based on a specific independent variable, identifying a linear relationship between the two. While it is efficient for linearly separable data, it is susceptible to overfitting and noise. Additionally, it assumes a linear relationship between the independent and dependent variables.
3. **Decision Trees:** The most reliable classification method in data mining is the decision tree. It is a flowchart that resembles a hierarchy. Each branch in this case represents the test's result (true or false), and every internal node denotes a test on a condition. In a decision tree, each leaf node has a class label. The decision tree can be used to divide the data into several classes. Based on the decision tree that was made, it would forecast the classes

to which a new data point would belong. Lines that are vertical and horizontal make up its prediction boundaries.

4. **Random Forest:** Several decision trees are fitted by the random forest classifier on various dataset subsamples. To improve its prediction accuracy and control overfitting, it makes use of the average. Although the samples are drawn with replacement, the sub-sample size is always equal to the input sample size. The random forest classifier has the unusual benefit of lessening overfitting. Furthermore, compared to decision trees, this classifier is substantially more accurate. Nevertheless, it is a much more complex and slower algorithm for real-time prediction, making its effective implementation extremely difficult.
5. **Naive Bayes:** According to the Naive Bayes algorithm, each feature contributes equally to the result and is independent of the others. This algorithm also works under the premise that each feature is equally important. In the modern world, it has a wide range of uses, including document classification and spam filtering. To estimate the necessary parameters, Naive Bayes only needs a modest amount of training data. A Naive Bayes classifier also performs noticeably faster than more complex and advanced classifiers. However, because it makes the assumption that every feature is equally important, which is untrue in the majority of real-world scenarios, the Naive Bayes classifier is notorious for being bad at estimation.
6. **Support Vector Machine:** The training data, which is divided into categories by wide gaps, is represented in space by the Support Vector Machine (SVM) algorithm. The categories of newly added data points are then projected based on which side of the gap they fall into after they have been mapped into the same area. Because the algorithm uses only a subset of training points in its decision function, it is particularly effective in high dimensional spaces and has a low memory footprint. Estimates of probability are not provided as quickly by this algorithm. It would be necessary to compute them using the very costly five-fold cross-validation method.
7. **K-Nearest Neighbors:** Since the k-nearest neighbor algorithm is a non-linear classifier, it has non-linear prediction boundaries. It determines the class of a new test data point by determining the class of its k closest neighbors. Using the Euclidean distance, you would choose a test data point's k closest neighbors. You would need to count the number of data points in each category in the k nearest neighbors, and then you would assign the new data point to the category with the greatest number of neighbors. Because it requires a lot of resources to find the value of k, the algorithm is fairly expensive. Its computing cost is further increased by the need to determine the separation between each instance and each training sample.

4.1.5. Applications of Classification of Data Mining Systems

Classification algorithms are used in many different contexts in daily life. The most popular ones are as follows:

- Classification algorithms are used by marketers to segment their audiences. They use these algorithms to categorize their target audiences in order to create more precise and successful marketing campaigns.
- These algorithms are used by meteorologists to forecast the weather based on a number of variables, including temperature and humidity.
- Public health experts utilize classifiers to predict the likelihood of different diseases and develop plans to reduce their transmission.
- Classification algorithms are utilized by financial institutions to identify potential defaulters for the purpose of approving credit cards and loans. Additionally, these algorithms aid in detecting fraudulent activity.

4.2. DECISION TREE CLASSIFIER

A non-parametric supervised learning technique for regression and classification is called a decision tree (DT). The objective is to build a model that, by utilizing basic decision rules deduced from the data features, predicts the value of a target variable. A piecewise constant approximation can be thought of as a tree. In the example below, for instance, decision trees use a series of if-then-else decision rules to approximate a sine curve based on data. The decision rules become more intricate and the model becomes more fitted as the tree gets deeper (Figure 4.1).

Some advantages of decision trees are:

- Simple to understand and to interpret. Trees can be visualized.
- Minimal data preparation is necessary. Other methods frequently call for the normalization of data, the creation of dummy variables, and the elimination of blank values. Missing values are supported by certain tree and algorithm combinations.
- The number of data points required to train the tree determines the logarithmic cost of using it, or the cost of predicting data.
- Capable of working with both categorical and numerical data. Nevertheless, categorical variables are not supported at this time by the scikit-learn implementation. Other methods are typically focused on examining datasets with a single kind of variable.
- Able to handle multi-output problems.
- Makes use of a white box model. When a condition is observable in a model, boolean logic provides a simple explanation for the state. In comparison, though, a black box model (e.g., results in an artificial neural network) could be more challenging to understand.
- It is feasible to use statistical tests to validate a model. This enables the model's dependability to be taken into consideration.
- Performs well even when the true model used to generate the data slightly deviates from its assumptions.

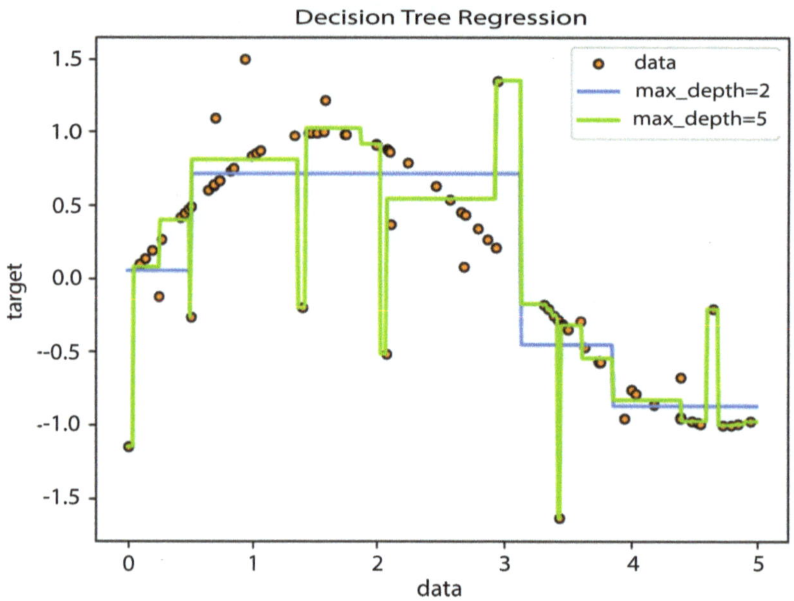

Figure 4.1. *Decision tree regression.*

Source: https://scikit-learn.org/stable/modules/tree.html.

The disadvantages of decision trees include:

- Decision-tree learners may produce trees that are overly complex and do not effectively represent the data, which is known as overfitting. To prevent overfitting, strategies such as pruning, specifying a minimum number of samples for a leaf node, or limiting the depth of the tree are essential.
- Because slight changes in the data could produce an entirely different tree, decision trees can be unstable. Decision trees used in an ensemble help to lessen this issue.
- As the above figure illustrates, decision tree predictions are piecewise constant approximations rather than smooth nor continuous. They are therefore not proficient in extrapolation.
- It is known that learning an optimal decision tree is an NP-complete problem under many optimality conditions, even for elementary concepts. As a result, heuristic algorithms like the greedy algorithm, which make locally optimal decisions at each node, serve as the foundation for practical decision-tree learning algorithms. The globally optimal decision tree cannot be guaranteed to be returned by such algorithms. Training several trees in an ensemble learner, where the features and samples are randomly sampled with replacement, can help to mitigate this.
- Certain concepts, like XOR, parity, and multiplexer problems, are challenging to learn because decision trees make it difficult to express them.
- If certain classes predominate, decision tree learners produce biased trees. Therefore, before fitting the decision tree, it is advised to balance the dataset.

4.2.1. Classification

A class called DecisionTreeClassifier can classify multiple classes in a dataset. DecisionTreeClassifier, like other classifiers, accepts two arrays as inputs: an array Y of integer values, shape (n_samples), that contains the class labels for the training samples, and an array X, sparse or dense, of shape (n_samples, n_features), holding the training samples.

```
>>> from sklearn import tree
>>> X = [[0, 0], [1, 1]]
>>> Y = [0, 1]
>>> clf = tree.DecisionTreeClassifier()
>>> clf = clf.fit(X, Y)
```

After being fitted, the model can then be used to predict the class of samples:

```
>>> clf.predict([[2., 2.]])
array()
```

The classifier will predict the class with the lowest index among those classes if there are multiple classes with the same and highest probability. The probability of each class, which is the fraction of training samples of the class in a leaf, can be predicted as an alternative to producing a specific class.

```
>>> clf.predict_proba([[2., 2.]])
array([[0., 1.]])
```

DecisionTreeClassifier is capable of both binary (where the labels are [-1, 1]) classification and multiclass (where the labels are [0, ..., K-1]) classification.

Using the Iris dataset, we can construct a tree as follows:

```
>>> from sklearn.datasets import load_iris
>>> from sklearn import tree
>>> iris = load_iris()
>>> X, y = iris.data, iris.target
>>> clf = tree.DecisionTreeClassifier()
>>> clf = clf.fit(X, y)
```

Once trained, you can plot the tree with the **plot_tree** function:

```
>>> tree.plot_tree(clf)
[..]
```

4.2.2. Regression

With the help of the Decision Tree Regressor class, regression issues can also be solved using decision trees. The fit method will accept arrays X and y as arguments, just as in the classification setting; however, in this instance, y is anticipated to have floating point values rather than integer values:

```
>>> from sklearn import tree
>>> X = [[0, 0], [2, 2]]
>>> y = [0.5, 2.5]
>>> clf = tree.DecisionTreeRegressor()
>>> clf = clf.fit(X, y)
>>> clf.predict([[1, 1]])
array([0.5])
```

4.2.3. Multi-Output Problems

When Y is a 2d array with shape (n_samples, n_outputs), we have a multi-output problem, which is a supervised learning problem with multiple outputs to predict. Building n independent models—one for each output—and using them to independently predict each of the n outputs is a very straightforward method of solving this kind of problem when there is no correlation between the outputs. However, creating a single model that can simultaneously predict all n outputs is frequently preferable because it is likely that the output values related to the same input are correlated. First off, because only one estimator is constructed, less training time is needed. Second, there's a good chance that the resulting estimator's generalization accuracy will improve.

This approach is easily adapted to support multi-output problems in decision trees. This calls for the alterations listed below:

- Store n output values in leaves, instead of 1;
- Employ division criteria that calculate the mean decrease for every n outputs.

This module implements this strategy in Decision Tree Classifier and Decision Tree Regressor, providing support for multi-output problems. The resulting estimator will be as follows if a decision tree is fitted on an output array Y of shape (n_samples, n_outputs).

- Output n_output values upon predict;

- Output a list of n_output arrays of class probabilities upon predict_proba.

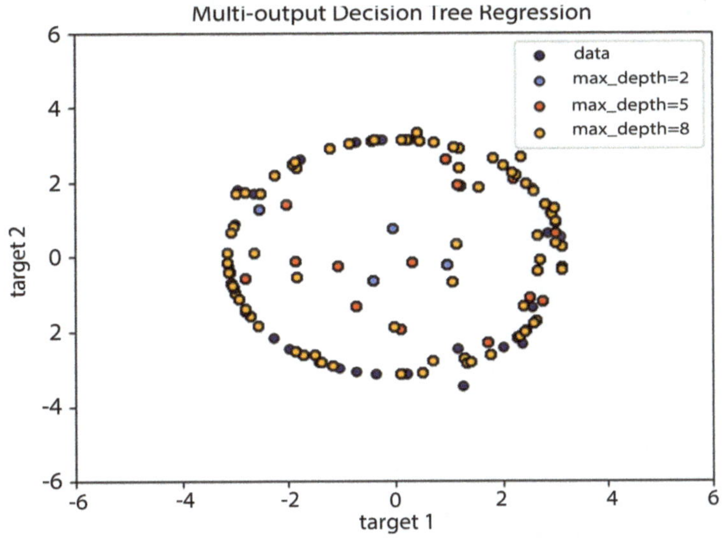

Figure 4.2. *Multi-output decision tree regression.*

Source: https://scikit-learn.org/stable/modules/tree.html.

Multi-output Decision Tree Regression provides an example of using multi-output trees for regression. The sine and cosine of the input, X, which in this case is a single real value, are the outputs, Y (Figure 4.2).

Face completion with a multi-output estimators provides an example of using multi-output trees for classification. The pixels of the upper half of the faces in this example are the inputs X, and the pixels of the lower half of those faces are the outputs Y (Figure 4.3).

Figure 4.3. *Face completion with a multi-output estimators.*

Source: https://scikit-learn.org/stable/modules/tree.html.

4.2.4. Complexity

Generally speaking, the run time cost of building a balanced binary tree is $O(n_{samples} nf_{eatures} \log(n_{samples}))$ and query time $O(\log(n_{samples}))$. Despite the algorithm's best efforts, balanced trees cannot always be produced by the tree construction process. By searching through $O(n_{features})$ for the feature that offers the greatest reduction in the impurity criterion, e.g., assuming that the subtrees stay roughly balanced. G. log loss, or the gain of information in its stead. This has a cost of $O(n_{features} n_{samples} \log(n_{samples}))$ at each node, resulting in a total cost over the entire trees (by summing the cost at each node) of $O(n_{features} n_{samples} 2\log(n_{samples}))$.

Tips on practical use:

- When dealing with large feature sets of data, decision trees often overfit. It's critical to get the ideal sample to feature ratio because overfitting is highly likely to occur in a tree with few samples in a high dimensional space.
- To improve your tree's chances of identifying discriminative features, think about completing dimensionality reduction (PCA, ICA, or feature selection) beforehand.
- Gaining a better understanding of the decision tree's structure will aid in learning more about how the tree makes predictions, which is crucial for identifying the key elements in the data.
- Utilize the export function to see your tree as you train. To gauge how well the tree is fitting your data, start with a max depth of 3 and gradually increase it.
- Keep in mind that for every level the tree grows to, twice as many samples are needed to populate it. Control the tree's size with max_depth to avoid overfitting.
- By limiting which splits are taken into consideration, min_samples_leaf or min_samples_split can help guarantee that multiple samples are taken into account for each decision made in the tree. A large number will stop the tree from learning the data, whereas a very small number will typically result in overfitting. Try setting the initial value of min_samples_leaf=5. A float number can be used as the percentage in these two parameters if there is a significant variation in the sample size. Min_samples_leaf ensures that every leaf has a minimum size, preventing low-variance, over-fit leaf nodes in regression problems, whereas min_samples_split can produce leaves that are arbitrary small. The best option is frequently min_samples_leaf=1 for classifications with few classes.

It should be noted that, if sample weight is supplied, min_samples_split evaluates samples independently and directly (a node with m weighted samples is still treated as having exactly m samples). If sample weights need to be taken into account at splits, take into consideration min_weight_fraction_leaf or min_impurity_decrease.

- To avoid the tree becoming biased toward the dominant classes, balance your dataset before training. Either sampling an equal number of samples from each class or, better yet, normalizing the sum of the sample weights (sample_weight) for every class to the same value can be used to achieve class balancing. Furthermore take note of the fact that weight-based pre-pruning criteria (like min_weight_ fraction_leaf) will then be less biased toward dominant classes than criteria (like min_samples_leaf) that are blind to sample weights.

- Weight-based pre-pruning criteria, such as min_weight_fraction_leaf, which guarantee that leaf nodes contain at least a fraction of the total sum of the sample weights, will make it easier to optimize the tree structure if the samples are weighted.
- Every decision tree employs internal arrays of np.float32. A duplicate of the dataset will be created if the training data is not in this format.
- It is advised to convert to sparse csc_matrix before calling fit and sparse csr_matrix before calling predict if the input matrix X is extremely sparse. When features have zero values in the majority of the samples, training times for a sparse matrix input can be orders of magnitude faster than for a dense matrix.

4.2.5. Tree algorithms: ID3, C4.5, C5.0 and CART

There are various decision tree algorithms:

Ross Quinlan created ID3 (Iterative Dichotomiser 3) in 1986. The method builds a multiway tree by determining for every node i.e., the categorical feature that will produce the greatest information gain for categorical targets (in a greedy way). After reaching their maximum size, trees are typically pruned in order to enhance their capacity to generalize to new data.

As the replacement for ID3, C4.5 dynamically defines a discrete attribute (based on numerical variables) that divides the continuous attribute value into a discrete set of intervals, thereby removing the requirement that features be categorical. Using C4.5, the trained trees (i.e., the ID3 algorithm's output) into sets of if-then instructions. Next, the order in which the rules should be applied is determined by assessing each rule's accuracy. If a rule's accuracy increases without a precondition, the rule can be pruned by removing it.

Quinlan's most recent version, available under a proprietary license, is C5.0. In comparison to C4.5, it is more accurate and requires less memory, building smaller rulesets.

The CART (Classification and Regression Trees) algorithm bears a resemblance to C4.5, however it distinguishes itself by accommodating numerical target variables for regression purposes and omitting the computation of rule sets. In each node, CART builds binary trees by selecting the feature and threshold combination that provides the greatest information gain. Although the CART algorithm is optimized in scikit-learn, categorical variables are not currently supported by the scikit-learn implementation.

4.2.6. Mathematical Formulation

A decision tree recursively partitions the feature space so that the samples with the same labels or similar target values are grouped together given training vectors $i \in R^n$, i=1,..., l and a label vector $y \in R^l$.

Let the data at node m be represented by Q_m with n_m samples. For each candidate split $\theta = (j,_m)$ consisting of a feature j and threshold t_m, partition the data into $Q_m^{left}(\theta)$ and $Q_m^{right}(\theta)$ subsets

$$Q_m^{left}(\theta) = \{(x, y) | x_j \leq t_m\}$$
$$Q_m^{right}(\theta) = Q_m \setminus Q_m^{left}(\theta)$$

Next, depending on the task being solved (classification or regression), the quality of a candidate split of node m is computed using an impurity function or loss function ().

$$G(Q_m,\theta) = \frac{n_m^{left}}{n_m} H(Q_m^{left}(\theta)) + \frac{n_m^{right}}{n_m} H(Q_m^{right}(\theta))$$

Select the parameters that minimizes the impurity

$\theta^{*}=\text{argmin}_{\theta}(Q_m,\theta)$

Recurse for subsets $Q_m{}^{left}(\theta*)$ and $Q_m{}^{right}(\theta*)$ until the maximum allowable depth is reached, $n_m<\min_{samples}$ or $n_m=1$.

- **Classification Criteria:**

Let's say that a target is a classification outcome for node m that can take on values 0,1,...,K-1.

$$p_{mk} = \frac{1}{n_m} \sum_{y \in Q_m} I(y=k)$$

be the percentage of observations from class k in node m. Predict_proba for this region is set to p_{mk} if m is a terminal node. These are typical impurity measurements.

Gini:

$$H(Q_m) = \sum_k p_{mk}(1-p_{mk})$$

Log Loss or Entropy:

$$H(Q_m) = -\sum_k p_{mk}\log(p_{mk})$$

- **Shannon Entropy:** The Shannon entropy of the potential classes is calculated using the entropy criterion. It determines their probability using the class frequencies of the training data points that arrived at a specific leaf m. The log loss (also called cross-entropy and multinomial deviance) between the true labels yi and the probabilistic predictions $T_k(x_i)$ of the tree model T for class k is minimized when the Shannon entropy is used as the tree node splitting criterion.

  To understand this, first keep in mind that the log loss of a tree model T calculated on a dataset D has the following definition:

$$\mathrm{LL}(D,T) = -\frac{1}{n} \sum_{(x_i,y_i)\in D} \sum_k I(y_i=k)\log(T_k(x_i))$$

Where; D is a training dataset of n pairs (x_i, y_i).

The expected class probabilities inside leaf nodes of a classification tree are constant, that is: for all $(x_i, {}_i) \in Q_m$, one has: $T_k(x_i)=p_{mk}$ for each class k.

Because of this characteristic, LL(x,y) can be rewritten as the sum of the Shannon entropies that were calculated for each leaf of y, weighted by the quantity of training data points that made it to each leaf.

$$\mathrm{LL}(D,T) = \sum_{m\in T} \frac{n_m}{n} H(Q_m)$$

- **Regression Criteria:** If the target is a continuous value, then mean squared error (MSE or L2 error), poisson deviance, and mean absolute error (MAE or L1 error) are common criteria to minimize for node m when deciding where to split in the future. While the MAE sets the predicted value of terminal nodes to the median $median(y)m$, MSE and Poisson deviance set the predicted value $\bar{y}_m$ of terminal nodes to the learned mean value of the node.

Mean Squared Error:

$$\bar{y}_m = \frac{1}{n_m} \sum_{y \in Q_m} y$$

$$H(Q_m) = \frac{1}{n_m} \sum_{y \in Q_m} (y - \bar{y}_m)^2$$

Half Poisson deviance:

$$H(Q_m) = \frac{1}{n_m} \sum_{y \in Q_m} (y \log \frac{y}{\bar{y}_m} - y + \bar{y}_m)$$

Setting criterion="poisson" might be a good choice if your target is a count or a frequency (count per some unit). In any case, $y>=0$ is a necessary condition to use this criterion. Note that it fits much slower than the MSE criterion.

Mean Absolute Error:

$$median(y)_m = \underset{y \in Q_m}{\mathrm{median}}(y)$$

$$H(Q_m) = \frac{1}{n_m} \sum_{y \in Q_m} |y - median(y)_m|$$

Note that it fits much slower than the MSE criterion.

4.2.7. Missing Values Support

The DecisionTreeClassifier and DecisionTreeRegressor models support missing values when using the 'best' splitter and 'gini,' 'entropy,' or 'log_loss' criteria for classification, or 'squared_error,' 'friedman_mse,' or 'poisson' criteria for regression.

The splitter will assess the split with all missing values going to either the left or right node for each possible threshold on the non-missing data.

Decisions are made as follows:

- The class used in the split discovered during training is automatically applied to the samples with missing values when predicting:

```
>>> from sklearn.tree import DecisionTreeClassifier
>>> import numpy as np
>>> X = np.array([0, 1, 6, np.nan]).reshape(-1, 1)
>>> y = [0, 0, 1, 1]
```

```
>>> tree = DecisionTreeClassifier(random_state=0).fit(X, y)
>>> tree.predict(X)
array([0, 0, 1, 1])
```

- The tie for missing value at predict time is broken by moving to the appropriate node if the criteria evaluation is the same for both nodes. Additionally, the splitter verifies the split in which non-missing values go to one child and all missing values go to the other:

```
>>> from sklearn.tree import DecisionTreeClassifier
>>> import numpy as np
>>> X = np.array([np.nan, -1, np.nan, 1]).reshape(-1, 1)
>>> y = [0, 0, 1, 1]
>>> tree = DecisionTreeClassifier(random_state=0).fit(X, y)
>>> X_test = np.array([np.nan]).reshape(-1, 1)
>>> tree.predict(X_test)
array()
```

- The child with the most samples is assigned to fill in the missing values during prediction if no missing values are observed for a particular feature during training:

```
>>> from sklearn.tree import DecisionTreeClassifier
>>> import numpy as np
>>> X = np.array([0, 1, 2, 3]).reshape(-1, 1)
>>> y = [0, 1, 1, 1]
>>> tree = DecisionTreeClassifier(random_state=0).fit(X, y)
>>> X_test = np.array([np.nan]).reshape(-1, 1)
>>> tree.predict(X_test)
array()
```

4.2.8. Minimal Cost-Complexity Pruning

An algorithm called minimal cost-complexity pruning is used to trim a tree in order to prevent over-fitting. The complexity parameter, denoted as $\alpha \geq 0$, is used to parameterize this algorithm. The cost-complexity measure, $R\alpha(T)$, of a particular tree T is defined by the complexity parameter:

$$R_\alpha(T) = R(T) + \alpha|\widetilde{T}|$$

Where; $|\widetilde{T}|$ is the total misclassification rate of the terminal nodes is the traditional definition of the number of terminal nodes in T and $R(T)$. As an alternative, scikit-learn calculates $R(T)$ using the terminal nodes' total sample weighted impurity. As previously demonstrated, the criterion determines a node's impurity. A subtree of T is found by minimal cost-complexity pruning, which minimizes $R_\alpha(T)$.

The cost complexity measure of a single node is $R_\alpha(t)=R(t)+\alpha$. The tree branch, T_t, is a tree with node t as its root. Generally, the impurity of a node is higher than the sum of impurities of its terminal nodes, $R(T_t)<R(t)$. However, the cost complexity measure of a node, t, and its branch, T_t, can be equal depending on the value of α. We define the effective α of a node to be the value where they are equal, $R(T_t)=R_\alpha(t)$ or $\alpha_{eff}(t) = \frac{R(t)-R(T_t)}{|T|-1}$. A non-terminal node with the smallest value of α_{eff} is the weakest link and will be pruned. This process stops when the pruned tree's minimal α_{eff} is greater than the ccp_alpha parameter.

4.3. MODEL OVERFITTING

When an algorithm fits training data too closely, or even exactly, it is said to be overfitting in machine learning. This leaves the model unable to draw valid inferences or predictions from any other type of data than the training set. The machine learning model's purpose is defeated by overfitting. The ability of a model to be applied to new data is ultimately what enables us to use machine learning algorithms on a daily basis for data classification and prediction. A sample dataset is used in the construction of machine learning algorithms in order to train the model. However, if the model is overly complex or trains on sample data for an extended period of time, it may begin to learn the "noise," or unimportant information, present in the dataset. The model becomes "overfitted," making it difficult for it to generalize effectively to new data, when it learns to recognize the noise and fits the training set too closely. A model will not be able to carry out the classification or prediction tasks for which it was designed if it does not generalize well to new data.

High variance and low error rates are reliable signs of overfitting. A portion of the training dataset is usually set aside as the "test set" to look for overfitting in order to stop this kind of behavior. Overfitting is indicated if the test data has a high error rate while the training data has a low error rate.

4.3.1. Overfitting Explained

The ultimate goal of machine learning is to develop models that perform well when applied to fresh data. When a model fits the training set too closely—capturing even the random fluctuations—this is known as overfitting. Imagine teaching a child to identify birds, but all you show them are pigeons instead of teaching them about general bird characteristics. Because that is all they know, even if they see an eagle, they might still believe it to be a pigeon.

The causes of overfitting can be numerous:

- **Complicated Models:** Employing a complex model for a straightforward task may result in overfitting, such as utilizing a high-degree polynomial regression for linear data.
- **Inadequate Information:** Insufficient data can lead to the model identifying fictitious patterns.
- **Noisy information:** An overfitted model will interpret errors or random fluctuations in the training data as patterns.

Overfitting has a substantial impact. A model that is overfitted may achieve high accuracy on its training data, but will struggle to perform well on unfamiliar data as it lacks generalization.

4.3.2. How to Detect Overfitting

An essential step in the machine learning process is identifying overfitting. Here's how to identify it:

- **Validation Group Assembled:** Make training and validation sets from your data. You can be pretty sure your model is overfitting if it does well on the training set but poorly on the validation.
- **Learning Curves:** Plot how well the model performed over time on the training and validation sets. Overfitting occurs when there is a divergence between the two curves.
- **Cross-Checking:** Make use of cross-validation, in which the model is assessed after the training data is divided into multiple segments.

It's especially important to check for overfitting when:

- You're using a complex model.
- You have a small amount of data.
- The stakes are high, like in medical diagnoses.

4.3.3. How to Prevent Overfitting

It is preferable to avoid overfitting than to treat it. The actions to take are as follows:

- **Early Stopping:** This method involves pausing the training process before the model begins to learn about internal noise. Measure the model's performance at each iteration while it is being trained in this manner. Proceed up to a predetermined number of times until a new iteration enhances the model's functionality. We have to stop the process before the learner reaches that point because that is when the model starts to overfit the training set.

  Early stopping is the practice of ending the training process before the model begins to extract noise from the data (Figure 4.4).

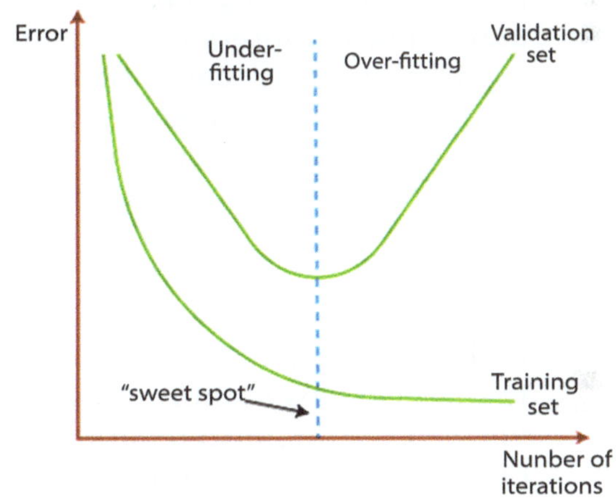

Figure 4.4. *Early stopping.*

Source: https://www.javatpoint.com/overfitting-in-machine-learning.

However, if training is stopped too soon, this method might result in the underfitting issue. Finding the ideal balance between underfitting and overfitting is therefore crucial.

- **Training with More Data:** Increasing the amount of data used for training is one strategy to avoid overfitting. Algorithms can more easily identify the signal with this option, reducing error rates. The model will have to generalize in order to produce results as the user adds more training data to it because it will be unable to overfit all the samples. Users can improve the accuracy of the model by consistently gathering more data. Users should make sure the data being used is clean and relevant, though, as this method is thought to be costly.

- **Data Augmentation:** An alternative to training with additional data is data augmentation, which is a more cost-effective option. If you are unable to continuously gather more data, you can create the illusion of diversity in existing data sets. Data augmentation alters each instance of data slightly each time it is processed by the model, ensuring that each data set appears unique and preventing the model from memorizing specific characteristics. Another similar option is to introduce noise into both input and output data. Adding noise to the input helps stabilize the model without compromising data quality or privacy, while adding noise to the output increases data diversity. It is important to be cautious with noise addition to avoid distorting the data or making it excessively different.
- **Data Simplification:** A model's complexity may lead to overfitting, whereby the model manages to overfit the training dataset despite having access to vast amounts of data. Using the data simplification method, overfitting is lessened by making the model simpler than necessary so that it does not overfit. A few of the things that can be done are use dropout on a neutral network, reduce the number of parameters in a neural network, and prune a decision tree. The model can operate more quickly and be lighter by simplifying it.
- **Ensembling:** A machine learning method called ensembling functions by merging predictions from two or more different models. The two most used assembling techniques are bagging and boosting. Boosting increases the aggregate complexity of simple base models through their use. It trains a large number of weak learners in a sequential fashion so that each learner gains knowledge from the errors made by the learner before them. By combining all of the sequence's weak learners, boosting produces a single strong learner. The antithesis of boosting, bagging, is the other ensembling technique. In order to maximize its predictions, bagging trains a large number of powerful learners in a parallel configuration.

4.3.4. Overfitting vs Underfitting

Underfitting is the opposite of overfitting, which is the over adaptation of a model to training data. Even the most fundamental patterns in the training set are missed by an underfitted model.

- **Overfitting:** On training data, high accuracy; on fresh data, low accuracy. Envision a GPS that functions flawlessly in your hometown but becomes disoriented in other locations.
- **Underfitting:** Low accuracy with fresh data, high accuracy with training data. Imagine having a GPS that is spot on in your hometown but misplaced everywhere else.

For different reasons, overfitting and underfitting result in inaccurate predictions when applied to fresh data. Underfitting can occur from an overly simple model or insufficient features, whereas overfitting is typically caused by an overly complex model or noisy data.

4.3.5. Overfitting: The Ongoing Struggle for ML Engineers

As engineers working in machine learning (ML), we are always trying to create the most accurate models we can. But one of the main dangers associated with aiming for high accuracy is overfitting. A lot of businesses make the mistake of overfitting. They believe they have created a superior model after observing the high training accuracy. Regretfully, the model completely fails when it is used in the real world. It's comparable to doing flawlessly on every practice test but failing the real one.

We as ML engineers must fight the urge to focus only on training data in order to achieve perfect accuracy. It is just not possible to achieve perfect accuracy on training data and then expect it to transfer to fresh data. To guarantee that our models generalize effectively, we must employ strategies like cross-validation, regularization, data augmentation, and ensembling. A common path in machine learning is to begin with an underfit model and gradually increase accuracy through iterations. However, there is a limit to how many adjustments before overfitting occurs. To create a Goldilocks model that works well in every circumstance, we must tread carefully to avoid both underfitting and overfitting.

4.4. MODEL EVALUATION

The process of evaluating a model using a metrics-driven analysis is known as model evaluation in machine learning. There are two approaches to doing it:

- **Offline:** During experimentation or ongoing retraining, the model is assessed following training.
- **Online:** Model monitoring includes the model's evaluation during production.

Depending on the data, algorithm, and use case, different metrics are chosen for the analysis.

The metrics are divided into categories based on regression and classification for supervised learning. Regression metrics, such as mean absolute error (MAE) and root mean squared errors (RMSE), are based on errors, whereas classification metrics, such as accuracy, precision, recall, and f1-score, are based on the confusion matrix. Metrics for unsupervised learning are designed to characterize the output's coherence, separation, confidence, and error. To gauge how similar a data point is to its own cluster in comparison to other clusters, the silhouette measure, for instance, is employed in clustering. Model evaluation metrics are expanded during experimentation with visualizations and manual analysis of (groups of) data points for both learning approaches, and inevitably for the latter. Experts in the field are frequently needed to assist with this assessment. Business metrics, such as increased revenue and decreased expenses, should also be defined and reported in addition to technical metrics and analysis. This makes it possible to comprehend the effects of implementing the model in production.

4.4.1. Importance

ML model evaluation ensures that production models' performance is:

- **Optimal:** The model(s) that have been put into production operate as well as is currently possible, usually when compared to several other trained models.
- **Reliable:** The produced model or models exhibit expected behavior. The model's behavioral profile provides a detailed analysis of how feature contribution, counterfactual analysis, and fairness tests define the model's mapping of inputs to outputs, both globally and with regard to particular data slices.

In particular for crucial applications requiring real-time inference, an inaccurate or inadequate model evaluation can have catastrophic effects on a company's revenue as well as user experience. Effective internal model evaluation streamlines development and management processes by ensuring that all stakeholders are aware of the use case's potential and are in favor of it.

4.4.2. Classification

The most widely used metrics to assess the effectiveness of classification systems are log-loss, accuracy, precision, confusion matrix, and AUC (area under the ROC curve).

- As accuracy is defined as the ratio of correct predictions to total predictions, it quantifies the frequency with which the classifier produces accurate predictions.
- The percentage of predicted Positives that are actually Positives is measured by precision. When you want to be absolutely certain of your prediction, precision is an excellent choice for an evaluation metric. For instance, you must be extremely certain of your prediction if you are developing a system to determine whether to lower the credit limit on a specific account. Otherwise, you risk upsetting your customers.
- Confusion tables, also known as confusion matrices, provide a more thorough breakdown of the right and wrong classifications for every class. When you have a lot more test data on one class than the other or when the cost of misclassification might vary for the two classes, using a confusion matrix can help you understand how the two classes differ from one another. For instance, there are significant differences in the repercussions of diagnosing cancer falsely as positive or negative.

4.4.3. Reporting on Model Evaluation

An ML model evaluation reporting template has not yet been agreed upon by the AI community. This is mostly because machine learning use case designs vary greatly. A one-page report is generally advised since it strikes a balance between being thorough and succinct. Technical and business metrics should be used in the report to clearly explain the model's performance. Relevant technical model aspects should be summed up with an emphasis on engineering requirements. The report's underlying template should ideally be reusable for all of the team's ML use cases. Before the model or models are put into production, the model evaluation report needs to be written and distributed. During the production phase, this procedure should be carried out regularly through continuous evaluation.

4.4.4. Pattern Evaluation Methods

Pattern evaluation in data mining is the process of rating the quality of patterns that are found. Determining the usefulness and trustworthiness of the patterns requires this process. Various metrics can be employed to assess patterns; the selection of a measure is contingent upon the specific use case. Pattern mining algorithms can be assessed in a few different methods:

4.4.4.1. Accuracy

A data mining model's accuracy is determined by how well it predicts the target values. A test dataset, distinct from the training dataset used to train the model, is used to gauge accuracy. Although there are several methods to gauge accuracy, the most popular one is to figure out what proportion of the predictions are accurate.

We call this the accuracy rate. The mean absolute error (MAE) and the root mean squared error (RMSE) are two additional accuracy metrics. The mean of the absolute errors is called the MAE, and the square root of the mean squared error is called the RMSE. While a data mining model's accuracy is a crucial factor, it is not the only one to take into account. Also, the model needs to be reliable and broadly applicable. A poor model is one that achieves 100% accuracy on training data but only 50% accuracy on test data. The model cannot be generalized to new data because it overfits the training set. A good model is one that achieves 80% accuracy on training data and 80% accuracy on test data. Predictions on new data can be made using the generalizable model.

4.4.4.2. Classification Accuracy

This gauges how well new data can be classified using the patterns the algorithm found. Usually, to accomplish this, a set of data with pre-identified class labels is used, and the patterns found in the data are then used to predict the data's class labels. Next, by contrasting the predicted and actual labels, the accuracy can be calculated.

One of the most widely used evaluation metrics for classification models is classification accuracy, which is just the model's percentage of accurate predictions. Classification accuracy is a simple and easy-to-understand metric, but it can be deceptive in some circumstances. For instance, a model that consistently predicts class 1 will attain a high classification accuracy of 90% if the dataset has a highly unbalanced class distribution, with 100 instances of class 0 and 1,000 instances of class 1. However, given that it is not producing any accurate predictions for class 0, it is evident that this model is not very useful.

Classification models can be evaluated in a few different ways; some methods, like recall and precision, are more useful in datasets that are not evenly distributed. Recall is the percentage of instances of a specific class that the model correctly predicted, while precision is the percentage of correct predictions the model made for a given class. The model in the aforementioned example has a precision of 0% and a recall of 0% if we were to examine precision and recall for class 0. A confusion matrix can also be used to assess classification models. A table that displays the number of accurate and inaccurate predictions the model made for each class is called a confusion matrix. This can be a useful technique to see how well a model is performing and pinpoint its areas of error. For instance, the confusion matrix in the example above would indicate that the model is only predicting for class 1, not for class 0.

When assessing classification models, classification accuracy is generally a useful metric to use. It's crucial to understand its limitations, though, and to employ different evaluation metrics in circumstances where classification accuracy can be deceptive.

4.4.4.3. Clustering Accuracy

This gauges how well new data can be clustered using the patterns the algorithm found. Usually, to do this, a set of data that has been labeled with known cluster labels is used, and the patterns found can then be used to predict the data's cluster labels. Next, by contrasting the predicted and actual labels, the accuracy can be calculated.

The accuracy of a clustering algorithm can be assessed in a few ways:

- **External Indices:** These indices make a comparison between the algorithm-generated clusters and a known ground truth. If the ground truth is known, for instance, the Jaccard coefficient or the Rand Index can be applied.
- **Internal Indices:** These indices evaluate the quality of clustering independently of any outside data. The Dunn index is the most widely used internal index.
- Stability: This gages the clustering's resilience to slight alterations in the data. If a clustering algorithm yields the same results when run on various samples of the same data, it is considered stable.
- Efficiency: This gages the speed at which the algorithm arrives at the ideal clustering.

4.4.4.4. Coverage

This indicates the number of potential patterns in the data that the algorithm is able to find. This can be calculated by dividing the total number of potential patterns by the number of patterns that the algorithm found. One kind of sequential pattern that can be discovered by searching for objects that frequently occur together in a sequential order is called a coverage pattern. A coverage pattern could be, for instance, "Customers who buy item A also tend to buy item B within the next month."

In order to assess a coverage pattern, analysts usually consider two factors: confidence and support. The proportion of transactions with the pattern is known as support. Confidence is calculated by dividing the total number of transactions containing the pattern by the percentage of transactions containing the first item in the pattern. Take the following coverage pattern, for instance: "Customers who buy item A also typically buy item B within the following month." If 0.1% of transactions support this pattern, then 0.1% of all transactions contain the pattern. 80% of the transactions containing item A also contain item B if the pattern's confidence level is 80%.

Generally speaking, a stronger pattern is indicated by higher support and confidence values. But when a pattern is discovered that is too particular to the data and cannot be extrapolated to other data sets, it is known as overfitting, and analysts need to exercise caution to prevent it.

4.4.4.5. Visual Inspection

This approach, in which the data miner merely examines the patterns to determine whether they make sense, is arguably the most popular. Visual inspection involves plotting the data in a graphical format and looking for patterns. When the data is easily plottable and not too big, this method is employed. When the data is categorical in nature, it is also employed. In data mining, visual inspection is a technique for evaluating patterns in patterns by visually inspecting the data. This can be accomplished by examining the raw data or by looking at a graph or plot of the data. This technique is frequently applied to identify anomalies or peculiar trends.

4.4.4.6. Running Time

This expresses the time it takes the algorithm to identify patterns in the given data. Usually, this is expressed in minutes or seconds. While there are several approaches to gauge a machine learning algorithm's effectiveness, one of the most popular ones is to just track how long it takes to train and predict a model. The running time pattern evaluation is the term for this.

A few different considerations need to be made when calculating an algorithm's running time. The time it takes to load the data into memory must be considered first. Secondly, you should factor in the time required for any necessary pre-processing of the data. The time required to train the model and generate predictions must also be taken into consideration. An algorithm's running time will typically grow as the amount of data increases. This is a result of the algorithm's need to process additional data in order to draw conclusions. Still, some algorithms are more effective than others and perform better when applied to big datasets. A crucial consideration when comparing various algorithms is the particular dataset being used. Certain kinds of data may lend themselves more to the use of some algorithms than others. Furthermore, the hardware being utilized may also have an impact on the running time.

4.4.4.7. Support

The proportion of all records that have the pattern in them is known as the pattern's support. The process of identifying intriguing and possibly helpful patterns in data is known as support pattern evaluation. The evaluation of support patterns aims to find intriguing patterns that could be helpful in making decisions. Applications such as data mining and machine learning often use support pattern evaluation. There are numerous approaches for assessing support patterns. Using a support metric, which counts the occurrences of a pattern in a dataset, is one popular method. Using a lift metric, which calculates the ratio of a pattern's actual occurrence to its expected occurrence, is another popular strategy.

A range of intriguing patterns in data, such as association rules, sequential patterns, and co-occurrence patterns, can be discovered using support pattern evaluation. A crucial component of data mining and machine learning, support pattern evaluation aids in decision-making.

4.4.4.8. Confidence

The percentage of times a pattern is determined to be accurate is its confidence level. A data mining technique called confidence pattern evaluation is used to rate the quality of patterns discovered in data. Typically, this assessment is carried out by figuring out the percentage of times a pattern appears in a data set and contrasting that number with the percentage of times the pattern should be present given the distribution of the data as a whole. A pattern is considered to be a strong confidence pattern if the percentage of times it is discovered is noticeably higher than the predicted percentage.

4.4.4.9. Lift

The ratio of the number of times a pattern is found to be correct to the number of times it is expected to be correct is called the lift of the pattern. One data mining method for assessing a predictive model's performance is Lift Pattern evaluation. A graphical depiction of the model's performance, the lift pattern can be used to spot possible issues with the model. Plotting the true positive rate (TPR) against the false positive rate (FPR) creates the lift pattern. The proportion of positive cases that the model correctly classifies is known as the TPR, whereas the proportion of negative cases that the model incorrectly classifies as positive is known as the FPR. In an ideal world, there would be no FPR and 100% TPR, but this is rarely the case in reality. One way to assess the model's proximity to this ideal is through the lift pattern.

A lifted pattern that approaches the diagonal line is indicative of a high-quality model. This indicates that the model is correctly classifying a similar percentage of positive and negative instances, and that the TPR and FPR are similar. A model that is far from the diagonal line and has an elevated pattern is not operating as well. Numerous things, such as uneven data, shoddy feature selection, or overfitting, can contribute to this. One helpful tool for spotting possible issues with a predictive model is the lift pattern. But keep in mind that the lift pattern should only be interpreted in conjunction with other evaluation metrics, as it is merely a graphical depiction of the model's performance.

4.4.4.10. Prediction

The percentage of times a pattern is discovered to be accurate is its prediction. A data mining technique called prediction pattern evaluation is used to evaluate how accurate predictive models are. It is used to assess how well a model, grounded in historical data, can forecast future results. Evaluation of prediction patterns can be used to assess a single model's performance or to compare several models.

A training set and a test set are created from the data set in order to evaluate the prediction pattern. The test set is used to evaluate the model's accuracy, whereas the training set is used to train the model. The prediction error is computed to assess the model's accuracy. Predictive models can be made more accurate by evaluating prediction patterns. Predictive models can be adjusted to more closely match the data by using a test set. This can be achieved by introducing new features to the data set or by adjusting the model's parameters.

4.4.4.11. Precision

One technique for examining data gathered from multiple sources is called precision pattern evaluation. This approach can be used to assess the accuracy of the data as well as spot patterns and trends in it. Precision Pattern Evaluation is a useful tool for locating errors in data and figuring out why they occur. The effect of the errors on the overall accuracy of the data can also be ascertained using this method. One useful tool for data mining and analysis is Precision Pattern Evaluation. This technique can be used to find patterns and trends in the data as well as increase the accuracy of the data.

4.4.4.12. Cross-Validation

Using this approach, the data is divided into two sets, one for model training and the other for testing. To obtain a more accurate estimate of the model's performance, this can be repeated several times with various partitions. A model validation technique called cross-validation is used to determine how well data mining analysis findings will transfer to a different set of data. It is mostly applied in situations where predicting outcomes is the main objective and one wishes to gauge how well a predictive model will work in real-world scenarios. Another name for cross-validation is out-of-sample testing. A pattern evaluation technique called cross-validation is used to gauge a model's accuracy. It accomplishes this by dividing the data into test and training sets. After that, the training set is used to fit the model, and the test set is used to gauge its accuracy. After that, this process is repeated several times, averaging the accuracy across all of the iterations.

4.4.4.13. Test Set

This approach entails dividing the data into two sets, using the full data set to train the model, and the held-out test set to test it. Although this can be more costly if the data set is large, it is more dependable than cross-validation. The effectiveness of a model on a test set can be assessed in a variety of ways. The most popular method involves calculating the percentage of correctly classified instances by simply comparing the predicted and true labels. We refer to this as accuracy. Precision is a widely used metric that is calculated by dividing the total number of true positives by the sum of true positives and false positives. Recall is calculated by dividing the total number of true positives and false negatives by the number of true positives. The F1 score, which is the harmonic mean of recall and precision, can be produced by combining these metrics.

4.4.4.14. Bootstrapping

Using this approach, the data is sampled at random using replacement, the model is trained on the sampled data, and the model is tested on the original data. This can be used to obtain a performance distribution for the model, which can help determine how reliable the model is. A resampling method called bootstrapping is used to gauge a model's accuracy. The process entails taking a random sample of data from the original dataset and using it to train the model. Next, a different set of data that was not used for training is used to test the model. The model's average accuracy is computed after this procedure is carried out several times.

4.5. PRESENCE OF HYPER-PARAMETERS

In the field of machine learning, hyperparameters are specific parameters like the learning rate or optimizer selection that dictate the learning process, hence earning the name "hyperparameters." These differ from the parameters that actually define the model itself.

Model hyperparameters are those that, because the objective function is usually non-differentiable with respect to them, cannot usually be inferred while the machine is being fitted to the training set. Gradient-based optimization techniques cannot therefore be used directly. A neural network's topology and size are two examples of model hyperparameters. Hyperparameters of an algorithm include things like learning rate, batch size, and mini-batch size. A mini-batch size would be a smaller sample set, whereas batch size can refer to the entire data sample. Certain basic algorithms (like ordinary least squares regression) require no hyperparameters, while other model training algorithms require different ones. The training algorithm determines the parameters from the data given these hyperparameters. For example, LASSO is an algorithm that, before estimating the parameters through the training algorithm, requires the setting of a regularization hyperparameter, which is added to ordinary least squares regression (Yang, Li; Shami, Abdallah, 2020).

4.5.1. Considerations

The selection of a model's hyperparameters can affect how long it takes to train and test. Typically, a hyperparameter is of an integer or continuous type, which results in optimization problems of mixed types. The existence of some hyperparameters is conditional upon the value of others, e.g., the size of each hidden layer in a neural network can be conditional upon the number of layers.

- **Difficulty Learnable Parameters:** Generally speaking, but not always, well-known gradient-based techniques (like gradient descent and LBFGS), which are frequently used to learn parameters, cannot be used to learn hyperparameters. These hyperparameters are those that describe a model representation and have an impact on the loss function but are not amenable to learning through standard optimization techniques. The tolerance hyperparameter for errors in support vector machines is one example.
- **Untrainable Parameters:** Because they aggressively boost a model's capacity and have the potential to push the loss function to an undesirable minimum (overfitting to and picking up noise in the data), hyperparameters can sometimes

prevent a model from learning from the training set by incorrectly mapping the richness of the structure in the data. The degree of a polynomial equation that fits a regression model, for instance, would increase until the model perfectly fit the data if we treated it as a trainable parameter. This would result in low training error but poor generalization performance.

- *Tunability:* A small number of hyperparameters account for the majority of the variation in performance. The amount of performance that can be increased by adjusting an algorithm, hyperparameter, or combination of hyperparameters is known as its tunability. While learning rate and network size are an LSTM's most important hyperparameters, batching and momentum have no discernible impact on the model's performance.
- *Robustness:* Learning has an inherent stochasticity, which suggests that the performance measured by empirical hyperparameters may not accurately reflect its true performance. Without substantial simplification and robustification, methods that are not resistant to straightforward modifications in hyperparameters, random seeds, or even distinct implementations of the same algorithm cannot be incorporated into mission-critical control systems.

In particular, algorithms for reinforcement learning need to have their performance evaluated across a large number of random seeds and their sensitivity to hyperparameter adjustments evaluated. Because of the high variance, their evaluation using a small number of random seeds is unable to fully capture performance. Certain techniques for reinforcement learning, like e.g., Deep Deterministic Policy Gradients, or DDPGs, are more susceptible to changes in hyperparameters than other models.

4.5.2. Optimization

The process of hyperparameter optimization identifies a pair of hyperparameters that, when applied to test data, produce an ideal model that minimizes a predetermined loss function. The goal function returns the corresponding loss after receiving a tuple of hyperparameters. These techniques are usually not gradient based, but rather use ideas from black box optimization or derivative-free optimization.

4.5.3. Reproducibility

In addition to fine-tuning hyperparameters, machine learning requires reproducibility assurance, parameter and result organization and storage. When a strong infrastructure isn't in place for this kind of thing, research code tends to change quickly and jeopardizes important things like reproducibility and bookkeeping. Machine learning online collaboration platforms go one step further by enabling scientists to automatically exchange, arrange, and communicate about experiments, data, and algorithms. Deep learning models can be especially challenging to reproduce (Villa, Jennifer; Zimmerman, Yoav (25 May 2018)). For instance, studies have demonstrated that deep learning models rely significantly even on the random number generator's random seed selection (Bethard, 2022).

CASE STUDY

SVM VS DECISION TREE IN MACHINE LEARNING

One case study that compares the performance of support vector machines (SVM) and decision trees is the classification of breast cancer tumors as benign or malignant based on various features.

In this study, a dataset of breast cancer patients was used, where each patient had several attributes such as tumor size, shape, and texture. The goal was to build a model that could accurately predict whether a tumor is benign or malignant based on these attributes.

First, a decision tree algorithm was applied to the dataset. The decision tree algorithm works by recursively splitting the data based on the attribute that provides the most information gain. This process continues until a stopping criterion is met, such as reaching a specific depth or having a minimum number of samples in each leaf node.

The decision tree model achieved an accuracy of 92% on the test set. However, it was observed that the decision tree model tended to overfit the training data, resulting in poor generalization performance on unseen data. To address this issue, an SVM algorithm was also applied to the same dataset. SVM is a binary classification algorithm that finds the optimal hyperplane that separates the data points of different classes with the maximum margin. It works by mapping the data into a high-dimensional feature space and finding the optimal separating hyperplane.

The SVM model achieved an accuracy of 95% on the test set, outperforming the decision tree model. Additionally, it was observed that the SVM model had better generalization performance and was less prone to overfitting compared to the decision tree model.

Decision Tree vs SVM stated that SVM uses a "kernel trick to solve non-linear problems whereas decision trees derive hyper-rectangles in input space to solve the problem" and "decision trees are better for categorical data and it deals with collinearity" better than SVM.

Overall, this case study highlights the differences in performance and generalization capabilities between SVM and decision tree algorithms. While decision trees are intuitive and easy to interpret, they can be prone to overfitting. On the other hand, SVMs can handle complex datasets and have better generalization performance but may be more computationally expensive and less interpretable. The selection of the algorithm depends on the specific requirements and goals of the classification task.

CLASS ACTIVITY

SUPERVISED LEARNING

Given a set of example data, which we will call training data, the goal is to learn a function/model that will compute a target value for new data. This is known as supervised learning. An example of supervised learning is predicting the sales price of a home. Example data for this task is shown in the table below.

SQFT	# of bedrooms	zip code	Sales price
1000	2	22999	160,000
2000	4	20111	450,000
2200	3	90210	850,000

When the predicted value is a real number (sales price), we call this regression. When the predicted value is a label, this is called classification, for example, identifying an email as spam or not spam. When only two labels are possible (as is the case with spam), this is called binary classification. A general approach to classification to shown on the left.

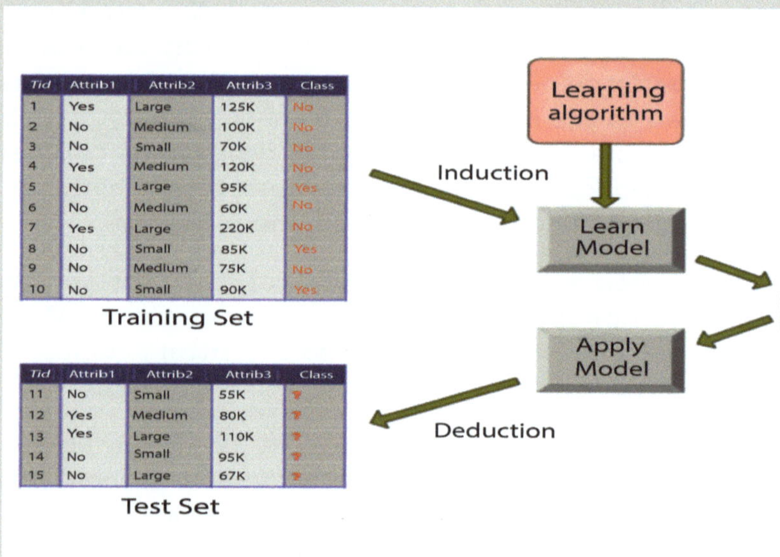

Source: Introduction to Data Mining. Pang-Ning Tan et. al. 2019.

1. List 3 possible uses of regression.
2. List 3 possible uses of classification.

SUMMARY

- Classification in data mining is a common technique that separates data points into different classes. It allows you to organize data sets of all sorts, including complex and large datasets as well as small and simple ones. It primarily involves using algorithms that you can easily modify to improve the data quality.
- Data classification systems have become a regular aspect of our everyday lives. The AI behind the spam folder in your inbox, for instance, uses data classification techniques to filter emails. The use of classification has become crucial to maintaining a clean and efficient data environment.
- DecisionTreeClassifier is a class capable of performing multi-class classification on a dataset. Decision trees can also be applied to regression problems, using the DecisionTreeRegressor class.
- A multi-output problem is a supervised learning problem with several outputs to predict, that is when Y is a 2d array of shape (n_samples, n_outputs).
- In machine learning, overfitting occurs when an algorithm fits too closely or even exactly to its training data, resulting in a model that can't make accurate predictions or conclusions from any data other than the training data. Overfitting defeats purpose of the machine learning model. Generalization of a model to new data is ultimately what allows us to use machine learning algorithms every day to make predictions and classify data.
- Model evaluation in machine learning is the process of determining a model's performance via a metrics-driven analysis. The most popular metrics for measuring classification performance include accuracy, precision, confusion matrix, log-loss, and AUC (area under the ROC curve).
- In machine learning, a hyperparameter is a parameter, such as the learning rate or choice of optimizer, which specifies details of the learning process, hence the name *hyper*parameter. This is in contrast to parameters which determine the model itself.

REVIEW QUESTIONS

1. What is classification in data mining?
2. What is the difference between linear regression and logistic regression?
3. Write the importance of classification in data mining?
4. Why use decision trees for classification?
5. Where is a decision tree used?
6. Why is the model overfitting?
7. How can you prevent overfitting?

REFERENCES

1. Bethard, S. (2022). We need to talk about random seeds. *ArXiv*, abs/2210.13393.
2. Bittner, T. (2001). Rough sets in spatio-temporal data mining. In *Proceedings of the First International Workshop on Temporal, Spatial, and Spatio-Temporal Data Mining-Revised Papers*. Springer-Verlag.
3. Danks, N. P., Sharma, P. N., & Sarstedt, M. (2020). Model selection uncertainty and multimodel inference in partial least squares structural equation modeling (PLS-SEM). *Journal of Business Research, 113*, 13–24.
4. Elias, B. (2003). Extracting landmarks with data mining methods. In W. Kuhn, M. Worboys, & S. Timpf (Eds.), *Spatial Information Theory: Foundations of Geographic Information Science; International Conference, COSIT 2003, Kartause Ittingen, Switzerland* (pp. 375–389). Springer-Verlag.
5. Ferreira de Oliveira, M. C., & Levkowitz, H. (2003). From visual data exploration to visual data mining: A survey. *IEEE Transactions on Visualization and Computer Graphics, 9*(3), 378.
6. Han, J., & Kamber, M. (2000). *Data Mining: Concepts and Techniques*. Morgan Kaufmann.
7. Han, J., Altman, R. B., Kumar, V., Mannila, H., & Pregibon, D. (2002). Emerging scientific applications in data mining. *Communications of the ACM, 45*(8), 54–58.
8. Hastie, T., Tibshirani, R., & Friedman, J. (2009). *Elements of Statistical Learning*. Springer.
9. Hastie, T., Tibshirani, R., & Friedman, J. H. (2001). *The Elements of Statistical Learning: Data Mining, Inference, and Prediction*. Springer.
10. Jinwook, S., & Shneiderman, B. (2002). Interactively exploring hierarchical clustering results [gene identification]. *Computer, 35*(7), 80.
11. Liengaard, B. D., Sharma, P. N., Hult, G. T. M., Jensen, M. B., Sarstedt, M., Hair, J. F., & Ringle, C. M. (2021). Prediction: Coveted, yet forsaken? Introducing a cross-validated predictive ability test in partial least squares path modeling. *Decision Sciences, 52*(2), 362–392.
12. Milligan, G. W., & Hirtle, S. C. (2003). Clustering and classification methods. In J. Schinka & W. Velicer (Eds.), *Comprehensive Handbook of Psychology* (Vol. 2, pp. 165–186). Wiley.
13. Mitra, S., Pal, S. K., & Mitra, P. (2002). Data mining in soft computing framework: A survey. *IEEE Transactions on Neural Networks, 13*(1), 3.
14. Mozer, M. C., Wolniewicz, R., Grimes, D. B., Johnson, E., & Kaushansky, H. (2000). Predicting subscriber dissatisfaction and improving retention in the wireless telecommunications industry. *IEEE Transactions on Neural Networks, 11*, 690–696.
15. Ng, R. T., & Han, J. (2002). Clarans: A method for clustering objects for spatial data mining. *IEEE Transactions on Knowledge and Data Engineering, 14*(5), 1003.

16. Rigdon, E., Sarstedt, M., & Moisescu, O.-I. (2023). Quantifying model selection uncertainty via bootstrapping and Akaike weights. *International Journal of Consumer Studies, 47*(4), 1596–1608.

17. Sharma, P. N., Liengaard, B. D., Hair, J. F., Sarstedt, M., & Ringle, C. M. (2022). Predictive model assessment and selection in composite-based modeling using PLS-SEM: Extensions and guidelines for using CVPAT. *European Journal of Marketing, 57*(6), 1662–1677.

18. Sharma, P. N., Sarstedt, M., Shmueli, G., Kim, K. H., & Thiele, K. O. (2019). PLS-based model selection: The role of alternative explanations in information systems research. *Journal of the Association for Information Systems, 20*(4), 346–397.

19. Sharma, P. N., Shmueli, G., Sarstedt, M., Danks, N., & Ray, S. (2021). Prediction-oriented model selection in partial least squares path modeling. *Decision Sciences, 52*(3), 567–607.

20. Shmueli, G., Ray, S., Estrada, J. M. V., & Chatla, S. B. (2016). The elephant in the room: Predictive performance of PLS models. *Journal of Business Research, 69*(10), 4552–4564.

21. Shmueli, G., Sarstedt, M., Hair, J. F., Cheah, J. H., Ting, H., Vaithilingam, S., & Ringle, C. M. (2019). Predictive model assessment in PLS-SEM: Guidelines for using PLSpredict. *European Journal of Marketing, 53*(11), 2322–2347.

22. Villa, J., & Zimmerman, Y. (2018). Reproducibility in ML: Why it matters and how to achieve it. *Determined AI Blog*. Retrieved from: https://determined.ai/blog/reproducibility-in-ml (accessed on 25 June 2024).

23. Yang, L., & Shami, A. (2020). On hyperparameter optimization of machine learning algorithms: Theory and practice. *Neurocomputing, 415*, 295–316. https://doi.org/10.1016/j.neucom.2020.07.061.

CHAPTER 5

Alternative Techniques

LEARNING OBJECTIVES

After studying this chapter, you will be able to:

- Discuss on rule-based classifier
- Learn about the nearest-neighbor classifiers
- Give an overview on artificial neural network

KEY TERMS FROM THIS CHAPTER

Fraud detection
Purchasing behavior
Operational efficiency
Customer segmentation
Noise sensitivity
Data mining
Network security
Marketing campaigns
Interpretability
Sequential covering algorithm
Machine learning algorithms

INTRODUCTION

One effective method for obtaining useful information from huge datasets is data mining. In addition to conventional approaches, a number of alternative strategies have surfaced, each with special benefits and uses. These methods include text mining, graph mining, anomaly detection, association rule learning, and cluster analysis. Finding intriguing connections between variables in big databases is the main goal of association rule learning. This method is frequently applied to market basket analysis in order to identify product sets that are frequently purchased in tandem. The classic illustration is noticing that consumers who purchase bread also frequently purchase butter. Product placement, marketing plans, and inventory management can all benefit from this understanding. Another essential data mining technique is anomaly detection, which identifies uncommon objects, occurrences, or observations that deviate markedly from the bulk of the data. This method is essential in many domains, including network security, fraud detection, and industrial system fault detection. Anomaly detection assists organizations in proactively addressing possible problems before they worsen by highlighting odd patterns. Using cluster analysis, a collection of items is grouped so that items within the same group (or cluster) are more similar to one another than they are to those outside of it. This method works especially well for customer classification, image analysis, and market segmentation. Businesses can use clustering, for instance, to divide their clientele into discrete groups according to how they make purchases, allowing for more specialized marketing efforts.

The process of extracting valuable information from text is called text mining, sometimes referred to as text analytics or text data mining. Usually, it entails organizing the text input, identifying patterns in the organized data, and then assessing and interpreting the results. Sentiment analysis, topic detection, and document classification make extensive use of this technique. With social media and digital communication becoming more prevalent, text mining offers vital insights into public opinion and new trends. The study of graph structures, which are just representations of networks made up of nodes (vertices) and edges (links), is the main focus of graph mining. This method is critical to the study of web structures, biological networks, and social networks. Identifying significant nodes and forecasting link formations are just two examples of how graph mining aids in the understanding of intricate relationships and interactions within networks. These alternative approaches to data mining each have unique benefits and uses that help organizations get more insights from a wider range of complicated and varied datasets. Leveraging these strategies is getting more and more important for maintaining an operational edge and competitive advantage as data continues to grow exponentially in volume and variety. Alternative data mining techniques offer effective tools to make sense of the deluge of data, whether it's by identifying anomalies, extracting insights from text, segmenting data into meaningful clusters, or analyzing network structures.

5.1. RULE-BASED CLASSIFIER

A data mining technique called a rule-based classifier uses a set of if-then rules that are extracted from the dataset to classify data. These rules are frequently chosen for numerous applications where interpretability and transparency are essential because they are generally simple to read and comprehend. Rule-based classifiers have applications in many different fields, including customer segmentation, credit scoring, and medical diagnosis. Fundamentally, a rule-based classifier uses the training data to create a set of rules. Every rule has the format if condition then outcome, where the class label is specified in the outcome part and a combination of attribute values is specified in the condition part. An example of a rule might be: high risk of heart disease if age > 50 and cholesterol > 200. Algorithms that look for patterns in the data that best distinguish between various classes are used to generate these rules. Rule generation and rule pruning are typically the two primary steps in the development of a rule-based classifier. The process of removing possible rules from the data is called rule generation. For this, a variety of algorithms can be applied, including the RIPPER algorithm (Repeated Incremental Pruning to Produce Error Reduction). These algorithms seek to identify rules that, while retaining accuracy, cover the greatest number of examples of a given class.

Rule pruning is used after the rules are created to eliminate or modify rules in order to enhance the classifier's functionality and avoid overfitting. When a classifier is overfit to the training set, noise is captured instead of the underlying patterns. This is known as overfitting. Pruning strategies can include grouping related rules together to create more general rules or eliminating rules that don't substantially improve classification accuracy. Interpretability is a primary benefit of rule-based classifiers. Stakeholders and domain experts can understand the simple if-then rules with ease. Because of this, rule-based classifiers are especially helpful in domains like medicine, where it's imperative to comprehend the rationale behind a classification. Rule-based classifiers are also adaptable and capable of handling both numerical and categorical data, which makes them useful for a variety of dataset types. Rule-based classifiers do, however, have certain drawbacks. In terms of predictive accuracy, they might not work as well as more sophisticated models, like ensemble approaches or deep learning algorithms. In very large or highly dimensional datasets, where the number of possible rules can become overwhelming, rule-based classifiers may also have difficulty. In these situations, more complex algorithms that can manage large amounts of data and high dimensionality may be favored. (Liu, Bing, et al., 2000).

5.1.1. Purpose

Rule-based classifiers are just another type of classifier which makes the class decision depending by using various "if else" rules. Since these rules are simple to understand, classifiers using them are typically used to create descriptive models. The expected class of each rule is referred to as the subsequent, and the condition used with "if" is referred to as the antecedent (Table 5.1).

- Coverage: The percentage of records which satisfy the antecedent conditions of a particular rule.
- The rules generated by the rule-based classifiers are generally not mutually exclusive, i.e., many rules can cover the same record.
- The rules generated by the rule-based classifiers may not be exhaustive, i.e., there may be some records which are not covered by any of the rules.
- The decision boundaries created by them is linear, but these can be much more complex than the decision tree because the many rules are triggered for the same record.

An obvious question, which comes into the mind after knowing that the rules are not mutually exclusive is that how the class would be decided in case different rules with different consequent cover the record.

There are two solutions to the above problem:

- Either rules can be ordered, i.e., the class corresponding to the highest priority rule triggered is taken as the final class.
- Otherwise, we can assign votes for each class depending on some their weights, i.e., the rules remain unordered.

Table 5.1. The Dataset to Classify Mushrooms as Edible or Poisonous

Class	Cap Shape	Cap Surface	Bruises	Odour	Stalk Shape	Population	Habitat
edible	flat	scaly	yes	anise	tapering	scattered	grasses
poisonous	convex	scaly	yes	pungent	enlargening	several	grasses
edible	convex	smooth	yes	almond	enlargening	numerous	grasses
edible	convex	scaly	yes	almond	tapering	scattered	meadows
edible	flat	fibrous	yes	anise	enlargening	several	woods
edible	flat	fibrous	no	none	enlargening	several	urban
poisonous	conical	scaly	yes	pungent	enlargening	scattered	urban
edible	flat	smooth	yes	anise	enlargening	numerous	meadows
poisonous	convex	smooth	yes	pungent	enlargening	several	urban

Source: https://www.geeksforgeeks.org/rule-based-classifier-machine-learning/.

- **Rules:**
  - o Odour = pungent and habitat = urban -> Class = poisonous
  - o Bruises = yes -> Class = edible: This rules covers both negative and positive records.

The given rules are not mutually exclusive.

- **How to Generate a Rule:** The general-to-specific and specific-to-general approaches can be used to create rules. To improve our evaluation metrics, begin with a rule in the general-to-specific approach that has no antecedents and gradually add conditions to it. In contrast, we continue to remove requirements from a rule that applies to a very particular set of circumstances. Accuracy, information gain, likelihood ratio, and other metrics can be used as evaluation metrics (Figure 5.1).

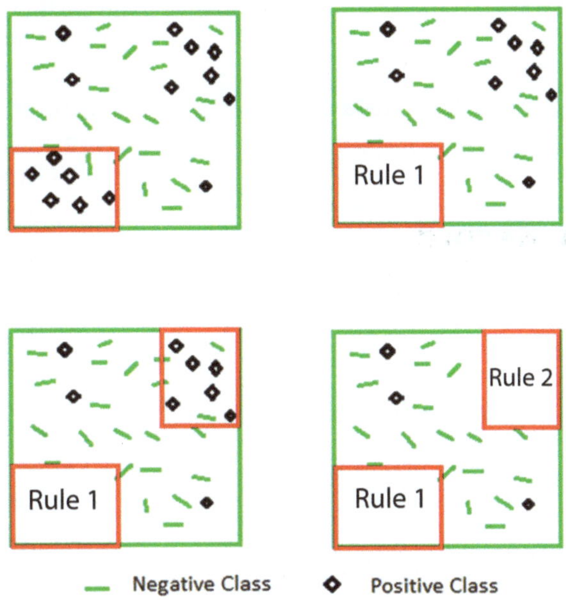

Figure 5.1. *Sequential rule generation.*

Source: https://media.geeksforgeeks.org/wp-content/uploads/20200402041013/Rule-Generation.png.

5.1.2. Algorithm for Generating the Model Incrementally

The algorithm given below generates a model with unordered rules and ordered classes, i.e., we can decide which class to give priority while generating the rules.

A <-Set of attributes

T <-Set of training records

Y <-Set of classes

Y' <-Ordered Y according to relevance

R <-Set of rules generated, initially to an empty list

for each class y in Y'

while the majority of class y records are not covered

generate a new rule for class y, using methods given above

Add this rule to R

Remove the records covered by this rule from T

end while

end for

Add rule {}->y' where y' is the default class

5.1.3. Classifying a Record

The classification algorithm described below assumes that the rules are unordered and the classes are weighted.

R <-Set of rules generated using training Set

T <-Test Record

W <-class name to Weight mapping, predefined, given as input

F <-class name to Vote mapping, generated for each test record, to be calculated

for each rule r in R

check if r covers T

if so then add W of predicted_class to F of predicted_class

end for

Output the class with the highest calculated vote in F

5.1.4. Properties of Rule-Based Classifiers

There are two significant properties of rule-based classification in data mining. They are:

1. **Rules May Not be Mutually Exclusive in Nature:** Since the dataset generates a large number of rules, it is likely that many of them will satisfy the same data record. This means that the rules are not exclusive of one another. We are unable to select classes that cover distinct data segments on separate rules because the rules do not conflict with one another. However, this was our primary goal. Thus, we have two options for resolving this issue:
   i. The first way is using an ordered set of rules. By ordering the rules, we set priority orders. Thus, this ordered rule set is called a decision list. So the class with the highest priority rule is taken as the final class.
   ii. The second solution can be assigning votes for each class depending on their weights. So, in this, the set of rules remains unordered.
2. **Rules May Not Be Exhaustive in Nature:** There is no assurance that every data entry will be covered by the rule. Any rule could leave some entries in the data. When this situation arises, the rules will become non-exhaustive. Thus, we too need to find a solution to this issue. So, we can use a default class to solve this issue. We can assign all the data entries that aren't covered by any rules to the

default class by using a default class. Therefore, the non-exhaustivity issue can be resolved by using the default class.

5.1.5. IF-THEN Rules

Rule-based classifier makes use of a set of IF-THEN rules for classification. We can express a rule in the following from:

IF condition THEN conclusion

Let us consider a rule R1,

R1: IF age = youth AND student = yes

THEN buy_computer = yes

Points to remember:

- The IF part of the rule is called rule antecedent or precondition.
- The THEN part of the rule is called rule consequent.
- The antecedent part the condition consist of one or more attribute tests and these tests are logically ANDed.
- The consequent part consists of class prediction.

Note – We can also write rule R1 as follows –

R1: (age = youth) ^ (student = yes))(buys computer = yes)

If the condition holds true for a given tuple, then the antecedent is satisfied.

5.1.6. Rule Extraction

Here we will learn how to build a rule-based classifier by extracting IF-THEN rules from a decision tree.

Points to remember:

To extract a rule from a decision tree:

- One rule is created for each path from the root to the leaf node.
- To form a rule antecedent, each splitting criterion is logically ANDed.
- The leaf node holds the class prediction, forming the rule consequent.

5.1.7. Rule Induction Using Sequential Covering Algorithm

The training data can be used to extract IF-THEN rules using the Sequential Covering Algorithm. It is not necessary for us to create a decision tree beforehand. Each rule in this algorithm covers a large number of tuples within a given class. The sequential Covering Algorithms include RIPPER, CN2, and AQ. The general strategy is to teach the rules one at a time. Every time a rule is learned, a tuple that it applies to is eliminated, and the process is then repeated for the remaining tuples. This is so because each leaf in a decision tree has a path that relates to a rule.

The Following is the sequential learning Algorithm where rules are learned for one class at a time. When learning a rule from a class Ci, we want the rule to cover all the tuples from class C only and no tuple form any other class.

Algorithm: Sequential Covering

```
Input:
D, a data set class-labeled tuples,
Att_vals, the set of all attributes and their possible values.
Output: A Set of IF-THEN rules.
Method:
Rule_set={ }; // initial set of rules learned is empty
for each class c do


repeat
Rule = Learn_One_Rule(D, Att_valls, c);
remove tuples covered by Rule form D;
until termination condition;


Rule_set=Rule_set+Rule; // add a new rule to rule-set
end for
return Rule_Set;
```

5.1.8. Rule Pruning

The rule is pruned is due to the following reason –

- The Assessment of quality is made on the original set of training data. The rule may perform well on training data but less well on subsequent data. That's why the rule pruning is required.
- The rule is pruned by removing conjunct. The rule R is pruned, if pruned version of R has greater quality than what was assessed on an independent set of tuples.

FOIL is one of the simple and effective method for rule pruning. For a given rule R,

FOIL_Prune = pos – neg / pos + neg

where pos and neg is the number of positive tuples covered by R, respectively.

Note – This value will increase with the accuracy of R on the pruning set. Hence, if the FOIL_Prune value is higher for the pruned version of R, then we prune R.

5.1.9. Implementation of Rule-Based Classifier

We have two different kinds of methods for implementing rule-based classification in data mining. They are:

- Direct Method
- Indirect Method

5.1.9.1. Direct Method

The direct method for rule-based classification in data mining contains algorithms that extract rules directly from the dataset. (Henri Prade et al., 2012)

The prominent among these are:

1. 1R Algorithm
2. Sequentia Covering Algorithm

1. **1R Algorithm:** The Learn One Rule Algorithm is another name for the 1R Algorithm. It is predicated on an easy classification principle. As a result, it's among the easiest algorithms. We create rules in this algorithm to test every attribute. When an attribute has a range of values, we use the frequency of occurrences of each class value to create rules. We take this action to determine its frequency and identify the class with the highest frequency. Next, we designate that class for the pair of attribute values. Next, we determine each attribute's error rate and choose the one with the lowest error rate. The 1R method is not without flaws; noise sensitivity and overfitting are major risks. Therefore, we employ the Sequential Covering Algorithm to get around these issues.
2. **Sequential Covering Algorithm:** The most popular algorithm for rule-based classification in data mining is the sequential covering algorithm. This algorithm specifies rules that cover no data records from other classes and the maximum number of records from one class. These algorithms grow rules one by one in a sequential fashion. All data records covered by a rule are removed once it has grown, and the process is then repeated for the remaining data records. At the point where we meet the stopping criteria, i.e., we reject the rule and end it there if its accuracy falls short of the necessary threshold. By taking the subsequent steps, we can comprehend how the sequential covering algorithm operates.

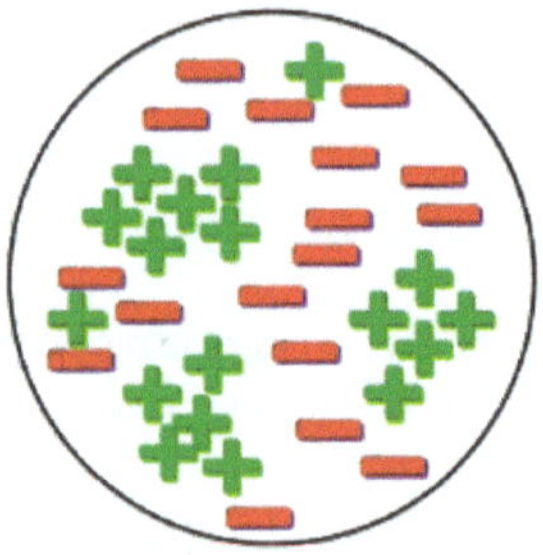

This is the original state

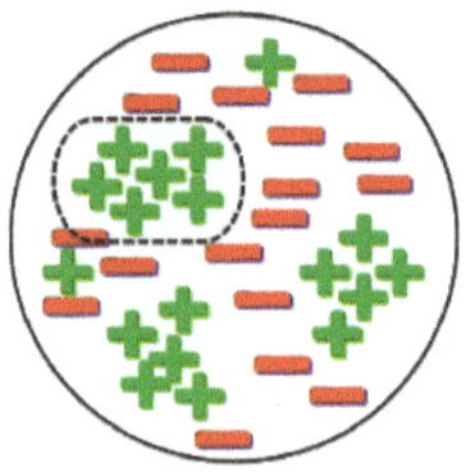

Rule Gowing (Rule 1)

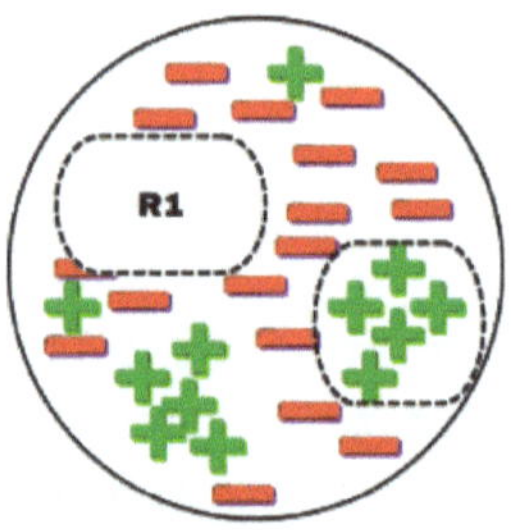

Instance Elimination (Removing Rule1 and growing Rule2)

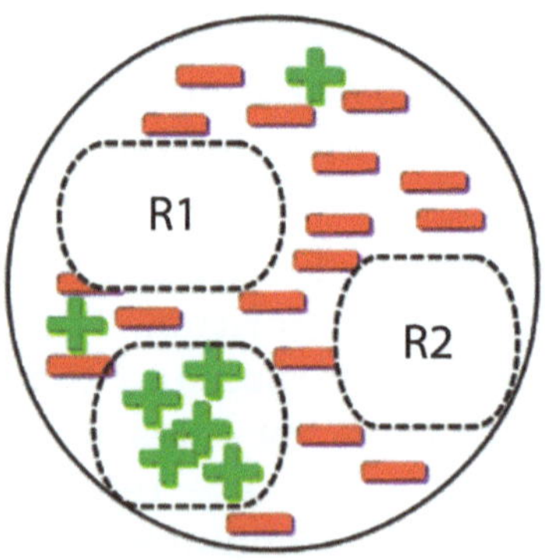

Continuing this process until meeting the stopping criteria.

5.1.9.2. Indirect Method

In the indirect method of rule-based classification in data mining, we extract rules from different other classification models. Some prominent classifications from which we extract the rules are decision trees and neural networks (Fausett, L.V 1993).

For example:

Converting the decision tree to the rule set.

5.1.10. Why We Use?

A straightforward, simple to comprehend, and simple to apply classification technique is rule-based classification. A human annotator or domain expert typically defines the rules for a rule-based classifier, and these rules are typically based on the features of the problem domain and the data set. Rule-based classifiers have the primary benefit of being simple to comprehend, elucidate, and debug. Additionally, they frequently outperform machine learning algorithms in precise and well-defined problem sets. Rule-based classifiers do, however, have certain drawbacks. They may be brittle, which means that when presented with fresh examples that don't adhere to the established guidelines, they may break easily. Additionally, they can be challenging to scale to large data sets and have a tendency to perform poorly when presented with more complex and varied data sets. The rules must also be defined and updated, which takes a great deal of experience and time. A straightforward, simple to comprehend, and simple to apply classification technique is rule-based classification. It tends to perform poorly on more complex and varied data sets, but it is helpful for small and well-defined problem sets.

There are several reasons why you might choose to use a rule-based classifier:

- Specific and well-defined problem sets: Rule-based classifiers are particularly useful for specific and well-defined problem sets, such as identifying spam emails or sentiment analysis, where the characteristics of the data set and the problem domain are well understood.
- Easy to understand and explain: Rule-based classifiers are easy to understand, explain, and debug. This makes them useful for applications where transparency and explainability are important.
- High accuracy: For specific and well-defined problem sets, rule-based classifiers can be more accurate than machine learning algorithms
- Easy to implement: Rule-based classifiers are relatively simple to implement and require less computational resources compared to machine learning algorithms.
- Cost-effective: Rule-based classifiers are generally less expensive to develop and maintain than machine learning algorithms.

Note: It's important to note that rule-based classifiers tend to perform poorly when faced with more complex and varied data sets, and they can be difficult to scale to large data sets. Additionally, they require a significant amount of expertise and time to define the rules and keep them updated.

5.1.11. Advantages of Rule-Based Classification

Let us see an example of rule-based classification in data mining to understand its advantages.

The significant advantages of rule-based classification in data mining, which we see through the example are:

- The rule-based classification is easy to generate.
- It is highly expressive in nature and very easy to understand.
- It assists in the classification of new records in significantly less time and very quickly.
- It helps us to handle redundant values during classification properly.
- The performance of the rule-based classification is comparable to that of a decision tree.

5.2. NEAREST-NEIGHBOR CLASSIFIERS

In data mining and machine learning, nearest-neighbor classifiers are a kind of instance-based learning algorithm used for classification and regression tasks. Classifying a data point according to the categories of its closest neighbors in the feature space is the fundamental principle of nearest-neighbor classifiers. The k-nearest neighbor (k-NN) algorithm, where "k" indicates the number of neighbors taken into consideration, is the most widely used and fundamental version of this classifier. In order to classify new cases (test data), a similarity measure—typically the Euclidean distance, though other distance metrics like Manhattan or Minkowski distances can also be used—must first be applied to all available cases (training data). The algorithm finds the 'k' training instances that are closest to a given test instance based on the selected distance metric. The majority class among these 'k' neighbors then determines the class label for the test instance. For instance, the test instance will be categorized as A if 'k' is set to 3 and the three closest neighbors are in classes A, B, and A. Nearest-neighbor classifiers are notable for a number of reasons. They are an accessible option for many applications because they are easy to understand and implement. Additionally, because they are non-parametric—that is, they don't assume anything about the data's underlying distribution—they function well in a variety of settings, particularly those with intricate, irregular decision boundaries. They are also very flexible; new data can be added to them without having to start the model over from scratch when it becomes available.

The nearest-neighbor classifiers, however (Djouadi & Bouktache, 1997) have a few drawbacks as well. Their computational inefficiency is a major drawback, particularly when dealing with big datasets. The algorithm can be computationally expensive in terms of time and memory because it needs to calculate the distance between each training instance and the test instance. The curse of dimensionality refers to this inefficiency, which is especially noticeable in high-dimensional spaces where nearest neighbors may not be as close as they are and the concept of distance loses significance. Furthermore, the selection of 'k' may have an impact on nearest-neighbor classifier performance. A large "k" value may smooth out the decision boundary too much, resulting in underfitting, while a small "k" value may make the classifier sensitive to noise in the training data, resulting in overfitting. Selecting the ideal "k" is important and is frequently accomplished using cross-validation. Additionally, since every feature has an equal impact on the distance calculation, these classifiers can be affected by the presence of redundant or irrelevant features. To make sure that features with larger ranges do not disproportionately affect the distance measurements, feature scaling or normalization is usually necessary.

Notwithstanding these difficulties, nearest-neighbor classifiers are still a preferred option in a number of fields, including pattern recognition, image and speech recognition, and recommendation systems, because of their adaptability and efficiency in specific situations. They offer useful insights into the data's structure and act as a foundation for more intricate algorithms. The efficiency of nearest-neighbor searches has increased due to developments in data structures and algorithms, such as KD-trees and Ball trees, which enable these classifiers to handle larger datasets more skillfully.

5.2.1. Basics

The two-step process for creating a classification model from data in the classification framework is called an inductive step, and the application of the model to test examples is called a deductive step. Eager learners include decision trees and rule-based classifiers, which are built to learn a model that instantly associates the input attributes with the class label upon the availability of training data. An alternative approach would be to postpone modeling the training set of data until after the test cases need to be classified.

Learners who use this tactic are referred to as lazy learners. The Rote classifier is an illustration of a lazy learner; it retains all of the training data and only classifies a test instance if its attributes precisely match one of the training examples. This approach has the obvious drawback of potentially leaving some test records unclassified if they don't match any training examples.

Finding all the training examples that have characteristics that are somewhat similar to those of the test example is one way to increase the flexibility of this strategy. The test example's class label can be ascertained using these instances, also referred to as nearest neighbors. It's easiest to apply the proverb "If it walks like a duck, quacks like a duck, and looks like a duck, then it's probably a duck" to support the use of nearest neighbors. Each example is represented by a data point in a d-dimensional space by a nearest neighbor classifier, where d is the number of attributes. We calculate a test example's proximity to every other data point in the training set. The k points that are closest to a given example z are called z's k-nearest neighbors. (Li, Yang, & Han, 2012)

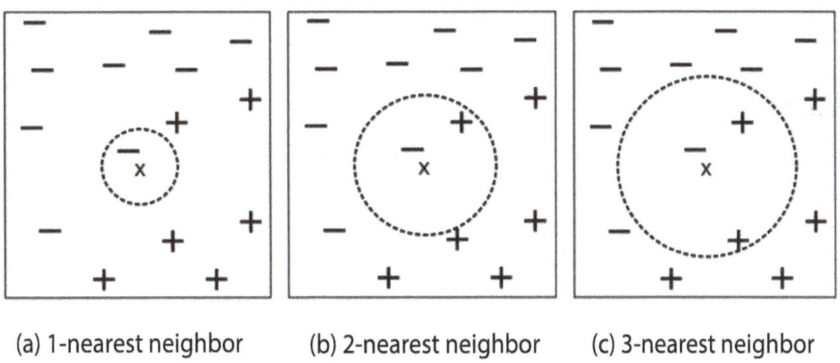

Figure 5.2. *The 1-, 2-, and 3-nearest neighbors of an instance.*

Source: http://www.gersteinlab.org/courses/545/07-spr/reading/tan-2005-chpt05.pdf.

The 1-, 2-, and 3-nearest neighbors of a data point at each circle's center are shown in Figure 5.2. The neighbors' class labels are used to classify the data point. The data point is assigned to the majority class of its closest neighbors when there are multiple labels present in the neighbors. The 1-nearest neighbor of the data point in Figure 5.2(a) serves as an illustration of a negative.

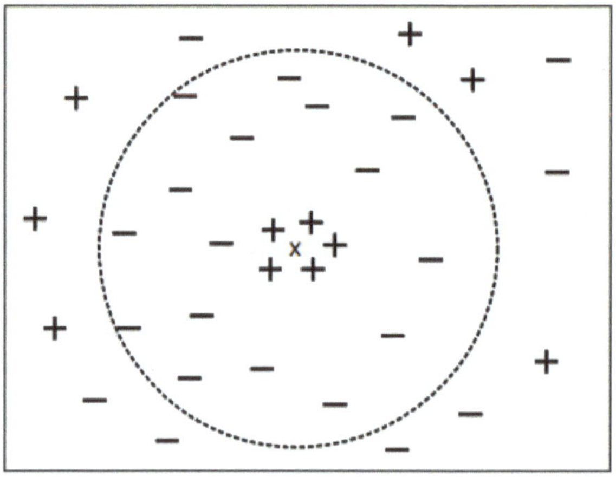

Figure 5.3. *k-nearest neighbor classification with large k.*

Source: http://www.gersteinlab.org/courses/545/07-spr/reading/tan-2005-chpt05.pdf.

As a result, the data point is classified as negative. Three neighbors, as indicated in Figure 5.2(c), indicates that there are two positive and one negative example in the neighborhood. The data point is allocated to the positive class by means of the majority voting scheme. We may select a class at random to classify the data point if there is a tie between them (see Figure 5.2(b)). The previous conversation emphasizes how crucial it is to select the appropriate value for k. The nearest-neighbor classifier may be prone to overfitting due to noise in the training set if k is too small. However, if k is too big, data points that are far from the test instance's neighborhood may be included in the nearest neighbors list, leading to a misclassification of the test instance by the nearest-neighbor classifier (see Figure 5.3).

5.2.2. Algorithm

Algorithm 5.1 provides a high-level overview of the nearest-neighbor classification technique. To determine its nearest-neighbor list, Dz, the algorithm calculates the distance (or similarity) between each test example, z = (x ′, y′), and all the training examples, x, y) ∈ D. In cases where there are a lot of training examples, this computation may be expensive. To find the closest neighbors of a test example, fewer calculations are required thanks to effective indexing techniques.

Algorithm 5.1. The k-nearest neighbor classification algorithm

```
Let k be the number of nearest neighbors and D be the set of training examples.
for each test example z = (x', y') do
   Compute d(x', x), the distance between z and every example, (x, y) ∈ D.
   Select D_z ⊆ D, the set of k closest training examples to z.
   y' = argmax_v Σ_{(x_i, y_i) ∈ D_z} I(v = y_i)
end for
```

Source: http://www.gersteinlab.org/courses/545/07-spr/reading/tan-2005-chpt05.pdf.

Once the nearest-neighbor list is obtained, the test example is classified based on the majority class of its nearest neighbors:

$$\text{Majority Voting: } y' = \underset{v}{\operatorname{argmax}} \sum_{(\mathbf{x}_i, y_i) \in D_z} I(v = y_i),$$

Where; v is a class label, y_i is the class label for one of the nearest neighbors, and $I(\cdot)$ is an indicator function that returns the value 1 if its argument is true and 0 otherwise.

With the majority voting method, the classification is affected equally by each neighbor. Because of this, the algorithm is sensitive to the selection of k. Weighing the influence of each closest neighbor xi based on their distance from you can help lessen the effect of k. $W_i = 1/d(x', x_i)^2$. Consequently, the impact of training examples located far from z on the classification is smaller than that of training examples located close to z. The class label can be ascertained as follows by applying the distance-weighted voting scheme:

$$\text{Distance-Weighted Voting: } y' = \underset{v}{\operatorname{argmax}} \sum_{(\mathbf{x}_i, y_i) \in D_z} w_i \times I(v = y_i)$$

5.2.3. Characteristics of Nearest-Neighbor Classifiers

The characteristics of the nearest-neighbor classifier are summarized below:

- Instance-based learning, a more comprehensive approach that employs particular training instances to generate predictions rather than requiring the maintenance of an abstraction (or model) derived from data, includes nearest-neighbor classification. A classification function that predicts a test instance's class based on its proximity to other instances and a proximity measure to assess the similarity or distance between instances are needed by instance-based learning algorithms.
- Model construction is not necessary for lazy learners like nearest-neighbor classifiers. However, because we have to calculate the proximity values between the test and training examples separately, classifying a test example can be

rather costly. On the other hand, motivated learners frequently dedicate most of their computer power to creating models. Classifying a test example is very fast once a model is built.

- While rule-based and decision tree classifiers try to find a global model that fits the entire input space, nearest-neighbor classifiers base their predictions on local data. Local decision-making regarding classification makes nearest-neighbor classifiers (with small values of k) highly vulnerable to noise.
- Decision boundaries of any shape can be produced by nearest-neighbor classifiers. When compared to decision trees and rule-based classifiers, which are frequently limited to rectilinear decision boundaries, such boundaries offer a more flexible model representation. Because nearest-neighbor classifier decision boundaries rely on the make-up of training examples, they are also highly variable. Raising the number of closest neighbors could lessen this fluctuation.
- Incorrect predictions may be generated by nearest-neighbor classifiers if the proper proximity measure and data preprocessing techniques are not followed. Assume, for instance, that we wish to categorize a group of individuals according to characteristics like weight (measured in pounds) and height (measured in meters). While the weight attribute can vary from 90 lb, the height attribute has a low variability, ranging from 1.5 m to 1.85 m. up to 250 lb. If the attribute scale is not taken into account, disparities in an individual's weights may dominate the proximity measure.

5.2.4. Nearest Neighbors Regression

When there are continuous data labels instead of discrete variables, neighbors-based regression can be applied. Based on the average of the labels of its closest neighbors, a query point's label is determined. Here, two distinct neighbors' regressors are implemented: KNeighborsRegressor, which learns about each query point's k nearest neighbors, where k is an integer value that the user specifies. With a fixed radius r around the query point—a floating-point value that the user specifies—Radius Neighbors Regressor provides learning based on the neighbors.

Every point in the local neighborhood contributes uniformly to the classification of a query point in the basic nearest neighbor's regression because uniform weights are used. It may be beneficial in some cases to weight the points so that closer points have a greater impact on the regression than farther points. The weights keyword can be used to achieve this. When weights = "distance" is used, the weights are proportionate to the inverse of the distance from the query point, whereas when weights = "uniform," all points are assigned equal weights. As an alternative, the weights can be calculated using a user-defined function of the distance (Figure 5.4).

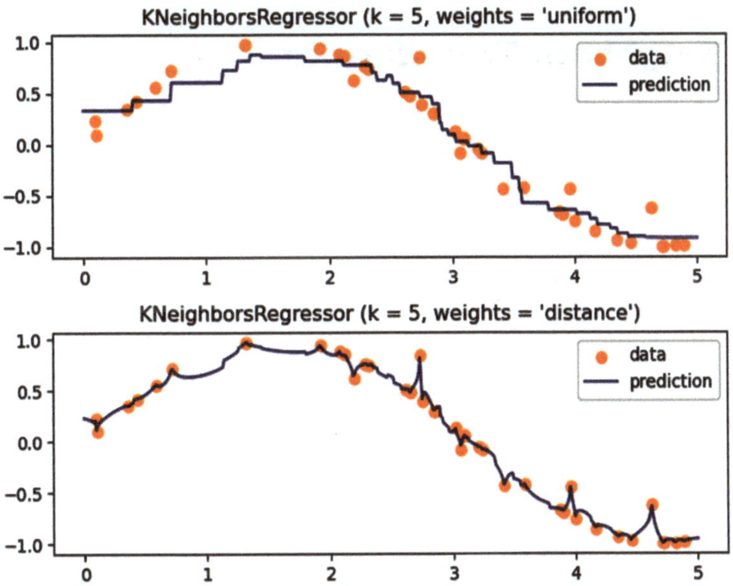

Figure 5.4. *Data prediction through neighbors-based regression.*

Source: https://scikit-learn.org/stable/_images/sphx_glr_plot_regression_001.png.

The use of multi-output nearest neighbors for regression is demonstrated in Face completion with a multi-output estimators. In this example, the inputs X are the pixels of the upper half of faces and the outputs Y are the pixels of the lower half of those faces (Figure 5.5).

Figure 5.5. *Face completion with a multi-output estimators.*

Source: https://scikit-learn.org/stable/_images/sphx_glr_plot_multioutput_face_completion_001.png.

5.2.5. Nearest Neighbors Transformer

Numerous estimators rely on nearest neighbors, including a number of classifiers and regressors like KNeighborsClassifier and KNeighborsRegressor, as well as a few manifold embeddings like TSNE and ISOmap and a few clustering techniques like DBSCAN and SpectralClustering. While most of these estimators accept precomputed nearest neighbors sparse graphs, provided by kneighbors_graph and radius_neighbors_graph, all of them are capable of internally computing the nearest neighbors. As needed, for example, in SpectralClustering, these functions return a binary adjacency sparse graph with mode mode='connectivity.' As needed, for example, in DBSCAN, they return a distance sparse graph when mode='distance' is used. The corresponding classes KNeighborsTransformer and RadiusNeighborsTransformer can also be used to incorporate these functions into a scikit-learn pipeline. This sparse graph API offers a number of advantages. Firstly, the precomputed graph can be used again and again, for example, when changing an estimator parameter.

This can be done manually by the user, or using the caching properties of the scikit-learn pipeline:

```
>>> import tempfile
>>> from sklearn.manifold import Isomap
>>> from sklearn.neighbors import KNeighborsTransformer
>>> from sklearn.pipeline import make_pipeline
>>> from sklearn.datasets import make_regression
>>> cache_path = tempfile.gettempdir() # we use a temporary folder here
>>> X, _ = make_regression(n_samples=50, n_features=25, random_state=0)
>>> estimator = make_pipeline(
...  KNeighborsTransformer(mode='distance'),
...  Isomap(n_components=3, metric='precomputed'),
...  memory=cache_path)
>>> X_embedded = estimator.fit_transform(X)
>>> X_embedded.shape
(50, 3)
```

Second, precalculating the graph can provide more precise control over the estimation of the nearest neighbors. For example, it can allow multiprocessing through the parameter n_jobs, which not all estimators may support. Last but not least, the precomputation can be carried out by custom estimators to employ various implementations, like implementation with unique data types or approximate nearest neighbors techniques. The neighbors sparse graph that was precomputed must be formatted as shown in radius_neighbors_graph output:

- a CSR matrix (although COO, CSC or LIL will be accepted).
- only explicitly store nearest neighborhoods of each sample with respect to the training data. This should include those at 0 distance from a query point, including the matrix diagonal when computing the nearest neighborhoods between the training data and itself.
- each row's data should store the distance in increasing order (optional. Unsorted data will be stable-sorted, adding a computational overhead).
- all values in data should be non-negative.
- there should be no duplicate indices in any row.
- if the algorithm being passed the precomputed matrix uses k nearest neighbors (as opposed to radius neighborhood), at least k neighbors must be stored in each row (or k+1, as explained in the following note).

5.2.6. Implementation of Nearest-Neighbor Classifiers

Implementing a nearest-neighbor classifier involves several steps: data preprocessing, selecting a distance metric, determining the value of 'k,' and classifying new instances based on the nearest neighbors. Here is a detailed explanation of the implementation process:

- **Data Preprocessing**: The dataset must be ready for the nearest-neighbor algorithm in the first place. Usually, this entails scaling or normalizing numerical features, handling missing values, and encoding categorical variables. The importance of normalization stems from nearest-neighbor classifiers (Ghosh A. K. Chaudhuri P. as well as Murthy C. A. (2005)) depend on distance measures that features with greater numerical ranges can disproportionately influence. Z-score standardization and min-max normalization are two popular scaling techniques.
- **Selecting a Distance Metric**: Selecting a suitable distance metric is crucial for ensuring that a nearest-neighbor classifier operates accurately. The Euclidean distance, which calculates the straight-line distance between two points in a multidimensional space, is the most widely used metric. Other metrics, however, might be more appropriate depending on the type of data, such as the Manhattan distance (sum of absolute differences), Minkowski distance (a generalization of Euclidean and Manhattan distances), or even cosine similarity (for text data).
- **Determining the Value of 'k'**: One crucial hyperparameter in nearest-neighbor classification is the value of 'k,' or the number of nearest neighbors to take into account. A tiny "k" (e.g., k=1) could cause overfitting by increasing the classifier's sensitivity to noise and outliers. On the other hand, a big "k" could produce a smoother decision boundary, which could cause underfitting. Cross-validation is typically used to determine the

optimal 'k,' testing different values of 'k' to see which one performs best on a validation set.

- **Classification Process**: Classifying new instances comes after the data has been preprocessed, the distance metric has been chosen, and 'k' has been established. Using the selected distance metric, the algorithm calculates the distance between each new instance and every instance in the training set. The next step involves finding the 'k' closest neighbors and looking at their class labels. The majority vote among these neighbors determines the classification of the new instance. The new instance will be categorized as class A, for instance, if 'k' is 5 and three of the closest neighbors are in class A and two are in class B.
- **Implementation in Code**: Nearest-neighbor classifiers can be implemented using various programming languages and libraries. In Python, the scikit-learn library provides a simple and efficient way to implement the k-nearest neighbors (k-NN) algorithm. Here is a basic implementation:

```
from sklearn.neighbors import KNeighborsClassifier

from sklearn.preprocessing import StandardScaler

from sklearn.model_selection import train_test_split

from sklearn.metrics import accuracy_score

# Load and preprocess the data

X, y = load_data() # Load your dataset

scaler = StandardScaler()

X_scaled = scaler.fit_transform(X)

# Split the data

X_train, X_test, y_train, y_test = train_test_split(X_scaled, y, test_size=0.2, random_state=42)

# Create and train the k-NN classifier

k = 5 # Optimal k determined via cross-validation

knn = KNeighborsClassifier(n_neighbors=k)

knn.fit(X_train, y_train)

# Make predictions and evaluate the model

y_pred = knn.predict(X_test)

accuracy = accuracy_score(y_test, y_pred)

print(f'Accuracy: {accuracy}')
```

This implementation uses train_test_split to divide the dataset into training and testing sets, StandardScaler to normalize the features, and KNeighborsClassifier to build the nearest-neighbor classifier. After the classifier has been trained on the training set of data, its performance is assessed using the accuracy score on the test set of data. The present procedure delineates the essential stages and factors to be taken into account when executing a nearest-neighbor classifier. It highlights the significance of distance metrics, hyper-parameter tuning, and preprocessing in attaining peak efficiency.

5.3. ARTIFICIAL NEURAL NETWORK

Units, or artificial neurons, are components of artificial neural networks. The Artificial Neural Network in a system is made up of these units arranged in a sequence of layers. The number of units in a layer can range from a few dozen to millions, depending on how many complex neural networks are needed to uncover the dataset's hidden patterns. Artificial neural networks typically consist of hidden layers, output layers, and input layers. The input layer is where external data is fed into the neural network for analysis or education. After that, the data goes through one or more hidden layers, which convert the input into useful data for the output layer. Ultimately, the Artificial Neural Networks' response to the supplied input data is provided as an output by the output layer. Units are connected from one layer to another in most neural networks. The weights assigned to each of these connections indicate how much influence each unit has over the others. The neural network gains knowledge about the data as it moves from one unit to the next, eventually producing an output from the output layer (Figure 5.6).

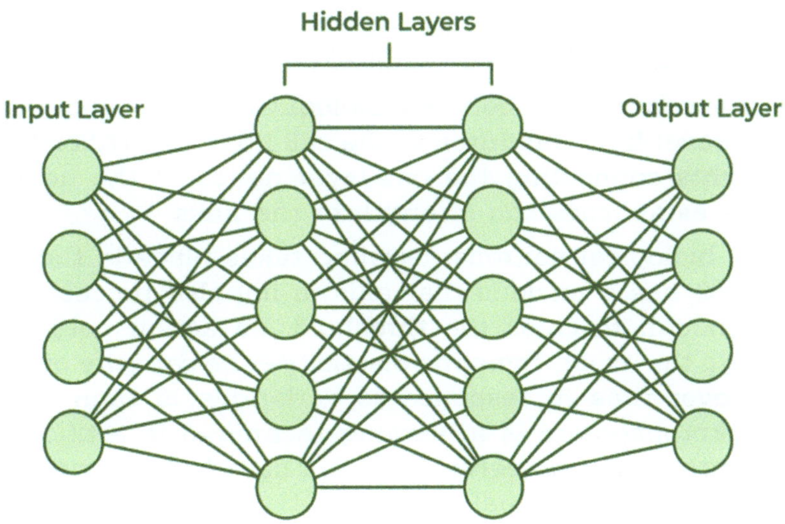

Figure 5.6. *Neural networks architecture.*

Source: https://media.geeksforgeeks.org/wp-content/cdn-uploads/20230602113310/Neural-Networks-Architecture.png.

Artificial neural networks are based on the architecture and functions of human neurons. Another name for it is neural nets or neural networks. An artificial neural network's first layer, known as the input layer, transfers data from outside sources to the second layer, known as the hidden layer.

Each neuron in the hidden layer takes in information from the neurons in the layer above, calculates the weighted sum, and then relays it to the neurons in the layer below. Because these connections are weighted, the effects of the inputs from the previous layer are essentially optimized by giving each input a unique weight, which is then modified during training to improve model performance.

5.3.1. Artificial Neurons vs Biological Neurons

The concept of artificial neural networks comes from biological neurons found in animal brains. So they share a lot of similarities in structure and function wise.

- **Structure**: Biological neurons serve as an inspiration for the architecture of artificial neural networks. An axon distributes the impulses to other neurons, dendrites receive the impulses, and a biological neuron's cell body, or soma, processes the impulses. Artificial neural network input nodes receive input signals, which are then computed by hidden layer nodes. The output layer nodes then use activation functions to process the results of the hidden layer to determine the final output.

Biological Neuron	Artificial Neuron
Dendrite	Inputs
Cell nucleus or Soma	Nodes
Synapses	Weights
Axon	Output

- **Synapses**: The connections between biological neurons known as synapses allow impulses to travel from dendrites to the cell body. In artificial neurons, synapses are the weights connecting the one-layer nodes to the next-layer nodes. The weight value establishes the strength of the links.
- **Learning**: In biological neurons, learning takes place in the soma, or cell body nucleus, which has a nucleus that aids in impulse processing. If the impulses are strong enough to cross the threshold, an action potential is created and moves through the axons. Synaptic plasticity—the capacity of synapses to change in strength over time in response to variations in their activity—makes this feasible. Backpropagation is a learning technique in artificial neural networks that modifies the weights between nodes based on the discrepancies or errors between predicted and actual outcomes.

Biological Neuron	Artificial Neuron
Synaptic plasticity	Backpropagations

- **Activation**: When an impulse is strong enough to cross the threshold, a biological neuron will fire at a rate known as activation. An activation function is a mathematical function that maps an input to an output in artificial neural networks and performs activations (Figure 5.7).

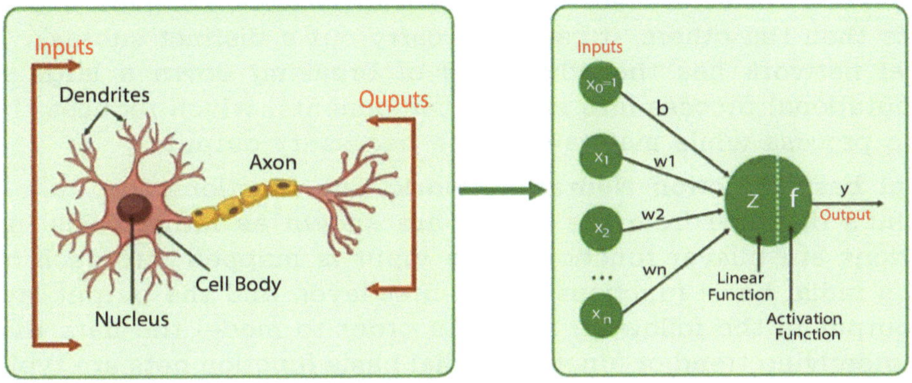

Figure 5.7. *Biological neurons to artificial neurons.*

Source: https://media.geeksforgeeks.org/wp-content/uploads/20230410104038/Artificial-Neural-Networks.webp.

5.3.2. Types of Artificial Neural Networks

A training set is used to train artificial neural networks. Let's say, for instance, that you wish to teach an ANN how to identify a cat. In order to train the network to recognize a cat, thousands of different cat images are then displayed to it. You must verify that the neural network can accurately identify cat images once it has had sufficient training with cat images. This is accomplished by asking the ANN to categorize the images it is given by determining whether or not they are images of cats. An explanation of whether or not the image is of a cat supplied by a human validates the output produced by the ANN. Backpropagation is used to modify the ANN's training data if it makes an incorrect identification. In order to perform backpropagation, ANN units' connection weights are adjusted based on the error rate recorded. Until the artificial neural network can accurately identify a cat in an image with the fewest possible error rates, this process is repeated.

- **Feedforward Neural Network:** One of the most fundamental types of artificial neural networks is the feedforward neural network. The data or input supplied to this ANN only moves in one direction. It may or may not have hidden layers; it enters the ANN through the input layer and leaves through the output layer. Thus, the feedforward neural network typically lacks backpropagation and only has front-propagated waves. .
- **Convolutional Neural Network:** Convolutional neural networks and feed-forward neural networks are similar in that they both use weighted connections between units to determine how much each unit influences the others. However, a CNN comprises one or more convolutional layers, each of which applies a convolution operation to the input before sending the output, or result, to the following layer. CNN has uses in image and speech processing, which is especially helpful for computer vision.

- **Modular Neural Network:** A modular neural network is made up of several separate neural networks that operate separately from one another to produce the desired result. Because each neural network receives a different set of inputs than the others, it can each carry out a distinct subtask. This modular neural network has the advantage of breaking down a large and complex computational process into smaller components, which reduces the complexity of the process while maintaining the necessary output.
- **Radial basis function Neural Network:** The functions that take into account a point's distance from the center are known as radial basis functions. RBF functions are bilayer functions. The input is mapped into each of the hidden layer's radial basis functions in the first layer, and the output layer computes the output in the following stage. In order to model the data that represents any underlying trend or function, radial basis function nets are typically utilized.
- **Recurrent Neural Network:** In order to improve layer prediction, the Recurrent Neural Network stores layer output and feeds it back into the input. The RNN's first layer is very similar to a feed-forward neural network, and after the first layer's output is calculated, the recurrent neural network begins. Each unit will retain some of the data from the preceding step after this layer, enabling it to function as a memory cell during computations.

5.3.3. Applications of Artificial Neural Networks

- **Social Media:** Social media makes extensive use of artificial neural networks. Take Facebook's "People you may know" feature, for instance, which recommends users you might know in real life and allows you to friend them. Artificial Neural Networks, which evaluate your profile, interests, current friends, their friends, and a host of other variables to determine who you might know, are used to create this magical effect. Facial recognition is another popular use of machine learning in social media. Convolutional neural networks are used to match the approximately 100 reference points on the subject's face with those already in the database.
- **Marketing and Sales:** Based on your past browsing activity, e-commerce websites such as Amazon and Flipkart will suggest products for you to purchase when you log in. In a similar vein, let's say you adore pasta. Try Zomato, Swiggy, etc., will suggest restaurants to you based on your order history and personal preferences. This holds true for all new-age marketing categories, such as movie services, book sites, hospitality sites, etc., and personalized marketing is used to achieve it. Artificial Neural Networks are used in this to determine the customer's preferences, dislikes, past purchasing behavior, etc., and subsequently modify the marketing campaigns in line with that.
- **Healthcare:** In Oncology, Artificial Neural Networks are used to train algorithms that can detect malignant tissue at the microscopic level with the same precision as medical professionals with training. Using Face Analysis on patient photos, a number of rare diseases that may show up as physical traits can be recognized in their early stages. Thus, the widespread application of artificial neural

networks in the healthcare sector can only improve the diagnostic skills of medical professionals and, in the end, raise the standard of healthcare globally.

- **Personal assistants:** I'm sure everyone has heard of Cortana, Alexa, Siri, and so forth., and also heard them from the phones you own! These are speech recognition examples of personal assistants that communicate with users through Natural Language Processing and then create a response based on that interaction. Artificial neural networks, which are designed to manage various tasks of these personal assistants, including correct speech, language syntax, semantics, and ongoing conversations, are used in Natural Language Processing.

5.3.4. Perceptron

Consider the diagram shown in Figure 5.8. The table on the left shows a data set containing three Boolean variables (x_1, x_2, x_3) and an output variable, y, that takes on the value −1 if at least two of the three inputs are zero, and +1 if at least two of the inputs are greater than zero.

X_1	X_2	X_3	y
1	0	0	−1
1	0	1	1
1	1	0	1
1	1	1	1
0	0	1	−1
0	1	0	−1
0	1	1	1
0	0	0	−1

(a) Data set.

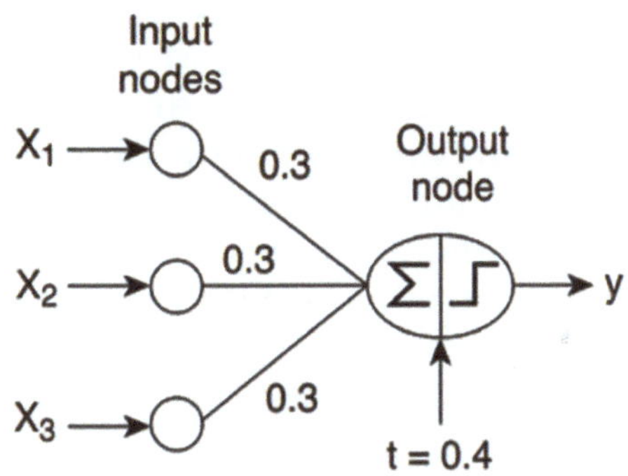

(b) Perceptron.

Figure 5.8. *Modeling a Boolean function using a perceptron.*

Source: http://www.gersteinlab.org/courses/545/07-spr/reading/tan-2005-chpt05.pdf.

A perceptron is a type of simple neural network architecture that is shown in Figure 5.8(b). The input nodes in a perceptron are used to represent the input attributes, while the output nodes in a perceptron are used to represent the model output. Neurons or units are the terms used to refer to the nodes in a neural network architecture. Every input node in a perceptron is linked to the output node by a weighted link. To simulate the strength of a synaptic connection between neurons, a weighted link is employed. Training a perceptron model involves adjusting the link weights until they match the input-output relationships of the underlying data, much like in biological neural systems.

A perceptron computes its output value, $\hat{y}$, by performing a weighted sum on its inputs, subtracting a bias factor t from the sum, and then examining the sign of the result. The model shown in Figure 5.8(b) has three input nodes, each of which has an identical weight of 0.3 to the output node and a bias factor of t = 0.4. The output computed by the model is:

$$\hat{y} = \begin{cases} 1, & \text{if } 0.3x_1 + 0.3x_2 + 0.3x_3 - 0.4 > 0; \\ -1, & \text{if } 0.3x_1 + 0.3x_2 + 0.3x_3 - 0.4 < 0. \end{cases}$$

For example, if $x_1 = 1$, $x_2 = 1$, $x_3 = 0$, then $\hat{y} = +1$ because $0.3x_1 + 0.3x_2 + 0.3x_3 - 0.4$ is positive. On the other hand, if $x_1 = 0$, $x_2 = 1$, $x_3 = 0$, then $\hat{y} = -1$ because the weighted sum subtracted by the bias factor is negative. Note the difference between the input and output nodes of a perceptron. An input node simply transmits the value it receives to the outgoing link without performing any transformation. The output node, on the other hand, is a mathematical device that computes the weighted sum of its inputs, subtracts the bias term, and then produces an output that depends on the sign of the resulting sum. More specifically, the output of a perceptron model can be expressed mathematically as follows:

$$\hat{y} = sign\big(w_d x_d + w_{d-1}x_{d-1} + \ldots + w_2 x_2 + w_1 x_1 - t\big)$$

where $w_1, w_2, \ldots, w_d$ are the weights of the input links and $x_1, x_2, \ldots, x_d$ are the input attribute values. The sign function, which acts as an activation function for the output neuron, outputs a value +1 if its argument is positive and –1 if its argument is negative. The perceptron model can be written in a more compact form as follows:

$$\hat{y} = sign[w_d x_d + w_{d-1}x_{d-1} + \ldots + w_1 x_1 + w_0 x_0] = sign(\mathbf{w} \cdot \mathbf{x}),$$

Where; $w_0 = -t$, $x_0 = 1$, and $w \cdot x$ is the dot product between the weight vector w and the input attribute vector x.

5.3.5. Multilayer Artificial Neural Network

The structure of an artificial neural network is more intricate than that of a perceptron model. There are several ways in which the extra complexities could appear:

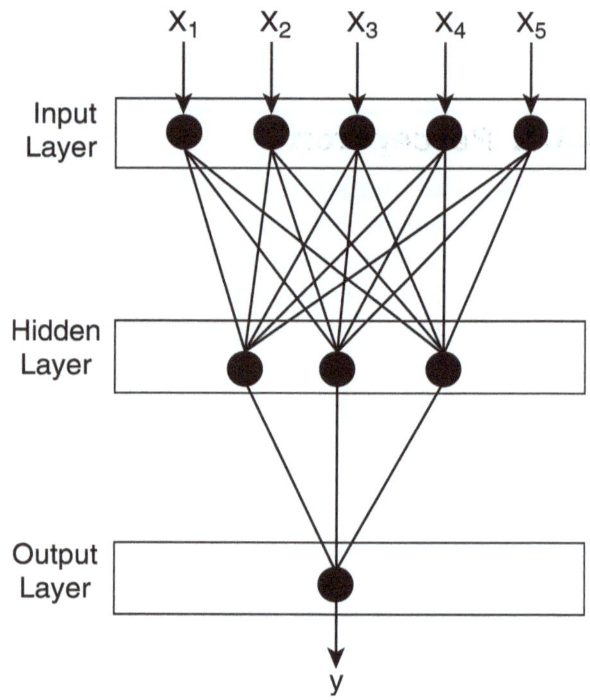

Figure 5.9. *Example of a multilayer feed-forward artificial neural network (ANN).*

Source: http://www.gersteinlab.org/courses/545/07-spr/reading/tan-2005-chpt05.pdf.

- Between its input and output layers, the network may have multiple intermediary layers. The nodes embedded in these intermediary layers are referred to as hidden nodes, and the layers themselves are referred to as hidden layers. A multilayer neural network is the name given to the resulting structure (see Figure 5.9). The nodes in one layer of a feed-forward neural network are only connected to the nodes in the layer below them. Because the perceptron only has one layer of nodes—the output layer—that is responsible for carrying out intricate mathematical operations, it is a single-layer, feed-forward neural network. Links in a recurrent neural network can link nodes from one layer to the layers above it or between nodes within the same layer.

- Other than the sign function, the network may employ other activation function types. As seen in Figure 5.10, additional activation functions include hyperbolic, sigmoid (logistic), and linear tangent functions. The hidden and output nodes can generate nonlinear output values based on their input parameters thanks to these activation functions.

More intricate relationships between the input and output variables can be modeled by multilayer neural networks thanks to these extra complexities. Take into consideration, for instance, the XOR issue from the previous section. Figure 5.11(a) illustrates how two hyperplanes that divide the input space into the appropriate classes can be used to classify the instances. A perceptron can only build one hyperplane, so it is unable to identify the best solution. As seen in Figure 5.11(b), a two-layer feed-forward neural network can be used to solve this issue. The output node merely combines the output of the perceptrons to produce the decision boundary depicted in Figure 5.11(a). It makes intuitive sense to think of each hidden node as a perceptron that attempts to build one of the two hyperplanes.

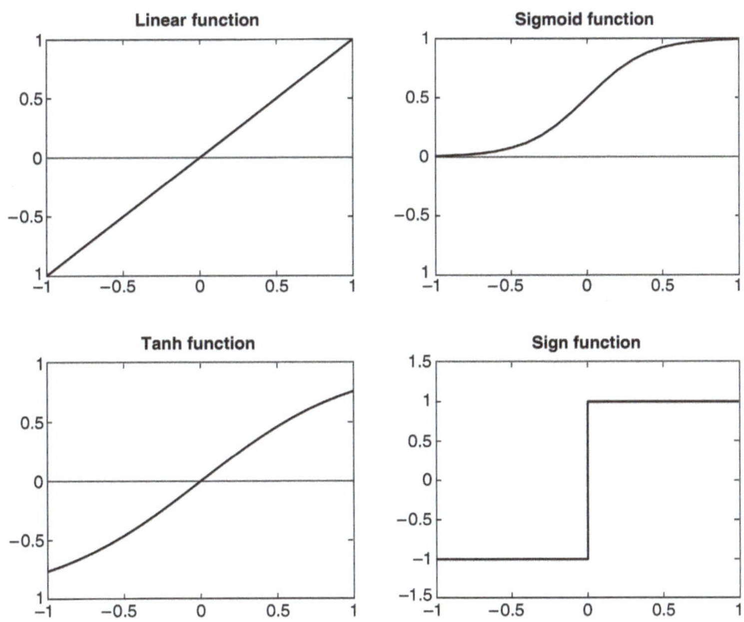

Figure 5.10. *Types of activation functions in artificial neural networks.*

Source: http://www.gersteinlab.org/courses/545/07-spr/reading/tan-2005-chpt05.pdf.

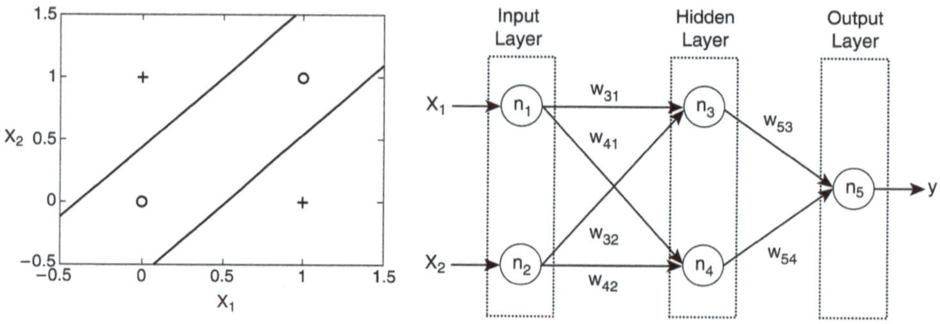

(a) Decision boundary.

(b) Neural network topology.

Figure 5.11. *A two-layer, feed-forward neural network for the XOR problem.*

Source: http://www.gersteinlab.org/courses/545/07-spr/reading/tan-2005-chpt05.pdf.

An effective algorithm that converges to the correct answer given enough training data is required to determine the weights of an ANN model. One method is to use Equation 1's weight update formula and treat each hidden node or output node in the network as a separate perceptron unit. This strategy will obviously fail because we do not know in advance what the true outputs of the hidden nodes are. As a result, figuring out the error term $(y - \hat{y})$, connected to every hidden node is challenging. The next section presents a gradient descent-based neural network weight learning methodology.

$$w_j^{(k+1)} = w_j^{(k)} + \lambda\big(y_i - \hat{y}_i^{(k)}\big)x_{ij}, \tag{1}$$

CASE STUDY

ARTIFICIAL NEURAL NETWORKS FOR CLASSIFYING CAUSE OF DEATH FROM VERBAL AUTOPSY

In many countries routine vital statistics are of poor quality, and often incomplete or unavailable. In countries where vital registration and routine health information systems are weak, the application of verbal autopsy (VA) in demographic surveillance systems or cross-sectional surveys has been suggested for assessing cause-specific burden of mortality. The technique involves taking an interviewer-led account of the symptoms and signs that were present preceding the death of individuals from their caretakers. Traditionally the information obtained from caretakers is analyzed by physicians and a cause(s) of death is reached if a majority of physicians on a panel agreed on a cause(s). The accuracy of physician reviews has been tested in several settings using causes of death assigned from hospital records as the 'gold standard.' Although physician reviews of VA gave robust estimates of cause-specific mortality fractions (CSMF) of several causes of death, the sensitivity, specificity and predictive values varied between causes of death and between populations and had poor repeatability of results.

Arguments to introduce opinion-based and/or data-derived algorithm methods of assigning cause of death from VA data are based on both the quest for accuracy and consistency, as well as the logistical difficulties in getting together a panel of physicians to review what are often large numbers of records. However, physician review performed better than set diagnostic criteria (opinion-based or data-derived) given in an algorithm to assign a cause of adult death. One promising approach to diagnose disease status has been artificial neural networks (ANN) which apply non-linear statistics to pattern recognition. For example, ANN predicted outcomes in cancer patients better than a logistic regression model. Duh *et al.* speculate that ANN will prove useful in epidemiological problems that require pattern recognition and complex classification techniques. In this report, we compare the performance of ANN and logistic regression models and physician review for reaching causes of adult death from VA.

- **An Overview of Neural Networks:** Although often referred to as black boxes, neural networks can in fact easily be understood by those versed in regression analysis techniques. In essence, they are complex non-linear modeling equations. The inputs, outputs and weights in a neural network are analogous to the input variables, outcome variables and coefficients in a regression analysis. The added complexity is largely the result of a layering of 'nodes' which provides a far more detailed map of the decision space. A single node neural network will produce a comparable output to logistic regression, where a function will combine the weights of the inputs to produce the output (Figure 5.12).

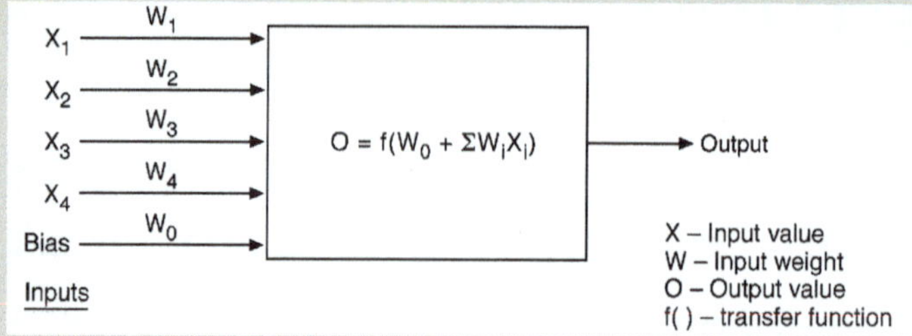

Figure 5.12. *Schematic representation of a single node in a neural network.*

Source: https://academic.oup.com/ije/article/30/3/515/736918.

Combining these nodes into multiple layers adds to the complexity of the model and hence the discriminatory power. In so doing, a number of elements, each receiving all of the inputs and producing an output, have these outputs sent as inputs to a further element(s). The architecture is called a multi-layer perceptron (Figure 5.13.).

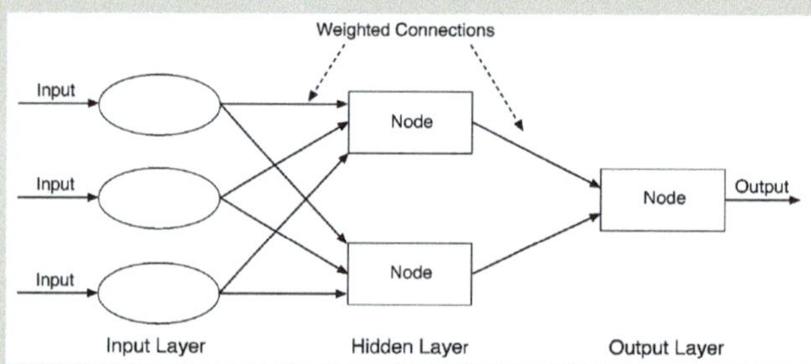

Figure 5.13. *Schematic representation of multi-layer perceptron.*

Source: https://academic.oup.com/ije/article/30/3/515/736918.

The study population and field procedures of the VA data used in this analysis are described elsewhere. In brief, data were collected at three sites (a regional hospital in Ethiopia, and two rural hospitals in Tanzania and Ghana). Adults dying at these hospitals who lived within a 60-km radius of the institution were included in the study. A VA questionnaire was administered by interviewers with at least 12 years of formal education. The reference diagnoses (gold standard) were obtained from a combination of hospital records and death certificates by one of the authors (DC) together with a local physician in each site. A panel of three physicians reviewed the VA data and reached a cause of death if any two agreed on a cause.

The method used to derive algorithms from the data using logistic regression models has been described elsewhere. Each subject was randomly assigned to the *train* dataset (n = 410) or *test* dataset (n = 386), such that the number of deaths due to each cause (gold standard) was the same in both datasets. If a cause of death had odd numbers, the extra subject was included in the train dataset. Symptoms (includes signs) with odds ratio (OR) ≥2 or ≤0.5 in univariate analyzes were included in a logistic model and then those symptoms that were not significant statistically ($P > 0.1$) were dropped from the model in a backward stepwise manner. Coefficients of each symptom remaining in the model were summed to obtain a score for each subject i.e., Score = $b_{1\times1}+b_{2\times2}+\ldots$, where $b_i x_i$ are the log OR b_i of symptoms x_i in the model. A cut-off score was identified for each cause of death (included 16 primary causes of adult death) that gave the estimated number of deaths closest to the true number of cause-specific deaths, such that the sensitivity was at least 50%.

We used the same train and test datasets used by Quigley *et al.* for training and testing an ANN. The data were ported to Microsoft Excel™ and analyzed using NeuroSolutions 3.0™ (Lefebvre WC. NeuroSolution Version 3.020, Neurodimension Inc., 1994.). All models were multi-layer perceptrons with a single hidden layer and trained with static backpropogation. The number of nodes in the hidden layer were varied according to the number of inputs and network performance. A learning rate of 0.7 was used throughout with the momentum learning rule. A sigmoid activation function was used for all processing elements.

Model inputs were based on those used in the logistic regression study, with further variables added to improve discrimination in instances when they improved the model performance. Sensitivity analysis provided the basis for evaluating the role of the inputs in the models.

For each diagnosis, the first 100 records of the training subset were used in the first training run of each model as a cross-validation set to determine the optimal number of hidden nodes and the training point at which the cross-validation mean squared error reached a trough. Thereafter the full training set was used to train the network to this point.

The output weights were then adjusted by a variable factor until the CSMF was as close as possible to 100% of the expected value in testing runs on the training set. At this point the network was tested on the unseen data in the test subset.

Weighted (by number of deaths) averages for sensitivity and specificity were calculated for each method. A summary measure for CSMF was calculated for each method by summing the absolute difference in observed and estimated number of cases for each cause of death, dividing by the total number of deaths, and converting to a percentage.

Results

The CSMF was estimated to within 10% of the true value in 8 out of 16 classes (causes of death) by the ANN. In a further six classes it was estimated to within 25% of the true value. In the remaining two classes the CSMF was extremely low (tetanus and rabies). The summary measure for CSMF favors those methods that are more accurate on the more frequently occurring classes and may mask poor performance on rare causes of death. In this measure however, calculated from the absolute number of over- or under-diagnosed cases, the neural network method performed better than logistic regression models (average error 11.27% versus 31.27%), and compared well with physician review (average error of 12.84%). In the assessment of chance agreement between ANN and gold-standard diagnoses, the kappa value was ≥0.5 for the following classes: rabies (0.86), injuries (0.76), tetanus (0.66), tuberculosis and AIDS (0.55), direct maternal causes (0.52), meningitis (0.50), and diarrhea (0.50).

There was a trade-off between specificity and sensitivity, and in some instances the neural network performed better than other techniques in one at the expense of the other. Compared to logistic regression, the networks performed better in both parameters for tuberculosis and AIDS, meningitis, cardiovascular disorders, diarrhea, and tetanus. They produced a lower sensitivity for malaria (compared with logistic regression), but a higher specificity. The overall and disease-specific sensitivities and specificities compared favorably with logistic regression, but did not match the performance of physician review.

Accuracy of CSMF Estimates:

One of the most significant findings of this analysis is the relative accuracy in assessing the fraction of deaths that are due to specific causes, especially for the more frequently occurring classes. The accuracy in this estimate does not always correlate with the reliability estimated by the kappa statistic. Care was taken to find a weighting for the output that would lead to a correct CSMF in the training set. The choice of this weight is analogous to selecting the minimum total score at which a case is defined in the logistic regression models. This then led to surprisingly good estimates in the testing set. It is a feature of the train and test subsets however that the number of members in each class is similar. Manipulating either subset so that the CSMF differed, by randomly removing or adding records of the class in question, did not alter the accuracy of the CSMF estimates if the number of training examples for the class was not decreased in the training subset. With less frequently occurring classes such as pneumonia, decreasing the number of training examples in the training set, reduced the accuracy of the CSMF estimate. This is essentially an issue of generalization, and it is to be expected that networks that are trained with fewer examples are less likely to be generalizable. It is suggested that it is for this reason that the CSMF estimates for the five most frequently occurring classes are all within 10% of the expected values. It would be expected furthermore that if the datasets were larger, that the generalizability of the CSMF estimates for the less frequently occurring classes would improve.

At the stage of data analysis the question can be asked as to whether or not there is an output level above which class membership is reasonably certain, and below which misclassification is more likely to occur. Looking at the tuberculosis-AIDS model (n = 71), as well as the meningitis model (n = 32), and ranking the top 20 test outputs in descending order by value (reflecting the certainty of the classification), 13/20 of these outputs correctly predict the class membership in both instances. The sensitivities for the models overall were 66% and 56% respectively. The implication is that without a gold standard result for comparison, it would be difficult to delineate the true positives from the false positives even in the least equivocal outputs. This is in keeping with observations that different data-derived methods arrive at their estimates differently. One study to predict an acute abdomen diagnosis from surgical admission records demonstrated that data-derived methods with similar overall performance correlated poorly as to which of the records they were correctly predicting.

Mechanisms of Improved Performance:

A single layer neural network (i.e., a network with only inputs, and one processing element) is isomorphic with logistic regression. A network with no hidden nodes produced almost identical results when comparing the input weights to the log(OR) for the four inputs used in the regression model to predict malaria as the cause of death. In those instances where the performance of logistic regression and neural network models differ, it is of interest as to know the mechanisms by which improvements are made. The results from this study indicate that the differences in performance of the neural networks are achieved both by improved fitting of those variables already known to be significantly predictive of class membership, through the modeling of interaction between them, and by additional discriminating power conferred by variables that are not significantly predictive on their own.

The first mechanism was borne out in one of the meningitis models in which the exact same inputs used in the logistic regression model were used in the neural network model with an improvement in performance. Exploring the sensitivity analysis for cardiovascular deaths, the network outputs are surprisingly sensitive to the absence of a tuberculosis history, which was not strongly predictive by itself. Age above 45 years old was the seventh most predictive input in the regression model, whereas it was the input to which the neural network model was second most sensitive. In the case of meningitis, presence of continuous fever was more important in the regression model, whilst presence or absence of recent surgery and abdominal distension were more significant in the ANN model. The network has mapped relationships between the inputs that were not predicted by the regression model.

Effect of Size of Dataset

Both data-derived methods stand to benefit from more training examples. In the regression models, some inputs not currently utilized may yield significant associations with outputs when larger datasets are used. With enough nodes and training time, it was possible in the course of this analysis to train a neural network to completely map the training set with 100% sensitivity and specificity. However, this level of sensitivity and specificity was not reproduced when these models were tested in the test dataset. What it did demonstrate is the ability of the method to map complex functions. The key point is one of generalizability. In the models presented above, training was stopped and the nodes limited to ensure that the generalizability was not compromised. With more training examples, it is likely that the networks would develop a better understanding of the relationships between inputs and outputs before over-training occurs. Arguably, the neural network models would stand to improve performance more than the regression models should larger training sets be available. However, further training may not achieve algorithms of sufficiently high sensitivity and specificity to obviate the need for algorithms with particular operating characteristics suitable for use in specific environments.

Physician Review

Only 78% of the reference diagnoses were confirmed by laboratory tests. Since 22% of the reference diagnoses were based on hospital physicians' clinical judgment, it is not surprising that physician review of VA performed better than the other methods. Nevertheless, physician review remains the optimal method of analysis, as far as overall performance is concerned, for gathering cause-specific mortality data as good as the data produced by routine health information systems. The technique by which physicians in this study came to their classification differed considerably, as they made extensive use of the open section of the questionnaire from which information was not coded for analysis by the other techniques. Interestingly though, other methods are able to come close if the CSMF is used as the outcome of choice, as indeed it often is. Thus ANN or logistic regression models based algorithms have the potential for substituting physician review of VA.

Limitations of the Technique

At various points we have alluded to some of the difficulties and limitations of using neural networks for the analysis.

Even with sensitivity analysis, we had no way of working out which were going to be the most important inputs prior to creating a model and conducting a sensitivity analysis on it. There is some correlation with linearly predictive inputs that helps in the initial stages.

Determining the weighting for the output for providing the optimum estimate of the CSMF was time-consuming. The software provides an option for prioritizing sensitivity over specificity, but no way of balancing the number of false positives and false negatives that would give an accurate CSMF estimate.

Designing the optimal network topology requires building numerous networks in search of the one with the lowest least mean squared error. The number of hidden nodes, inputs and training time all affect the performance of the network. Whilst training is relatively quick compared to the many hours it took to train ANN in the early days of their development, it is still time-consuming to build and train multiple networks for each model.

Cross-validation to prevent over-training required compromising the number of training examples to allow for a cross-validation dataset.

Sensitivity and specificity of the ANN algorithms were not high enough to be generalizable to a variety of settings. Furthermore, the accuracy of individual and summary estimates of CSMF obtained in this study could be due to the similarity in the CSMF between the training and test datasets. Thus large datasets from a variety of settings are needed to identify optimal algorithms for each site with different distributions of causes of death.

CLASS ACTIVITY

UNDERSTANDING AND IMPLEMENTING ARTIFICIAL NEURAL NETWORKS

To introduce students to the basic concepts of artificial neural networks, their structure, and how they are used in machine learning. By the end of this activity, students should be able to build a simple neural network model using a machine learning library.

Materials Needed:

- Computers with internet access
- Python installed (Anaconda distribution recommended)
- Jupyter Notebooks or any Python IDE
- Access to Google Colab (optional)
- Data set for training the neural network (e.g., MNIST dataset for handwritten digit recognition)

SUMMARY

- Data mining is a powerful process that involves extracting valuable information from large datasets. Beyond traditional methods, several alternative techniques have emerged, each offering unique advantages and applications.
- Anomaly detection is another crucial data mining technique, which involves identifying rare items, events, or observations that differ significantly from the majority of the data.
- Cluster analysis groups a set of objects in such a way that objects in the same group (or cluster) are more similar to each other than to those in other groups. This technique is particularly useful in market segmentation, image analysis, and customer classification.
- A rule-based classifier is a data mining technique that classifies data based on a set of if-then rules derived from the dataset. These rules are typically easy to interpret and understand, making them a popular choice for many applications where transparency and interpretability are crucial.
- The process of creating a rule-based classifier generally involves two main steps: rule generation and rule pruning. Rule generation is the process of extracting potential rules from the data.
- Sequential Covering Algorithm can be used to extract IF-THEN rules form the training data. We do not require to generate a decision tree first. In this algorithm, each rule for a given class covers many of the tuples of that class.
- The 1R Algorithm is also known as the Learn One Rule Algorithm. It is based on a simple classification rule. Thus it is one of the simplest algorithms. In this algorithm, we make rules to test each attribute. If the attribute has a range of values, we make rules by counting how often each class value appears.
- The sequential covering algorithm is the most widely used algorithm in rule-based classification in data mining. This algorithm defines rules to cover the maximum data records of one class and no data records of other classes.

REVIEW QUESTION

1. How is the algorithm for generating the model incrementally implemented?
2. What are the properties of rule-based classifiers?
3. How does rule induction work using the sequential covering algorithm?
4. What are the characteristics of nearest-neighbor classifiers?
5. How do artificial neurons differ from biological neurons?
6. What are the applications of artificial neural networks?

REFERENCES

1. Ankerst, M., Kastenmuller, G., Kriegel, H.-P., & Seidl, T. (1999). Nearest neighbor classification in 3D protein databases. In *Proceedings of the 7th International Conference on Intelligent Systems for Molecular Biology* (pp. 34–43).
2. Bear, M. F., Connors, B. W., & Pradiso, M. A. (2001). *Neuroscience: Exploring the Brain* (2nd ed.). Williams and Wilkins.
3. Behera, D. K., & Patra, P. K. (2014). Clustering based on fuzzy rule-based classifier. In *Computational Intelligence in Data Mining–Volume 1* (pp. 233–242). Springer India. http://dx.doi.org/10.1007/978-81-322-2205-7_22.
4. Bounhas, M., Prade, H., Serrurier, M., & Mellouli, K. (2012). A possibilistic rule-based classifier. In *Communications in Computer and Information Science* (pp. 21–31). Springer Berlin Heidelberg. http://dx.doi.org/10.1007/978-3-642-31709-5_3.
5. Chen, J., Zheng, H., Li, P., Zhang, Z., Li, H., & Liu, W. (2020). Fuzzy association rule mining algorithm based on load classifier. In *Communications in Computer and Information Science* (pp. 178–191). Springer Singapore. http://dx.doi.org/10.1007/978-981-15-2810-1_18.
6. Djouadi, A., & Bouktache, E. (1997). A fast algorithm for the nearest-neighbor classifier. *IEEE Transactions on Pattern Analysis and Machine Intelligence, 19*(3), 277–282.
7. Duda, R. O., Hart, P. E., & Stork, D. G. (2001). *Pattern Classification* (2nd ed.). Wiley.
8. Efros, A. A., Berg, A. C., Mori, G., & Malik, J. (2003). Recognizing action at a distance. In *Proceedings of the 9th IEEE Conference on Computer Vision* (pp. 726–733).
9. Fausett, L. V. (1993). *Fundamentals of Neural Networks: Architectures, Algorithms and Applications*. Prentice-Hall.
10. Ghosh, A. K., Chaudhuri, P., & Murthy, C. A. (2005). On visualization and aggregation of nearest neighbor classifiers. *IEEE Transactions on Pattern Analysis and Machine Intelligence, 27*(10), 1592–1602.
11. Han, J., & Kamber, M. (2006). *Data Mining: Concepts and Techniques* (2nd ed.). Elsevier.
12. Hastie, T., Tibshirani, R., & Friedman, J. (2001). *The Elements of Statistical Learning: Data Mining, Inference, and Prediction*. Springer.
13. Kriegel, H.-P., Pryakhin, A., & Schubert, M. (2005). Multi-represented kNN-classification for large class sets. In *Proceedings of the 10th International Conference on Database Systems for Advanced Applications* (pp. 511–522).
14. Li, Y., Yang, J., & Han, J. (2004). Continuous K-nearest neighbor search for moving objects. In *Proceedings of the 16th International Conference on Scientific and Statistical Database Management* (pp. 123–126).
15. Liu, B., Ma, Y., & Wong, C. K. (2000). Improving an association. In *Principles of Data Mining and Knowledge Discovery* (pp. 504–509). Springer Berlin Heidelberg. http://dx.doi.org/10.1007/3-540-45372-5_58.

16. Negnevitsky, M. (2002). *Artificial Intelligence: A Guide to Intelligent Systems*. Addison-Wesley/Pearson Education.

17. Rosenblatt, F. (1958). The perceptron: A probabilistic model for information storage and organization in the brain. *Psychological Review, 65*, 386–408.

18. Shah, D. J., & Agarwal, N. (2020). Multiclass weighted associative classifier with application-based rule selection for data gathered using wireless sensor networks. In *Evolutionary Computing and Mobile Sustainable Networks* (pp. 737–745). Springer Singapore. http://dx.doi.org/10.1007/978-981-15-5258-8_68.

19. Shibata, T., Kato, T., & Wada, T. K. (2003). K-D decision tree: An accelerated and memory efficient nearest neighbor classifier. In *Proceedings of the 2003 IEEE International Conference on Data Mining* (pp. 641–644).

20. Shimada, K., Arahira, T., & Hanioka, T. (2017). Association rule-based classifier using artificial missing values. In *Advances in Data Mining. Applications and Theoretical Aspects* (pp. 57–67). Springer International Publishing. http://dx.doi.org/10.1007/978-3-319-62701-4_5.

21. Sta⊠czyk, U. (2017). Ranking-based rule classifier optimization. In *Advances in Feature Selection for Data and Pattern Recognition* (pp. 113–131). Springer International Publishing. http://dx.doi.org/10.1007/978-3-319-67588-6_7.

22. Veenman, C. J., & Reinders, M. J. T. (2005). The nearest subclass classifier: A compromise between the nearest mean and nearest neighbor classifier. *IEEE Transactions on Pattern Analysis and Machine Intelligence, 27*(9), 1417–1429.

CHAPTER 6

Association Analysis: Basic Concepts and Algorithms

LEARNING OBJECTIVES

After studying this chapter, you will be able to:

- Discuss the basic concepts and algorithms
- Explain the frequent itemset generation
- Focus on rule generation
- Describe the association analysis – function, algorithms and application

KEY TERMS FROM THIS CHAPTER

Algorithm
Customer behavior
Lexicographic
Single transaction
Apriori algorithm
Enterprises
Medical diagnosis
Web mining

INTRODUCTION

One data mining technique that can be used to find interesting relationships between variables in large datasets is association analysis. Finding associations or patterns between objects, occurrences, or variables is its main goal, especially in transactional databases like retail sales where customers purchase multiple items in a single transaction. The foundational ideas and algorithms of association analysis are confidence, support, and the Apriori algorithm.

The frequency with which a specific group of items appears together in the dataset is called support. It is computed as the percentage of dataset transactions that contain the set of items. A high support value implies a strong correlation between the items and suggests that the itemset occurs frequently. The frequency with which items in a given set occur together in transactions containing a particular item is measured by confidence. It is computed as the ratio of transactions with the particular item to transactions with all the items in the set. One can measure the degree of association between items with the help of confidence. When one item is present in the transaction, it is likely that another item is there as well, according to a high confidence value.

One of the most popular algorithms for association analysis is the Apriori algorithm. It generates candidate itemsets iteratively and filters out those that don't meet minimum support thresholds in order to find frequently occurring itemsets using a breadth-first search strategy. The algorithm begins by determining the frequency of each individual item, and iteratively expands to larger itemsets until no more extensions are feasible. By taking advantage of the Apriori property, which stipulates that any subset of a frequent itemset must likewise be frequent, this method aids in narrowing the search space.

Creating frequent itemsets and creating association rules are the two main stages of the Apriori algorithm. By gradually creating larger itemsets based on the frequently found ones from the previous iteration, the algorithm finds all frequent itemsets in the first phase. Until no more frequent itemsets can be found, the process is repeated. Using predetermined support and confidence thresholds, the frequent itemsets are used to generate association rules in the second phase. These guidelines give businesses information about the connections between products, enabling them to plan targeted marketing campaigns, cross-sell products, and arrange products in the best possible ways.

Numerous fields, such as market basket analysis, customer relationship management, web usage mining, and bioinformatics, use association analysis. It aids companies in better understanding consumer behavior, enhancing decision-making procedures, and developing sales strategies. But there are other difficulties with association analysis as well, like managing big datasets, mining intricate relationships, and scalability. Novel algorithms and methodologies, such as distributed and parallel computing, are under development to tackle these obstacles and facilitate scalable and effective association analysis in practical situations.

6.1. BASIC CONCEPTS AND ALGORITHMS

Large amounts of data are gathered by many businesses from their daily operations. For instance, enormous volumes of consumer purchase information are gathered every day at grocery store checkout counters. An example of this type of data, also referred to as market basket transactions, is shown in Table 6.1. Every row in this table represents a transaction, which includes a set of goods purchased by a specific customer and a unique identification labeled TID. Retailers are curious to know more about their customers' purchasing habits through data analysis. Numerous business-related applications, including marketing campaigns, inventory control, and customer relationship management, can be supported by such important data.

Table 6.1. An Example of Market Basket Transactions

TID	Items
1	{Bread, Milk}
2	{Bread, Diapers, Beer, Eggs}
3	{Milk, Diapers, Beer, Cola}
4	{Bread, Milk, Diapers, Beer}
5	{Bread, Milk, Diapers, Cola}

Which is helpful in identifying intriguing connections that are concealed in big data sets. The relationships that have been discovered can be shown as sets of frequently occurring objects or association rules. For instance, the data set displayed in Table 6.1 can be used to extract the following rule:

$$\{\text{Diapers}\} \longrightarrow \{\text{Beer}\}.$$

Because many customers who purchase diapers also purchase beer, the rule implies a strong correlation between the sales of diapers and beer. Retailers can find new opportunities to cross-sell their products to customers by using these kinds of rules.

Association analysis is useful not only for market basket data but also for other application domains like scientific data analysis, Web mining, medical diagnosis, and bioinformatics. For instance, the association patterns in the analysis of Earth science data may highlight intriguing relationships between processes occurring on land, in the ocean, and in the atmosphere. Earth scientists may be able to better understand how the various components of the Earth system interact with one another with the aid of such information. For illustrative purposes, we will primarily discuss market basket data, but the techniques discussed here can be applied to a wider range of data sets.

The application of association analysis to market basket data raises two important issues that must be resolved. First, it can be computationally costly to extract patterns from a big transaction data set.

6.1.1. Problem Definition

The basic terminology used in association analysis and presents a formal description of the task.

6.1.1.1. Binary Representation

As demonstrated in Table 6.2, market basket data can be expressed in a binary format where each row denotes a transaction and each column denotes an item. When an item is included in a transaction, its value is one; otherwise, it is zero. This can be thought of as a binary variable. An item is an asymmetric binary variable since its presence in a transaction is frequently regarded as more significant than its absence.

Table 6.2. A Binary 0/1 Representation of Market Basket Data

TID	Bread	Milk	Diapers	Beer	Eggs	Cola
1	1	1	0	0	0	0
2	1	0	1	1	1	0
3	0	1	1	1	0	1
4	1	1	1	1	0	0
5	1	1	1	0	0	1

This representation is perhaps a very simplistic view of real market basket data because it ignores certain important aspects of the data such as the quantity of items sold or the price paid to purchase them.

6.1.1.2. Itemset and Support Count

Let $I = \{i_1, i_2, \ldots, i_d\}$ be the set of all items in a market basket data and $T = \{t_1, t_2, \ldots, t_N\}$ be the set of all transactions. In association analysis, a transaction ti includes a selection of items from set I. An itemset is a collection of zero or more items. If an itemset consists of k items, it is referred to as a k-itemset. For example, {Beer, Diapers, Milk} represents a 3-itemset. The empty set is an itemset that has no items.

The number of items in a transaction is known as the transaction width. If X is a subset of tj, then a transaction tj is said to contain an itemset X. For instance, the itemset {Bread, Diapers} is present in the second transaction displayed in Table 6.2, but not {Bread, Milk}. The number of transactions that contain a specific itemset, or its "support count," is a crucial aspect of an itemset.

Mathematically, the support count, $\sigma(X)$, for an itemset X can be stated as follows:

$$\sigma(X) = \left|\{t_i | X \subseteq t_i,\ t_i \in T\}\right|,$$

Where the number of elements in a set is indicated by the symbol $|\cdot|$. Because there are only two transactions that contain all three items, the support count for {Beer, Diapers, Milk} in the data set displayed in Table 6.2 is equal to two.

6.1.1.3. Association Rule

When X and Y are disjoint itemsets, i.e., an implication expression of the form $X \rightarrow Y$ is used as an association rule, i.e., $X \cap Y = \emptyset$. An association rule's confidence and support can be used to gauge how strong it is. Whereas confidence measures the frequency with which items in Y occur in transactions that contain X, support measures the frequency with which a rule is applicable to a specific data set.

The formal definitions of these metrics are

$$\text{Support, } s(X \longrightarrow Y) = \frac{\sigma(X \cup Y)}{N}; \quad (1)$$

$$\text{Confidence, } c(X \longrightarrow Y) = \frac{\sigma(X \cup Y)}{\sigma(X)}. \quad (2)$$

Example 6.1. Consider the rule {Milk, Diapers} → {Beer}. Since the support count for {Milk, Diapers, Beer} is 2 and the total number of transactions is 5, the rule's support is 2/5=0.4. The rule's confidence is obtained by dividing the support count for {Milk, Diapers, Beer} by the support count for {Milk, Diapers}. Since there are 3 transactions that contain milk and diapers, the confidence for this rule is 2/3=0.67.

- **Why Use Support and Confidence?**

Support is a crucial metric because a rule with very little support could exist by accident. From a business standpoint, a low support rule is also probably uninteresting because it might not be profitable to promote products that customers seldom purchase together. Support is frequently used to get rid of boring rules because of these reasons. Additionally, support has a desirable property that can be used to efficiently find association rules.

Conversely, confidence quantifies how trustworthy an inference drawn by a rule is. The greater the confidence level for a particular rule X → Y, the greater the probability that Y will be found in transactions that involve X. An estimate of the conditional probability of Y given X is also provided by confidence. Results of association analyzes should be interpreted cautiously. An association rule's conclusion does not always imply causation. Rather, it implies a robust co-occurrence connection between the elements in the rule's antecedent and consequent. Contrarily, causality usually refers to relationships that develop over time and necessitates knowledge of the causal and effect characteristics in the data (e.g., the loss of ozone causes global warming).

6.1.1.4. Formulation of Association Rule Mining Problem

The association rule mining problem can be formally stated as follows:

- **Definition 6.1 (Association Rule Discovery).** Given a set of transactions T, find all the rules having support ≥ minsup and confidence ≥ minconf, where minsup and minconf are the corresponding support and confidence thresholds.

Calculating the support and confidence for each potential rule is a brute-force method for mining association rules. Because there are an infinite number of rules that can be extracted from a data set, this method is unaffordable. To be more precise, the total number of rules that can be extracted from a data set with d items is.

$$R = 3^d - 2^{d+1} + 1. \quad (3)$$

The proof for this equation is left as an exercise to the readers. Even for the small data set shown in Table 6.1, this approach requires us to compute the support and confidence for $3^6 - 2^7 + 1 = 602$ rules. More than 80% of the rules are discarded after applying minsup = 20% and minconf = 50%, thus making most of the computations become wasted. To avoid performing needless computations, it would be useful to prune the rules early without having to compute their support and confidence values.

To start enhancing the efficiency of association rule mining algorithms, the support and confidence requirements should be separated. It is evident from Equation 6.2 that the endorsement of a rule X → Y is contingent solely upon the endorsement of its corresponding itemset, X ∪ Y. For instance, because they deal with items from the same itemset, {Beer, Diapers, Milk}, the following rules have the same support:

$$
\begin{array}{ll}
\{\texttt{Beer, Diapers}\} \longrightarrow \{\texttt{Milk}\}, & \{\texttt{Beer, Milk}\} \longrightarrow \{\texttt{Diapers}\},\\
\{\texttt{Diapers, Milk}\} \longrightarrow \{\texttt{Beer}\}, & \{\texttt{Beer}\} \longrightarrow \{\texttt{Diapers, Milk}\},\\
\{\texttt{Milk}\} \longrightarrow \{\texttt{Beer,Diapers}\}, & \{\texttt{Diapers}\} \longrightarrow \{\texttt{Beer,Milk}\}.
\end{array}
$$

If the itemset is infrequent, then all six candidate rules can be pruned immediately without our having to compute their confidence values. Therefore, a common strategy adopted by many association rule mining algorithms is to decompose the problem into two major subtasks:

- Frequent Itemset Generation, whose objective is to find all the itemsets that satisfy the minsup threshold. These itemsets are called frequent itemsets.
- Rule Generation, whose objective is to extract all the high-confidence rules from the frequent itemsets found in the previous step. These rules are called strong rules.

Generally speaking, frequent itemset generation requires more computational resources than rule generation. Effective methods for producing association rules and frequent itemsets, respectively.

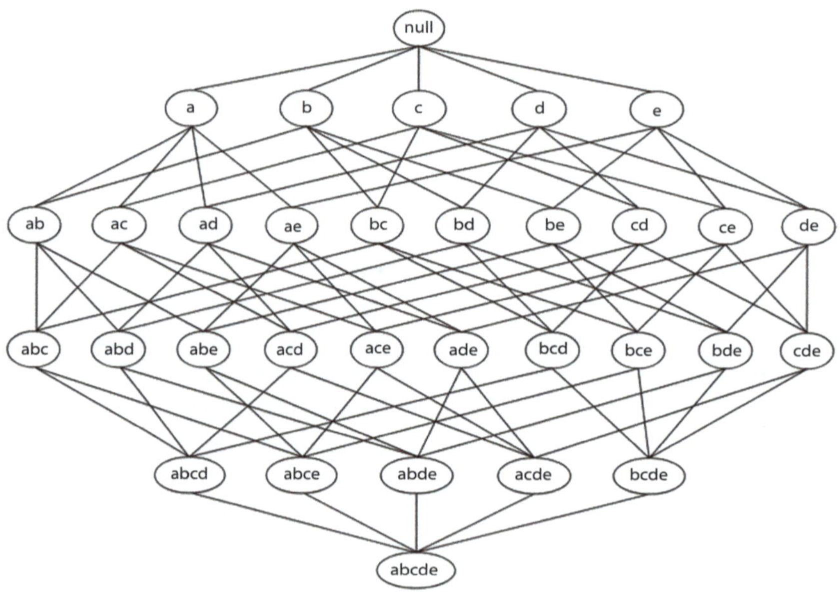

Figure 6.1. *An itemset lattice.*

Source: https://www.cs.helsinki.fi/group/bioinfo/teaching/dami_s10/dami_lecture4.pdf.

6.2. FREQUENT ITEMSET GENERATION

To list every possible itemset, a lattice structure can be utilized. An itemset lattice for I = {a, b, c, d, e} is displayed in Figure 6.1. With the exception of the null set, a data set with k items can generally produce up to $2^k - 1$ frequent itemsets. The search space of itemsets to be explored is exponentially large because in many practical applications k can be very large.

Finding the support count for each candidate itemset in the lattice structure is a brute-force method for locating frequently occurring itemsets. In order to accomplish this, we must compare each candidate with each transaction—an operation that Figure 6.2 illustrates. The candidate's support count will increase if it is a part of a transaction. For instance, because the itemset is present in transactions 1, 4, and 5, the support for {Bread, Milk} is increased three times. Because it necessitates O(NMw) comparisons—where N is the number of transactions, $M = 2^k - 1$ is the number of candidate itemsets, and w is the maximum transaction width—such an approach may be highly costly.

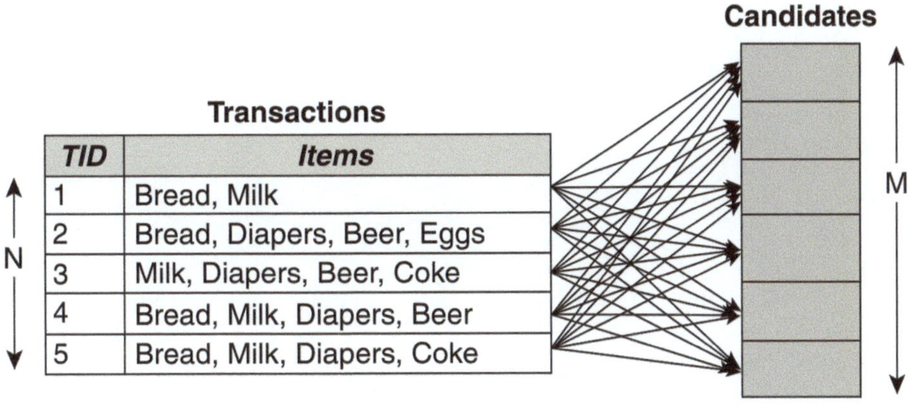

Figure 6.2. *Counting the support of candidate itemsets.*

Source: https://www.researchgate.net/profile/Darshan-Tank/publication/276231946/figure/fig1/AS:406644845498371@1473963094731/Counting-the-support-of-candidate-itemsets.png.

There are several ways to reduce the computational complexity of frequent itemset generation.

- Reduce the number of candidate itemsets (M). The Apriori principle, is an effective way to eliminate some of the candidate itemsets without counting their support values.
- Reduce the number of comparisons. Instead of matching each candidate itemset against every transaction, we can reduce the number of comparisons by using more advanced data structures, either to store the candidate itemsets or to compress the data set.

6.2.1. The Apriori Principle

During frequent itemset generation, the number of candidate itemsets explored is decreased with the aid of the support measure. The following idea directs the use of support for candidate itemset pruning.

- **Theorem 6.1 (Apriori Principle).** Every subset of a frequent itemset must likewise be frequent. The itemset lattice depicted in Figure 6.3 serves as an example of the concept underlying the Apriori principle. Assume the itemset {c, d, e} is a frequent one. It is obvious that any transaction containing {c, d, e} must also contain {c, d}, {c, e}, {d, e}, {c}, {d}, and {e}, as well as its subsets. Consequently, in the event that {c, d, e} is frequent, all subsets of {c, d, e} (i.e., the item sets that are shaded in this figure) need to be common as well.

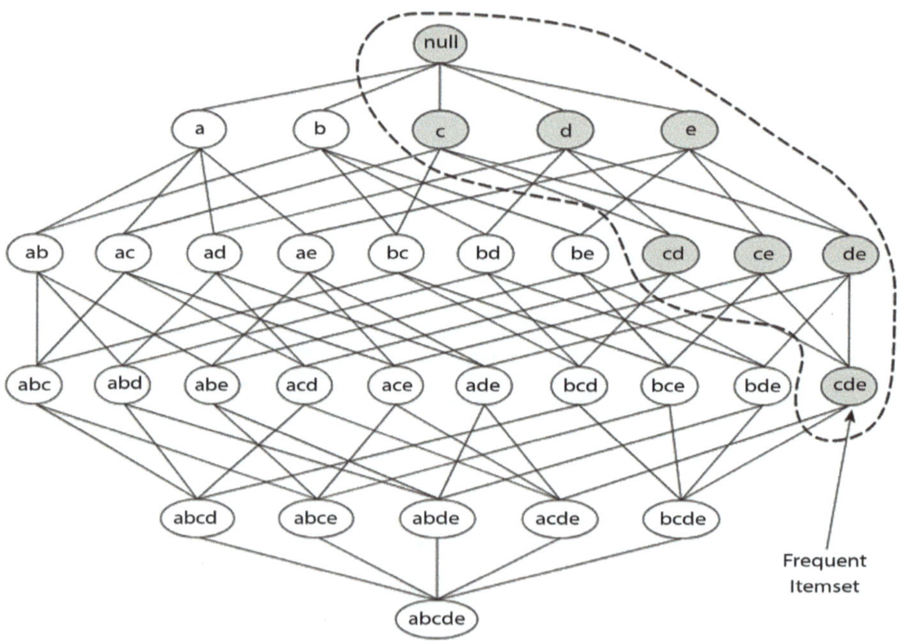

Figure 6.3. *An illustration of the Apriori principle. If {c, d, e} is frequent, then all subsets of this itemset are frequent.*

Source: https://www.researchgate.net/profile/Darshan-Tank/publication/276231946/figure/fig2/AS:406644845498372@1473963094797/An-illustration-of-the-Apriori-principle.png.

On the other hand, all of an itemset's supersets must also be infrequent if the itemset {a, b} is infrequent. Once {a, b} is found to be infrequent, the entire subgraph containing the supersets of {a, b} can be pruned immediately, as Figure 6.4 illustrates. Support-based pruning is the process of reducing the exponential search space according to the support measure. A crucial characteristic of the support measure is that the support for an itemset never surpasses the support for its subsets, which allows for such a pruning strategy. The anti-monotone property of the support measure is another name for this characteristic.

- **Definition 6.2 (Monotonicity Property).** Let I be a set of items, and $J = 2^I$ be the power set of I. A measure f is monotone (or upward closed) if

  $\forall X, Y \in J: (X \subseteq Y) \rightarrow f(X) \leq f(Y);$

  Which means that if X is a subset of Y, then f(X) must not exceed f(Y). On the other hand, f is anti-monotone (or downward closed) if;

  $\forall X, Y \in J: (X \subseteq Y) \longrightarrow f(Y) \leq f(X);$

  Which means that if X is a subset of Y, then f(Y) must not exceed f(X).

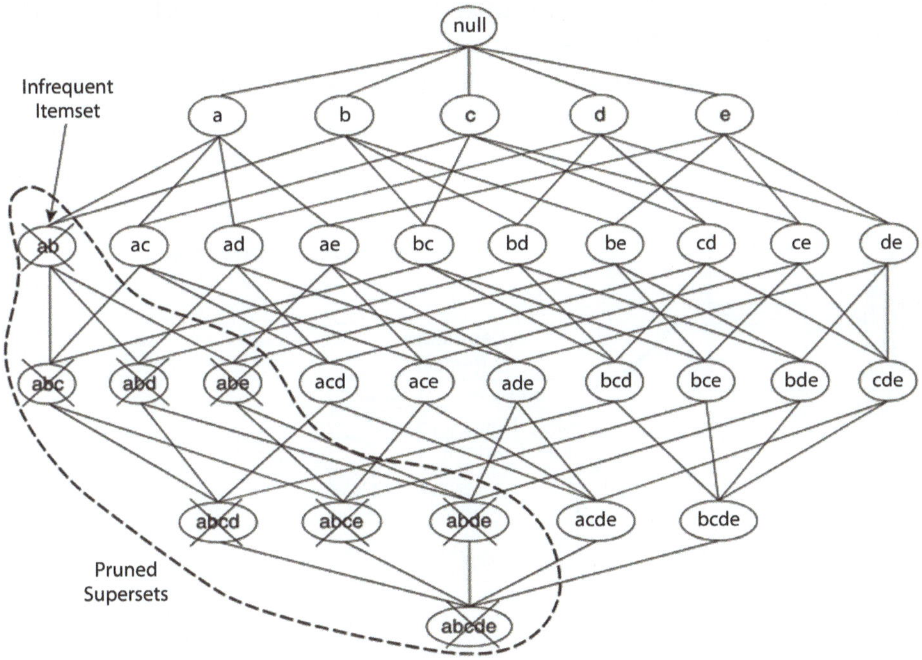

Figure 6.4. *An illustration of support-based pruning. If {a, b} is infrequent, then all supersets of {a, b} are infrequent.*

Source: https://i0.wp.com/studynotesnepal.com/wp-content/uploads/2022/05/support-based-pruning.png?resize=640%2C461&ssl=1.

To efficiently prune the exponential search space of candidate itemsets, the mining algorithm can incorporate any measure with an anti-monotone property directly.

6.2.2. Frequent Itemset Generation in the Apriori Algorithm

The first association rule mining algorithm, Apriori, invented support-based pruning, which is a methodical way to manage the exponential expansion of candidate itemsets. For the transactions listed in Table 6.1, Figure 6.5 offers a high-level representation of the Apriori algorithm's frequent itemset generation phase. We take it for granted that the support threshold is 60%, corresponding to a minimum support count of three.

Initially, every item is considered as a candidate 1-itemset. After counting their supports, the candidate itemsets {Cola} and {Eggs} are discarded because they appear in fewer than three transactions. In the next iteration, candidate 2-itemsets are generated using only the frequent 1-itemsets because the Apriori principle ensures that all supersets of the infrequent 1-itemsets must be infrequent. Because there are only four frequent 1-itemsets, the number of candidate 2-itemsets generated by the algorithm is $\binom{4}{2} = 6$. Two of these six candidates, {Beer, Bread} and {Beer, Milk}, are subsequently found to be infrequent after computing their support values. The remaining four candidates are frequent, and thus will be used to generate candidate 3-itemsets. Without support-based pruning, there are $\binom{6}{3} = 20$ candidate 3-itemsets that can be formed using the six items given in this example. With the Apriori principle, we only need to keep candidate 3-itemsets whose subsets are frequent. The only candidate that has this property is {Bread, Diapers, Milk}.

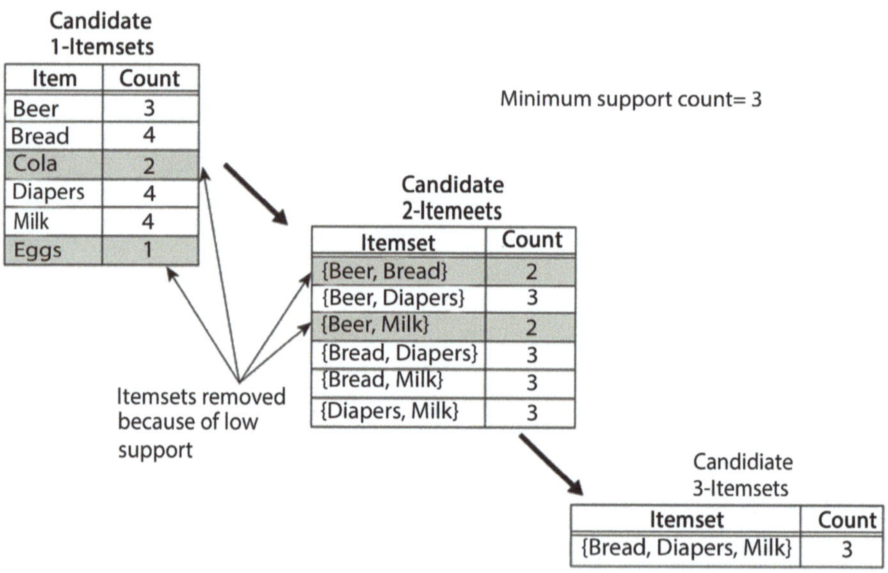

Figure 6.5. *Illustration of frequent itemset generation using the Apriori algorithm.*

Source: https://www.researchgate.net/profile/Darshan-Tank/publication/276231946/figure/fig4/AS:668703708438528@1536442796001/Illustration-of-frequent-itemset-generation-using-the-Apriori-algorithm.jpg.

The effectiveness of the Apriori pruning strategy can be shown by counting the number of candidate itemsets generated.

A brute-force strategy of enumerating all itemsets (up to size 3) as candidates will produce;

$$\binom{6}{1} + \binom{6}{2} + \binom{6}{3} = 6 + 15 + 20 = 41$$

candidates. With the Apriori principle, this number decreases to;

$$\binom{6}{1} + \binom{4}{2} + 1 = 6 + 6 + 1 = 13$$

candidates, which represents a 68% reduction in the number of candidate itemsets even in this simple example.

The pseudocode for the frequent itemset generation part of the Apriori algorithm is shown in Algorithm 6.1. Let C_k denote the set of candidate k-itemsets and F_k denote the set of frequent k-itemsets:

- The algorithm initially makes a single pass over the data set to determine the support of each item. Upon completion of this step, the set of all frequent 1-itemsets, F_1, will be known (steps 1 and 2).
- Next, the algorithm will iteratively generate new candidate k-itemsets using the frequent (k – 1)-itemsets found in the previous iteration (step 5). Candidate generation is implemented using a function called apriorigen.
- To count the support of the candidates, the algorithm needs to make an additional pass over the data set (steps 6–10). The subset function is used to determine all the candidate itemsets in C_k that are contained in each transaction t.
- After counting their supports, the algorithm eliminates all candidate itemsets whose support counts are less than minsup (step 12).
- The algorithm terminates when there are no new frequent itemsets generated, i.e., $F_k = \emptyset$ (step 13).

Algorithm 6.1 Frequent itemset generation of the *Apriori* algorithm.

1: $k = 1$.
2: $F_k = \{ i \mid i \in I \wedge \sigma(\{i\}) \geq N \times minsup\}$. {Find all frequent 1-itemsets}
3: **repeat**
4: $k = k + 1$.
5: $C_k =$ apriori-gen(F_{k-1}). {Generate candidate itemsets}
6: **for** each transaction $t \in T$ **do**
7: $C_t =$ subset(C_k, t). {Identify all candidates that belong to t}
8: **for** each candidate itemset $c \in C_t$ **do**
9: $\sigma(c) = \sigma(c) + 1$. {Increment support count}
10: **end for**
11: **end for**
12: $F_k = \{ c \mid c \in C_k \wedge \sigma(c) \geq N \times minsup\}$. {Extract the frequent k-itemsets}
13: **until** $F_k = \emptyset$
14: Result $= \bigcup F_k$.

There are two key features of the Apriori algorithm's frequent itemset generation phase. It is a level-wise algorithm, to start with; i.e., it moves from frequent 1-itemsets to the maximum size of frequent itemsets by going through the itemset lattice one level at a time. Secondly, it utilizes a generate-and-test approach to identify frequently occurring itemsets. New candidate itemsets are created from the frequently occurring itemsets discovered in the preceding iteration for every iteration. Next, each candidate's support is tallied and compared to the minsup threshold. The total number of iterations needed by the algorithm is $k_{max} + 1$, where k_{max} is the maximum size of the frequent itemsets.

6.2.3. Candidate Generation and Pruning

The apriori-gen function shown in Step 5 of Algorithm 6.1 generates candidate itemsets by performing the following two operations:

- **Candidate Generation:** This operation generates new candidate kitemsets based on the frequent (k – 1)-itemsets found in the previous iteration.
- **Candidate Pruning:** This operation eliminates some of the candidate k-itemsets using the support-based pruning strategy.

To illustrate the candidate pruning operation, consider a candidate k-itemset, $X = \{i_1, i_2,..,i_k\}$. The algorithm must determine whether all of its proper subsets, $X - \{i_j\}$ ($\forall j = 1, 2,..,k$), are frequent.

X is immediately pruned if any of them are rare. This method can successfully lower the total number of candidate itemsets taken into account when calculating support counts. For every candidate k-itemset, this operation has an O(k) complexity. But as we'll see later, we don't need to look at every one of a given candidate itemset's k subsets. During candidate pruning, we only need to examine the k – m subsets that remain if m of the k subsets were used to generate a candidate. In principle, there are many ways to generate candidate itemsets. The following is a list of requirements for an effective candidate generation procedure:

1. It should avoid generating too many unnecessary candidates. A candidate itemset is unnecessary if at least one of its subsets is infrequent. Such a candidate is guaranteed to be infrequent according to the antimonotone property of support.
2. It must ensure that the candidate set is complete, i.e., no frequent itemsets are left out by the candidate generation procedure. To ensure completeness, the set of candidate itemsets must subsume the set of all frequent itemsets, i.e., $\forall k$: $F_k \subseteq C_k$.
3. It should not generate the same candidate itemset more than once. For example, the candidate itemset {a, b, c, d} can be generated in many ways—by merging {a, b, c} with {d}, {b, d} with {a, c}, {c} with {a, b, d}, etc. Generation of duplicate candidates leads to wasted computations and thus should be avoided for efficiency reasons.

Next, we will briefly describe several candidate generation procedures, including the one used by the apriori-gen function.

6.2.3.1. Brute-Force Method

The brute-force method considers every k-itemset as a potential candidate and then applies the candidate pruning step to remove any unnecessary candidates (see Figure 6.6). The number of candidate itemsets generated at level k is equal to $\binom{d}{k}$, where d is the total number of items. Although candidate generation is rather trivial, candidate pruning becomes extremely expensive because a large number of itemsets must be examined. Given that the amount of computations needed for each candidate is O(k), the overall complexity of this method is $O\left(\sum_{k=1}^{d} k \times \binom{d}{k}\right) = O(d \cdot 2^{d-1})$.

6.2.3.2. F_k–1 × F_1 Method

An alternative method for candidate generation is to extend each frequent (k – 1)-itemset with other frequent items. Figure 6.7 illustrates how a frequent 2-itemset such as {Beer, Diapers} can be augmented with a frequent item such as Bread to produce a candidate 3-itemset {Beer, Diapers, Bread}. This method will produce $O(|F_{k-1}| \times |F_1|)$ candidate k-itemsets, where $|F_j|$ is the number of frequent j-itemsets. The overall complexity of this step is $O(\sum_k k|F_{k-1}||F_1|)$.

The procedure is complete because every frequent k-itemset is composed of a frequent (k – 1)-itemset and a frequent 1-itemset. Therefore, all frequent k-itemsets are part of the candidate k-itemsets generated by this procedure.

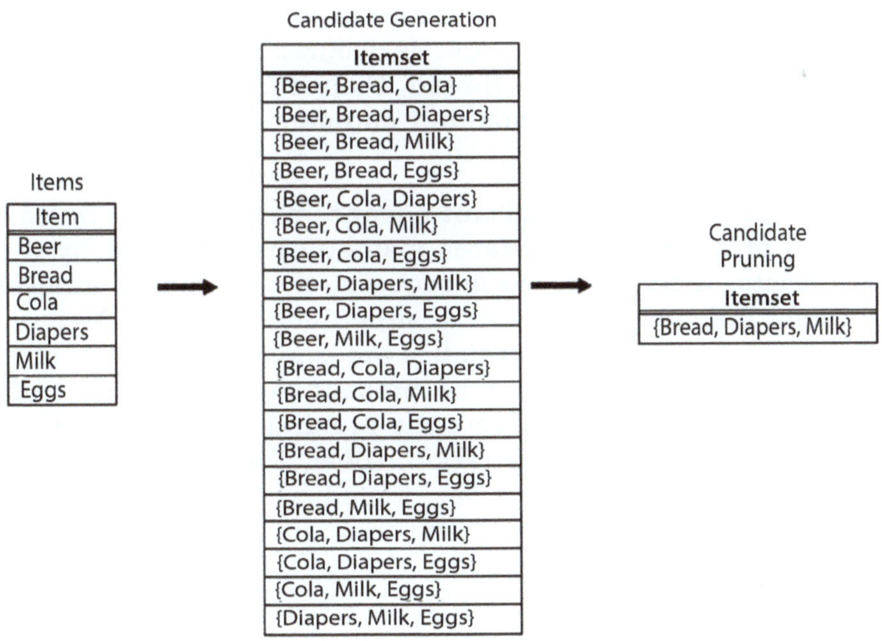

Figure 6.6. *A brute-force method for generating candidate 3-itemsets.*

Source: https://slideplayer.com/slide/13192245/79/images/23/Brute-force+Method.jpg.

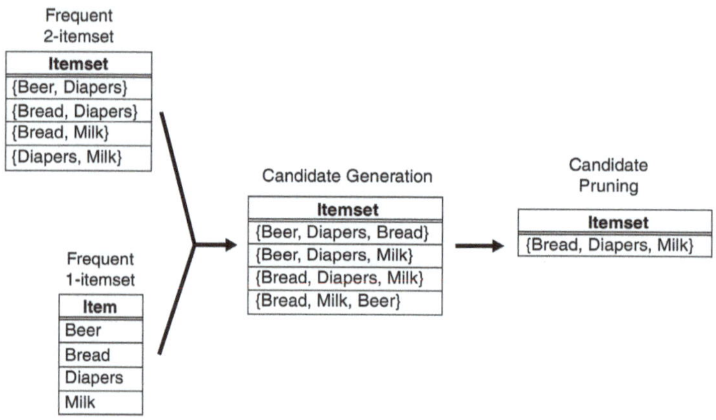

Figure 6.7. *Generating and pruning candidate k-itemsets by merging a frequent (k−1)-itemset with a frequent item. Note that some of the candidates are unnecessary because their subsets are infrequent.*

Source: https://www-users.cse.umn.edu/~kumar001/dmbook/ch6.pdf.

Nevertheless, this method does not stop the generation of the same candidate itemset more than once. By combining {Bread, Diapers} with {Milk}, {Bread, Milk} with {Diapers}, or {Diapers, Milk} with {Bread}, for example, {Bread, Diapers, Milk} can be created. Maintaining the lexicographic order of the items in each frequent itemset is one technique to prevent the generation of duplicate candidates. Next, frequent items that are lexicographically larger than the items in each frequent (k−1)-itemset X are added. For instance, since Milk has a larger lexicographic space than both Bread and Diapers, it can be added to the itemset {Bread, Diapers}. But since they both break the lexicographic ordering condition, we shouldn't augment {Diapers, Milk} with {Bread} or {Bread, Milk} with {Diapers}.

Even though this process is a significant advancement over the brute-force method, a significant number of needless candidates may still be produced by it. For instance, since one of its subsets, {Beer, Milk}, is infrequent, the candidate itemset that results from combining {Beer, Diapers} with {Milk} is superfluous. To cut down on the quantity of unneeded candidates, a number of heuristics are available. For instance, observe that each item in a candidate k-itemset must be present in at least k − 1 of the frequent (k − 1)-itemsets for the candidate to survive the pruning step. If not, the candidate will undoubtedly be uncommon. As an illustration, {Beer, Diapers, Milk} is only a feasible candidate 3-itemset if each item in the set, including Beer, appears in two or more frequent 2-itemsets. Beer appears in only one frequent 2-itemset, so all possible item sets containing Beer have to be uncommon.

6.3.3.3. F_k−1×F_k−1 Method

The candidate generation procedure in the apriori-gen function merges a pair of frequent (k−1)-itemsets only if their first k−2 items are identical. Let A = $\{a_1, a_2,..,a_{k-1}\}$ and B = $\{b_1, b_2,..,b_{k-1}\}$ be a pair of frequent (k − 1)-itemsets. A and B are merged if they satisfy the following conditions:

$$a_i = b_i \text{ (for } i = 1, 2, \ldots, k-2) \text{ and } a_{k-1} \neq b_{k-1}.$$

The frequently occurring itemsets {Bread, Diapers} and {Bread, Milk} are combined in Figure 6.8 to create a potential 3-itemset {Bread, Diapers, Milk}. {Beer, Diapers} and {Diapers, Milk} do not need to be combined by the algorithm because the first item in each itemset is distinct. In fact, if {Beer, Diapers, Milk} is a good fit, {Beer, Diapers} and {Beer, Milk} would have merged to get it instead. This example demonstrates the benefits of employing lexicographic ordering to avoid duplicate candidates as well as the thoroughness of the candidate generation process. To guarantee that the remaining k – 2 subsets of the candidate are frequent, an extra candidate pruning step is required, as each candidate is obtained by merging a pair of frequent (k–1)-itemsets.

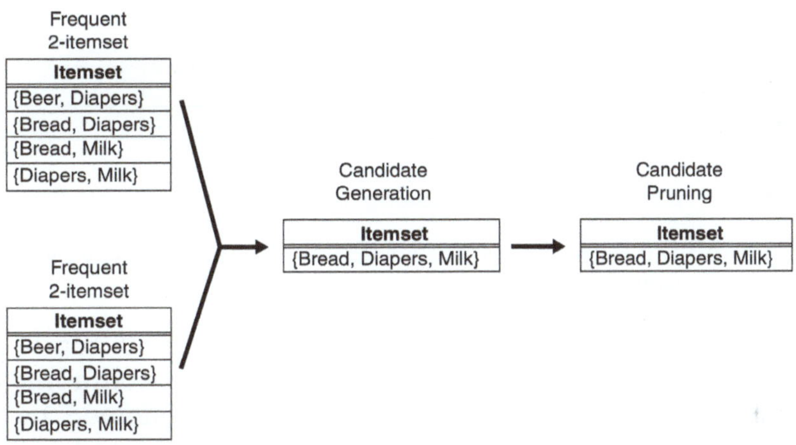

Figure 6.8. *Generating and pruning candidate k-itemsets by merging pairs of frequent (k–1)-itemsets.*

Source: https://www-users.cse.umn.edu/~kumar001/dmbook/slides/chap5_basic_association_analysis.pdf.

6.2.4. Support Counting

Finding the frequency of occurrence for each candidate itemset that makes it past the candidate pruning stage of the apriori-gen function is known as support counting. Algorithm 6.1's steps 6 through 11 implement support counting. One way to accomplish this is to update the support counts of the candidates included in the transaction and compare each transaction to each candidate itemset (refer to Figure 6.2). This method is computationally expensive, particularly for large numbers of candidate itemsets and transactions.

An alternative approach is to enumerate the itemsets contained in each transaction and use them to update the support counts of their respective candidate itemsets. To illustrate, consider a transaction t that contains five items, {1, 2, 3, 5, 6}. There are $\binom{5}{3} = 10$ itemsets of size 3 contained in this transaction. Some of the itemsets may correspond to the candidate 3-itemsets under investigation, in which case, their support counts are incremented. Other subsets of t that do not correspond to any candidates can be ignored.

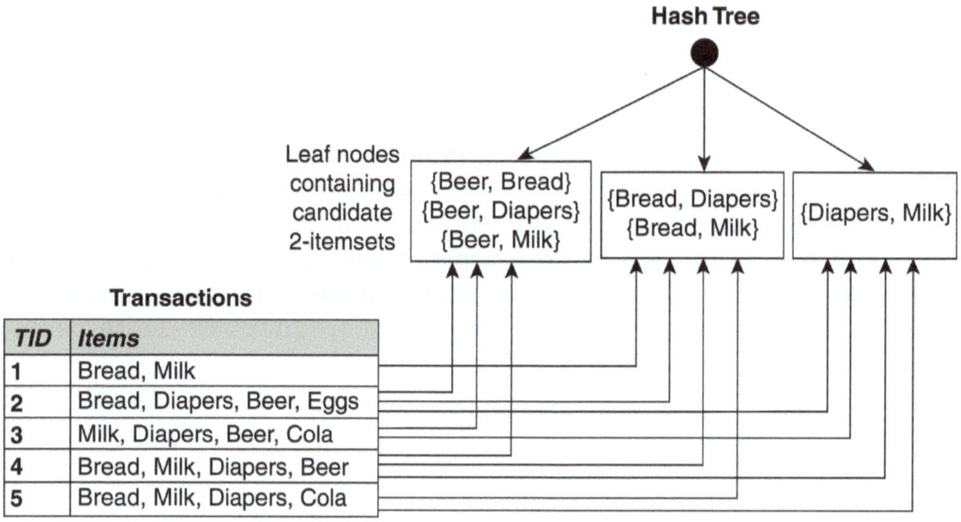

Figure 6.9. *Counting the support of itemsets using hash structure.*

Source: https://encrypted-tbn0.gstatic.com/images?q=tbn:ANd9GcRlg4LVDkU2WF63cmdSawEZshBZmvEu6K0AsjFRhtLBBTEH9lS51UdjyJK1Xq2ZzNtaSpo&usqp=CAU.

Figure 6.9 shows a systematic way for enumerating the 3-itemsets contained in t. Assuming that each itemset keeps its items in increasing lexicographic order, an itemset can be enumerated by specifying the smallest item first, followed by the larger items. For instance, given t = {1, 2, 3, 5, 6}, all the 3- itemsets contained in t must begin with item 1, 2, or 3. It is not possible to construct a 3-itemset that begins with items 5 or 6 because there are only two items in t whose labels are greater than or equal to 5. The number of ways to specify the first item of a 3-itemset contained in t is illustrated by the Level 1 prefix structures depicted in Figure 6.9. For instance, 1 2 3 5 6 represents a 3-itemset that begins with item 1, followed by two more items chosen from the set {2, 3, 5, 6}.

After fixing the first item, the prefix structures at Level 2 represent the number of ways to select the second item. For example, 1 2 3 5 6 corresponds to itemsets that begin with prefix (1 2) and are followed by items 3, 5, or 6. Finally, the prefix structures at Level 3 represent the complete set of 3-itemsets contained in t. For example, the 3-itemsets that begin with prefix {1 2} are {1, 2, 3}, {1, 2, 5}, and {1, 2, 6}, while those that begin with prefix {2 3} are {2, 3, 5} and {2, 3, 6}.

Figure 6.9's prefix structures illustrate how itemsets within a transaction can be methodically listed, i.e., listing each of their items individually, starting with the item on the left and moving rightward. It remains to be seen if every listed 3-itemset matches an already-existing candidate itemset. The corresponding candidate's support count is increased if it corresponds with one of the candidates. We demonstrate how a hash tree structure can be used to efficiently carry out this matching operation.

6.2.4.1. Support Counting Using a Hash Tree

Candidate itemsets are divided into various buckets and kept in a hash tree by the Apriori algorithm. Each transaction's itemsets are hashed into the proper buckets during the support counting process. In this manner, as illustrated in Figure 6.9, each itemset in the transaction is matched only against candidate itemsets that belong to the same bucket, as opposed to being compared with every candidate itemset.

Here is an illustration of a hash tree structure in Figure 6.10. The hash function h(p) = p mod 3 is used by each internal node of the tree to determine which branch of the current node should be followed next. For instance, the hashes of items 1, 4, and 7 point to the same branch (i.e., the branch on the left) since, when the number is divided by 3, their remainders are equal. The leaf nodes of the hash tree hold all candidate itemsets. There are 15 candidate 3-itemsets, distributed ac, in the hash tree displayed in Figure 6.10.

Assume that t = {1, 2, 3, 5, 6} is a transaction. The hash tree must be traversed so that every leaf node holding candidate 3-itemsets belonging to t must be visited at least once in order to update the support counts of the candidate itemsets. Remember that the Level 1 prefix structures in Figure 6.9 indicate that the 3-itemsets in t must start with either item 1 or item 2. As a result, items 1, 2, and 3 of the transaction are hashed independently at the hash tree's root node. The root node's left child is hashed for item 1, the middle child for item 2, and the right child for item 3. The transaction is hashed on the second item listed in the Level 2 structures depicted in Figure 6.9 at the next level of the tree. For instance, items 2, 3, and 5 of the transaction are hashed at the root node following hashing on item 1. As seen in Figure 6.11, items 2 and 5 are hashed to the middle child and item 3 is hashed to the right child. Until the hash tree's leaf nodes are reached, this process keeps going. The transaction is compared with the candidate itemsets kept at the visited leaf nodes. A candidate's support count is increased if it comprises a portion of the transaction. 19 itemsets out of 15 are compared to the transaction in this example, and five of the nine leaf nodes are visited.

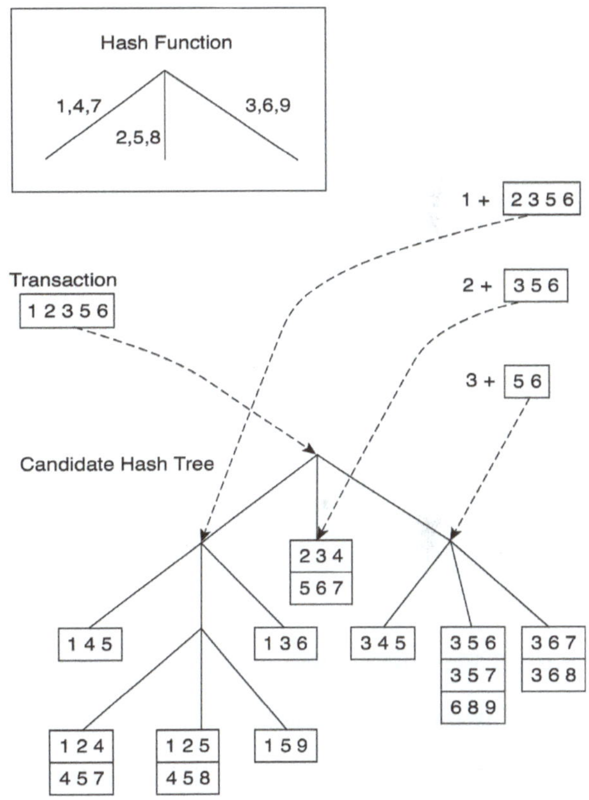

Figure 6.10. *Hashing a transaction at the root node of a hash tree.*

Source: https://www-users.cse.umn.edu/~kumar001/dmbook/ch6.pdf.

6.2.5. Computational Complexity

The computational complexity of the Apriori algorithm can be affected by the following factors.

- **Support Threshold:** When the support threshold is lowered, more itemsets are frequently declared as frequent. As seen in Figure 6.12, this has a negative impact on the algorithm's computational complexity since more candidate itemsets need to be created and counted. Lower support thresholds also tend to increase the maximum size of frequent itemsets. The algorithm will have to run through the data set more times as the maximum size of the frequent itemsets grows.

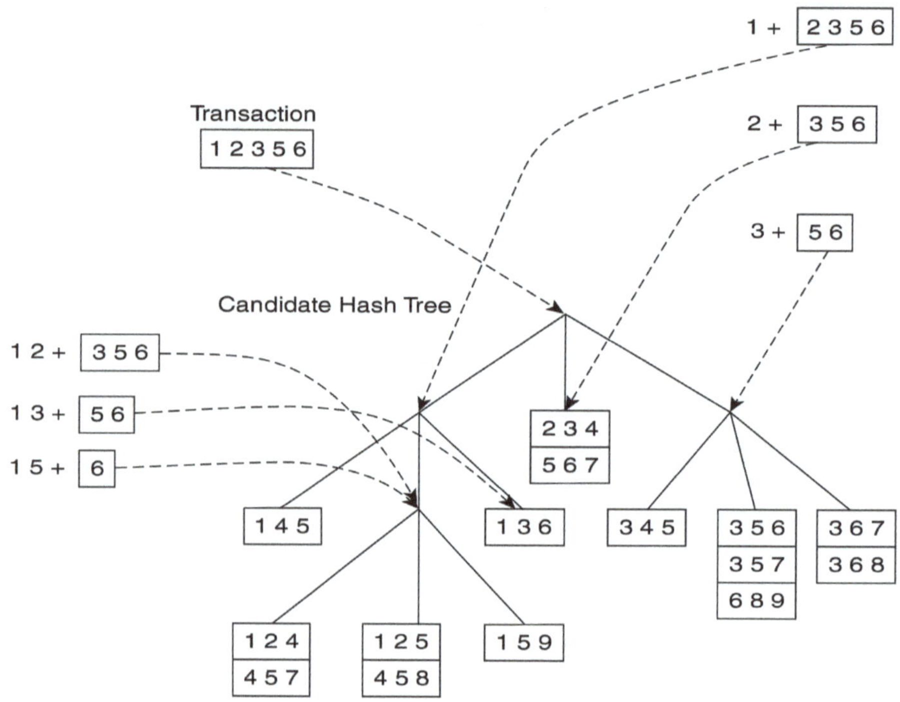

Figure 6.11. *Subset operation on the leftmost subtree of the root of a candidate hash tree.*

Source: https://csdl-images.ieeecomputer.org/trans/tk/2000/03/figures/k03373.gif.

- **Number of Items (Dimensionality):** More room will be required to hold the support counts of items as the number of items rises. The more candidate itemsets the algorithm generates, the higher the computation and I/O costs will be if the number of frequent items increases along with the dimensionality of the data.
- **Number of Transactions:** Since the Apriori algorithm makes repeated passes over the data set, its run time increases with a larger number of transactions.
- **Average Transaction Width:** The average transaction width can be very large for dense data sets. This has two effects on the Apriori algorithm's complexity. First, when the average transaction width rises, the maximum size of frequent itemsets tends to rise as well. Consequently, as Figure 6.13 illustrates, more candidate itemsets need to be looked at in order to generate candidates and count the number of candidates. Second, the transaction contains a greater number of

itemsets as the transaction width grows. As a result, during support counting, more hash tree traversals will be made.

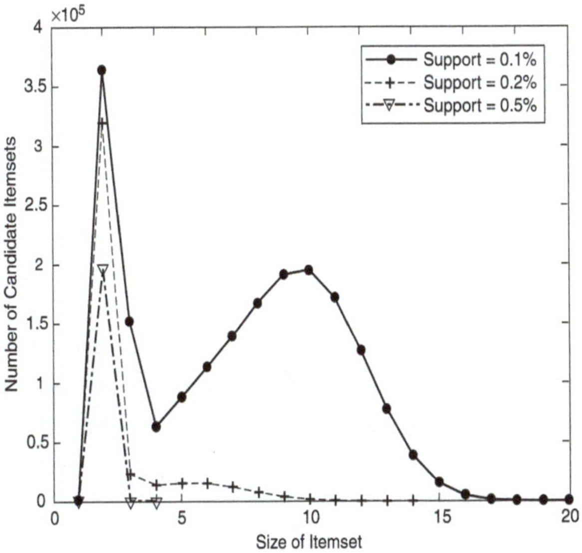

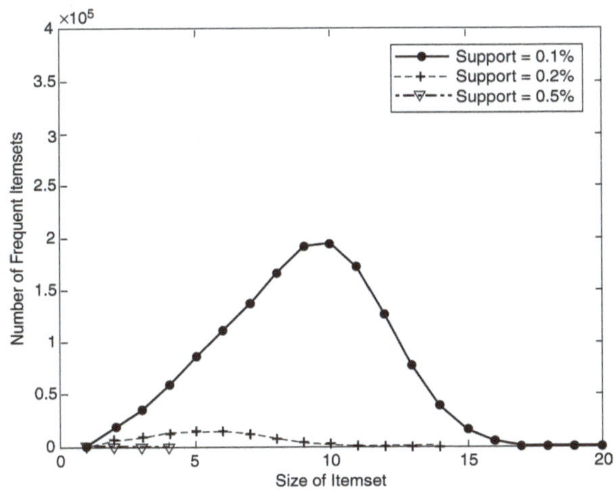

(b) Number of frequent itemsets.

Figure 6.12. *Effect of support threshold on the number of candidate and frequent itemsets.*

Source: https://www-users.cse.umn.edu/~kumar001/dmbook/ch6.pdf.

- **Generation of Frequent 1-itemsets:** We must update the number of supports for each item included in each transaction. This operation takes O(Nw) time, where N is the total number of transactions, assuming that w is the average transaction width.
- **Candidate generation:** Pairs of frequent (k – 1)-itemsets are merged to see if they have at least k – 2 items in common, which generates candidate k-itemsets. At most k – 2 equality comparisons are needed for each merging operation. Every merging step, in the best-case scenario, results in a feasible candidate k-itemset. In the worst-case situation, all pairs of frequent (k–1)-itemsets discovered in the preceding iteration must be merged by the algorithm. Therefore, the overall cost of merging frequent itemsets is

$$\sum_{k=2}^{w}(k-2)|C_k| < \text{Cost of merging} < \sum_{k=2}^{w}(k-2)|F_{k-1}|^2.$$

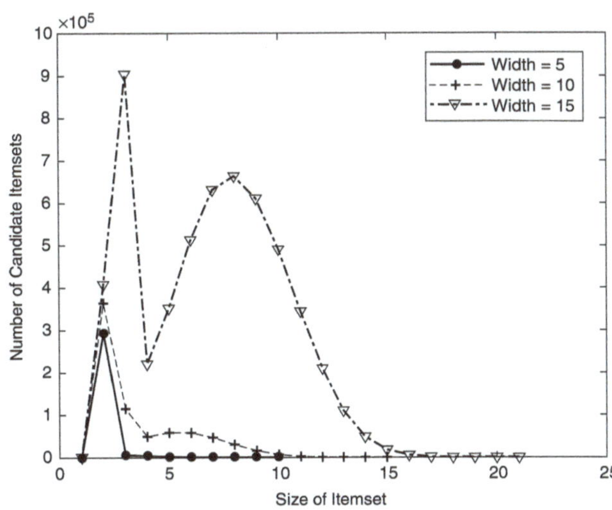

(a) Number of candidate itemsets.

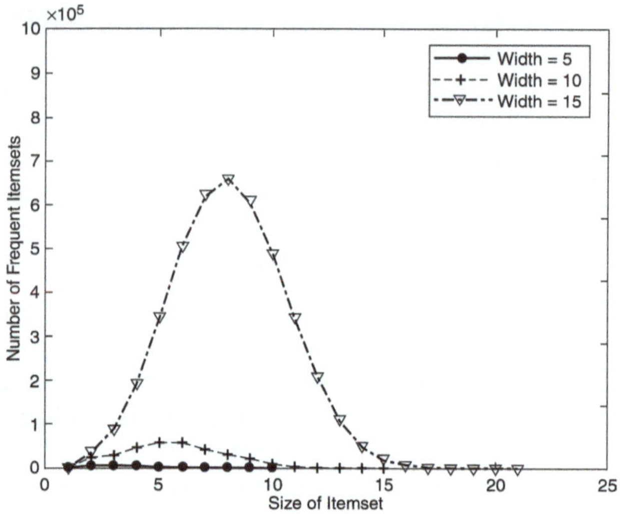

(b) Number of Frequent Itemsets.

Figure 6.13. *Effect of average transaction width on the number of candidate and frequent itemsets.*

Source: https://www-users.cse.umn.edu/~kumar001/dmbook/ch6.pdf.

A hash tree is also constructed during candidate generation to store the candidate itemsets. Because the maximum depth of the tree is k, the cost for populating the hash tree with candidate itemsets is $O(\sum_{k=2}^{w} k|C_k|)$. During candidate pruning, we need to verify that the k – 2 subsets of every candidate k-itemset are frequent. Since the cost for looking up a candidate in a hash tree is O(k), the candidate pruning step requires $O(\sum_{k=2}^{w} k(k-2)|C_k|)$ time.

- **Support Counting:** Each transaction of length |t| produces $\binom{|t|}{k}$ itemsets of size k. This is also the effective number of hash tree traversals performed for each transaction. The cost for support counting is $O(N \sum_k \binom{w}{k} \alpha_k)$, where w is the maximum transaction width and αk is the cost for updating the support count of a candidate k-itemset in the hash tree.

6.3. RULE GENERATION

Each frequent k-itemset, Y, can produce up to 2^k-2 association rules, ignoring rules that have empty antecedents or consequents ($\emptyset \rightarrow Y$ or $Y \rightarrow \emptyset$). An association rule can be extracted by partitioning the itemset Y into two non-empty subsets, X and Y −X, such that X → Y −X satisfies the confidence threshold. Note that all such rules must have already met the support threshold because they are generated from a frequent itemset.

Example 6.2. Let X = {1, 2, 3} be a frequent itemset. There are six candidate association rules that can be generated from X: {1, 2} → {3}, {1, 3} → {2}, {2, 3} → {1}, {1} → {2, 3}, {2} → {1, 3}, and {3} → {1, 2}. As each of their support is identical to the support for X, the rules must satisfy the support threshold.

Computing the confidence of an association rule does not require additional scans of the transaction data set. Consider the rule {1, 2} → {3}, which is generated from the frequent itemset X = {1, 2, 3}. The confidence for this rule is $\sigma(\{1, 2, 3\})/\sigma(\{1, 2\})$. Because {1, 2, 3} is frequent, the anti-monotone property of support ensures that {1, 2} must be frequent, too. Since the support counts for both itemsets were already found during frequent itemset generation, there is no need to read the entire data set again.

6.3.1. Confidence-Based Pruning

Unlike the support measure, confidence does not have any monotone property. For example, the confidence for X −→ Y can be larger, smaller, or equal to the confidence for another rule $\tilde{X} \rightarrow \tilde{Y}, where\ \tilde{X} \subseteq X\ and\ \tilde{Y} \subseteq Y$. Nevertheless, if we compare rules generated from the same frequent itemset Y, the following theorem holds for the confidence measure.

- **Theorem 6.2:**

  If a rule X −→ Y −X does not satisfy the confidence threshold, then any rule X' −→ Y − X,' where X' is a subset of X, must not satisfy the confidence threshold as well.

  To prove this theorem, consider the following two rules: X′→ Y −X′ and X −→ Y −X, where $X' \subset X$. The confidence of the rules are $\sigma(Y)/\sigma(X')$ and $\sigma(Y)/\sigma(X)$, respectively. Since X′ is a subset of X, $\sigma(X') \geq \sigma(X)$. Therefore, the former rule cannot have a higher confidence than the latter rule.

6.3.2. Rule Generation in Apriori Algorithm

The Apriori algorithm creates association rules level-by-level, with each level denoting the quantity of items that make up the rule consequent. First, every high-confidence rule with a single item in the rule consequent is taken out. Next, new candidate rules are generated using these rules. For instance, if {acd} → {b} and {abd} → {c} are high-confidence rules, combining the consequents of both rules yields the candidate rule {ad} –→ {bc}. A lattice structure for the association rules produced by the frequent itemset {a, b, c, d} is displayed in Figure 6.14. Theorem 6.2 states that if a node in the lattice has low confidence, the entire subgraph that the node spans can be pruned right away. Assume that there is little confidence for {bcd} → {a}. You can discard all the rules that have item a in their consequent, such as {cd} → {ab}, {bd} → {ac}, {bc} → {ad}, and {d} → {abc}.

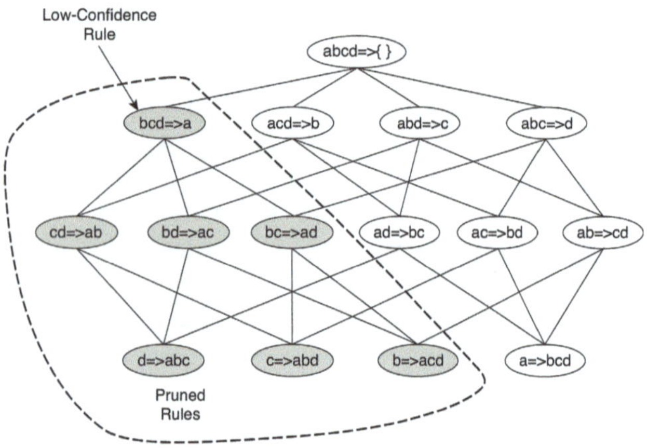

Figure 6.14. *Pruning of association rules using the confidence measure.*

Source: https://www-users.cse.umn.edu/~kumar001/dmbook/ch6.pdf.

The rule generation step's pseudocode can be seen in Algorithms 6.2 and 6.3. Take note of how the frequent itemset generation process in Algorithm 6.1 and the ap-genrules procedure in Algorithm 6.3 are similar. The only distinction is that in rule generation, calculating the confidence of the candidate rules does not require additional passes over the data set. Rather, we use the support counts computed during frequent itemset generation to determine the confidence of each rule.

Algorithm 6.2 Rule generation of the *Apriori* algorithm.

for each frequent k-itemset f_k, $k \geq 2$ **do**
  $H_1 = \{i \mid i \in f_k\}$ {1-item consequents of the rule.}
  call ap-genrules$(f_k, H_1.)$
end for

Algorithm 6.3 Procedure ap-genrules(f_k, H_m).

$k = |f_k|$ {size of frequent itemset.}
$m = |H_m|$ {size of rule consequent.}
if $k > m + 1$ **then**
  $H_{m+1} = \text{apriori-gen}(H_m)$.
  for each $h_{m+1} \in H_{m+1}$ **do**
    $conf = \sigma(f_k)/\sigma(f_k - h_{m+1})$.
    if $conf \geq minconf$ **then**
      output the rule $(f_k - h_{m+1}) \longrightarrow h_{m+1}$.
    else
      delete h_{m+1} from H_{m+1}.
    end if
  end for
  call ap-genrules$(f_k, H_{m+1}.)$
end if

6.3.3. Compact Representation of Frequent Itemsets

When using a transaction data set, a large number of frequent itemsets may actually be generated. Finding a small representative set of itemsets that all other frequently occurring itemsets can be derived from is helpful. The maximal and closed frequent itemsets are two examples of these representations.

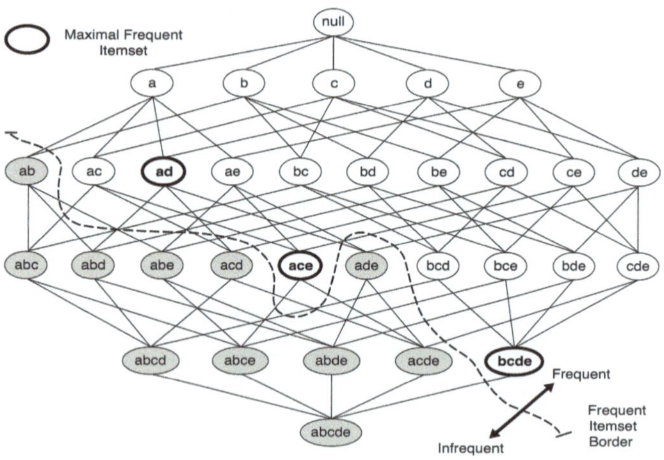

Figure 6.15. Maximal frequent itemset.

Source: https://www-users.cse.umn.edu/~kumar001/dmbook/ch6.pdf.

6.3.4. Maximal Frequent Itemsets

Definition 6.3 (Maximal Frequent Itemset). A frequent itemset for which none of its immediate supersets are frequent is called a maximal frequent itemset. Figure 6.15's itemset lattice serves as an example of this idea. The frequent and the infrequent itemsets in the lattice are separated into two categories. The diagram also shows a frequent itemset border, which is represented by a dashed line. While the itemsets below the border (the shaded nodes) are infrequent, every itemset above the border is frequent. Because their immediate supersets are infrequent, the itemsets {a, d}, {a, c, e}, and {b, c, d, e}, which are located close to the border, are regarded as maximal frequent itemsets. Because all of its immediate supersets—{a, b, d}, {a, c, d}, and {a, d, e}—are infrequent, an itemset like {a, d} is maximally frequent. On the other hand, because {a, c} is frequent, one of its immediate supersets, {a, c, e}, is not maximal.

Maximal frequent itemsets effectively provide a compact representation of frequent itemsets. In other words, they form the smallest set of itemsets from

Which all frequent itemsets can be derived. For example, the frequent itemsets shown in Figure 6.15 can be divided into two groups:

- Frequent itemsets that begin with item a and that may contain items c, d, or e. This group includes itemsets such as {a}, {a, c}, {a, d}, {a, e}, and {a, c, e}.
- Frequent itemsets that begin with items b, c, d, or e. This group includes itemsets such as {b}, {b, c}, {c, d},{b, c, d, e}, etc.

Frequent itemsets that belong in the first group are subsets of either {a, c, e} or {a, d}, while those that belong in the second group are subsets of {b, c, d, e}. Hence, the maximal frequent itemsets {a, c, e}, {a, d}, and {b, c, d, e} provide a compact representation of the frequent itemsets shown in Figure 6.15.

Because there are exponentially many frequent itemsets in data sets that can produce very long itemsets, maximal frequent itemsets offer a useful representation for those types of data. However, this method is only useful if there is a reliable algorithm that can identify the maximal frequent itemsets explicitly without requiring the enumeration of all of their subsets.

Maximal frequent itemsets, although offering a compact representation, lack the support data of their subsets. For instance, there is no indication of the support of their subsets in the maximal frequent itemsets {a, c, e}, {a, d}, and {b, c, d, e} support. Therefore, in order to ascertain the support counts of the non-maximal frequent itemsets, one more pass over the data set is required. Sometimes it would be preferable to have a simple representation of common itemsets while retaining the supporting data.

6.4. ASSOCIATION ANALYSIS – FUNCTION, ALGORITHMS AND APPLICATION

One of the most important resources in our time is data, which has long since become so. But this value only materializes when the proper inferences are made and the frequently overlooked correlations are identified. An interdisciplinary field of study in computer science and statistics has emerged as a result of this extremely complex undertaking: data mining. Data mining uses a variety of computer-aided methods to unlock the secrets of the data treasure trove. Particularly effective has been association analysis, which applies some remarkably basic principles.

6.4.1. What Is an Association Analysis?

One data mining technique for finding correlations between items in a database is association analysis. It can be used to ascertain whether various combinations occur with a given probability based on frequencies. Establishing association rules is the ultimate goal, and this is usually expressed in the form of basic if-then sentences (X → Y). Conversely, other techniques like variance analysis focus more on target values and numerical characteristics.

Many algorithms can be used to automate association analysis to a large extent. This is machine learning in the traditional sense since it entails computer-controlled data analysis with forecasts and decisions made from it. The method's roots are in shopping basket analysis, a study that looks at the connections between purchases. This use case will increasingly be used as an example here because it is still the most prevalent one today. But since then, other data structures have been added to the concept.

6.4.2. Important Basic Terms

Their mathematical-logical linking ultimately forms the actual process of association analysis.

- **Items:** These are the objects in the population between which the association analysis examines relationships. When it comes to items in a supermarket, this often involves over 10,000 units. For e-commerce providers such as Amazon, however, shopping basket analysis quickly becomes a big data project with several hundred million products.
- **Item Set:** This refers to a combination of items – usually to express that they have appeared or been purchased together with a certain frequency (e.g., {milk, bread, butter}). The frequency of the set also determines whether an association rule can be derived from it.
- **Support:** More meaningful than the absolute frequency is its ratio to all transactions, i.e., the relative frequency. For the binary decision as to whether an item set is considered frequent, a corresponding threshold value of the *minimal support* be set.
- **Confidence:** This key figure corresponds to the relative frequency with which different item sets occur together or are found in a transaction. To calculate the confidence, the frequency of the set (or its support) is divided by the frequency of an individual item in the association analysis. This results in values up to a maximum of 1 – in this case there would only be common transactions.
- **Lift:** Not every association rule has a high information content. To map this, the confidence of a rule is divided by an expected confidence value. This results in a metric that indicates whether a data-based finding is of particular relevance. A lift of 1 means that the rule corresponds to the statistical expectation. The higher the lift, the more significant the established correlation.

6.4.3. Derive Association Rules

In the end, significant association rules are derived using each of the displayed key figures. These represent the likelihood that item Y will be added to item X and have the standard form X → Y(Support, Confidence). This can be expressed linguistically as hypotheses like If (premise), then (as a result). Several processes that are predicated on an item-by-item structured data set are required in order to accomplish this goal of association analysis.

1. **Identify Frequent Item Set:** Each rule begins with a suspicion or hypothesis. A simple frequency count of various item sets can be used for this, which can also be formed from parts of existing transactions/sets. If, in addition to a certain frequency, there is also a high *Support* before, confirms the suspicion that X → Y. In this way, an algorithm would filter out as many conspicuous item sets as possible.
2. **Examine Rule:** The *Confidence* now forms the next examination instance and reveals more about the accuracy of a rule. Here you can sort out again so that only correlations with a confidence level of a desired low difference to the value 1 remain. Just because a rule is established does not mean that it is relevant for the planned investigation.
3. **Evaluate and Apply Rule:** All that remains are association rules

that correspond to the previously defined metrics. Often, however, one is aware of some correlations from the outset, so that a gain in knowledge only arises from an unexpectedly high effect strength. For this assessment, the *Lift,* which merely compares the confidence level with the expectation. If this is exceeded, business processes, inventories or supply chains can be adjusted accordingly.

- **Example:**

The following list of shopping baskets has resulted from transactions in a supermarket:

Transaction ID	Items
1	Bread, milk
2	Bread, eggs, beer
3	Milk, eggs, cola
4	Bread, milk, eggs, beer
5	Bread, milk, eggs, cola

Even a simple frequency count shows that, for example, the item set {bread, milk} appears quite frequently, namely in three out of five transactions. The minimum support is Smin=50%.

The support of {bread, milk} S = $^3/_5$ = 60% > 50%. So there is actually a frequency of interest for the investigation. We therefore assume the rule bread → milk (60%, C%). Confidence C is still unknown.

We want to change this and divide the support of {bread, milk} by the support of {bread}: C = 60% / 80% = 75%. The complete association rule is thus Bread → Milk (60%, 75%). This seems convincing, as three quarters of bread purchases are also accompanied by milk.

In order to take measures to increase sales, the supermarket operators only want to consider the most meaningful rules. The items bread and milk have often been seen together on the checkout conveyor belt and a confidence level of 60% was assumed. This results in a *Lift* L = 75% / 60% = 1.25 > 1. time to move the bread shelf in the direction of the milk.

6.4.4. Three Common Algorithms

Real-world applications, of course, are considerably more complicated and difficult to resolve with such manual computations. For this reason, appropriate algorithms are typically used to perform association analysis. This makes it possible to analyze much larger amounts of data and find correlations across large item sets.

1. **Apriori:** One of the first algorithms of its kind, the Apriori algorithm is still widely used today. This is especially because of how simple it is to use and put into practice. The minimal support and the minimum confidence are the only additional inputs required in addition to the database. The program finds all frequent item sets in the data and removes rules that match the input in line with the procedure outlined. The examination of the so-called a priori principle is one of this case's unique features. This says that only frequent items are included in frequent item sets. If this isn't the case, the software uses a process known as pruning to clean up the data and maximize the quality of the selection.
2. **FP-Growth:** FP-Growth is an extension of Apriori that improves speed and scalability while handling

exponentially increasing data volumes. An additional consequence, though, is a more intricate implementation. An item is represented by each of the connecting nodes in a so-called frequent pattern tree, which is used to organize the original item sets. The benefits of this compression extend to data collection and storage, where using Apriori would necessitate numerous scan runs. Each matching item set of a transaction is assigned a common prefix, with the root serving as the tree's branches. In the end, this aids the algorithm in eliminating all common patterns.

3. **ECLAT:** Equivalence Class Clustering and Bottom-Up Lattice Traversal is a contemporary algorithm that is just as effective as FP-Growth. It does not rely on multiple scans of the original data, instead analyzing an independently generated data set. This algorithm uses a vertical format, with items listed in a table on the left and their corresponding transactions on the right. ECLAT examines these tidsets to create item pairs with matching tidsets, indicating a potential connection between items based on common transactions.

6.4.5. Areas of Application

It should come as no surprise that the method's most popular application is in the retail sector, where association rules are used to analyze shopping baskets in an effort to promote cross-selling and make decisions easier for customers. This is not, however, the only advantage of rule-based data mining. The following areas of application particularly benefit from association analysis:

- **Medicine:** Initially, it is frequently unknown precisely which traits could serve as risk factors or indicators of a given illness. The use of association rules based on health data can help with prevention and diagnosis. Indian researchers demonstrated how to extract these correlations by combining natural language processing with the above-discussed algorithms.
- **UX Design:** A crucial component of websites and other digital products is the user experience. In order to help users find exactly what they're looking for, the application and navigation are designed to be as enjoyable and easy to use as possible. Association analysis based on past usage data can help with this, for instance by customizing buttons and links. What use is a shopping basket analysis, after all, if the route to the online retailer is too difficult?
- **Warehouse Management:** The arrangement of the goods in big warehouses greatly affects how efficiently the business operates. Large orders, as well as frequently requested goods and frequent sequences, should ideally be processed as quickly as possible. The distances needed for this can be significantly reduced with the help of algorithms like Apriori.

CASE STUDY

OPTIMIZING DELIVERY ROUTES WITH ALGORITHMS

- **Background:** A mid-sized logistics company, FastTrack Deliveries, was facing challenges in optimizing its delivery routes. With an expanding customer base and increasing order volume, the company needed a more efficient system to manage its fleet and ensure timely deliveries.
- **Problem:** FastTrack Deliveries relied on manual route planning, leading to inefficiencies, higher fuel costs, and delayed deliveries. The goal was to implement an algorithmic solution to optimize delivery routes, minimize costs, and improve customer satisfaction.
- **Solution:** The company decided to implement a combination of algorithms:
  1. *Dijkstra's Algorithm*: Used for finding the shortest path between delivery points on a graph representing the city's road network.
  2. *Traveling Salesman Problem (TSP) Solver*: Applied to minimize the total distance traveled by each delivery vehicle.
  3. *K-means Clustering*: Used to group deliveries into clusters, ensuring that each vehicle covers a specific area, reducing overall travel time.
- **Implementation:**
  1. **Data Collection:** FastTrack collected data on delivery locations, traffic patterns, and delivery time windows.
  2. **Graph Construction:** They built a graph model of the city's road network, with nodes representing delivery points and edges representing the distance and travel time between them.
  3. **Route Optimization:** Using Dijkstra's Algorithm, the shortest paths between all nodes were calculated. The TSP solver then optimized the routes for each vehicle, considering delivery time windows and capacity constraints.
  4. **Clustering:** Deliveries were grouped using K-means clustering to balance the workload among the fleet.
- **Results:**
  1. **Efficiency Gains:** The algorithmic approach reduced total travel distance by 20% and fuel costs by 15%.
  2. **Time Savings:** Delivery times improved by 25%, leading to higher customer satisfaction.
  3. **Scalability:** The system could easily scale with the growing number of deliveries and expand to new cities.

- **Conclusion**:

  By leveraging algorithms like Dijkstra's, TSP solvers, and K-means clustering, FastTrack Deliveries successfully optimized its delivery routes, reducing costs and improving service quality. This case study demonstrates the practical application of algorithms in solving complex logistical problems and enhancing operational efficiency.

CLASS ACTIVITY

Association analysis is a data mining technique used to discover interesting relationships, or associations, between variables in large datasets. In a classroom activity, students can explore market basket analysis, a common application, by examining transaction data to identify frequent itemsets and generate association rules. This process involves calculating metrics like support, confidence, and lift to evaluate the strength and relevance of the associations. Through hands-on practice with real-world data, students learn to uncover patterns and insights that can inform decision-making in various fields such as retail, healthcare, and finance.

SUMMARY

- Association analysis is a data mining technique that uncovers interesting relationships between variables in large datasets.
- The Apriori algorithm is one of the most widely used algorithms for association analysis. It employs a breadth-first search strategy to discover frequent itemsets by iteratively generating candidate itemsets and pruning those that do not meet minimum support thresholds.
- Apriori is the first association rule mining algorithm that pioneered the use of support-based pruning to systematically control the exponential growth of candidate itemsets.
- Support counting is the process of determining the frequency of occurrence for every candidate itemset that survives the candidate pruning step of the apriori-gen function.
- The Apriori algorithm uses a level-wise approach for generating association rules, where each level corresponds to the number of items that belong to the rule consequent.

REVIEW QUESTIONS

1. What is Association Analysis?
2. Define association analysis and explain its primary goal in data mining.
3. What is an Itemset?
4. Describe what an itemset is and provide an example.
5. What are Frequent Itemsets?
6. Explain what constitutes a frequent itemset and how the support measure is used to identify them.
7. What is a Rule in Association Analysis?
8. What are Support, Confidence, and Lift?
9. What is the Apriori Algorithm?
10. What is the Downward Closure Property?

REFERENCES

1. Aggarwal, C. C., & Yu, P. S. (2001). Mining associations with the collective strength approach. *IEEE Transactions on Knowledge and Data Engineering, 13*(6), 863–873.
2. Potter, C., Klooster, S., Steinbach, M., Tan, P. N., Kumar, V., Shekhar, S., & Carvalho, C. (2004). Understanding global teleconnections of climate to regional model estimates of Amazon ecosystem carbon fluxes. *Global Change Biology, 10*(5), 693–703.
3. Bárbara, D., Couto, J., Jajodia, S., & Wu, N. (2001). ADAM: A testbed for exploring the use of data mining in intrusion detection. *SIGMOD Record, 30*(4), 15–24.

4. Dokas, P., Ertöz, L., Kumar, V., Lazarevic, A., Srivastava, J., & Tan, P. N. (2002). Data mining for network intrusion detection. In *Proceedings of the NSF Workshop on Next Generation Data Mining* (pp. 21–30), Baltimore, MD.

5. Agarwal, R. C., Aggarwal, C. C., & Prasad, V. V. V. (2001). A tree projection algorithm for generation of frequent itemsets. *Journal of Parallel and Distributed Computing, 61*(3), 350–371.

6. Bolton, R. J., Hand, D. J., & Adams, N. M. (2002). Determining hit rate in pattern search. In *Proceedings of the ESF Exploratory Workshop on Pattern Detection and Discovery in Data Mining* (pp. 36–48), London, UK.

7. Bay, S. D., & Pazzani, M. (2001). Detecting group differences: Mining contrast sets. *Data Mining and Knowledge Discovery, 5*(3), 213–246.

8. Jaroszewicz, S., & Simovici, D. (2004). Interestingness of frequent itemsets using Bayesian networks as background knowledge. In *Proceedings of the 10th International Conference on Knowledge Discovery and Data Mining* (pp. 178–186), Seattle, WA.

9. DuMouchel, W., & Pregibon, D. (2001). Empirical Bayes screening for multi-item associations. In *Proceedings of the 7th International Conference on Knowledge Discovery and Data Mining* (pp. 67–76), San Francisco, CA.

10. Huang, Y., Shekhar, S., & Xiong, H. (2004). Discovering co-location patterns from spatial datasets: A general approach. *IEEE Transactions on Knowledge and Data Engineering, 16*(12), 1472–1485.+++

CHAPTER 7

Association Analysis: Advanced Concepts

LEARNING OBJECTIVES

After studying this chapter, you will be able to:

- Define handling categorical attributes
- Explain the sequential patterns
- Discus subgraph patterns

KEY TERMS FROM THIS CHAPTER

Apriori algorithm	Association analysis
Data sequences	Database systems
Maxgap constraints	Sequential patterns
Telecommunications networks	Web sequence

INTRODUCTION

Association analysis is a fundamental technique in data mining and machine learning, used primarily to uncover interesting relationships and patterns within large datasets. It extends beyond the simple identification of frequent itemsets, which are groups of items that commonly co-occur in transactions, by exploring intricate associations and correlations between different variables. Association analysis aims to discover rules that highlight the probability of the occurrence of an item based on the presence of other items. This is especially useful in market basket analysis, where understanding the products often bought together can inform strategic business decisions such as cross-selling, promotions, and inventory management.

7.1. HANDLING CATEGORICAL ATTRIBUTES

Symmetric binary and nominal attributes are present in a lot of applications. In addition to nominal attributes like state and level of education, the Internet survey data displayed in Table 7.1 includes symmetric binary attributes like gender, computer at home, chat online, shop online, and privacy concerns. We may find out fascinating details about the traits of Internet users, like these, by using association analysis.

$$\{\text{Shop Online} = \text{Yes}\} \longrightarrow \{\text{Privacy Concerns} = \text{Yes}\}.$$

This rule suggests that most Internet users who shop online are concerned about their personal privacy.

Table 7.1. Internet Survey Data with Categorical Attributes

Gender	Level of Education	State	Computer at Home	Chat Online	Shop Online	Privacy Concerns
Female	Graduate	Illinois	Yes	Yes	Yes	Yes
Male	College	California	No	No	No	No
Male	Graduate	Michigan	Yes	Yes	Yes	Yes
Female	College	Virginia	No	No	Yes	Yes
Female	Graduate	California	Yes	No	No	Yes
Male	College	Minnesota	Yes	Yes	Yes	Yes
Male	College	Alaska	Yes	Yes	Yes	No
Male	High School	Oregon	Yes	No	No	No
Female	Graduate	Texas	No	Yes	No	No
...	...	...	...	...	...	...

Source: Pang-Ning Tan, Michael Steinbach, Vipin Kumar; Introduction to Data Mining; ISBN 10: 1–292–02615–4.

The categorical and symmetric binary attributes are first converted into "items" in order to make use of the association rule mining algorithms already in place for extracting such patterns. To carry out this kind of transformation, a new item must be made for every unique attribute-value pair. Three binary items, for instance, can be used to substitute the nominal attribute Level of Education: Education = College, Education = Graduate, and Education = High School. In a similar vein, binary attributes that are symmetric, like gender, can be transformed into the binary items Male and Female. The outcome of binarizing the Internet survey data is displayed in Table 7.2.

There are several issues to consider when applying association analysis to the binarized data:

- It's possible that some attribute values don't occur frequently enough to form a regular pattern. When it comes to nominal attributes with a wide range of possible values, such as e.g., state titles. Reducing the support threshold leads to exponentially more frequent patterns—many of which might be spurious—and increases the cost of the computation, so it is ineffective. Sorting related attribute values into a limited number of categories is a more doable solution. For instance, the names of the corresponding geographic regions, such as the Midwest, Pacific Northwest, Southwest, and East Coast, could be used in place of each state. As illustrated in Figure 7.1, another option is to combine the less common attribute values into a single category named others.

Table 7.2. Internet Survey Data After Binarizing Categorical and Symmetric Binary Attributes

Male	Female	Education = Graduate	Education = College	...	Privacy = Yes	Privacy = No
0	1	1	0	...	1	0
1	0	0	1	...	0	1
1	0	1	0	...	1	0
0	1	0	1	...	1	0
0	1	1	0	...	1	0
1	0	0	1	...	1	0
1	0	0	1	...	0	1
1	0	0	0	...	0	1
0	1	1	0	...	0	1
...	...	...	...	...	...	...

Source: Pang-Ning Tan, Michael Steinbach, Vipin Kumar; Introduction to Data Mining; ISBN 10: 1-292-02615-4.

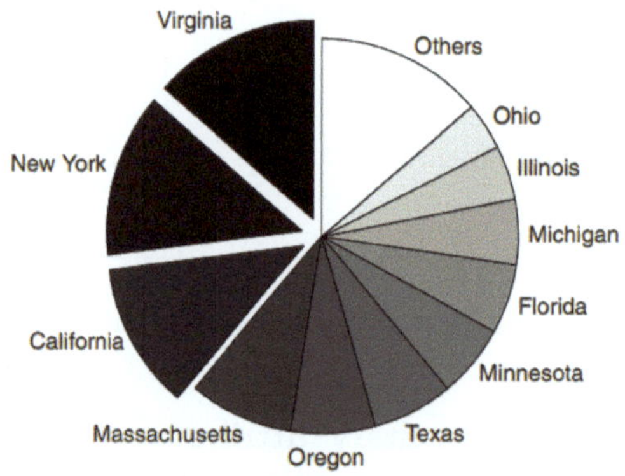

Figure 7.1. *A pie chart with a merged category called others.*

Source: Pang-Ning Tan, Michael Steinbach, Vipin Kumar; Introduction to Data Mining; ISBN 10: 1-292-02615-4.

- It's possible for some attribute values to occur much more frequently than others. Let's take an example where 85% of respondents to the survey own a home computer. We may possibly produce a large number of redundant patterns if we create a binary item for every attribute value that frequently occurs in the data, as the following example shows:

{Computer at home = Yes, Shop Online = Yes} –→ {Privacy Concerns = Yes}.

  This rule is unnecessary since it is covered by the more comprehensive rule provided at the start of this section. The high-frequency items rarely contain any new information that can aid in our understanding of the pattern because they typically correspond to the values of an attribute. Therefore, eliminating such items before using common association analysis algorithms might be helpful.

- Even though each transaction has the same width as the total number of attributes in the original data, there may be a rise in computation time, particularly if a large number of the newly created items start to occur frequently. This is due to the fact that handling the extra candidate itemsets that these items generate requires more time. Avoiding creating candidate itemsets with multiple items from the same attribute is one technique to speed up computation. It is not necessary, for instance, to create a candidate itemset with the format {State = X, State = Y, ...}. since the itemset has zero support counts.

7.2. SEQUENTIAL PATTERNS

Market basket data frequently includes temporal details regarding the time at which a customer made a purchase. With the use of this data, a customer's transaction history over a specific time period can be assembled. Similar to this, event-based data gathered from research projects or the observation of real-world systems like computer, wireless sensor, and telecommunications networks are inherently sequential. This indicates that there is an ordinal relation between the events that occur in such data, typically based on temporal or spatial precedence. The notions of association patterns that have been covered thus far, however, only focus on co-occurrence relationships and ignore the data's sequential information. The latter data could be useful for forecasting the future occurrence of specific events or identifying recurrent characteristics of a dynamic system.

7.2.1. Problem Formulation

A sequence data set is the input for the problem of finding sequential patterns; it is depicted on the left side of Figure 7.2. Every row documents the events that are connected to a specific object at a specific moment in time. For instance, the events that happened for object A at timestamp t = 10 are contained in the first row. A sequence for object A is produced by ordering all of the events connected to it according to increasing timestamps, as seen on the right side of Figure 7.2.

Sequence Database:

Object	Timestamp	Events
A	10	2, 3, 5
A	20	6, 1
A	23	1
B	11	4, 5, 6
B	17	2
B	21	7, 8, 1, 2
B	28	1, 6
C	14	1, 8, 7

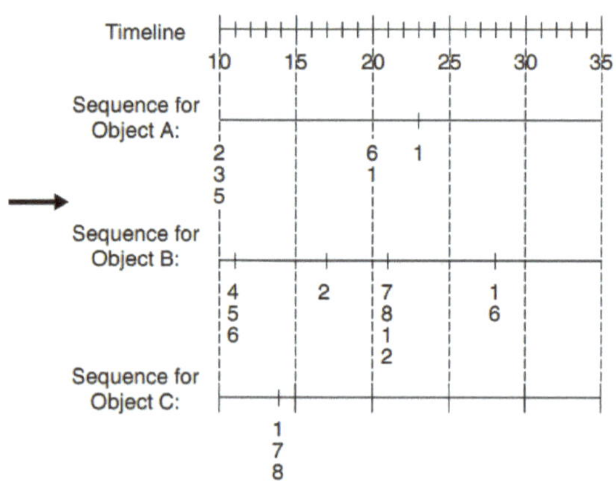

Figure 7.2. *Example of a sequence database.*

Source: Pang-Ning Tan, Michael Steinbach, Vipin Kumar; Introduction to Data Mining; ISBN 10: 1-292-02615-4.

Generally speaking, a sequence is an ordered list of elements. A sequence can be denoted as $s = \langle e_1 e_2 e_3 \ldots e_n \rangle$, where each element e_j is a collection of one or more events, i.e., $e_j = \{i_1, i_2, \ldots, i_k\}$. The following is a list of examples of sequences:

- Sequence of Web pages viewed by a Web site visitor:

  ⟨ {Homepage} {Electronics} {Cameras and Camcorders} {Digital Cameras} {Shopping Cart} {Order Confirmation} {Return to Shopping} ⟩

- Sequence of events leading to the nuclear accident at Three-Mile Island:

  ⟨ {clogged resin} {outlet valve closure} {loss of feedwater} {condenser polisher outlet valve shut} {booster pumps trip} {main waterpump trips} {main turbine trips} {reactor pressure increases} ⟩

- Sequence of classes taken by a computer science major:

  ⟨ {Algorithms and Data Structures, Introduction to Operating Systems} {Database Systems, Computer Architecture} {Computer Networks, Software Engineering} {Computer Graphics, Parallel Programming} ⟩

A sequence's length and the quantity of occurrences can be used to define it. A sequence's length is determined by the number of elements it contains; on the other hand, a k-sequence is made up of k events. The preceding example's Web sequence has seven elements and seven events; the Three-Mile Island event sequence has eight elements and eight events; and the class sequence has four elements and eight events.

Examples of elements, events, and sequences defined for various application domains are shown in Figure 7.3. Calendar time is the ordinal attribute associated with each of the first three domains, with the exception of the last row. The ordinal attribute for the final row reflects where bases (A, C, G, and T) are located in the gene sequence. While temporal events are the main focus of the discussion of sequential patterns, it can also be extended to the case where the events have spatial ordering.

Sequence Database	Sequence	Element (Transaction)	Event (Item)
Customer	Purchase history of a given customer	A set of items bought by a customer at time t	Books, diary products, CDs, etc
Web Data	Browsing activity of a particular Web visitor	The collection of files viewed by a Web visitor after a single mouse click	Home page, index page, contact info, etc
Event data	History of events generated by a given sensor	Events triggered by a sensor at time t	Types of alarms generated by sensors
Genome sequences	DNA sequence of a particular species	An element of the DNA sequence	Bases A,T,G,C

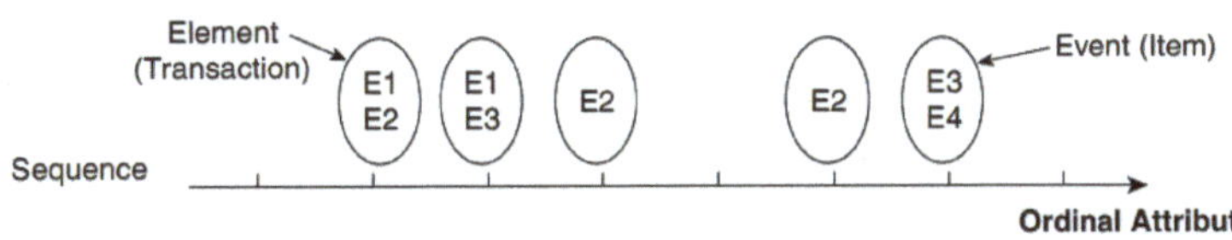

Figure 7.3. *Examples of elements and events in sequence data sets.*

Source: Pang-Ning Tan, Michael Steinbach, Vipin Kumar; Introduction to Data Mining; ISBN 10: 1-292-02615-4.

- **Subsequences:** A sequence t is a subsequence of another sequence s if each ordered element in t is a subset of an ordered element in s. Formally, the sequence t = $\langle t_1 t_2 \ldots t_m \rangle$ is a subsequence of $s = \langle s_1 s_2 \ldots s_n \rangle$ if there exist integers $1 \le j_1 < j_2 < \cdots < j_m \le n$ such that $t_1 \subseteq s_{j1}$, $t_2 \subseteq s_{j2}, \ldots, tm \subseteq s_{jm}$. If t is a subsequence of s, then we say that t is contained in s. The following table gives examples illustrating the idea of subsequences for various sequences.

Sequence, *s*	Sequence, *t*	Is *t* a subsequence of *s*?
<{2,4} {3,5,6} {8} >	< {2} {3,6} {8} >	Yes
<{2,4} {3,5,6} {8} >	< {2} {8} >	Yes
<{1,2} {3,4} >	< {1} {2} >	No
<{2,4} {2,4} {2,5} >	< {2} {4} >	Yes

7.2.2. Sequential Pattern Discovery

Consider a data set D that consists of one or more data sequences. A data sequence is defined as a list of events corresponding to a single data object in a specific order. For instance, in the data set illustrated in Figure 7.2, there are three data sequences representing objects A, B, and C, respectively. The support of a sequence s is the fraction of all data sequences that contain s. If the support for s is greater than or equal to a user-specified threshold minsup, then s is declared to be a sequential pattern (or frequent sequence).

Definition (Sequential Pattern Discovery). Given a sequence data set D and a user-specified minimum support threshold minsup, the task of sequential pattern discovery is to find all sequences with support ≥ minsup.

Figure 7.4 illustrates an example of a data set that contains five data sequences. The support for the sequence < {1}{2} > is equal to 80% because it occurs in four of the five data sequences (every object except for D). Assuming that the minimum support threshold is 50%, any sequence that appears in at least three data sequences is considered to be a sequential pattern. Examples of sequential patterns extracted from the given data set include < {1}{2} >, < {1, 2} >, <{2, 3}>, < {1, 2}{2, 3}>, etc.

Object	Timestamp	Events
A	1	1, 2, 4
A	2	2, 3
A	3	5
B	1	1, 2
B	2	2, 3, 4
C	1	1, 2
C	2	2, 3, 4
C	3	2, 4, 5
D	1	2
D	2	3, 4
D	3	4, 5
E	1	1, 3
E	2	2, 4, 5

Minsup = 50%

Examples of Sequential Patterns:

<{1,2}>	s=60%
<{2,3}>	s=60%
<{2,4}>	s=80%
<{3} {5}>	s=80%
<{1} {2}>	s=80%
<{2} {2}>	s=60%
<{1} {2,3}>	s=60%
<{2} {2,3}>	s=60%
<{1,2} {2,3}>	s=60%

Figure 7.4. *Sequential patterns derived from a data set that contains five data sequences.*

Source: Pang-Ning Tan, Michael Steinbach, Vipin Kumar; Introduction to Data Mining; ISBN 10: 1-292-02615-4.

Sequential pattern discovery is a computationally challenging task because there are exponentially many sequences contained in a given data sequence. For example, the data sequence <{a,b} {c,d,e} {f} {g,h,i}> contains sequences such as <{a} {c,d} {f} {g}>, <{c,d,e}>, <{b} {g}>, etc. It can be easily shown that the total number of k-sequences present in a data sequence with n events is $\binom{n}{k}$. A data sequence with nine events therefore contains distinct sequences.

$$\binom{9}{1} + \binom{9}{2} + \ldots + \binom{9}{9} = 2^9 - 1 = 511$$

A brute-force approach for generating sequential patterns is to enumerate all possible sequences and count their respective supports. Given a collection of n events, candidate 1-sequences are generated first, followed by candidate 2-sequences, candidate 3-sequences, and so on:

$$\begin{array}{ll}
\text{1-sequences:} & < i_1 >, < i_2 >, \ldots, < i_n > \\
\text{2-sequences:} & < \{i_1, i_2\} >, < \{i_1, i_3\} >, \ldots, < \{i_{n-1}, i_n\} >, \\
 & < \{i_1\}\{i_1\} >, < \{i_1\}\{i_2\} >, \ldots, < \{i_{n-1}\}\{i_n\} > \\
\text{3-sequences:} & < \{i_1, i_2, i_3\} >, < \{i_1, i_2, i_4\} >, \ldots, < \{i_1, i_2\}\{i_1\} >, \ldots, \\
 & < \{i_1\}\{i_1, i_2\} >, \ldots, < \{i_1\}\{i_1\}\{i_1\} >, \ldots, < \{i_n\}\{i_n\}\{i_n\} >
\end{array}$$

Notice that the number of candidate sequences is substantially larger than the number of candidate itemsets. There are two reasons for the additional number of candidates:

1. An item can appear at most once in an itemset, but an event can appear more than once in a sequence. Given a pair of items, i_1 and i_2, only one candidate 2-itemset, $\{i_1, i_2\}$, can be generated. On the other hand, there are many candidate 2-sequences, such as $< \{i_1, i_2\} >$, $< \{i_1\}\{i_2\} >$, $< \{i_2\}\{i_1\} >$, and $< \{i_1, i_1\} >$, that can be generated.
2. Order matters in sequences, but not for itemsets. For example, {1, 2} and {2, 1} refers to the same itemset, whereas $< \{i_1\}\{i_2\} >$ and $< \{i_2\}\{i_1\} >$ correspond to different sequences, and thus must be generated separately.

The Apriori principle holds for sequential data because any data sequence that contains a particular k-sequence must also contain all of its (k – 1)- subsequences. An Apriori-like algorithm can be developed to extract sequential patterns from a sequence data set. The basic structure of the algorithm is shown in Algorithm 7.1.

- **Candidate Generation:** A candidate k-sequence is created by merging two frequent (k –1)-sequences. Remember that the classic Apriori algorithm only combines two frequent k-itemsets if their first k – 1 items are the same in order to prevent producing duplicate candidates. Sequences can be approached in a manner similar to this. The following process outlines the requirements for combining sequences.

Algorithm 7.1. Apriori-Like Algorithm for Sequential Pattern Discovery

$k = 1$.
$F_k = \{\, i \mid i \in I \wedge \frac{\sigma(\{i\})}{N} \geq minsup\}$. {Find all frequent 1-subsequences.}
repeat
  $k = k + 1$.
  $C_k = \text{apriori-gen}(F_{k-1})$. {Generate candidate k-subsequences.}
  for each data sequence $t \in T$ **do**
    $C_t = \text{subsequence}(C_k, t)$. {Identify all candidates contained in t.}
    for each candidate k-subsequence $c \in C_t$ **do**
      $\sigma(c) = \sigma(c) + 1$. {Increment the support count.}
    end for
  end for
  $F_k = \{\, c \mid c \in C_k \wedge \frac{\sigma(c)}{N} \geq minsup\}$. {Extract the frequent k-subsequences.}
until $F_k = \emptyset$
Answer $= \bigcup F_k$.

Figure 7.5 illustrates examples of candidate 4-sequences obtained by merging pairs of frequent 3-sequences. The first candidate ⟨{1}{2}{3}{4}⟩ is obtained by merging ⟨(1)(2)(3)⟩ with ⟨(2)(3)(4)⟩. Since events 3 and 4 belong to different elements of the second sequence, they also belong to separate elements in the merged sequence. On the other hand, merging ⟨{1}{5}{3}⟩ with ⟨{5}{3, 4}⟩ produces the candidate 4-sequence ⟨{1}{5}{3, 4}⟩. In this case, since events 3 and 4 belong to the same element of the second sequence, they are combined into the same element in the merged sequence. Finally, the sequences ⟨{1}{2}{3}⟩ and ⟨{1}{2, 5}⟩ do not have to be merged because removing the first event from the first sequence does not give the same subsequence as removing the last event from the second sequence. Although ⟨{1}{2, 5}{3}⟩ is a viable candidate, it is generated by merging a different pair of sequences, ⟨{1}{2, 5}⟩ and ⟨{2, 5}{3}⟩. This example shows that the sequence merging procedure is complete; i.e., it will not miss any viable candidate, while at the same time, it avoids generating duplicate candidate sequences.

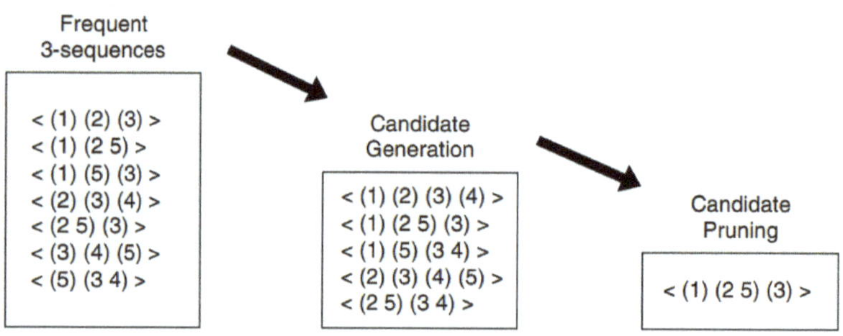

Figure 7.5. *Example of the candidate generation and pruning steps of a sequential pattern mining algorithm.*

Source: Pang-Ning Tan, Michael Steinbach, Vipin Kumar; Introduction to Data Mining; ISBN 10: 1–292–02615–4.

- **Candidate Pruning:** A candidate k-sequence is pruned if at least one of its (k–1)-sequences is infrequent. For example, suppose ⟨{1}{2}{3}{4}⟩ is a candidate 4-sequence. We need to check whether ⟨{1}{2}{4}⟩ and ⟨{1}{3}{4}⟩ are frequent

3-sequences. Since both are infrequent, the candidate ⟨{1}{2}{3}{4} can be eliminated. Readers should be able to verify that the only candidate 4-sequence that survives the candidate pruning step in Figure 7.5 is ⟨{1}{2 5}{3}⟩.

- **Support Counting:** The algorithm will count every candidate k-sequence that is a part of a specific data sequence during the support counting phase. These candidates will receive more support. The algorithm may count the candidates' supports, find the frequently occurring k-sequences, and then eliminate any candidates whose support counts are below the minsup threshold.

7.2.3. Timing Constraints

A sequential pattern formulation with timing constraints applied to pattern elements and events is presented in this section. The courses that two students who enrolled in a data mining class took can be seen as illustrative of why timing constraints are necessary.

Student A: ⟨ {Statistics} {Database Systems} {Data Mining} ⟩.
Student B: ⟨ {Database Systems} {Statistics} {Data Mining} ⟩.

The sequential pattern of interest is ⟨{Statistics, Database Systems} {Data Mining} ⟩, which means that students who are enrolled in the data mining class must have previously taken a course in statistics and database systems. Clearly, the pattern is supported by both students even though they do not take statistics and database systems at the same time. In contrast, a student who took a statistics course 10 years earlier should not be considered as supporting the pattern because the time gap between the courses is too long.

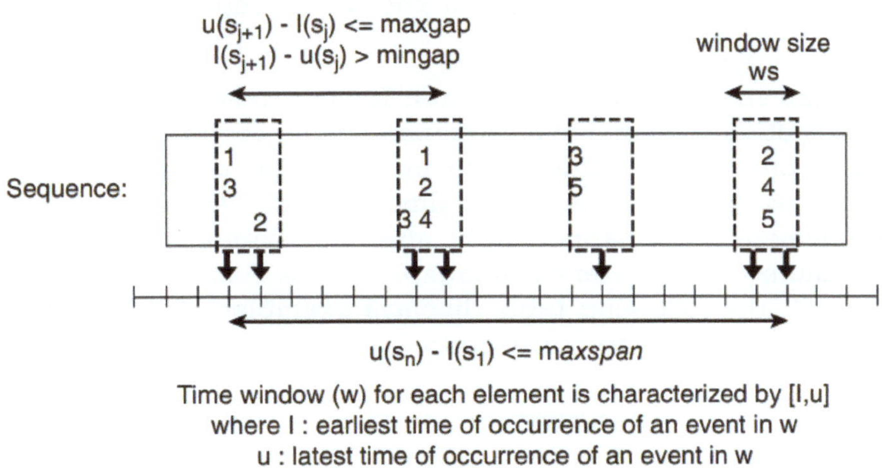

Figure 7.6. *Timing constraints of a sequential pattern.*

Source: https://www.ceom.ou.edu/media/docs/upload/Pang-Ning_Tan_Michael_Steinbach_Vipin_Kumar_-_Introduction_to_Data_Mining-Pe_NRDK4fi.pdf.

Figure 7.6 illustrates some of the timing constraints that can be imposed on a pattern. The definition of these constraints and the impact they have on sequential pattern discovery algorithms will be discussed in the next sections. Note that each element of the sequential pattern is associated with a time window [l, u], where l is the earliest occurrence of an event within the time window and u is the latest occurrence of an event within the time window.

- **The Maxspan Constraint:** The maxspan constraint specifies the maximum allowed time difference between the latest and the earliest occurrences of events in the entire sequence. For example, suppose the following data sequences contain events that occur at consecutive time stamps (1, 2, 3,...). Assuming that maxspan = 3, the following table contains sequential patterns that are supported and not supported by a given data sequence.

Data Sequence, s	Sequential Pattern, t	Does s support t?
<{1,3} {3,4} {4} {5} {6,7} {8} >	< {3} {4} >	Yes
<{1,3} {3,4} {4} {5} {6,7} {8} >	< {3} {6} >	Yes
<{1,3} {3,4} {4} {5} {6,7} {8} >	< {1,3} {6} >	No

In general, the likelihood of finding a pattern in a data sequence increases with maxspan length. However, because a longer maxspan increases the likelihood that two unrelated events are temporally related, it can also capture spurious patterns. Furthermore, the pattern might include already-outdated events.

Sequential pattern discovery algorithms' support counting step is impacted by the maxspan constraint. As demonstrated by the examples above, applying the maxspan constraint causes some data sequences to stop supporting a candidate pattern. Some patterns may have overestimated support counts if we just use Algorithm 7.1. The algorithm needs to be changed to ignore situations in which the time between an event's first and last occurrence in a given pattern is longer than maxspan in order to avoid this issue.

- **The Mingap and Maxgap Constraints:** To limit the amount of time that separates two consecutive elements of a sequence, timing constraints can also be specified. Events in one element must take place within a week of the events in the preceding element if the maximum time difference (maxgap) is one week. Events in one element must happen right after the events in the previous element if the minimum time difference (mingap) is zero. Assuming that maxgap = 3 and mingap = 1, the following table displays examples of patterns that pass or fail the maxgap and mingap constraints.

Data Sequence, s	Sequential Pattern, t	*maxgap*	*mingap*
<{1,3} {3,4} {4} {5} {6,7} {8} >	< {3} {6} >	Pass	Pass
<{1,3} {3,4} {4} {5} {6,7} {8} >	< {6} {8} >	Pass	Fail
<{1,3} {3,4} {4} {5} {6,7} {8} >	< {1,3} {6} >	Fail	Pass
<{1,3} {3,4} {4} {5} {6,7} {8} >	< {1} {3} {8} >	Fail	Fail

Similar to maxspan, the presence of mingap and maxgap constraints will cause some data sequences to no longer support a candidate pattern, which will have an impact on the support counting step of sequential pattern discovery algorithms. To make sure that the timing restrictions are respected when counting a pattern's support, these algorithms must be adjusted. If not, some rare sequences might be incorrectly identified as common patterns.

A side effect of using the maxgap constraint is that the Apriori principle might be violated. To illustrate this, consider the data set shown in Figure 7.4. Without mingap or maxgap constraints, the support for ⟨{2}{5}⟩ and ⟨{2}{3}{5}⟩ are both equal to 60%. However, if mingap = 0 and maxgap = 1, then the support for ⟨{2}{5}⟩ reduces to 40%, while the support for ⟨{2}{3}{5}⟩ is still 60%. In other words, support has increased when the number of events in a sequence increases—which contradicts the Apriori principle. The violation occurs because the object D does not support the pattern ⟨{2}{5}⟩ since the time gap between events 2 and 5 is greater than maxgap. This problem can be avoided by using the concept of a contiguous subsequence.

Definition (Contiguous Subsequence). A sequence s is a contiguous subsequence of w = ⟨$e_1e_2 \ldots e_k$⟩ if any one of the following conditions hold:

1. s is obtained from w after deleting an event from either e_1 or e_k,
2. s is obtained from w after deleting an event from any element $e_i \in$ w that contains at least two events, or
3. s is a contiguous subsequence of t and t is a contiguous subsequence of w.

The following examples illustrate the concept of a contiguous subsequence:

Data Sequence, s	Sequential Pattern, t	Is t a contiguous subsequence of s?
<{1} {2,3}>	< {1} {2} >	Yes
<{1,2} {2} {3} >	< {1} {2} >	Yes
<{3,4} {1,2} {2,3} {4} >	< {1} {2} >	Yes
<{1} {3} {2} >	< {1} {2} >	No
<{1,2} {1} {3} {2} >	< {1} {2} >	No

Using the concept of contiguous subsequences, the Apriori principle can be modified to handle maxgap constraints in the following way.

Definition (Modified Apriori Principle). If a k-sequence is frequent, then all of its contiguous k – 1-subsequences must also be frequent.

The modified Apriori principle can be applied to the sequential pattern discovery algorithm with minor modifications. During candidate pruning, not all k-sequences need to be verified since some of them may violate the maxgap constraint. For example, if maxgap = 1, it is not necessary to check whether the subsequence ⟨{1}{2, 3}{5}⟩ of the candidate ⟨{1}{2, 3}{4}{5}⟩ is frequent since the time difference between elements {2, 3} and {5} is greater than one time unit. Instead, only the contiguous subsequences of ⟨{1}{2, 3}{4}{5}⟩ need to be examined. These subsequences include ⟨{1}{2, 3}{4}⟩, ⟨{2, 3}{4}{5}⟩, ⟨{1}{2}{4}{5}⟩, and ⟨{1}{3}{4}{5}⟩.

- **The Window Size Constraint:** Finally, events within an element s_j do not have to occur at the same time. A window size threshold (ws) can be defined to specify the maximum allowed time difference between the latest and earliest occurrences of events in any element of a sequential pattern. A window size of 0 means all events in the same element of a pattern must occur simultaneously.

  The following example uses ws = 2 to determine whether a data sequence supports a given sequence (assuming mingap = 0, maxgap = 3, and maxspan = ∞).

Data Sequence, *s*	Sequential Pattern, *t*	Does *s* support *t*?
<{1,3} {3,4} {4} {5} {6,7} {8} >	< {3,4} {5} >	Yes
<{1,3} {3,4} {4} {5} {6,7} {8} >	< {4,6} {8} >	Yes
<{1,3} {3,4} {4} {5} {6,7} {8} >	< {3, 4, 6} {8} >	No
<{1,3} {3,4} {4} {5} {6,7} {8} >	< {1,3,4} {6,7,8} >	No

The pattern {1,3,4} {6,7,8} in the last example satisfies the window size constraint, but it violates the maxgap constraint because there is a maximum time difference of 5 units between events in the two elements. Sequential pattern discovery algorithms' support counting step is also impacted by the window size constraint. The support counts for some of the candidate patterns may be underestimated if Algorithm 7.1 is used without enforcing the window size constraint, which could lead to the loss of some interesting patterns.

7.2.4. Alternative Counting Schemes

There are several methods available for counting the support of a candidate k-sequence from a database of sequences. For illustrative purposes, consider the problem of counting the support for sequence ⟨{p}{q}⟩, as shown in Figure 7.7. Assume that ws = 0, mingap = 0, maxgap = 1, and maxspan = 2.

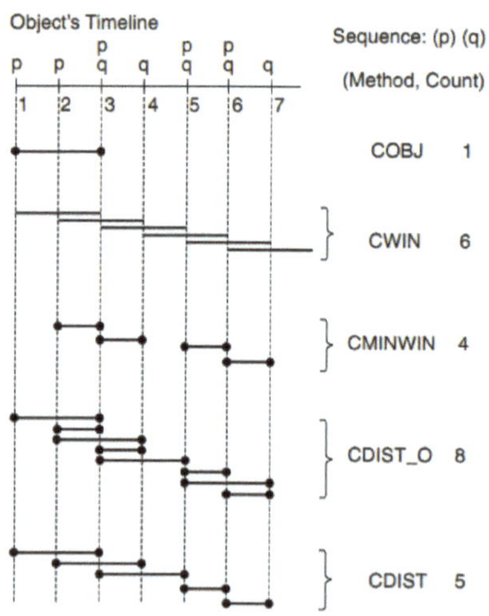

Figure 7.7. *Comparing different support counting methods.*

Source: https://www.ceom.ou.edu/media/docs/upload/Pang-Ning_Tan_Michael_Steinbach_Vipin_Kumar_-_Introduction_to_Data_Mining-Pe_NRDK4fi.pdf.

- **COBJ: One Occurrence Per Object:** This method looks for at least one occurrence of a given sequence in an object's timeline. In Figure 7.7, even though the sequence ⟨(p) (q)⟩ appears several times in the object's timeline, it is counted only once— with p occurring at t = 1 and q occuring at t = 3.
- **CWIN: One Occurrence Per Sliding Window:** In this approach, a sliding time window of fixed length (maxspan) is moved across an object's timeline, one unit at a time. The support count is incremented each time the sequence is encountered in the sliding window. In Figure 7.7, the sequence ⟨{p}{q}⟩ is observed 6 times using this method.
- CMINWIN: Number of minimal windows of occurrence.

  A minimal window of occurrence is the smallest window in which the sequence occurs given the timing constraints. In other words, a minimal window is the time interval such that the sequence occurs in that time interval, but it does not occur in any of the proper subintervals of it. This definition can be considered as a restrictive version of CWIN, because its effect is to shrink and collapse some of the windows that are counted by CWIN. For example, sequence {p}{q} has four minimal window occurrences: (1) the pair (p: t = 2, q: t = 3), (2) the pair (p: t = 3, q: t = 4), (3) the pair (p: t = 5, q: t = 6), and (4) the pair (p: t = 6, q: t = 7). The occurrence of event p at t = 1 and event q at t = 3 is not a minimal window occurrence because it contains a smaller window with (p: t = 2, q: t = 3), which is indeed a minimal window of occurrence.
- CDIST O: Distinct occurrences with possibility of event-timestamp overlap.

  A distinct occurrence of a sequence is defined to be the set of event-timestamp pairs such that there has to be at least one new event-timestamp pair that is different from a previously counted occurrence. Counting all such distinct occurrences results in the CDIST O method. If the occurrence time of events p and q is denoted as a tuple (t(p), t(q)), then this method yields eight distinct occurrences of sequence ⟨{p}{q}⟩ at times (1,3), (2,3), (2,4), (3,4), (3,5), (5,6), (5,7), and (6,7).
- CDIST: Distinct occurrences with no event-timestamp overlap allowed. In CDIST O above, two occurrences of a sequence were allowed to have overlapping event-timestamp pairs, e.g., the overlap between (1,3) and (2,3). In the CDIST method, no overlap is allowed. Effectively, when an event-timestamp pair is considered for counting, it is marked as used and is never used again for subsequent counting of the same sequence. As an example, there are five distinct, non-overlapping occurrences of the sequence ⟨{p}{q}⟩ in the diagram shown in Figure 7.7. These occurrences happen at times (1,3), (2,4), (3,5), (5,6), and (6,7). Observe that these occurrences are subsets of the occurrences observed in CDIST O.

One final point regarding the counting methods is the need to determine the baseline for computing the support measure. For frequent itemset mining, the baseline is given by the total number of transactions. For sequential pattern mining, the baseline depends on the counting method used. For the COBJ method, the total number of objects in the input data can be used as the baseline. For the CWIN and CMINWIN methods, the baseline is given by the sum of the number of time windows possible in all objects. For methods such as CDIST and CDIST O, the baseline is given by the sum of the number of distinct timestamps present in the input data of each object.

7.3. SUBGRAPH PATTERNS

Subgraph patterns in data mining involve finding significant and repeating substructures in graph data. These patterns aid in comprehending intricate relationships and structures within the data. Instances include chemical compounds, 3-D protein configurations, network layouts, and tree structured XML files. These entities can be represented using a graph model, as detailed in Table 7.3.

Table 7.3. Graph Representation of Entities in Various Application Domains

Application	Graphs	Vertices	Edges
Web mining	Web browsing patterns	Web pages	Hyperlink between pages
Computational chemistry	Structure of chemical compounds	Atoms or ions	Bond between atoms or ions
Network computing	Computer networks	Computers and servers	Interconnection between machines
Semantic Web	Collection of XML documents	XML elements	Parent-child relationship between elements
Bioinformatics	Protein structures	Amino acids	Contact residue

Source: Pang-Ning Tan, Michael Steinbach, Vipin Kumar; Introduction to Data Mining; ISBN 10: 1–292–02615–4.

A useful data mining task to perform on this type of data is to derive a set of common substructures among the collection of graphs. Such a task is known as frequent subgraph mining. A potential application of frequent subgraph mining can be seen in the context of computational chemistry. Each year, new chemical compounds are designed for the development of pharmaceutical drugs, pesticides, fertilizers, etc. Although the structure of a compound is known to play a major role in determining its chemical properties, it is difficult to establish their exact relationship. Frequent subgraph mining can aid this undertaking by identifying the substructures commonly associated with certain properties of known compounds. Such information can help scientists to develop new chemical compounds that have certain desired properties.

The section begins with a review of some of the basic graph-related concepts and definitions. The frequent subgraph mining problem is then introduced, followed by a description of how the traditional Apriori algorithm can be extended to discover such patterns.

7.3.1. Graphs and Subgraphs

A graph is a data structure that can be used to represent the relationships among a set of entities. Mathematically, a graph is composed of a vertex set V and a set of edges E connecting between pairs of vertices. Each edge is denoted by a vertex pair (v_i, v_j), where $v_i, v_j \in V$. A label $l(v_i)$ can be assigned to each vertex vi representing the name of an entity. Similarly each edge (v_i, v_j) can also be associated with a label $l(v_i, v_j)$ describing the relationship between a pair of entities. Table 7.3 shows the vertices and edges associated with different types of graphs. For example, in a Web graph, the vertices correspond to Web pages and the edges represent the hyperlinks between Web pages.

Definition (Subgraph). A graph G' = (V', E') is a subgraph of another graph G' = (V,E) if its vertex set V' is a subset of V and its edge set E' is a subset of E. The subgraph relationship is denoted as G' ⊆S G.

Figure 7.8 shows a graph that contains 6 vertices and 11 edges along with one of its possible subgraphs. The subgraph, which is shown in Figure 7.8(b), contains only 4 of the 6 vertices and 4 of the 11 edges in the original graph.

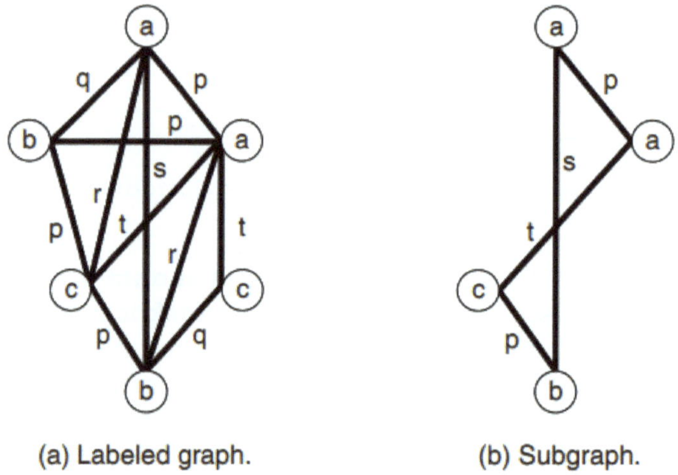

Figure 7.8. *Example of a subgraph.*

Source: Pang-Ning Tan, Michael Steinbach, Vipin Kumar; Introduction to Data Mining; ISBN 10: 1–292–02615–4.

Definition (Support). Given a collection of graphs G, the support for a subgraph g is defined as the fraction of all graphs that contain g as its subgraph, i.e., (Figure 7.9);

$$s(g) = \frac{|\{G_i | g \subseteq_S G_i,\ G_i \in \mathcal{G}\}|}{|\mathcal{G}|}.$$

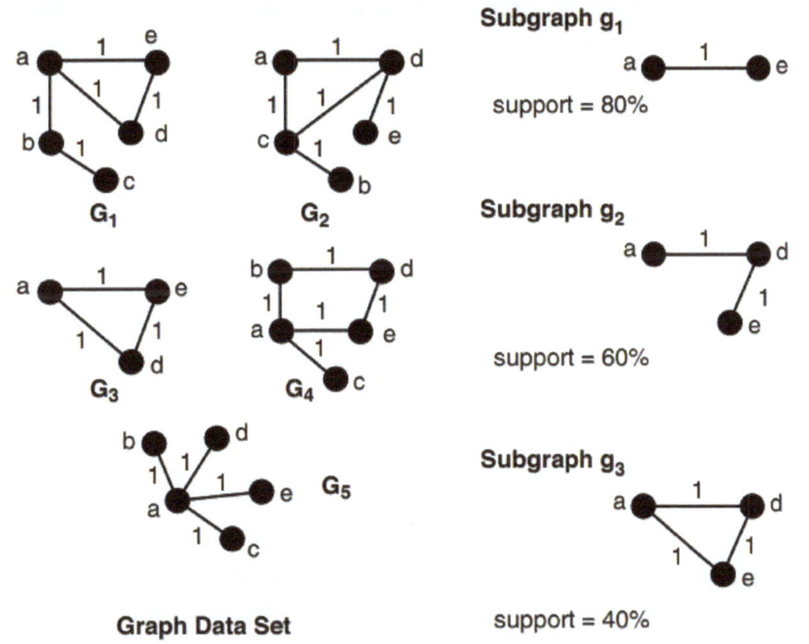

Figure 7.9. *Computing the support of a subgraph from a set of graphs.*

Source: https://www.ceom.ou.edu/media/docs/upload/Pang-Ning_Tan_Michael_Steinbach_Vipin_Kumar_-_Introduction_to_Data_Mining-Pe_NRDK4fi.pdf.

7.3.2. Frequent Subgraph Mining

Definition (Frequent Subgraph Mining). Given a set of graphs G and a support threshold, minsup, the goal of frequent subgraph mining is to find all subgraphs g such that s(g) ≥ minsup.

While this formulation is generally applicable to any type of graph, the discussion presented in this chapter focuses primarily on undirected, connected graphs. The definitions of these graphs are given below:

1. A graph is connected if there exists a path between every pair of vertices in the graph, in which a path is a sequence of vertices $< v_1 v_2 .. v_k >$ such that there is an edge connecting between every pair of adjacent vertices (v_i, v_{i+1}) in the sequence.
2. A graph is undirected if it contains only undirected edges. An edge (v_i, v_j) is undirected if it is indistinguishable from (v_j, v_i).

Mining frequent subgraphs is a computationally expensive task because of the exponential scale of the search space. To illustrate the complexity of this task, consider a data set that contains d entities. In frequent itemset mining, each entity is an item and the size of the search space to be explored is 2^d, which is the number of candidate itemsets that can be generated. In frequent subgraph mining, each entity is a vertex and can have up to d −1 edges to other vertices. Assuming that the vertex labels are unique, the total number of subgraphs is;

$$\sum_{i=1}^{d} \binom{d}{i} \times 2^{i(i-1)/2},$$

Where; $\binom{d}{i}$ is the number of ways to choose i vertices to form a subgraph and $2^{i(i-1)/2}$ is the maximum number of edges between vertices. Table 7.4 compares the number of itemsets and subgraphs for different values of d.

Table 7.4. A Comparison Between Number of Itemsets and Subgraphs for Different Dimensionality, d.

Number of entities, d	1	2	3	4	5	6	7	8
Number of itemsets	2	4	8	16	32	64	128	256
Number of subgraphs	2	5	18	113	1,450	40,069	2,350,602	28,619,2513

The number of candidate subgraphs is actually much smaller because the numbers given in Table 7.4 include subgraphs that are disconnected. Disconnected subgraphs are usually ignored because they are not as interesting as connected subgraphs.

A brute-force method for doing this is to generate all connected subgraphs as candidates and count their respective supports. For example, consider the graphs shown in Figure 7.10(a). Assuming that the vertex labels are chosen from the set {a, b} and the edge labels are chosen from the set {p, q}, the list of connected subgraphs with one vertex up to three vertices is shown in Figure 7.10(b).

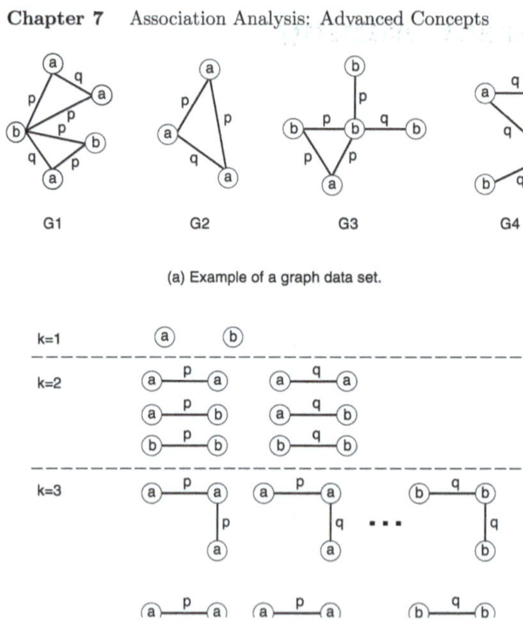

Figure 7.10. *Brute-force method for mining frequent subgraphs.*

Source: https://www.ceom.ou.edu/media/docs/upload/Pang-Ning_Tan_Michael_Steinbach_Vipin_Kumar_-_Introduction_to_Data_Mining-Pe_NRDK4fi.pdf.

The number of candidate subgraphs is considerably larger than the number of candidate itemsets in traditional association rule mining for the following reasons:

1. An item can appear at most once in an itemset, whereas a vertex label can appear more than once in a graph.
2. The same pair of vertex labels can have multiple choices of edge labels.

Given the large number of candidate subgraphs, a brute-force method may break down even for moderately sized graphs.

7.3.3. Apriori-like Method

7.3.3.1. Data Transformation

One possible approach is to transform each graph into a transaction-like format so that existing algorithms such as Apriori can be applied. Figure 7.11 illustrates how to transform a collection of graphs into its equivalent market basket representation. In this representation, each combination of edge label l(e) with its corresponding vertex labels, $(l(v_i), l(v_j))$, is mapped into an "item." The width of the "transaction" is given by the number of edges in the graph. Despite its simplicity, this approach works only if every edge in a graph has a unique combination of vertex and edge labels. Otherwise, such graphs cannot be accurately modeled using this representation.

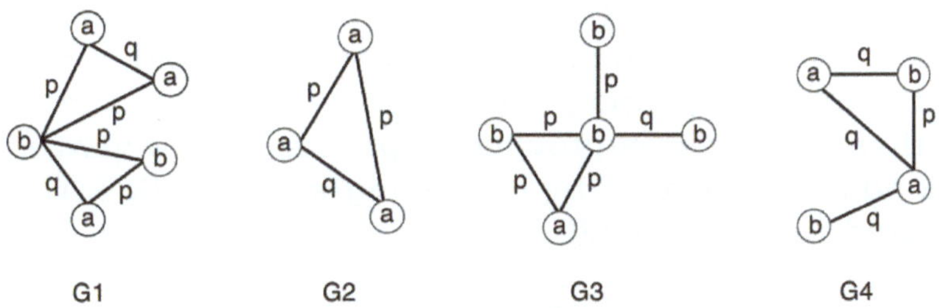

	(a,b,p)	(a,b,q)	(a,b,r)	(b,c,p)	(b,c,q)	(b,c,r)	...	(d,e,r)
G1	1	0	0	0	0	1	...	0
G2	1	0	0	0	0	0	...	0
G3	0	0	1	1	0	0	...	0
G4	0	0	0	0	0	0	...	0

Figure 7.11. *Mapping a collection of graph structures into market basket transactions.*

Source: https://www.ceom.ou.edu/media/docs/upload/Pang-Ning_Tan_Michael_Steinbach_Vipin_Kumar_-_Introduction_to_Data_Mining-Pe_NRDK4fi.pdf.

7.3.3.2. General Structure of the Frequent Subgraph Mining Algorithm

An Apriori-like algorithm for mining frequent subgraphs consists of the following steps:

1. Candidate generation, which is the process of merging pairs of frequent (k – 1)-subgraphs to obtain a candidate k-subgraph.

2. Candidate pruning, which is the process of discarding all candidate k-subgraphs that contain infrequent (k – 1)-subgraphs.
3. Support counting, which is the process of counting the number of graphs in G that contain each candidate.
4. Candidate elimination, which discards all candidate subgraphs whose support counts are less than minsup.

7.3.4. Candidate Generation

During candidate generation, a pair of frequent (k – 1)-subgraphs are merged to form a candidate k-subgraph. The first question is how to define k, the size of a subgraph. In the example shown in Figure 7.10, k refers to the number of vertices in the graph. This approach of iteratively expanding a subgraph by adding an extra vertex is known as vertex growing. Alternatively, k may refer to the number of edges in the graph. This approach of adding an extra edge to the existing subgraphs is known as edge growing. To avoid generating duplicate candidates, we may impose an additional condition for merging, that the two (k – 1)-subgraphs must share a common (k–2)-subgraph. The common (k–2)-subgraph is known as their core.

7.3.4.1. Candidate Generation via Vertex Growing

Vertex growing is the process of generating a new candidate by adding a new vertex into an existing frequent subgraph. Before describing this approach, let us first consider the adjacency matrix representation of a graph. Each entry M(i, j) in the matrix contains either the label of the edge connecting between the vertices v_i and v_j, or zero, if there is no edge between them. The vertex-growing approach can be viewed as the process of generating a k × k adjacency matrix by combining a pair of (k – 1) × (k – 1) adjacency matrices, as illustrated in Figure 7.12.

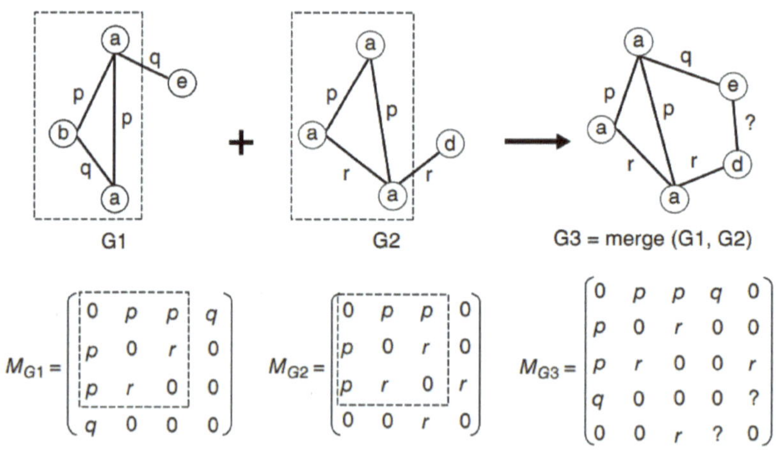

Figure 7.12. *Vertex-growing strategy.*

Source: Pang-Ning Tan, Michael Steinbach, Vipin Kumar; Introduction to Data Mining; ISBN 10: 1–292–02615–4.

G1 and G2 are two graphs whose adjacency matrices are given by M(G1) and M(G2), respectively. The core for the graphs is indicated by dashed lines in the diagram. The procedure for generating candidate subgraphs via vertex growing is presented next.

The resulting graph contains one or two edges more than the original graphs. In Figure 7.12, both G1 and G2 contain four vertices and four edges. After merging, the resulting graph G3 has five vertices. The number of edges in G3 depends on whether the vertices d and e are connected. If d and e are disconnected, then G3 has five edges and the corresponding matrix entry for (d, e) is zero. Otherwise, G3 has six edges and the matrix entry for (d, e) corresponds to the label for the newly created edge. Since the edge label is unknown, we need to consider all possible edge labels for (d, e), thus increasing the number of candidate subgraphs substantially.

7.3.4.2. Candidate Generation via Edge Growing

Edge growing inserts a new edge to an existing frequent subgraph during candidate generation. Unlike vertex growing, the resulting subgraph does not necessarily increase the number of vertices in the original graphs. Figure 7.13 shows two possible candidate subgraphs obtained by merging G1 and G2 via the edge-growing strategy. The first candidate subgraph, G3, has one extra vertex, while the second candidate subgraph, G4, has the same number of vertices as the original graphs. The core for the graphs is indicated by dashed lines in the diagram.

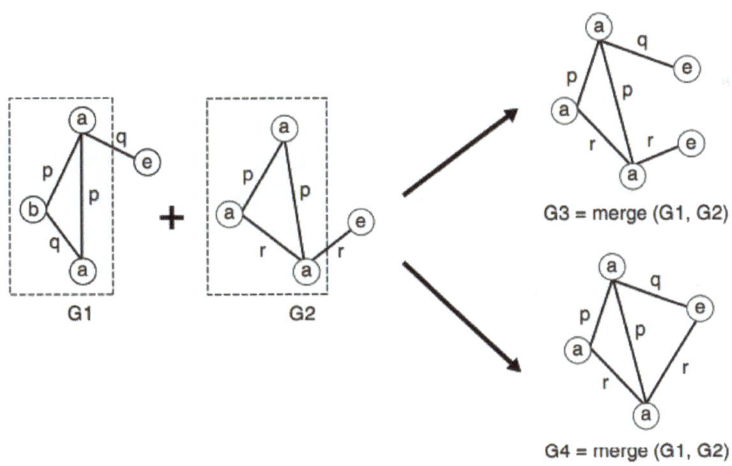

Figure 7.13. *Edge-growing strategy.*

Source: Pang-Ning Tan, Michael Steinbach, Vipin Kumar; Introduction to Data Mining; ISBN 10: 1-292-02615-4.

The graphs to be merged may contain several vertices that are topologically equivalent to each other. To illustrate the concept of topologically equivalent vertices, consider the graphs shown in Figure 7.14. The graph G1 contains four vertices with identical vertex labels, "a." If a new edge is at tached to any one of the four vertices, the resulting graph will look the same. The vertices in G1 are therefore topologically equivalent to each other.

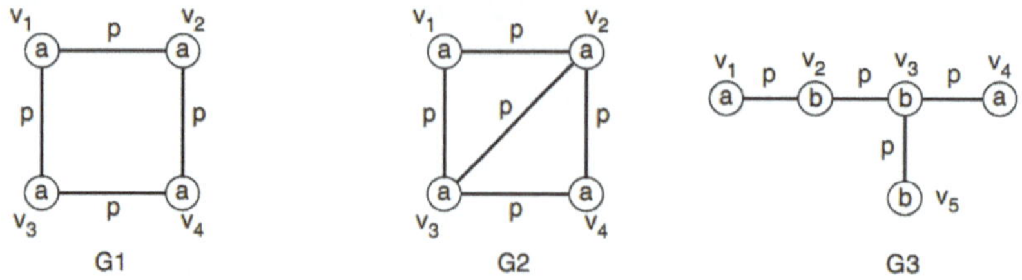

Figure 7.14. *Illustration of topologically equivalent vertices.*

Source: https://www.ceom.ou.edu/media/docs/upload/Pang-Ning_Tan_Michael_Steinbach_Vipin_Kumar_-_Introduction_to_Data_Mining-Pe_NRDK4fi.pdf.

The graph G2 has two pairs of topologically equivalent vertices, v_1 with v_4 and v_2 with v_3, even though the vertex and edge labels are identical. It is easy to see that v_1 is not topologically equivalent to v_2 because the number of edges incident on the vertices is different. Therefore, attaching a new edge to v_1 results in a different graph than attaching the same edge to v_2. Meanwhile, the graph G3 does not have any topologically equivalent vertices. While v_1 and v_4 have the same vertex labels and number of incident edges, attaching a new edge to v_1 results in a different graph than attaching the same edge to v_4.

The notion of topologically equivalent vertices can help us understand why multiple candidate subgraphs can be generated during edge growing. Consider the (k – 1)-subgraphs G1 and G2 shown in Figure 7.15. To simplify the notation, their core, which contains k – 2 common edges between the two graphs, is drawn as a rectangular box. The remaining edge in G1 that is not included in the core is shown as a dangling edge connecting the vertices a and b.

Similarly, the remaining edge in G2 that is not part of the core is shown as a dangling edge connecting vertices c and d. Although the cores for G1 and G2 are identical, a and c may or may not be topologically equivalent to each other. If a and c are topologically equivalent, we denote them as a = c. For vertices outside the core, we denote them as b = d if their labels are identical.

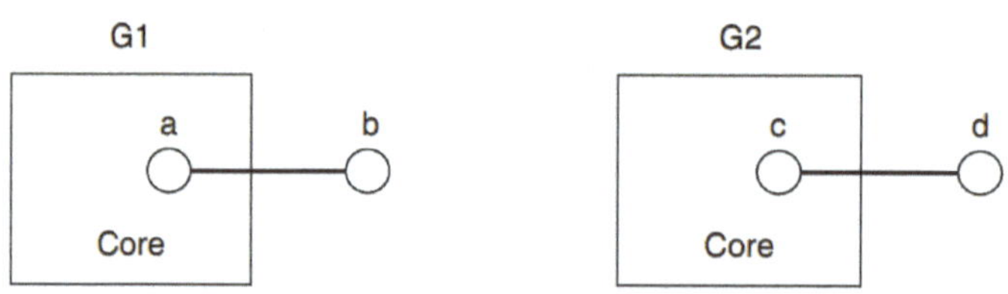

Figure 7.15. *General approach for merging a pair of subgraphs via edge growing.*

Source: https://www.ceom.ou.edu/media/docs/upload/Pang-Ning_Tan_Michael_Steinbach_Vipin_Kumar_-_Introduction_to_Data_Mining-Pe_NRDK4fi.pdf.

The following rule of thumb can be used to determine the candidate subgraphs obtained during candidate generation:

1. If a ≠ c and b ≠ d, then there is only one possible resulting subgraph, as shown in Figure 7.16(a).
2. If a = c but b ≠ d, then there are two possible resulting subgraphs, as shown in Figure 7.16(b).
3. If a ≠ c but b = d, then there are two possible resulting subgraphs, as shown in Figure 7.16(c).
4. If a = c and b = d, then there are three possible resulting subgraphs, as shown in Figure 7.16(d).

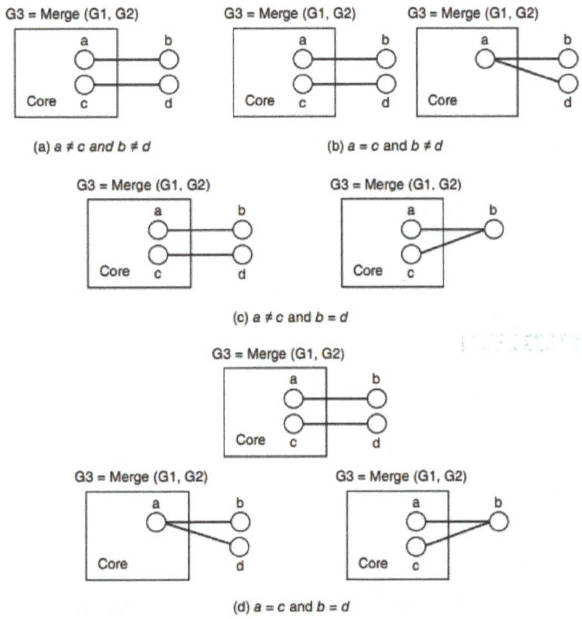

Figure 7.16. *Candidate subgraphs generated via edge growing.*

Source: Pang-Ning Tan, Michael Steinbach, Vipin Kumar; Introduction to Data Mining; ISBN 10: 1-292-02615-4.

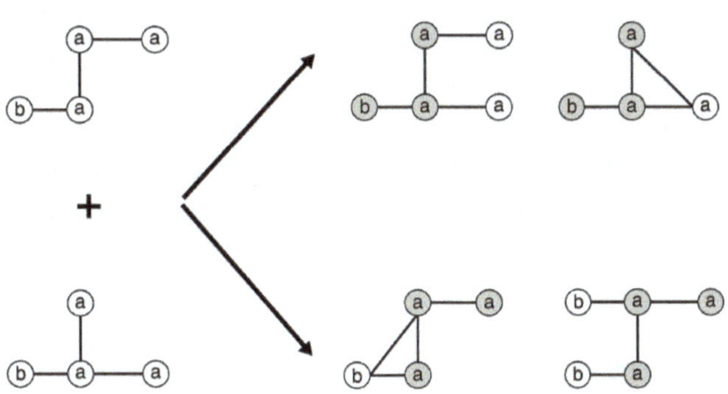

Figure 7.17. *Multiplicity of candidates during candidate generation.*

Source: https://www.ceom.ou.edu/media/docs/upload/Pang-Ning_Tan_Michael_Steinbach_Vipin_Kumar_-_Introduction_to_Data_Mining-Pe_NRDK4fi.pdf.

Multiple candidate subgraphs can also be generated when there is more than one core associated with the pair of (k–1)-subgraphs, as shown in Figure 7.17. The shaded vertices correspond to those vertices whose edges form a core during the merging operation. Each core may lead to a different set of candidate subgraphs. In principle, if a pair of frequent (k – 1)-subgraphs is merged, there can be at most k–2 cores, each of which is obtained by removing an edge from one of the merged graphs. Although the edge-growing procedure can produce multiple candidate subgraphs, the number of candidate subgraphs tends to be smaller than those produced by the vertex-growing strategy.

7.3.5. Candidate Pruning

After the candidate k-subgraphs are generated, the candidates whose (k – 1)-subgraphs are infrequent need to be pruned. The pruning step can be performed by successively removing an edge from the candidate k-subgraph and checking whether the corresponding (k – 1)-subgraph is connected and frequent. If not, the candidate k-subgraph can be discarded.

To check whether the (k – 1)-subgraph is frequent, it should be matched against other frequent (k–1)-subgraphs. Determining whether two graphs are topologically equivalent (or isomorphic) is known as the graph isomorphism problem. To illustrate the difficulty of solving the graph isomorphism problem, consider the two graphs shown in Figure 7.18. Even though both graphs look different, they are actually isomorphic to each other because there is a one-to-one mapping between vertices in both graphs.

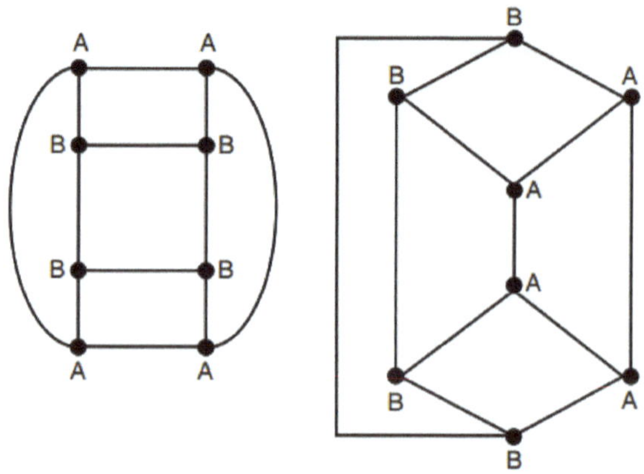

Figure 7.18. *Graph isomorphism.*

Source: https://www.ceom.ou.edu/media/docs/upload/Pang-Ning_Tan_Michael_Steinbach_Vipin_Kumar_-_Introduction_to_Data_Mining-Pe_NRDK4fi.pdf.

7.3.5.1. Handling Graph Isomorphism

A standard approach for handling the graph isomorphism problem is to map each graph into a unique string representation known as its code or canonical label. A canonical label has the property that if two graphs are isomorphic, then their codes must be the same. This property allows us to test for graph isomorphism by comparing the canonical labels of the graphs.

The first step toward constructing the canonical label of a graph is to find an adjacency matrix representation for the graph. Figure 7.19 shows an example of such a matrix for the given graph. In principle, a graph can have more than one adjacency matrix representation because there are multiple ways to order the vertices in the adjacency matrix. In the example shown in Figure 7.19, the first row and column correspond to the vertex a that has 3 edges, the second row and column correspond to another vertex a that has 2 edges, and so on. To derive all the adjacency matrix representations for a graph, we need to consider all possible permutations of rows (and their corresponding columns) of the matrix.

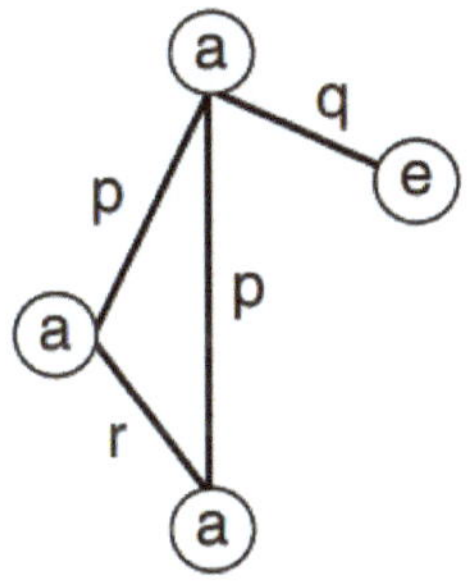

$$M = \begin{pmatrix} 0 & p & p & q \\ p & 0 & r & 0 \\ p & r & 0 & 0 \\ q & 0 & 0 & 0 \end{pmatrix}$$

Figure 7.19. *Adjacency matrix representation of a graph.*

Source: https://www.ceom.ou.edu/media/docs/upload/Pang-Ning_Tan_Michael_Steinbach_Vipin_Kumar_-_Introduction_to_Data_Mining-Pe_NRDK4fi.pdf.

Mathematically, each permutation corresponds to a multiplication of the initial adjacency matrix with a corresponding permutation matrix, as illustrated in the following example.

Example; Consider the following matrix:

$$M = \begin{pmatrix} 1 & 2 & 3 & 4 \\ 5 & 6 & 7 & 8 \\ 9 & 10 & 11 & 12 \\ 13 & 14 & 15 & 16 \end{pmatrix}$$

The following permutation matrix can be used to exchange the first row (and column) with the third row (and column) of M:

$$P_{13} = \begin{pmatrix} 0 & 0 & 1 & 0 \\ 0 & 1 & 0 & 0 \\ 1 & 0 & 0 & 0 \\ 0 & 0 & 0 & 1 \end{pmatrix},$$

Where; P_{13} is obtained by swapping the first and third row of the identity matrix. To exchange the first and third rows (and columns), the permutation matrix is multiplied with M:

$$M' = P_{13}^T \times M \times P_{13} = \begin{pmatrix} 11 & 10 & 9 & 12 \\ 7 & 6 & 5 & 8 \\ 3 & 2 & 1 & 4 \\ 15 & 14 & 13 & 16 \end{pmatrix}.$$

Note that multiplying M from the right with P_{13} exchanges the first and third columns of M, while multiplying M from the left with P_{13}^T exchanges the first and third rows of

M. If all three matrices are multiplied, this will produce a matrix M' whose first and third rows and columns have been swapped.

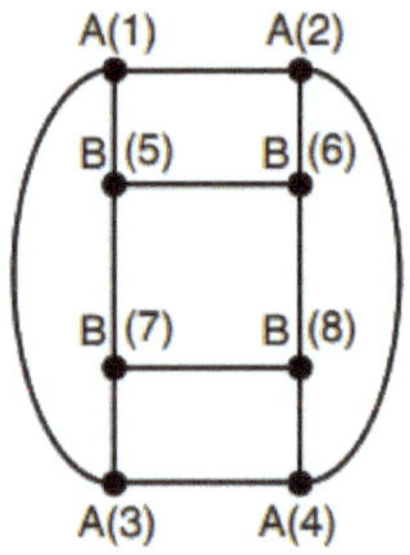

	A(1)	A(2)	A(3)	A(4)	B(5)	B(6)	B(7)	B(8)
A(1)	0	1	1	0	1	0	0	0
A(2)	1	0	0	1	0	1	0	0
A(3)	1	0	0	1	0	0	1	0
A(4)	0	1	1	0	0	0	0	1
B(5)	1	0	0	0	0	1	1	0
B(6)	0	1	0	0	1	0	0	1
B(7)	0	0	1	0	1	0	0	1
B(8)	0	0	0	1	0	1	1	0

Code = 1100111000010010010100001011

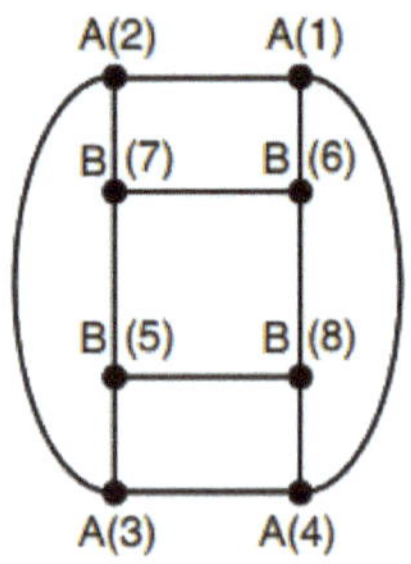

	A(1)	A(2)	A(3)	A(4)	B(5)	B(6)	B(7)	B(8)
A(1)	0	1	0	1	0	1	0	0
A(2)	1	0	1	0	0	0	1	0
A(3)	0	1	0	1	1	0	0	0
A(4)	1	0	1	0	0	0	0	1
B(5)	0	0	1	0	0	0	1	1
B(6)	1	0	0	0	0	0	1	1
B(7)	0	1	0	0	1	1	0	0
B(8)	0	0	0	1	1	1	0	0

Code = 1011010010100000100110001110

Figure 7.20. *String representation of adjacency matrices.*

Source: https://www.ceom.ou.edu/media/docs/upload/Pang-Ning_Tan_Michael_Steinbach_Vipin_Kumar_-_Introduction_to_Data_Mining-Pe_NRDK4fi.pdf.

The second step is to determine the string representation for each adjacency matrix. Since the adjacency matrix is symmetric, it is sufficient to construct the string representation based on the upper triangular part of the matrix. In the example shown in Figure 7.20, the code is obtained by concatenating the entries of the upper triangular matrix in a column-wise fashion. The final step is to compare all the string representations of the graph and choose the one that has the lowest (or highest) lexicographic value.

The preceding approach seems expensive because it requires us to examine all possible adjacency matrices of a graph and to compute each of their string representation in order to find the canonical label. More specifically, there are k! permutations that must be considered for every graph that contains k vertices. Some of the methods developed to reduce the complexity of this task include caching the previously computed canonical label (so that we do not have to recompute it again when performing an isomorphism test on the same graph) and reducing the number of permutations needed to determine the canonical label by incorporating additional information such as vertex labels and the degree of a vertex.

7.3.6. Support Counting

Support counting is also a potentially costly operation because all the candidate subgraphs contained in each graph $G \in \mathcal{G}$ must be determined. One way to speed up this operation is to maintain a list of graph IDs associated with each frequent $(k - 1)$-subgraph. Whenever a new candidate k-subgraph is generated by merging a pair of frequent $(k-1)$-subgraphs, their corresponding lists of graph IDs are intersected. Finally, the subgraph isomorphism tests are performed on the graphs in the intersected list to determine whether they contain a particular candidate subgraph.

ROLE MODEL

IAN H. WITTEN IS A PROMINENT FIGURE IN THE FIELD OF COMPUTER SCIENCE, PARTICULARLY RENOWNED FOR HIS CONTRIBUTIONS TO DATA MINING, MACHINE LEARNING, AND INFORMATION RETRIEVAL.

Early Life and Education

Ian H. Witten was born on February 22, 1947, in Glasgow, Scotland. He completed his undergraduate studies in mathematics at the University of Cambridge, graduating with a Bachelor of Arts degree. He then pursued postgraduate studies at the University of Edinburgh, where he obtained his Ph.D. in computer science in 1976.

Career and Contributions

Ian Witten has had a distinguished career in academia and research. He has held various academic positions, including serving as a professor at the University of Waikato in New Zealand, where he co-founded the renowned Waikato Environment for Knowledge Analysis (WEKA) software for data mining and machine learning.

Witten's research interests span a wide range of topics within computer science, with a particular focus on data mining, machine learning, and information retrieval. He has made significant contributions to the development of algorithms and techniques for text mining, web mining, and structured data analysis. His work has been instrumental in advancing the field of data science and has had practical applications in areas such as healthcare, finance, and social media analysis.

One of Ian Witten's most notable contributions is his co-authorship of the widely acclaimed textbook "Data Mining: Practical Machine Learning Tools and Techniques," along with Eibe Frank and Mark Hall. This book has become a standard reference in the field and is used by students, researchers, and practitioners worldwide.

Achievements and Recognition

Ian Witten's contributions to computer science have been widely recognized. He is a Fellow of the Association for Computing Machinery (ACM) and the Royal Society of New Zealand. He has received numerous awards and honors for his work, including the prestigious Rutherford Medal, New Zealand's highest scientific honor.

Legacy:

Ian Witten's work has had a profound impact on the field of computer science, particularly in the areas of data mining and machine learning. His research, publications, and software tools have helped shape the way data is analyzed, interpreted, and utilized in various domains. His commitment to advancing the field and sharing knowledge through teaching and writing has inspired countless students and researchers around the world.

CLASS ACTIVITY

SEQUENTIAL PATTERNS

To understand and identify sequential patterns in data using sequential pattern mining techniques.

Materials Needed:

- Computer with internet access
- Spreadsheet software (e.g., Microsoft Excel, Google Sheets)
- Access to sequential pattern mining tools (e.g., Python with libraries like pandas and mlxtend)

SUMMARY

- Association analysis aims to discover rules that highlight the probability of the occurrence of an item based on the presence of other items. This is especially useful in market basket analysis, where understanding the products often bought together can inform strategic business decisions such as cross-selling, promotions, and inventory management.
- Market basket data often contains temporal information about when an item was purchased by customers. Such information can be used to piece together the sequence of transactions made by a customer over a certain period of time.
- The maxspan constraint affects the support counting step of sequential pattern discovery algorithms. As shown in the preceding examples, some data sequences no longer support a candidate pattern when the maxspan constraint is imposed.
- Timing constraints can also be specified to restrict the time difference between two consecutive elements of a sequence. If the maximum time difference (maxgap) is one week, then events in one element must occur within a week's time of the events occurring in the previous element.
- Subgraph patterns in data mining refer to the discovery of meaningful and recurrent substructures within graph data. These patterns help in understanding complex relationships and structures within the data. Examples include chemical compounds, 3-D protein structures, network topologies, and tree structured XML documents.
- Multiple candidate subgraphs can also be generated when there is more than one core associated with the pair of (k–1)-subgraphs. The shaded vertices correspond to those vertices whose edges form a core during the merging operation. Each core may lead to a different set of candidate subgraphs.
- After the candidate k-subgraphs are generated, the candidates whose (k – 1)-subgraphs are infrequent need to be pruned. The pruning step can be performed by successively removing an edge from the candidate k-subgraph and checking whether the corresponding (k – 1)-subgraph is connected and frequent. If not, the candidate k-subgraph can be discarded.
- A standard approach for handling the graph isomorphism problem is to map each graph into a unique string representation known as its code or canonical label. A canonical label has the property that if two graphs are isomorphic, then their codes must be the same. This property allows us to test for graph isomorphism by comparing the canonical labels of the graphs.

REVIEW QUESTIONS

1. How can handling categorical attributes affect the performance of machine learning models?
2. Define sequential pattern mining and its importance.
3. What are subgraph patterns, and where are they commonly used?

4. Explain the concept of 'graph isomorphism' and its relevance in subgraph pattern mining.
5. What is alternative counting schemes?
6. What is frequent subgraph mining, and why is it important?

REFERENCES

1. Antonie, M.-L., & Zaïane, O. R. (2004). Mining positive and negative association rules: An approach for confined rules. In *Proceedings of the 8th European Conference on Principles and Practice of Knowledge Discovery in Databases* (pp. 27–38), Pisa, Italy.
2. Aumann, Y., & Lindell, Y. (1999). A statistical theory for quantitative association rules. In *Proceedings of the 5th ACM SIGKDD International Conference on Knowledge Discovery and Data Mining* (pp. 261–270), San Diego, CA.
3. Ayres, J., Flannick, J., Gehrke, J., & Yiu, T. (2002). Sequential pattern mining using a bitmap representation. In *Proceedings of the 8th International Conference on Knowledge Discovery and Data Mining* (pp. 429–435), Edmonton, Canada.
4. Boulicaut, J.-F., Bykowski, A., & Jeudy, B. (2000). Towards the tractable discovery of association rules with negations. In *Proceedings of the 4th International Conference on Flexible Query Answering Systems* (pp. 425–434), Warsaw, Poland.
5. Cheng, H., Yan, X., & Han, J. (2004). IncSpan: Incremental mining of sequential patterns in large databases. In *Proceedings of the 10th International Conference on Knowledge Discovery and Data Mining* (pp. 527–532), Seattle, WA.
6. Fukuda, T., Morimoto, Y., Morishita, S., & Tokuyama, T. (1996). Mining optimized association rules for numeric attributes. In *Proceedings of the 15th Symposium on Principles of Database Systems* (pp. 182–191), Montreal, Canada.
7. Garofalakis, M. N., Rastogi, R., & Shim, K. (1999). SPIRIT: Sequential pattern mining with regular expression constraints. In *Proceedings of the 25th VLDB Conference* (pp. 223–234), Edinburgh, Scotland.
8. Inokuchi, T., Washio, T., & Motoda, H. (2000). An Apriori-based algorithm for mining frequent substructures from graph data. In *Proceedings of the 4th European Conference on Principles and Practice of Knowledge Discovery in Databases* (pp. 13–23), Lyon, France.
9. Joshi, M. V., Karypis, G., & Kumar, V. (2001). A universal formulation of sequential patterns. In *Proceedings of the KDD'2001 Workshop on Temporal Data Mining*, San Francisco, CA.
10. Kuramochi, M., & Karypis, G. (2001). Frequent subgraph discovery. In *Proceedings of the 2001 IEEE International Conference on Data Mining* (pp. 313–320), San Jose, CA.
11. Kuramochi, M., & Karypis, G. (2002). Discovering frequent geometric subgraphs. In *Proceedings of the 2002 IEEE International Conference on Data Mining* (pp. 258–265), Maebashi City, Japan.

12. Lent, B., Swami, A., & Widom, J. (1997). Clustering association rules. In *Proceedings of the 13th International Conference on Data Engineering* (pp. 220–231), Birmingham, U.K.

13. Mannila, H., Toivonen, H., & Verkamo, A. I. (1997). Discovery of frequent episodes in event sequences. *Data Mining and Knowledge Discovery, 1*(3), 259–289.

14. Miller, R. J., & Yang, Y. (1997). Association rules over interval data. In *Proceedings of the 1997 ACM-SIGMOD International Conference on Management of Data* (pp. 452–461), Tucson, AZ.

15. Parthasarathy, S., & Coatney, M. (2002). Efficient discovery of common substructures in macromolecules. In *Proceedings of the 2002 IEEE International Conference on Data Mining* (pp. 362–369), Maebashi City, Japan.

16. Pei, J., Han, J., Mortazavi-Asl, B., Chen, Q., Dayal, U., & Hsu, M. (2001). PrefixSpan: Mining sequential patterns efficiently by prefix-projected pattern growth. In *Proceedings of the 17th International Conference on Data Engineering* (pp. 215–224), Heidelberg, Germany.

17. Savasere, A., Omiecinski, E., & Navathe, S. (1998). Mining for strong negative associations in a large database of customer transactions. In *Proceedings of the 14th International Conference on Data Engineering* (pp. 494–502), Orlando, Florida.

18. Seno, M., & Karypis, G. (2002). SLPMiner: An algorithm for finding frequent sequential patterns using length-decreasing support constraint. In *Proceedings of the 2002 IEEE International Conference on Data Mining* (pp. 418–425), Maebashi City, Japan.

19. Srikant, R., & Agrawal, R. (1996). Mining quantitative association rules in large relational tables. In *Proceedings of the 1996 ACM-SIGMOD International Conference on Management of Data* (pp. 1–12), Montreal, Canada.

20. Srikant, R., & Agrawal, R. (1996). Mining sequential patterns: Generalizations and performance improvements. In *Proceedings of the 5th International Conference on Extending Database Technology (EDBT'96)* (pp. 18–32), Avignon, France.

21. Tan, P. N., Kumar, V., & Srivastava, J. (2000). Indirect association: Mining higher order dependencies in data. In *Proceedings of the 4th European Conference on Principles and Practice of Knowledge Discovery in Databases* (pp. 632–637), Lyon, France.

22. Teng, W. G., Hsieh, M. J., & Chen, M.-S. (2002). On the mining of substitution rules for statistically dependent items. In *Proceedings of the 2002 IEEE International Conference on Data Mining* (pp. 442–449), Maebashi City, Japan.

23. Wang, K., Tay, S. H., & Liu, B. (1998). Interestingness-based interval merger for numeric association rules. In *Proceedings of the 4th International Conference on Knowledge Discovery and Data Mining* (pp. 121–128), New York, NY.

24. Webb, G. I. (2001). Discovering associations with numeric variables. In *Proceedings of the 7th International Conference on Knowledge Discovery and Data Mining* (pp. 383–388), San Francisco, CA.

CHAPTER 8

Cluster Analysis: Basic Concepts and Algorithms

LEARNING OBJECTIVES

After studying this chapter, you will be able to:

- Discuss about cluster analysis
- Define K-means
- Explain agglomerative hierarchical clustering

KEY TERMS FROM THIS CHAPTER

Centroid
Clustering algorithm
DBSCAN
Euclidean distance
K-means
Partitional clustering
Segmentation
Time complexity
Cluster analysis
Data compression
Dendrogram
Hierarchical clustering
Medoid
Proximity function
Suboptimal clustering

INTRODUCTION

Cluster analysis, a fundamental technique in data mining and machine learning, aims to group a set of objects in such a way that objects in the same group (or cluster) are more similar to each other than to those in other groups. This method is pivotal in identifying patterns and structures in data without prior knowledge of the categories. Applications of cluster analysis span various fields including market research, biology, pattern recognition, and image processing.

At its core, cluster analysis involves three main steps: selecting features, choosing a clustering algorithm, and validating the results. Features are the measurable properties or characteristics of the data, chosen based on their relevance to the problem at hand. The clustering algorithm then partitions the data into clusters based on these features. Finally, validation ensures the clusters are meaningful and useful for the intended application. Several algorithms are used in cluster analysis, each with its strengths and weaknesses. K-means clustering is one of the most widely used algorithms due to its simplicity and efficiency. It partitions the data into K clusters by minimizing the sum of squared distances between data points and their respective cluster centroids. However, it requires the number of clusters, K, to be specified in advance and is sensitive to the initial placement of centroids.

Hierarchical clustering builds a tree-like structure of nested clusters, either by progressively merging smaller clusters into larger ones (agglomerative approach) or by splitting larger clusters into smaller ones (divisive approach). This method does not require the number of clusters to be predefined, but it can be computationally intensive for large datasets. Cluster analysis is a versatile tool for uncovering hidden patterns in data. By choosing appropriate features, algorithms, and validation methods, it provides valuable insights across various domains, facilitating informed decision-making and deeper understanding of complex datasets.

8.1. CLUSTER ANALYSIS

Only data that describes the objects and their relationships can be used to group data objects in a cluster analysis. The idea is for the objects in a group to be distinct from (or unrelated to) the objects in other groups, while remaining similar to (or related to) one another. The better or more distinct the clustering, the greater the similarity (or homogeneity) within a group and the greater the difference between groups.

The concept of a cluster is not well defined in many applications. Take a look at Figure 8.1, which displays twenty points and three possible cluster divisions, to get a better idea of how difficult it is to determine what defines a cluster. Membership in a cluster is indicated by the markers' shapes. The data is divided into two parts in Figure 8.1(b) and six parts in Figure 8.1(d). The apparent separation of each of the two larger clusters into three smaller clusters, though, might just be a visual system artifact. Furthermore, as illustrated in Figure 8.1(c), it might not be implausible to claim that the points form four clusters. This figure demonstrates how a cluster's definition is ill-defined and how the ideal definition varies depending on the type of data and the intended outcomes.

There is a connection between cluster analysis and other methods of grouping data objects. For example, because clustering assigns class (cluster) labels to objects, it can be thought of as a type of classification. It only obtains these labels from the data, though. Classification, on the other hand, is supervised classification; that is, i.e., utilizing a model created from objects with established class labels, new, unlabeled objects are given a class label. For this reason, unsupervised classification is another name for cluster analysis. In data mining, supervised classification is usually meant when the term "classification" is used without any qualification.

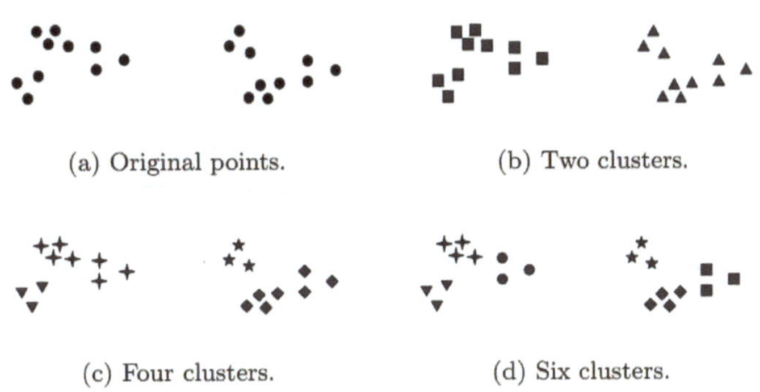

Figure 8.1. *Different ways of clustering the same set of points.*

Source: https://www.ceom.ou.edu/media/docs/upload/Pang-Ning_Tan_Michael_Steinbach_Vipin_Kumar_-_Introduction_to_Data_Mining-Pe_NRDK4fi.pdf.

Although segmentation and partitioning are occasionally used interchangeably with clustering, they often refer to methods that fall outside the typical realm of cluster analysis. Partitioning, for example, is frequently associated with dividing graphs into subgraphs rather than clustering. Segmentation typically involves grouping data using basic techniques, such as splitting an image based on pixel attributes or organizing people based on income levels. However, some research in graph partitioning, image segmentation, and market segmentation does overlap with cluster analysis.

8.1.1. Different Types of Clusterings

A clustering is a collection of all the clusters together. In this section, we differentiate between three types of clusterings: partitional (unnested) versus hierarchical (nested), fuzzy versus exclusive, and complete versus partial.

8.1.1.1. Hierarchical versus Partitional

The most often discussed difference between various clustering types is whether the set of clusters is nested or unnested, or alternatively, partitional or hierarchical, to use more conventional language. The division of the set of data objects into non-overlapping subsets (clusters) so that each data object is in exactly one subset is known as partitional clustering. When viewed separately, every cluster collection in Figures 8.1 (b–d) represents a partitional clustering.

A hierarchical clustering, or a collection of nested clusters arranged like a tree, is produced when we allow clusters to have subclusters. With the exception of leaf nodes, every node (cluster) in the tree is the union of all of its offspring (subclusters), and the cluster that contains every object in the tree is its root. The leaves of the tree are typically singleton clusters of distinct data objects, but this is not always the case. Figure 8.1(a) can be interpreted as having two subclusters (Figure 8.1(b)), each of which has three subclusters (Figure 8.1(d)) if we allow clusters to be nested. When viewed in that order, the clusters in Figures 8.1 (a–d) also create a hierarchical (nested) clustering, with 1, 2, 4, and 6 clusters on each level, respectively. Lastly, keep in mind that a partitional clustering can be created by taking any member of the sequence, i.e., a hierarchical clustering can be understood as a series of partitional clusterings. i.e., through chopping off a specific level of the hierarchical tree.

8.1.1.2. Exclusive Versus Overlapping Versus Fuzzy

Since each object is assigned to a single cluster, the clusterings displayed in Figure 8.1 are all exclusive. Non-exclusive clustering is a better option for handling the numerous scenarios where a point could logically be assigned to more than one cluster. Generally speaking, an overlapping or non-exclusive clustering is employed to represent the possibility of an object having multiple group (class) memberships at the same time. For example, an individual at a university may be both an employee of the university and an enrolled student. When an object is, for instance, "between" two or more clusters and could plausibly be assigned to any of these clusters, non-exclusive clustering is also frequently used. Consider a point that is midway between two of Figure 8.1's clusters. The object is distributed among all of the "equally good" clusters rather than being arbitrarily assigned to one.

Every object in a fuzzy clustering has a membership weight between 0 (absolutely doesn't belong) and 1 (absolutely belongs), meaning that every object belongs to every cluster. To put it another way, clusters are handled like fuzzy sets. (An object in a fuzzy set, mathematically speaking, can belong to any set with a weight between 0 and 1. An additional restriction that is frequently imposed in fuzzy clustering is that the total of the weights assigned to each object must equal 1. Similarly, each point's probability of belonging to each cluster is calculated using probabilistic clustering techniques, and these probabilities also need to add up to 1. A fuzzy or probabilistic clustering does not handle real multiclass situations, like the case of a student employee, where an object belongs to multiple classes, because the membership weights or probabilities for any object sum to 1. These methods are better suited for preventing the arbitrary assignment of an object to a single cluster when it may be near multiple clusters. An exclusive clustering is typically created in practice by allocating each object to the cluster in which its membership weight or probability is highest, from a fuzzy or probabilistic clustering.

8.1.1.3. Complete versus Partial

Every object is assigned to a cluster in a complete clustering, but not in a partial one. The possibility that some objects in a data set do not belong to clearly defined groups is what drives partial clustering. Objects within the data set frequently reflect noise, anomalies, or "uninteresting background." For instance, while some newspaper articles are more generic or unique, others may have a common theme, like global warming. Therefore, we might want to limit our search to document clusters that are closely related to one another through a common theme in order to identify the key themes in last month's stories. Other times, it's preferable for the items to be completely clustered. For instance, an application that arranges documents for browsing using clustering must ensure that every document is viewable.

8.1.2. Different Types of Clusters

Clustering seeks to identify meaningful groups of objects (clusters), with their usefulness determined by the objectives of the data analysis. There are various concepts of clusters that are valuable in practice. To visually demonstrate the distinctions between these types of clusters, we employ two-dimensional points in Figure 8.2 as our data points. It should be noted that the types of clusters discussed here are applicable to other types of data as well.

8.1.2.1. Well-Separated

An object is said to be in a cluster if all of its members are more similar to one another than they are to any other object. Occasionally, a threshold is employed to indicate that every object within a cluster needs to be sufficiently near (or comparable) to each other. Only when the data contains naturally occurring clusters that are relatively far from one another does this idealistic definition of a cluster hold true. An illustration of a well-separated cluster, which consists of two sets of points in a two-dimensional space, is shown in Figure 8.2(a). Any two points outside of groups are separated from each other more widely than any two points inside a group. Any shape will do; globular clusters are not required for well-separated clusters.

8.1.2.2. Prototype-Based

A cluster is a collection of items where each item is more similar to the prototype that defines the cluster than it is to any other cluster's prototype. A centroid, i.e., the center of a cluster, is frequently the prototype for data with continuous attributes. e. the cluster's mean, or average, of all its points. The prototype is frequently a medoid, i.e., when a centroid is not meaningful, as in the case of data with categorical attributes. e. the cluster's most representative point. The prototype can be thought of as the most central point for a variety of data types; in these cases, prototype-based clusters are also known as center-based clusters. The tendency of these clusters to be globular is not surprising. In Figure 8.2(b), a center-based cluster is demonstrated.

8.1.2.3. Graph-Based

If data is depicted in a graph with nodes representing objects and links showing connections between objects, a cluster can be identified as a connected component. This means it is a group of objects connected to each other but not to objects outside the group. An example of graph-based clusters is contiguity-based clusters, where two objects are linked only if they are within a set distance of each other. This indicates that each object in a contiguity-based cluster is closer to another object within the cluster than to any point in a different cluster. In Figure 8.2(c), there is an illustration of such clusters for two-dimensional points. This definition of a cluster is helpful for irregular or intertwined clusters but may struggle with noise as seen in the two spherical clusters in Figure 8.2(c), where a small bridge of points could merge two distinct clusters.

There are more kinds of graph-based clusters that can be created. According to one such method, a cluster is a clique; i.e., a group of nodes that are fully connected to one another in a graph. In particular, when a group of objects forms a clique, a cluster is created if we add connections between the objects in the order of their distance from one another. These clusters typically have globular shapes, just like prototype-based clusters.

8.1.2.4. Density-Based

A cluster is an area with a high concentration of objects encircled by a low density area. Some density-based clusters for the data produced by introducing noise to the data in Figure 8.2(c) are displayed in Figure 8.2(d). Because the bridge connecting the two circular clusters fades into the noise, they are not combined, as shown in Figure 8.2(c). Similarly, the curve in Figure 8.2(c) does not form a cluster in Figure 8.2(d); instead, it fades into the noise. When there is noise and outliers, as well as when the clusters are erratic or entangled, a density-based definition of a cluster is frequently used. In contrast, the data in Figure 8.2(d) would not lend themselves well to a contiguity-based definition of a cluster because the noise would tend to create bridges between clusters.

8.1.2.5. Shared-Property (Conceptual Clusters)

A cluster is more broadly defined as a collection of objects that have a common attribute. This definition of a cluster includes every definition that came before it, such as e.g., The characteristic that unites the objects in a center-based cluster is their proximity to the same centroid, also known as the medoid. The shared-property strategy does, however, also incorporate new kinds of clusters. Think about the clusters depicted in Figure 8.2(e).

Two entwined circles (clusters) and a triangle area (cluster) next to a rectangle area. For a clustering algorithm to identify these clusters in both scenarios, a very specific definition of a cluster would be required. Conceptual clustering is the method used to locate these clusters.

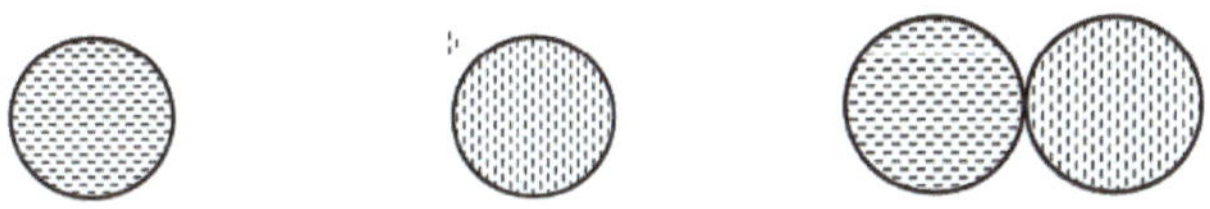

(a) Well-separated clusters. Each point is closer to all of the points in its cluster than to any point in another cluster.

(b) Center-based clusters. Each point is closer to the center of its cluster than to the center of any other cluster.

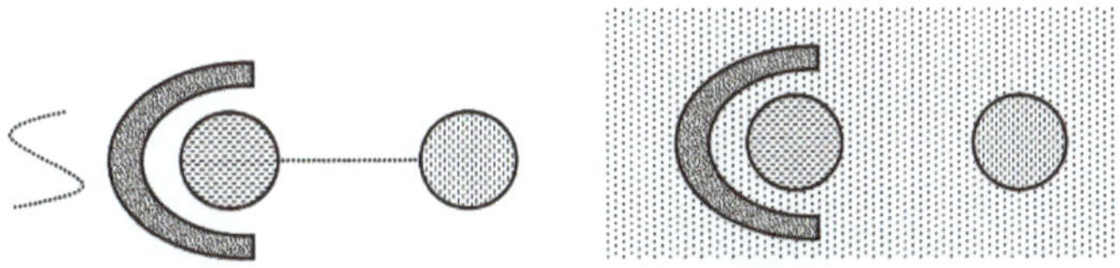

(c) Contiguity-based clusters. Each point is closer to at least one point in its cluster than to any point in another cluster.

(d) Density-based clusters. Clusters are regions of high density separated by regions of low density.

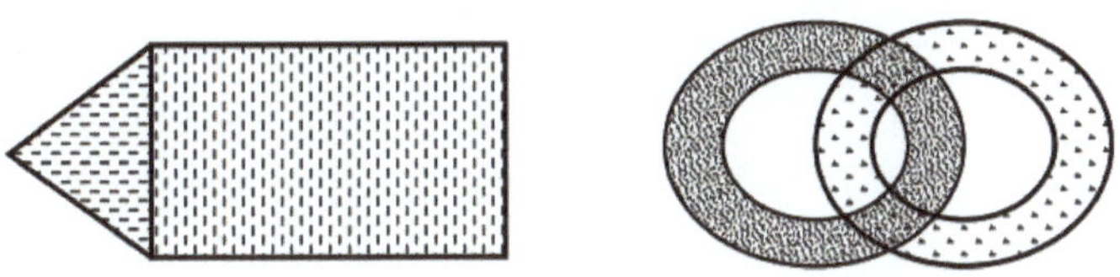

(e) Conceptual clusters. Points in a cluster share some general property that derives from the entire set of points. (Points in the intersection of the circles belong to both.)

Figure 8.2. *Different types of clusters as illustrated by sets of two-dimensional points.*

Source. https://www.ceom.ou.edu/media/docs/upload/Pang-Ning_Tan_Michael_Steinbach_Vipin_Kumar_-_Introduction_to_Data_Mining-Pe_NRDK4fi.pdf.

We use the following three simple, but important techniques to introduce many of the concepts involved in cluster analysis.

- **K-means**: This is a prototype-based, partitional clustering technique that attempts to find a user-specified number of clusters (K), which are represented by their centroids.
- **Agglomerative Hierarchical Clustering**: This clustering approach refers to a collection of closely related clustering techniques that produce a hierarchical clustering by starting with each point as a singleton cluster and then repeatedly merging the two closest clusters until a single, all-encompassing cluster remains. Some of these techniques have a natural interpretation in terms of graph-based clustering, while others have an interpretation in terms of a prototype-based approach.

- **DBSCAN**: This is a density-based clustering algorithm that produces a partitional clustering, in which the number of clusters is automatically determined by the algorithm. Points in low-density regions are classified as noise and omitted; thus, DBSCAN does not produce a complete clustering.

8.2. K-MEANS

Prototype-based clustering methods divide the data objects into one level. While there are many such methods, K-means and K-medoid are two of the most well-known. K-means is commonly applied to objects in a continuous n-dimensional space and defines a prototype in terms of a centroid, which is typically the mean of a group of points. Since K-medoid only needs a proximity measure for a pair of objects, it can be applied to a wide range of data and defines a prototype in terms of a medoid, which is the most representative point for a group of points. A medoid, by definition, has to be an actual data point, whereas a centroid almost never matches one. This section will only address K-means, one of the most popular and established clustering algorithms.

8.2.1. The Basic K-means Algorithm

The K-means clustering method is straightforward, and we start with an explanation of the fundamental algorithm. First, we select K initial centroids, where K is the number of desired clusters, a user-specified parameter. The nearest centroid is then assigned to each point, and a cluster is formed when a group of points is assigned to a single centroid. Next, each cluster's centroid is updated in accordance with the points allocated to it. Until no point changes clusters, or equivalently, until the centroids stay the same, we repeat the assignment and update steps.

In formal terms, Algorithm 8.1 describes K-means. Figure 8.3 provides an illustration of how K-means works. It shows how the final clusters are found in four assignment-update steps, starting with three centroids. Each subfigure in these and other K-means clustering figures displays two things: (1) the centroids at the beginning of the iteration, and (2) the points assigned to those centroids. The "+" symbol designates the centroids, and the marker shape is consistent across all points that belong to the same cluster.

Algorithm 8.1. Basic K-Means Algorithm

```
Select K points as initial centroids.
repeat
   Form K clusters by assigning each point to its closest centroid.
   Recompute the centroid of each cluster.
until Centroids do not change.
```

Points are allocated to the initial centroids, all of which are part of the larger group of points, in the first step, as illustrated in Figure 8.3(a). The mean serves as the centroid in this instance. A centroid is updated following the assignment of points to it. Once more, the centroid at the start of each step and the points assigned to those centroids are displayed in the figure. The updated centroids are updated once more and given points in the subsequent step.

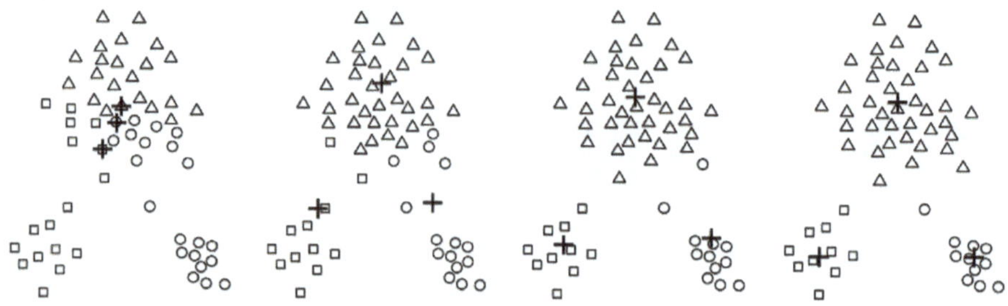

(a) Iteration 1. (b) Iteration 2. (c) Iteration 3. (d) Iteration 4.

Figure 8.3. *Using the K-means algorithm to find three clusters in sample data.*

Source: https://www.ceom.ou.edu/media/docs/upload/Pang-Ning_Tan_Michael_Steinbach_Vipin_Kumar_-_Introduction_to_Data_Mining-Pe_NRDK4fi.pdf.

In Figures 8.3 (b), (c), and (d), respectively, steps 2, 3, and 4 depict two of the centroids moving to the two small groups of points at the bottom of the figures. The centroids have determined the natural groupings of points when the K-means algorithm stops in Figure 8.3(d) due to the absence of any more changes.

K-means always converges to a solution for certain combinations of centroids and proximity functions; i.e., K-means finds a state where the centroids remain unchanged because no points are moving from one cluster to another. However, the condition on line 5 of Algorithm 8.1 is frequently substituted with a weaker condition, e, because the majority of convergence happens in the early steps. Continue until a mere 1 percent of the points exhibit cluster switching.

We consider each of the steps in the basic K-means algorithm in more detail and then provide an analysis of the algorithm's space and time complexity.

8.2.2. Assigning Points to the Closest Centroid

We require a proximity measure that expresses the concept of "closest" in terms of the particular data being examined in order to allocate a point to the closest centroid. For data points in Euclidean space, Euclidean (L_2) distance is frequently utilized, but cosine similarity is better suited for documents. Nonetheless, different proximity measure types might be suitable for a particular kind of data. For Euclidean data, for instance, the Manhattan (L_1) distance can be utilized, whereas the Jaccard measure is frequently used for documents.

The similarity measures typically used for K-means are generally straightforward, as the algorithm regularly computes the similarity between each point and each centroid. However, in certain situations, like when the data is in a low-dimensional format, more complex similarity measures may be required.

Table 8.1. Table of Notation

Symbol	Description
$\mathbf{x}$	An object.
C_i	The ith cluster.
$\mathbf{c}_i$	The centroid of cluster C_i.
$\mathbf{c}$	The centroid of all points.
m_i	The number of objects in the ith cluster.
m	The number of objects in the data set.
K	The number of clusters.

Source. https://www.ceom.ou.edu/media/docs/upload/Pang-Ning_Tan_Michael_Steinbach_Vipin_Kumar_-_Introduction_to_Data_Mining-Pe_NRDK4fi.pdf.

The K-means algorithm can be substantially accelerated by avoiding computing many of the similarities in Euclidean space. Another method that accelerates K-means by lowering the total number of similarities computed is bisecting K-means.

8.2.3. Centroids and Objective Functions

Since the centroid can change based on the proximity measure for the data and the clustering goal, step 4 of the K-means algorithm was described rather broadly as "recompute the centroid of each cluster." Typically, the objective function used to express the clustering goal depends on how close the points are to each other or to the cluster centroids; e.g., reduce each point's squared distance from its nearest centroid. We provide two instances to demonstrate this. But the important thing to remember is that we can usually calculate the centroid of our choice using mathematics once we have defined an objective function and a proximity measure.

8.2.3.1. Data in Euclidean Space

Take data that have Euclidean distance as their proximity measure. The sum of squared errors, or SSE for short, is what we use as our objective function to gauge the quality of a clustering. Stated differently, we compute the error of every data point, i.e., the closest centroid's Euclidean distance, and finally calculate the sum of the squared errors. We choose the cluster with the smallest squared error between two distinct sets of clusters generated by separate K-means runs because it indicates that the prototypes (centroids) of this clustering are a more accurate representation of the points in their cluster. Using the notation in Table 8.1, the SSE is formally defined as follows:

$$\text{SSE} = \sum_{i=1}^{K} \sum_{x \in C_i} dist(c_i, x)^2 \qquad (1)$$

Where; dist is the standard Euclidean (L_2) distance between two objects in Euclidean space.

Given these assumptions, it can be shown that the centroid that minimizes the SSE of the cluster is the mean. Using the notation in Table 8.1, the centroid (mean) of the i th cluster is defined by Equation 2.

$$\mathbf{c}_i = \frac{1}{m_i} \sum_{\mathbf{x} \in C_i} \mathbf{x} \qquad (2)$$

To illustrate, the centroid of a cluster containing the three two-dimensional points, (1,1), (2,3), and (6,2), is ((1 + 2 + 6)/3,((1 + 3 + 2)/3) = (3, 2). The SSE (or, more broadly, the objective function) is directly attempted to be minimized in steps 3 and 4 of the K-means algorithm. In step three, the SSE for the given set of centroids is minimized by allocating points to the clusters' nearest centroid. In order to further reduce the SSE, the centroids are recomputed in Step 4. However, because Steps 3 and 4 of K-means rely on optimizing the SSE for particular choices of the centroids and clusters rather than for all possible choices, they can only be relied upon to find a local minimum with respect to the SSE. We'll see an example later on where this results in a clustering that isn't ideal.

8.2.3.2. Document Data

We take document data and the cosine similarity measure to show that K-means is not limited to data in Euclidean space. Our goal is to maximize the cohesion of a cluster, which is measured by how similar the documents in the cluster are to its centroid. It can be demonstrated for this purpose that the cluster centroid is the mean for Euclidean data. Equation 3 provides the total cohesion, which is the equivalent quantity to the total SSE.

$$\text{Total Cohesion} = \sum_{i=1}^{K} \sum_{\mathbf{x} \in C_i} cosine(\mathbf{x}, \mathbf{c}_i) \qquad (3)$$

8.2.3.3. The General Case

The basic K-means algorithm can be applied with a variety of guaranteed to converge proximity function, centroid, and objective function choices. A few options, including the two we just covered, are displayed in Table 8.2. You'll see that the median of a cluster's points serves as the proper centroid for the Manhattan (L_1) distance and the goal of minimizing the sum of the distances.

Table 8.2. K-Means: COMMON Choices for Proximity, Centroids, and Objective Functions

Proximity Function	Centroid	Objective Function
Manhattan (L_1)	median	Minimize sum of the L_1 distance of an object to its cluster centroid
Squared Euclidean (L_2^2)	mean	Minimize sum of the squared L_2 distance of an object to its cluster centroid
cosine	mean	Maximize sum of the cosine similarity of an object to its cluster centroid
Bregman divergence	mean	Minimize sum of the Bregman divergence of an object to its cluster centroid

Source. Source. https://www.ceom.ou.edu/media/docs/upload/Pang-Ning_Tan_Michael_Steinbach_Vipin_Kumar_-_Introduction_to_Data_Mining-Pe_NRDK4fi.pdf.

In reality, a class of proximity measures that includes the squared Euclidean distance, L_2^2, the Mahalanobis distance, and cosine similarity is represented by the table's final entry, Bregman divergence. Bregman divergence functions are important because they can be the foundation of any K-means style clustering algorithm where the mean is the centroid. To be more precise, the resulting clustering algorithm has the typical K-means characteristics in terms of convergence, local minima, etc., if we utilize a Bregman divergence as our proximity function. Additionally, all potential Bregman divergences can have their clustering algorithm's properties developed. In fact, a general clustering algorithm based on Bregman divergences is embodied in K-means algorithms that employ either squared Euclidean distance or cosine similarity.

Since two-dimensional data makes it easier to understand K-means and its properties, we will use it for the remainder of our discussion of K-means. However, as the preceding paragraphs have indicated, K-means is a very general clustering algorithm that can be applied to a wide range of data types, including time series and documents.

8.2.4. Choosing Initial Centroids

Generally, different K-means runs yield different total SSEs when random initialization of centroids is applied. The set of two-dimensional points with three naturally occurring point clusters in Figure 8.3 serves as an example of this. Figure 8.4(b) depicts a suboptimal clustering that is only a local minimum, whereas Figure 8.4(a) depicts a clustering solution that is the global minimum of the SSE for three clusters.

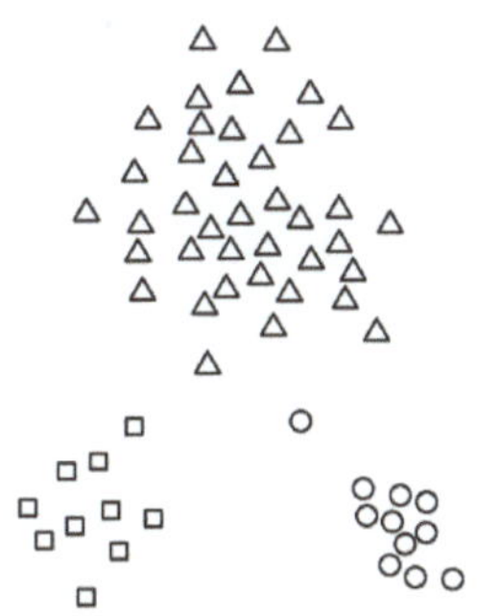

(a) Optimal clustering.

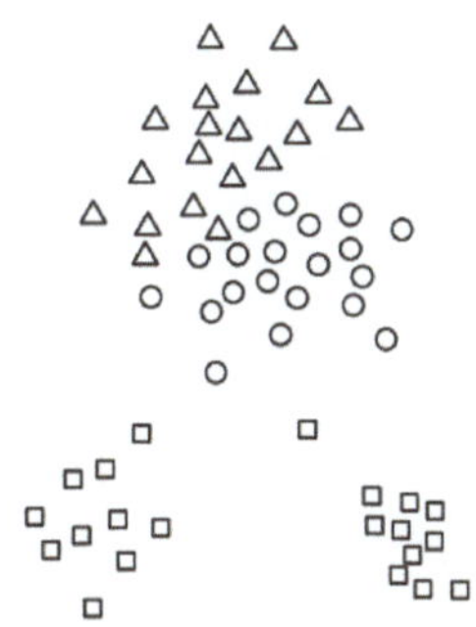

(b) Suboptimal clustering.

Figure 8.4. *Three optimal and non-optimal clusters.*

Source: https://www.ceom.ou.edu/media/docs/upload/Pang-Ning_Tan_Michael_Steinbach_Vipin_Kumar_-_Introduction_to_Data_Mining-Pe_NRDK4fi.pdf.

Selecting the correct initial centroids is crucial for the basic K-means algorithm. While a common method is to randomly select initial centroids, this often leads to subpar clusters.

- **Example 1 (Poor Initial Centroids):** Poor initial centroids may have been chosen at random. Using the same data set as Figures 8.3 and 8.4, we demonstrate this. The resulting clusters from two different initial centroid selections are displayed in Figures 8.3 and 8.5. (Crosses denote where the cluster centroids were in each of the iterations for both figures). The minimum SSE clustering is still found in Figure 8.3, despite the fact that all of the initial centroids are from a single natural cluster. However, in Figure 8.5, we obtain a suboptimal clustering with higher squared error, despite the initial centroids appearing to be better distributed.
- **Example 2 (Limits of Random Initialization):** Performing several runs, each with a different set of randomly selected initial centroids, is one method that is frequently used to solve the problem of initial centrogenesis. The set of clusters with the lowest SSE is then chosen. Despite being straightforward, the effectiveness of this strategy may vary based on the data set and the number of clusters being sought. We use the sample data set displayed in Figure 8.6(a) to illustrate this. There are two pairs of clusters in the data, and each pair's clusters are closer to the other pair's clusters than they are to each other (top-bottom). According to Figure 8.6(b–d), if each pair of clusters has two initial centroids, the centroids will redistribute themselves to find the "true" clusters even if they are in the same cluster. On the other hand, Figure 8.7 illustrates that two of the genuine clusters will merge and one true cluster will split if two clusters have one initial centroid while the other pair has three.

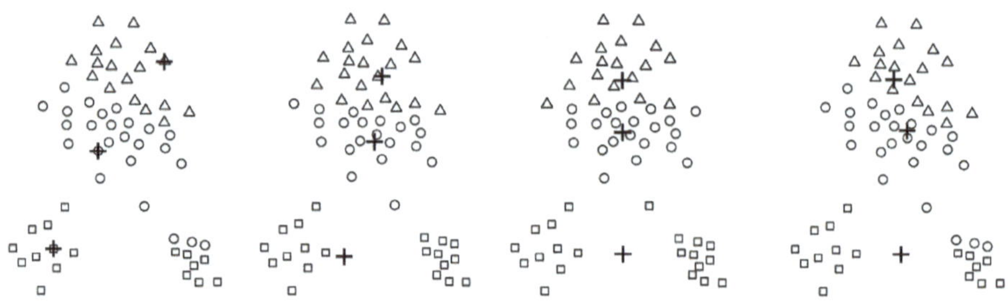

(a) Iteration 1. (b) Iteration 2. (c) Iteration 3. (d) Iteration 4.

Figure 8.5. *Poor starting centroids for K-means.*

Source: https://www.ceom.ou.edu/media/docs/upload/Pang-Ning_Tan_Michael_Steinbach_Vipin_Kumar_-_Introduction_to_Data_Mining-Pe_NRDK4fi.pdf.

Because the centroids will redistribute, one to each cluster, an ideal clustering will be achieved as long as two initial centroids fall anywhere in a pair of clusters. Unfortunately, it is more likely that at least one pair of clusters will have only one initial centroid as the number of clusters increases. The K-means algorithm will not redistribute the centroids between pairs of clusters in this instance because the pairs of clusters are farther apart than the clusters within a pair. As a result, only a local minimum will be reached.

Other methods are often used for initialization because of the issues with using randomly selected initial centroids, which may not be resolved even after several runs. Using a hierarchical clustering technique to cluster a sample of points is one efficient method. The initial centroids are the centroids of K clusters that are taken out of the hierarchical clustering. This method is frequently effective, but it is only useful in the following situations: (1) the sample is small, e.g., several hundred to several thousand (the cost of hierarchical clustering), and (2) K is comparatively small in relation to the sample size.

Another method for choosing initial centroids is the one that follows. At random, choose the first point, or take the centroid of all the points. Next, choose the point that is farthest from any of the previously chosen initial centroids for each subsequent initial centroid. By doing this, we are able to produce a set of initial centroids that are both well separated and assured to be chosen at random. Regretfully, this method may choose outliers over points in dense regions (clusters). The computation of the farthest point from the current set of initial centroids is also costly. This method is frequently used on a subset of the points in order to get around these issues. Outliers are uncommon, so a random sample is unlikely to contain them. On the other hand, unless the sample size is extremely small, points from every dense region are likely to be included. Because the sample size is usually much smaller than the number of points, there is also a significant reduction in the computation required to find the initial centroids.

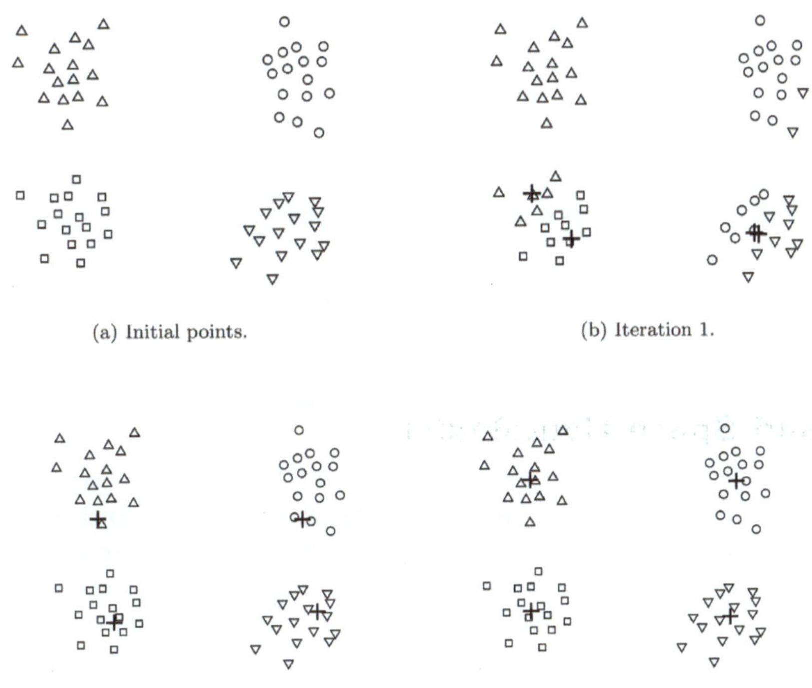

(a) Initial points. (b) Iteration 1.

(c) Iteration 2. (d) Iteration 3.

Figure 8.6. *Two pairs of clusters with a pair of initial centroids within each pair of clusters.*

Source. Source. https://www.ceom.ou.edu/media/docs/upload/Pang-Ning_Tan_Michael_Steinbach_Vipin_Kumar_-_Introduction_to_Data_Mining-Pe_NRDK4fi.pdf.

Two other strategies that are helpful in generating higher-quality (lower SSE) clusterings will be covered later on: bisecting K-means, a K-means variant that is less prone to initialization issues, and post-processing to "fixup" the generated set of clusters.

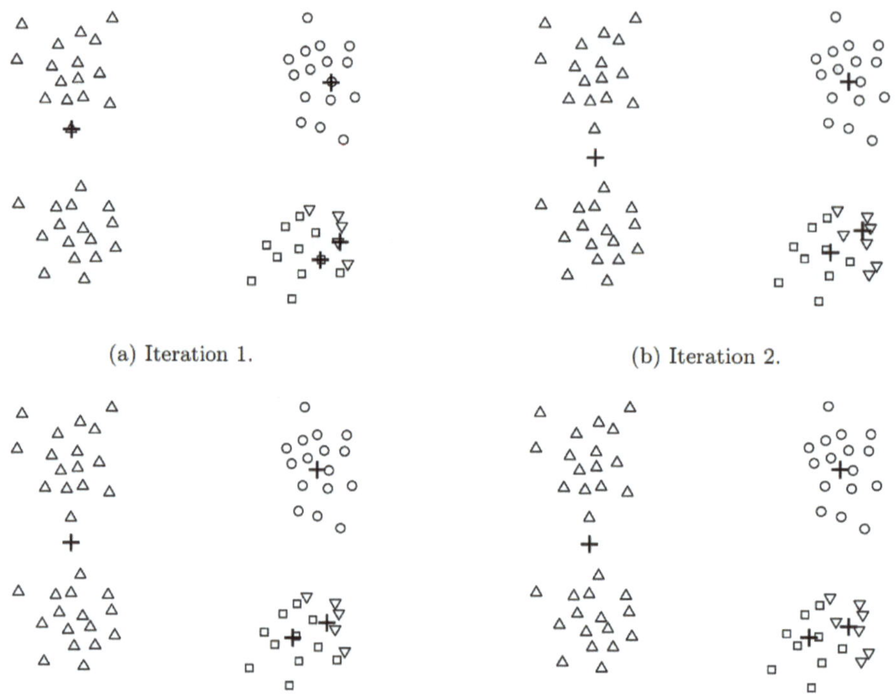

(a) Iteration 1. (b) Iteration 2. (c) Iteration 3. (d) Iteration 4.

Figure 8.7. *Two pairs of clusters with more or fewer than two initial centroids within a pair of clusters.*

Source: https://www.ceom.ou.edu/media/docs/upload/Pang-Ning_Tan_Michael_Steinbach_Vipin_Kumar_-_Introduction_to_Data_Mining-Pe_NRDK4fi.pdf.

8.2.5. Time and Space Complexity

Since K-means only stores the centroids and data points, its space requirements are negligible. O((m + K)n), where m is the number of points and n is the number of attributes, is the exact amount of storage needed. K-means also has reasonable time requirements, which are essentially linear in the number of data points. Specifically, O(I *K *m*n) time is needed, where I is the number of iterations needed to reach convergence. As previously indicated, I is frequently small and can be safely bounded because the majority of changes happen during the first several iterations. As a result, K-means is efficient and straightforward as long as K, the number of clusters, is substantially less than m. It is also linear in m, the number of points.

8.2.6. K-Means: Additional Issues

8.2.6.1. Handling Empty Clusters

One issue with the previously described basic K-means algorithm is that it can result in empty clusters if no points are assigned to any clusters at the assignment step. In the event that this occurs, a replacement centroid selection strategy is required because the squared error would otherwise be greater than required. Selecting the point that is farthest from any existing centroid is one method. This removes the point that presently adds the greatest amount to the total squared error, if nothing else. Selecting the replacement centroid from the cluster with the highest SSE is an alternative strategy. Usually, this will split the cluster and lower the clustering's overall SSE. This process can be repeated numerous times if there are several empty clusters.

8.2.6.2. Outliers

Outliers have the potential to unduly affect the clusters that are found when the squared error criterion is applied. Outliers in particular can make the cluster centroids (prototypes) that result from them less representative than they otherwise would be, which raises the SSE. This is why it is frequently helpful to identify and get rid of outliers in advance. But it's crucial to understand that in some cases, clustering applications call for leaving outliers in place. Every point must be clustered when using clustering for data compression; in certain situations, like financial analysis, apparent outliers, e.g., remarkably lucrative clients may be the most intriguing aspects.

A clear problem is how to recognize outliers. In Chapter 10, several methods for locating outliers will be covered. We can prevent clustering points that won't cluster well by employing strategies that eliminate outliers prior to clustering. As an alternative, outliers may be found during a postprocessing stage. For example, we can monitor the SSE that each point contributes and remove points that have disproportionately large contributions, especially over several runs. Additionally, since small clusters typically represent collections of outliers, we might want to remove them.

8.2.6.3. Reducing the SSE with Postprocessing

Clearly, increasing the number of clusters is one way to lower the SSE, i.e., to employ a bigger K. On the other hand, we frequently want to raise the SSE without growing the number of clusters. Since K-means usually converges to a local minimum, this is frequently feasible. The resultant clusters are "fixed up" using a variety of methods to create a clustering with a lower SSE. Since the total SSE is just the sum of the SSE contributed by each cluster, the strategy is to concentrate on individual clusters. To prevent any misunderstandings, we will refer to total SSE and cluster SSE, respectively. By dividing or merging clusters, among other operations on the clusters, we can alter the total SSE. Using different phases for cluster splitting and merging is one popular strategy. Clusters split up during a splitting phase and come together during a merging phase. By doing this, it is frequently possible to avoid local SSE minima while still obtaining the required number of clusters in the clustering solution. Some strategies employed during the division and consolidation stages are listed below. Two strategies that decrease the total SSE by increasing the number of clusters are the following:

- **Split a Cluster:** The cluster with the largest SSE is usually chosen, but we could also split the cluster with the largest standard deviation for one particular attribute.
- **Introduce a New Cluster Centroid:** Often the point that is farthest from any cluster center is chosen. We can easily determine this if we keep track of the SSE contributed by each point. Another approach is to choose randomly from all points or from the points with the highest SSE.

Two strategies that decrease the number of clusters, while trying to minimize the increase in total SSE, are the following:

- **Disperse a Cluster:** This is accomplished by removing the centroid that corresponds to the cluster and reassigning the points to other clusters. Ideally, the cluster that is dispersed should be the one that increases the total SSE the least.
- **Merge Two Clusters:** The clusters with the closest centroids are typically chosen, although another, perhaps better, approach is to merge the two clusters that result in the smallest increase in total SSE. These two merging strategies are the same ones that are used in the hierarchical clustering techniques known as the centroid method and Ward's method, respectively.

8.2.6.4. Updating Centroids Incrementally

The cluster centroids can be updated incrementally following each point assignment to a cluster, as an alternative to updating them all at once. Because a point either moves to a new cluster (requiring two updates) or stays in its current cluster (requiring zero updates), it is important to note that this requires either zero or two updates to cluster centroids at each step. Since each cluster begins with a single point and is guaranteed to always have that point reassigned to the same cluster, using an incremental update strategy ensures that no empty clusters are created.

Furthermore, the relative weight of the point being added may change if incremental updating is applied; e.g., as the clustering progresses, the weight of the points is frequently reduced. Even though this can lead to faster convergence and improved accuracy, choosing the right relative weight can be challenging, particularly in a range of scenarios. The problems with updating these updates are comparable to those with updating artificial neural network weights. Using goals other than "minimize SSE" is yet another advantage of incremental updates. Assume that an arbitrary objective function is provided to us in order to gauge how good a collection of clusters is. After processing a single point, we can determine which cluster assignment would maximize the objective by computing the value of the objective function for each potential cluster assignment.

However, there is a drawback: updating centroids progressively results in an order dependency. Put another way, the order in which the points are processed may affect the clusters that are generated. The basic K-means approach of updating the centroids after all points have been assigned to clusters has no order dependency, though this can be addressed by varying the order in which the points are processed. Incremental updates also cost a little bit extra. On the other hand, K-means converges fairly quickly, which means that the number of points that switch clusters gets relatively small very quickly.

8.2.7. Bisecting K-Means

A straightforward extension of the fundamental K-means algorithm, the bisecting K-means algorithm is based on a straightforward principle: in order to produce K clusters, divide the set of all points into two clusters, choose one of these clusters to split, and so on, until K clusters are generated. The information about splitting K-means is provided by Algorithm 8.2.

Algorithm 8.2. Bisecting K-Means Algorithm

```
Initialize the list of clusters to contain the cluster consisting of all points.
repeat
    Remove a cluster from the list of clusters.
    {Perform several "trial" bisections of the chosen cluster.}
    for i = 1 to number of trials do
        Bisect the selected cluster using basic K-means.
    end for
    Select the two clusters from the bisection with the lowest total SSE.
    Add these two clusters to the list of clusters.
until Until the list of clusters contains K clusters.
```

Selecting which cluster to split can be done in a number of ways. At every stage, we have the option of selecting the largest cluster, the one with the highest SSE, or a criterion that takes into account both size and SSE. Various decisions lead to various clusters.

To improve the clusters, we utilize the centroids as initial centroids for the basic K-means algorithm. While the K-means algorithm is reliable in finding a clustering that signifies a local minimum in terms of SSE, bisecting K-means requires using the algorithm on a local scale to split individual clusters. As a result, the final clusters do not necessarily represent a local minimum in regard to total SSE.

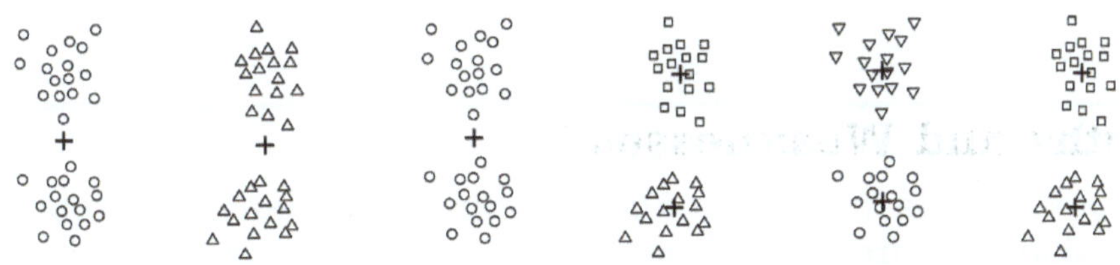

(a) Iteration 1. (b) Iteration 2. (c) Iteration 3.

Figure 8.8. *Bisecting K-means on the four clusters example.*

Source: https://www.ceom.ou.edu/media/docs/upload/Pang-Ning_Tan_Michael_Steinbach_Vipin_Kumar_-_Introduction_to_Data_Mining-Pe_NRDK4fi.pdf.

- **Example 3 (Bisecting K-means and Initialization):** The benefits of using bisecting K-means to address initialization issues are demonstrated in Figure 8.8. By applying this method to the data set from Figure 8.6(a), four clusters are successfully identified. Initially, two pairs of clusters are found in iteration 1, followed by the splitting of the rightmost pair in iteration 2, and finally the splitting of the leftmost pair in iteration 3. The advantage of bisecting K-means lies in its ability to try multiple bisections and select the one with the lowest sum of squared errors (SSE), as well as having only two centroids at each step.

Additionally, we can create a hierarchical clustering by recording the sequence of clusterings generated as K-means bisects clusters.

8.2.8. K-Means and Different Types of Clusters

There are several restrictions on the types of clusters that can be found using K-means and its variants. In particular, when clusters have non-spherical shapes, significantly different sizes, or densities, K-means has trouble identifying the "natural" clusters. Figures 8.9–8.11 provide examples of this. Because one of the clusters in Figure 8.9 is significantly larger than the other two, K-means is unable to identify the three natural clusters; as a result, the larger cluster is broken, and one of the smaller clusters is combined with a portion of the larger cluster. Because the two smaller clusters in Figure 8.10 are significantly denser than the larger cluster, K-means is unable to identify the three natural clusters. Ultimately, because the two natural clusters' shapes are not globular, K-means discovers two clusters in Figure 8.11 that combine elements of the two original clusters.

The challenge in these three scenarios arises from the fact that the K-means objective function is not well-suited for identifying the types of clusters we are seeking. This is because the function is designed to minimize globular clusters of uniform size and density, or clusters that are widely spaced apart. However, it is possible to overcome these limitations to some extent by accepting a clustering that divides the natural clusters into multiple subclusters. In Figure 8.12, the outcomes of the three previous data sets are depicted when six clusters are identified instead of two or three. Each smaller cluster is considered pure as it consists solely of data points from one of the natural clusters.

8.2.9. Strengths and Weaknesses

K-means is an easy-to-use algorithm that works with many different kinds of data. Despite the fact that it is frequently run multiple times, it is also very efficient. Some variations are even more effective and less prone to initialization issues, such as bisecting K-means. However, K-means is not appropriate for all kinds of data. It can usually find pure subclusters if a large enough number of clusters are specified, but it cannot handle non-globular clusters or clusters of different sizes and densities. Additionally, K-means struggles to cluster data with outliers. In these circumstances, outlier detection and removal can be quite beneficial. Lastly, K-means can only be applied to data that have a known center, or centroid. Although more expensive, a related method called K-medoid clustering does not have this limitation.

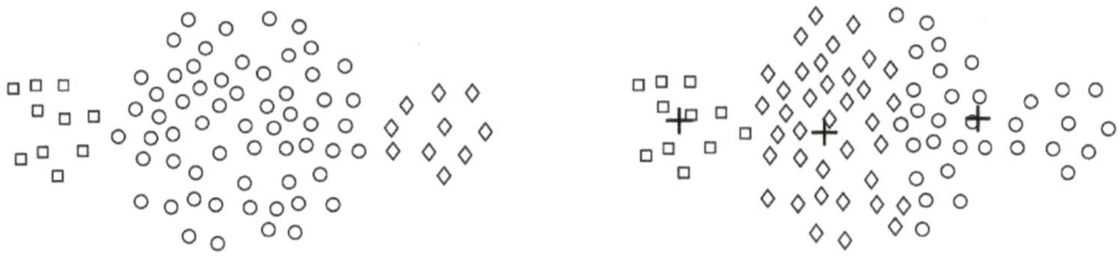

(a) Original points. (b) Three K-means clusters.

Figure 8.9. *K-means with clusters of different size.*

Source: https://www.ceom.ou.edu/media/docs/upload/Pang-Ning_Tan_Michael_Steinbach_Vipin_Kumar_-_Introduction_to_Data_Mining-Pe_NRDK4fi.pdf.

(a) Original points. (b) Three K-means clusters.

Figure 8.10. *K-means with clusters of different density.*

Source: https://www.ceom.ou.edu/media/docs/upload/Pang-Ning_Tan_Michael_Steinbach_Vipin_Kumar_-_Introduction_to_Data_Mining-Pe_NRDK4fi.pdf.

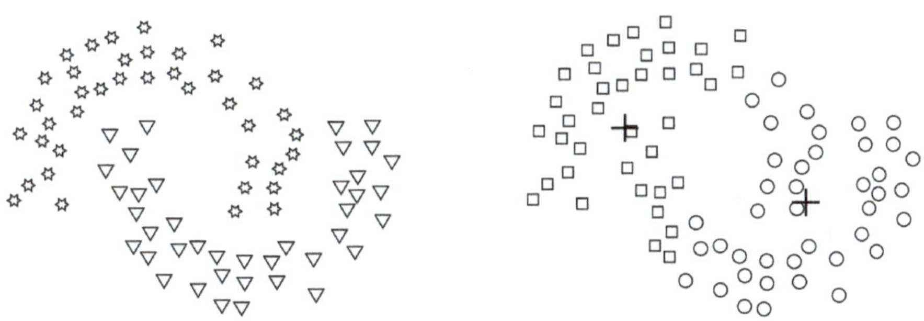

(a) Original points. (b) Two K-means clusters.

Figure 8.11. *K-means with non-globular clusters.*

Source: https://www.ceom.ou.edu/media/docs/upload/Pang-Ning_Tan_Michael_Steinbach_Vipin_Kumar_-_Introduction_to_Data_Mining-Pe_NRDK4fi.pdf.

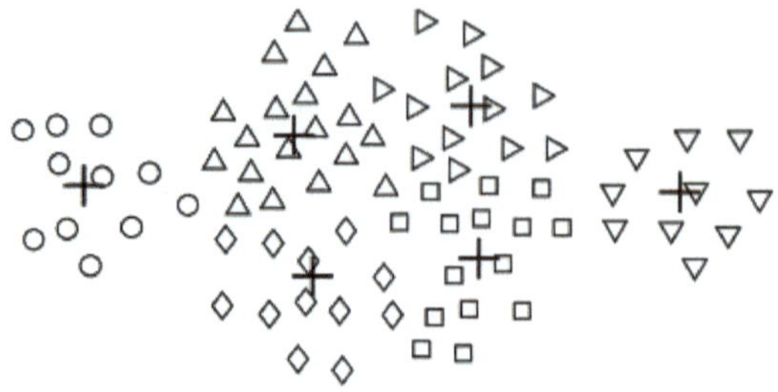

(a) Unequal sizes.

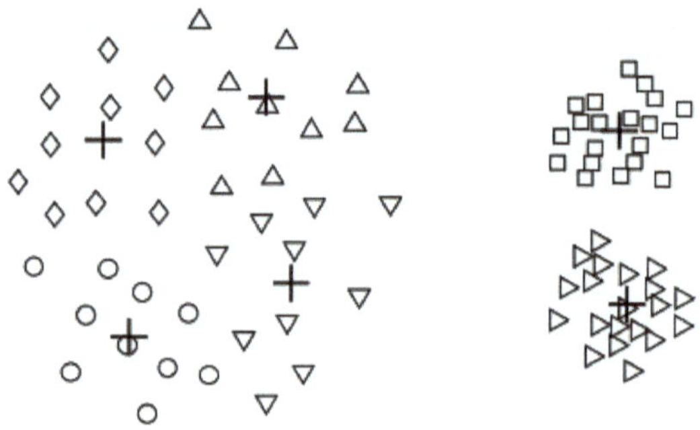

(b) Unequal densities.

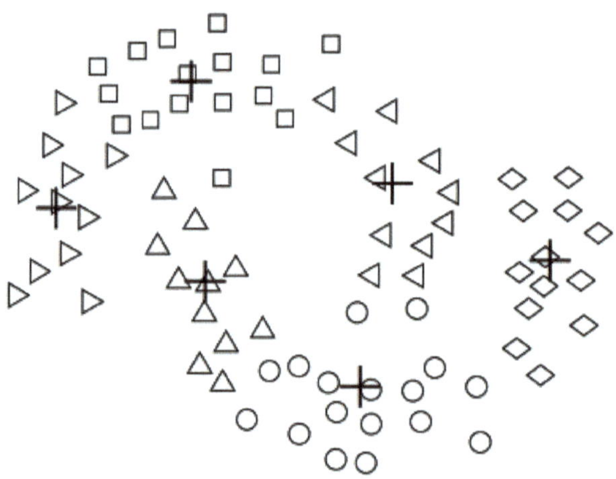

(c) Non-spherical shapes.

Figure 8.12. *Using K-means to find clusters that are subclusters of the natural clusters.*

Source: https://www.ceom.ou.edu/media/docs/upload/Pang-Ning_Tan_Michael_Steinbach_Vipin_Kumar_-_Introduction_to_Data_Mining-Pe_NRDK4fi.pdf.

8.2.10. K-means as an Optimization Problem

We now examine the underlying mathematics of K-means. This is a non-continuous section that requires some calculus knowledge through partial derivatives. It could also be beneficial to be familiar with optimization techniques, particularly those that rely on gradient descent.

As previously mentioned, when faced with an objective function such as "minimize SSE," clustering can be viewed as an optimization problem. In order to find the global optimum, one approach is to consider all possible ways of grouping the points into clusters and select the set of clusters that most effectively meets the objective function, such as minimizing the total SSE. However, due to the impractical nature of exhaustively trying all possibilities, a more feasible solution is required, even if it may not guarantee optimal results. One practical method, known as gradient descent, involves selecting an initial solution and then iteratively performing two steps: evaluating the change needed to optimize the objective function and adjusting the solution accordingly.

We assume that the data is one-dimensional, i.e., dist(x, y)=$(x - y)^2$. This does not change anything essential, but greatly simplifies the notation.

8.2.10.1. Derivation of K-means as an Algorithm to Minimize the SSE

When the goal is to minimize the SSE and the proximity function is Euclidean distance, we demonstrate how the centroid of the K-means algorithm can be obtained mathematically. In particular, we study the optimal way to update a cluster centroid to minimize the cluster SSE. To put it mathematically, we want to minimize Equation 1, which we reiterate for one-dimensional data here.

$$\text{SSE} = \sum_{i=1}^{K} \sum_{x \in C_i} (c_i - x)^2 \qquad (4)$$

Here, C_i is the i th cluster, x is a point in C_i, and ci is the mean of the i th cluster. See Table 8.1 for a complete list of notation. We can solve for the kth centroid c_k, which minimizes Equation 4, by differentiating the SSE, setting it equal to 0, and solving, as indicated below.

$$\begin{aligned}
\frac{\partial}{\partial c_k}\text{SSE} &= \frac{\partial}{\partial c_k}\sum_{i=1}^{K} \sum_{x \in C_i} (c_i - x)^2 \\
&= \sum_{i=1}^{K} \sum_{x \in C_i} \frac{\partial}{\partial c_k}(c_i - x)^2 \\
&= \sum_{x \in C_k} 2 * (c_k - x_k) = 0
\end{aligned}$$

$$\sum_{x \in C_k} 2 * (c_k - x_k) = 0 \Rightarrow m_k c_k = \sum_{x \in C_k} x_k \Rightarrow c_k = \frac{1}{m_k} \sum_{x \in C_k} x_k$$

Thus, as previously indicated, the best centroid for minimizing the SSE of a cluster is the mean of the points in the cluster.

8.2.10.2. Derivation of K-means for SAE

In this study, we show that the K-means algorithm is versatile and can be used with different objective functions. Our goal is to divide the data into K clusters in a way that minimizes the total Manhattan (L_1) distances between the data points and the centers of their clusters. We aim to minimize the sum of the L_1 absolute errors (SAE) using the equation below, where distL_1 represents the L_1 distance.

Again, for notational simplicity, we use one-dimensional data, i.e., $dist_{L1} = |c_i - x|$.

$$\text{SAE} = \sum_{i=1}^{K} \sum_{x \in C_i} dist_{L_1}(c_i, x) \quad (5)$$

We can solve for the kth centroid c_k, which minimizes Equation 5, by differentiating the SAE, setting it equal to 0, and solving.

$$\begin{aligned} \frac{\partial}{\partial c_k} \text{SAE} &= \frac{\partial}{\partial c_k} \sum_{i=1}^{K} \sum_{x \in C_i} |c_i - x| \\ &= \sum_{i=1}^{K} \sum_{x \in C_i} \frac{\partial}{\partial c_k} |c_i - x| \\ &= \sum_{x \in C_k} \frac{\partial}{\partial c_k} |c_k - x| = 0 \end{aligned}$$

$$\sum_{x \in C_k} \frac{\partial}{\partial c_k} |c_k - x| = 0 \Rightarrow \sum_{x \in C_k} sign(x - c_k) = 0$$

If we solve for c_k, we find that $c_k = \text{median}\{x \in C_k\}$, the median of the points in the cluster. The median of a group of points is straightforward to compute and less susceptible to distortion by outliers.

8.3. AGGLOMERATIVE HIERARCHICAL CLUSTERING

Another significant class of clustering techniques is hierarchical clustering. Similar to K-means, these methods are not as new as many clustering algorithms, but they are still widely used. There are two basic approaches for generating a hierarchical clustering:

- **Agglomerative:** Start with the points as individual clusters and, at each step, merge the closest pair of clusters. This requires defining a notion of cluster proximity.
- **Divisive:** Start with one, all-inclusive cluster and, at each step, split a cluster until only singleton clusters of individual points remain. In this case, we need to decide which cluster to split at each step and how to do the splitting.

The most popular approach is agglomerative hierarchical clustering, which is the only thing we will cover in this section.

A dendrogram, a tree-like diagram that shows the relationships between clusters and the order in which the clusters were split (divisive view) or merged (agglomerative view), is a common graphic representation of a hierarchical clustering. A nested cluster diagram can also be used to graphically depict a hierarchical clustering for sets of two-dimensional points, like the ones we'll use as examples. An illustration of these two figure types for a set of four two-dimensional points can be found in Figure 8.13.

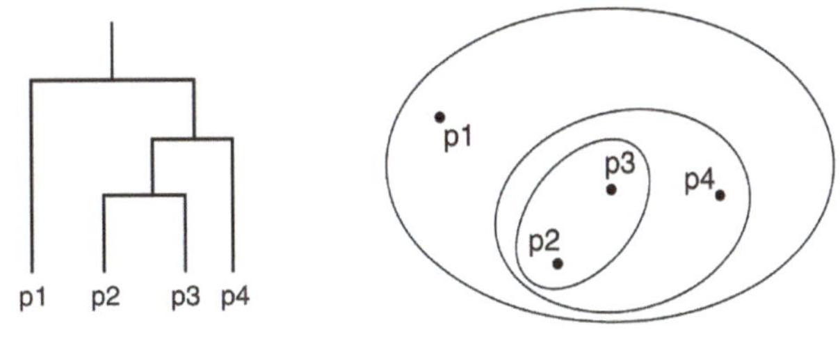

(a) Dendrogram. (b) Nested cluster diagram.

Figure 8.13. *A hierarchical clustering of four points shown as a dendrogram and as nested clusters.*

Source. https://www.ceom.ou.edu/media/docs/upload/Pang-Ning_Tan_Michael_Steinbach_Vipin_Kumar_-_Introduction_to_Data_Mining-Pe_NRDK4fi.pdf.

8.3.1. Basic Agglomerative Hierarchical Clustering Algorithm

A common method used in many agglomerative hierarchical clustering techniques is to start with individual points as clusters and then merge the two closest clusters one at a time until only one cluster is left. Algorithm 8.3 provides a more formal expression of this strategy.

Algorithm 8.3. Basic Agglomerative Hierarchical Clustering Algorithm

```
Compute the proximity matrix, if necessary.
repeat
    Merge the closest two clusters.
    Update the proximity matrix to reflect the proximity between the new
    cluster and the original clusters.
until Only one cluster remains.
```

8.3.1.1. Defining Proximity between Clusters

Computing the proximity between two clusters is the main function of Algorithm 8.3, and the definition of cluster proximity sets the different agglomerative hierarchical techniques apart that we will talk about. Typically, a specific kind of cluster is taken into consideration when defining cluster proximity. For instance, a graph-based view of clusters is the basis for numerous agglomerative hierarchical clustering techniques, including MIN, MAX, and Group Average. Cluster proximity, or the shortest edge between two nodes in different subsets of nodes, is defined by MIN as the distance between the closest two points that are in different clusters. The result is contiguity-based clusters, as Figure 8.2(c) illustrates. Alternatively, MAX defines cluster proximity as the longest edge between two nodes in different subsets of nodes, or, in graph terms, the proximity between the farthest two points in different clusters. MIN and MAX are brief and evocative names if our proximities are distances. However, the names appear to be reversed for similarities, where closer points are indicated by higher values. Because of this, we typically favor using the alternate terms, complete link and single link, respectively. Cluster proximity is defined as the average pairwise proximities (average length of edges) of all pairs of points from various clusters by another graph-based technique called the group average technique. Figure 8.14 provides examples of these three strategies.

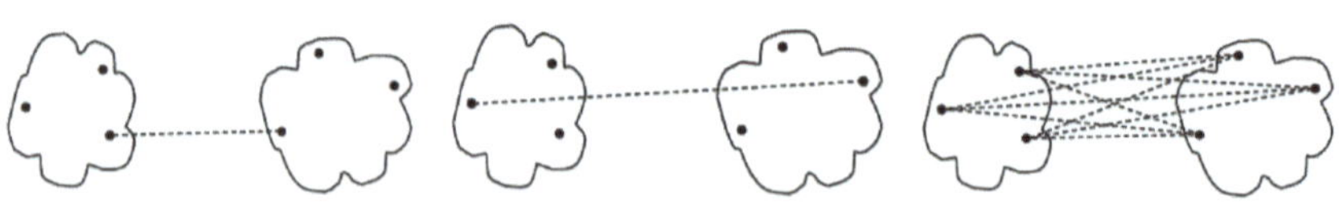

(a) MIN (single link.) (b) MAX (complete link.) (c) Group average.

Figure 8.14. *Graph-based definitions of cluster proximity.*

Source. https://www.ceom.ou.edu/media/docs/upload/Pang-Ning_Tan_Michael_Steinbach_Vipin_Kumar_-_Introduction_to_Data_Mining-Pe_NRDK4fi.pdf.

Different definitions of cluster proximity make more sense if we adopt a prototype-based perspective, in which a centroid represents each cluster. The proximity between cluster centroids is the standard definition of cluster proximity when using centroids. Ward's method is an alternative technique that also uses the centroid of a cluster to represent it. However, instead of using the centroid, Ward's method measures the proximity between two clusters by calculating the increase in the SSE that occurs when the two clusters merge. Ward's technique, like K-means, aims to reduce the total squared distance between a point and its cluster centroids.

8.3.1.2. Time and Space Complexity

A proximity matrix is used in the fundamental agglomerative hierarchical clustering algorithm that was just described. If the proximity matrix is symmetric, then storing $\frac{1}{2}m^2$ proximities is necessary, where m is the total number of data points. With the exception of singleton clusters, the amount of space required to maintain track of the clusters is m−1. Therefore, $O(m^2)$ is the total space complexity.

In terms of computational complexity, the analysis of the fundamental agglomerative hierarchical clustering algorithm is also simple. The proximity matrix must be computed in $O(m^2)$ time. Following that, since there are m clusters at the beginning and two clusters are merged during each iteration, there are m – 1 iterations involving steps 3 and 4. Step 3 takes $O((m-i+1)^2)$ time for the i th iteration if the proximity matrix is searched linearly. This time is proportional to the square of the current number of clusters. After two clusters merge, Step 4 only needs $O(m - i + 1)$ time to update the proximity matrix. (For the methods we consider, a cluster merger affects only $O(m-i+1)$ proximities. If left unchanged, this would result in an $O(m^3)$ time complexity. The cost of locating the two closest clusters can be lowered to $O(m - i + 1)$ if the distances between each cluster and every other cluster are kept as a sorted list (or heap). However, the total time needed for a hierarchical clustering based on Algorithm 8.3 is $O(m^2 \log m)$ due to the added complexity of maintaining data in a sorted list or heap. The amount of data sets that can be processed is severely constrained by the space and time complexity of hierarchical clustering.

8.3.2. Specific Techniques

8.3.2.1. Sample Data

In order to demonstrate how different hierarchical clustering algorithms work, we will be using a set of sample data containing 6 two-dimensional points. These points are displayed in Figure 8.15, with their respective x and y coordinates listed in Table 8.3 and the Euclidean distances between them shown in Table 8.4.

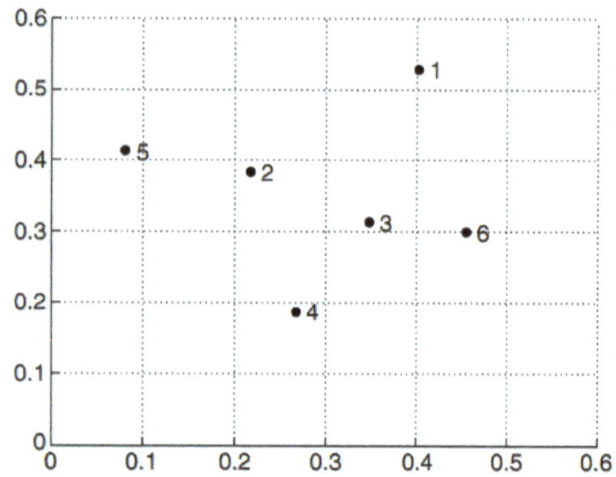

Figure 8.15. *Set of 6 two-dimensional points.*

Source. https://www.ceom.ou.edu/media/docs/upload/Pang-Ning_Tan_Michael_Steinbach_Vipin_Kumar_-_Introduction_to_Data_Mining-Pe_NRDK4fi.pdf.

Table 8.3. XY Coordinates of 6 Points

Point	x Coordinate	y Coordinate
p1	0.40	0.53
p2	0.22	0.38
p3	0.35	0.32
p4	0.26	0.19
p5	0.08	0.41
p6	0.45	0.30

Source. https://www.ceom.ou.edu/media/docs/upload/Pang-Ning_Tan_Michael_Steinbach_Vipin_Kumar_-_Introduction_to_Data_Mining-Pe_NRDK4fi.pdf.

Table 8.4. Euclidean Distance Matrix for 6 Points

	p1	p2	p3	p4	p5	p6
p1	0.00	0.24	0.22	0.37	0.34	0.23
p2	0.24	0.00	0.15	0.20	0.14	0.25
p3	0.22	0.15	0.00	0.15	0.28	0.11
p4	0.37	0.20	0.15	0.00	0.29	0.22
p5	0.34	0.14	0.28	0.29	0.00	0.39
p6	0.23	0.25	0.11	0.22	0.39	0.00

Source. https://www.ceom.ou.edu/media/docs/upload/Pang-Ning_Tan_Michael_Steinbach_Vipin_Kumar_-_Introduction_to_Data_Mining-Pe_NRDK4fi.pdf.

8.3.2.2. Single Link or MIN

The proximity of two clusters is determined by taking the minimum of the distance (maximum of the similarity) between any two points in the two distinct clusters in the single link or MIN version of hierarchical clustering. To put it in terms of graphs, if you begin with all the points as singleton clusters and then add links, shortest links first, one at a time, the points will eventually combine into clusters. Although the single link technique is sensitive to noise and outliers, it performs well when handling non-elliptical shapes.

- **Example 4 (Single Link):** The outcome of using the single link technique on our six-point example data set is displayed in Figure 8.16. The nested clusters are depicted as a series of nested ellipses in Figure 8.16(a), with the numbers corresponding to the ellipses designating the clustering order. In Figure 8.16(b), the same data is displayed as a dendrogram. The distance between two clusters is reflected in the dendrogram by the height at which they merge. As an example, Table 8.4 shows that the height at which points 3 and 6 are connected to form a single cluster in the dendrogram is 0.11. As an additional illustration, the separation between clusters {3, 6} and {2, 5} is provided by.

$$\begin{aligned} dist(\{3,6\},\{2,5\}) &= \min(dist(3,2), dist(6,2), dist(3,5), dist(6,5)) \\ &= \min(0.15, 0.25, 0.28, 0.39) \\ &= 0.15. \end{aligned}$$

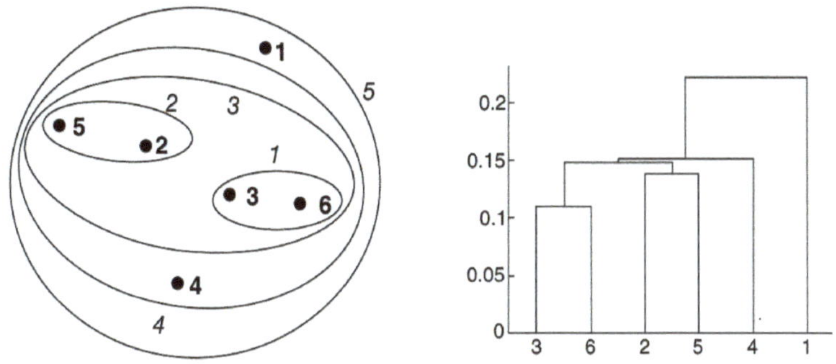

(a) Single link clustering. (b) Single link dendrogram.

Figure 8.16. *Single link clustering of the six points shown in Figure 8.15.*

Source: https://www.ceom.ou.edu/media/docs/upload/Pang-Ning_Tan_Michael_Steinbach_Vipin_Kumar_-_Introduction_to_Data_Mining-Pe_NRDK4fi.pdf.

8.3.2.3. Complete Link or MAX or CLIQUE

The proximity of two clusters is determined by taking the maximum of the distance (minimum of the similarity) between any two points in the two distinct clusters in the complete link or MAX version of hierarchical clustering. In graph language, a collection of points is not considered a cluster until every single point within it is fully linked, i.e., if you begin with all points as singleton clusters and add links between points one at a time, shortest links first. establish a clique. Although complete link tends to favor globular shapes and can break large clusters, it is less vulnerable to noise and outliers.

- **Example 5 (Complete Link):** The results of applying MAX to the six-point sample data set are displayed in Figure 8.17. As with a single link, the merging of points 3 and 6 occurs first. But rather than combining with {2, 5} or {1}, {3, 6} is combined with {4}.

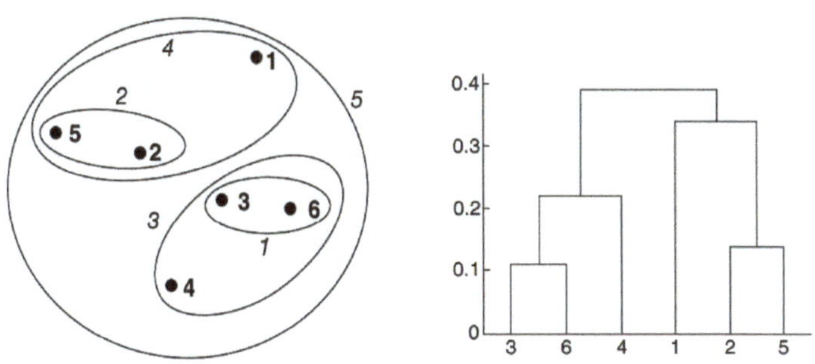

(a) Complete link clustering. (b) Complete link dendrogram.

Figure 8.17. *Complete link clustering of the six points shown in Figure 8.15.*

Source: https://www.ceom.ou.edu/media/docs/upload/Pang-Ning_Tan_Michael_Steinbach_Vipin_Kumar_-_Introduction_to_Data_Mining-Pe_NRDK4fi.pdf.

$$\begin{aligned}
dist(\{3,6\},\{4\}) &= \max(dist(3,4), dist(6,4)) \\
&= \max(0.15, 0.22) \\
&= 0.22. \\
dist(\{3,6\},\{2,5\}) &= \max(dist(3,2), dist(6,2), dist(3,5), dist(6,5)) \\
&= \max(0.15, 0.25, 0.28, 0.39) \\
&= 0.39. \\
dist(\{3,6\},\{1\}) &= \max(dist(3,1), dist(6,1)) \\
&= \max(0.22, 0.23) \\
&= 0.23.
\end{aligned}$$

8.3.2.4. Group Average

In hierarchical clustering, the group average version calculates the proximity of two clusters as the average pairwise proximity among all pairs of points in the clusters. This method falls between the single and complete link approaches. The cluster proximity (C_i, C_j) for two clusters C_i and C_j, with sizes m_i and m_j, is then determined using the following equation.

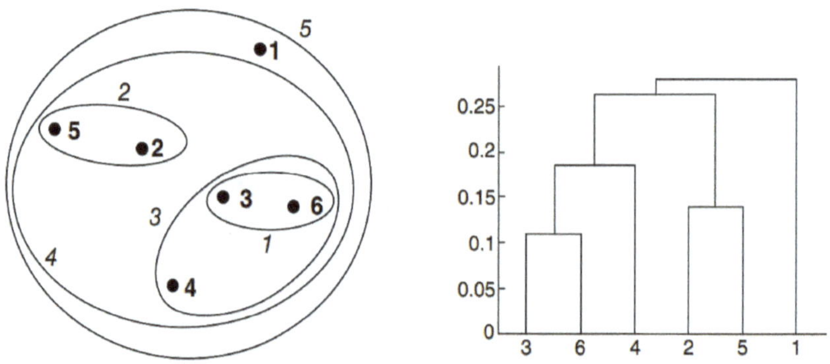

(a) Group average clustering. (b) Group average dendrogram.

Figure 8.18. *Group average clustering of the six points shown in Figure 8.15.*

Source: https://www.ceom.ou.edu/media/docs/upload/Pang-Ning_Tan_Michael_Steinbach_Vipin_Kumar_-_Introduction_to_Data_Mining-Pe_NRDK4fi.pdf.

$$proximity(C_i, C_j) = \frac{\sum_{\substack{\mathbf{x}\in C_i \\ \mathbf{y}\in C_j}} proximity(\mathbf{x}, \mathbf{y})}{m_i * m_j}. \quad (6)$$

- **Example 6 (Group Average):** The results of utilizing the group average method on a sample data set of six points is depicted in Figure 8.18. To demonstrate the application of the group average technique, we examine the distances between various clusters.

$$
\begin{aligned}
dist(\{3,6,4\},\{1\}) &= (0.22+0.37+0.23)/(3*1)\\
&= 0.28\\
dist(\{2,5\},\{1\}) &= (0.2357+0.3421)/(2*1)\\
&= 0.2889\\
dist(\{3,6,4\},\{2,5\}) &= (0.15+0.28+0.25+0.39+0.20+0.29)/(6*2)\\
&= 0.26
\end{aligned}
$$

Because dist({3, 6, 4}, {2, 5}) is smaller than dist({3, 6, 4}, {1}) and dist({2, 5}, {1clusters {3, 6, 4} and {2, 5} are merged at the fourth stage.

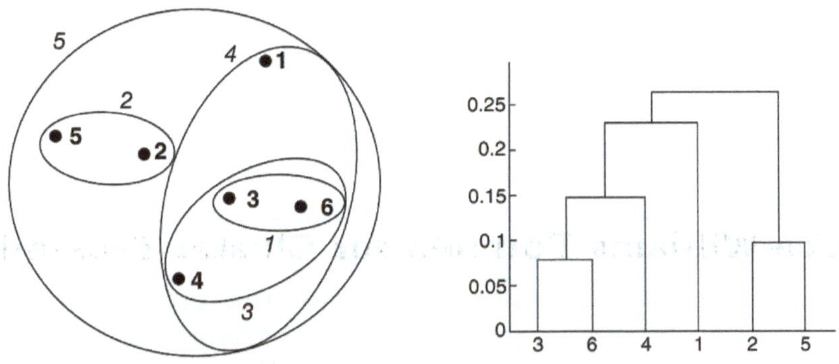

(a) Ward's clustering. (b) Ward's dendrogram.

Figure 8.19. *Ward's clustering of the six points shown in Figure 8.15.*

Source: https://www.ceom.ou.edu/media/docs/upload/Pang-Ning_Tan_Michael_Steinbach_Vipin_Kumar_-_Introduction_to_Data_Mining-Pe_NRDK4fi.pdf.

8.3.2.5. Ward's Method and Centroid Methods

Ward's method defines the proximity between two clusters as the increase in squared error when they are merged. This method shares the same objective function as K-means clustering, making it distinct from other hierarchical techniques. However, mathematically, Ward's method is shown to be very similar to the group average method when the proximity between points is considered as the square of the distance between them.

- **Example 7 (Ward's Method):** The results of applying Ward's method to the six-point sample data set are displayed in Figure 8.19. Compared to clustering generated by a single link, complete link, and group average, this clustering is distinct.

By measuring the separation between the centroids of clusters, centroid methods determine the proximity between two clusters. These methods might look like K-means, but Ward's method is the correct hierarchical analog, as we have pointed out.

The potential for inversions is another feature of centroid methods that sets them apart from the other hierarchical clustering strategies we have covered and is frequently viewed negatively. To be more precise, two merged clusters might be closer in nature than the pair that underwent a previous step of merging.

With the other approaches, as we move from singleton clusters to a single all-inclusive cluster, the distance between the merged clusters grows monotonically (or, at worst, is non-increasing).

Table 8.5. Table of Lance-Williams Coefficients for Common Hierarchical Clustering Approaches

Clustering Method	α_A	α_B	β	γ
Single Link	1/2	1/2	0	−1/2
Complete Link	1/2	1/2	0	1/2
Group Average	$\frac{m_A}{m_A+m_B}$	$\frac{m_B}{m_A+m_B}$	0	0
Centroid	$\frac{m_A}{m_A+m_B}$	$\frac{m_B}{m_A+m_B}$	$\frac{-m_A m_B}{(m_A+m_B)^2}$	0
Ward's	$\frac{m_A+m_Q}{m_A+m_B+m_Q}$	$\frac{m_B+m_Q}{m_A+m_B+m_Q}$	$\frac{-m_Q}{m_A+m_B+m_Q}$	0

Source: https://www.ceom.ou.edu/media/docs/upload/Pang-Ning_Tan_Michael_Steinbach_Vipin_Kumar_-_Introduction_to_Data_Mining-Pe_NRDK4fi.pdf.

8.3.3. The Lance-Williams Formula for Cluster Proximity

In the Lance-Williams formula (equation 7), any of the cluster proximities we have covered in this section can be seen as an option for varying the parameters pertaining to the proximity between clusters Q and R, where R is the result of the merger of clusters A and B. This formula uses p(., .) is a proximity function, and the numbers m_A, m_B, and m_Q denote the points in clusters A, B, and Q, in that order. To put it another way, when clusters A and B combine to form cluster R, the distance between the new cluster and an existing cluster, Q, is determined by the linear relationship between Q's proximities to the original clusters A and B. Table 8.5 displays these coefficient values for the techniques we have covered.

$$p(R,Q) = \alpha_A\, p(A,Q) + \alpha_B\, p(B,Q) + \beta\, p(A,B) + \gamma\, |p(A,Q) - p(B,Q)| \quad (7)$$

The original data points need not be retained in any hierarchical clustering method that can be expressed using the Lance-Williams formula. Rather, as clustering takes place, the proximity matrix is updated. Although there is appeal to a general formula, particularly in the context of implementation, it is easier to comprehend the various hierarchical methods by examining the definition of cluster proximity that is employed by each method.

8.3.4. Key Issues in Hierarchical Clustering

8.3.4.1. Lack of a Global Objective Function

As we have stated earlier, it is not possible to consider agglomerative hierarchical clustering as globally optimizing an objective function. Agglomerative hierarchical clustering techniques, on the other hand, make local decisions at each step about which clusters to merge (or split, in the case of divisive approaches) based on a variety of criteria. Using this method produces clustering algorithms without having to deal with the challenges of trying to solve a challenging combinatorial optimization problem. (It can be demonstrated that the general clustering problem is computationally impractical for an objective function like "minimize SSE." Moreover, these methods do not encounter issues with local minima or challenges in selecting starting points. Naturally, in many situations, the space complexity of $O(m^2)$ and the time complexity of $O(m^2 \log m)$ are prohibitive.

8.3.4.2. Ability to Handle Different Cluster Sizes

We have not yet covered the treatment of the relative sizes of the merged cluster pairs in agglomerative hierarchical clustering. Only cluster proximity schemes involving sums, like centroid, Ward's, and group average, are covered in this discussion. There are two methods: unweighted, which considers the total number of points in each cluster, and weighted, which treats each cluster equally. Keep in mind that the terms weighted and unweighted relate to the individual data points rather than the clusters. Stated differently, points within different clusters receive different weights when clusters of unequal size are treated equally, whereas points within different clusters receive the same weight when cluster size is taken into consideration.

We will illustrate this using the group average technique discussed in Section 8.3.2, which is the unweighted version of the group average technique. In the clustering literature, the full name of this approach is the Unweighted Pair Group Method using Arithmetic averages (UPGMA). In Table 8.5, which gives the formula for updating cluster similarity, the coefficients for UPGMA involve the size of each of the clusters that were merged: $\alpha_A = \frac{m_A}{m_A+m_B}, \alpha_B = \frac{m_B}{m_A+m_B}, \beta = 0, \gamma = 0$. For the weighted version of group average—known as WPGMA—the coefficients are constants: $\alpha_A = 1/2$, $\alpha_B = 1/2$, $\beta = 0$, $\gamma = 0$. In general, unweighted approaches are preferred unless there is reason to believe that individual points should have different weights; e.g., perhaps classes of objects have been unevenly sampled.

8.3.4.3. Merging Decisions Are Final

Due to their ability to utilize information regarding the pairwise similarity of all points, agglomerative hierarchical clustering algorithms typically produce good local decisions when merging two clusters. Nevertheless, the choice to combine two clusters cannot be reversed after it is made. By using this method, it is impossible for a local optimization criterion to turn into a global one. For instance, although Ward's method uses the K-means "minimize squared error" criterion to determine which clusters to merge, the clusters at each level do not represent local minima with regard to the overall SSE. A point in one cluster might actually be closer to the centroid of another cluster than it is to the centroid of its current cluster, indicating that the clusters are not even stable. However, Ward's approach is frequently employed as a reliable way to start a K-means clustering, showing that there is a relationship between a local "minimize squared error" objective function and a global "minimize squared error" objective function. Certain strategies aim to get around the restriction that merges are final. In an attempt to improve a global objective function, one method involves rearranging the tree's branches in order to correct the hierarchical clustering. Another method divides the data into numerous small clusters using a partitional clustering technique like K-means. These clusters are then used as the basis for hierarchical clustering.

8.3.5. Strengths and Weaknesses

We have already covered the advantages and disadvantages of various agglomerative hierarchical clustering algorithms. More generally, these kinds of algorithms are employed because the underlying program, e.g., a hierarchy is necessary for the creation of a taxonomy. Furthermore, some research indicates that these algorithms may be able to generate clusters of higher quality. However, in terms of processing power and storage needs, agglomerative hierarchical clustering algorithms are costly. The finality of all merges may also be problematic for high-dimensional, noisy data, like document data. These two issues can then be partially resolved by first using a different method, like K-means, to partially cluster the data.

CASE STUDY

CUSTOMER SEGMENTATION FOR E-COMMERCE

- **Objective:** To segment customers based on their purchasing behavior to enhance personalized marketing strategies.
- **Background:** An e-commerce company aims to understand its customer base better to tailor marketing efforts, increase customer satisfaction, and improve sales. The company has a large dataset of customer transactions, including variables such as purchase frequency, average transaction value, and product categories.
- **Methodology:**
  1. **Data Collection:** Transaction data collected from the company's online platform.
  2. **Feature Selection:** Selected features such as purchase frequency, average transaction value, number of distinct products purchased, and categories of products bought.
  3. **Algorithm Used:** K-means clustering.
  4. **Number of Clusters:** Determined using the Elbow method, which involves plotting the within-cluster sum of squares against the number of clusters and looking for the "elbow" point where the rate of decrease sharply changes.
- **Implementation:**
  1. Applied K-means clustering to the selected features.
  2. Used PCA for dimensionality reduction to visualize the clusters.
- **Results:**

1. Identified four distinct customer segments:
   - i. **Frequent Shoppers:** High purchase frequency, moderate transaction value.
   - ii. **High-Value Customers:** Low purchase frequency, high transaction value.
   - iii. **Bargain Hunters:** Moderate purchase frequency, low transaction value, primarily shop during sales.
   - iv. **Diverse Shoppers:** Moderate frequency, diverse product categories.

- **Conclusion**: The e-commerce company implemented personalized marketing strategies for each segment, such as loyalty programs for frequent shoppers and targeted promotions for bargain hunters, leading to increased engagement and sales.

CLASS ACTIVITY

To understand the fundamental concepts of cluster analysis, including selecting features, applying different clustering algorithms, and evaluating cluster validity. Students will work in groups to apply cluster analysis to a dataset, interpret the results, and present their findings. Demonstration of how to apply K-means clustering to a simple dataset using Python. Groups will choose one or more clustering algorithms (K-means, hierarchical clustering, DBSCAN) to apply to their dataset.

SUMMARY

- Cluster analysis groups data objects based only on information found in the data that describes the objects and their relationships.
- A partitional clustering is simply a division of the set of data objects into non-overlapping subsets (clusters) such that each data object is in exactly one subset.
- A fuzzy or probabilistic clustering is often converted to an exclusive clustering by assigning each object to the cluster in which its membership weight or probability is highest.
- A cluster is a set of objects in which each object is closer (or more similar) to every other object in the cluster than to any object not in the cluster.
- A cluster is a dense region of objects that is surrounded by a region of low density.
- K-medoid defines a prototype in terms of a medoid, which is the most representative point for a group of points, and can be applied to a wide range of data since it requires only a proximity measure for a pair of objects.
- The cluster with the largest SSE is usually chosen, but we could also split the cluster with the largest standard deviation for one particular attribute.

REVIEW QUESTIONS

1. What is cluster analysis?
2. Explain the different types of clusterings.
3. Describe the basic K-means algorithm.
4. Write the derivation of K-means as an algorithm to minimize the SSE.
5. What is agglomerative hierarchical clustering algorithm?

REFERENCES

1. Aldenderfer, M. S., & Blashfield, R. K. (1985). *Cluster Analysis*. Sage Publications, Los Angeles.
2. Anderberg, M. R. (1973). *Cluster Analysis for Applications*. Academic Press, New York.
3. Ankerst, M., Breunig, M. M., Kriegel, H.-P., & Sander, J. (1999). OPTICS: Ordering points to identify the clustering structure. In *Proceedings of the 1999 ACM-SIGMOD International Conference on Management of Data* (pp. 49–60). Philadelphia, Pennsylvania. ACM Press.
4. Arabie, P., Hubert, L., & Soete, G. D. (1996). An overview of combinatorial data analysis. In P. Arabie, L. Hubert, & G. D. Soete (Eds.), *Clustering and Classification* (pp. 188–217). World Scientific, Singapore.
5. Ball, G., & Hall, D. (1967). A clustering technique for summarizing multivariate data. *Behavior Science, 12*, 153–155.
6. Banerjee, A., Merugu, S., Dhillon, I. S., & Ghosh, J. (2004). Clustering with Bregman divergences. In *Proceedings of the 2004 SIAM International Conference on Data Mining* (pp. 234–245), Lake Buena Vista, FL.
7. Berkhin, P. (2002). Survey of clustering data mining techniques. Technical report, Accrue Software, San Jose, CA.
8. Boley, D. (1998). Principal direction divisive partitioning. *Data Mining and Knowledge Discovery, 2*(4), 325–344.
9. Bradley, P. S., & Fayyad, U. M. (1998). Refining initial points for k-means clustering. In *Proceedings of the 15th International Conference on Machine Learning* (pp. 91–99). Madison, WI. Morgan Kaufmann Publishers Inc.
10. Dhillon, I. S., & Modha, D. S. (2001). Concept decompositions for large sparse text data using clustering. *Machine Learning, 42*(1/2), 143–175.
11. Dhillon, I. S., Guan, Y., & Kogan, J. (2002). Iterative clustering of high dimensional text data augmented by local search. In *Proceedings of the 2002 IEEE International Conference on Data Mining* (pp. 131–138). IEEE Computer Society.
12. Duda, R. O., Hart, P. E., & Stork, D. G. (2001). *Pattern Classification* (2nd ed.). John Wiley & Sons, Inc., New York.
13. Ester, M., Kriegel, H.-P., Sander, J., & Xu, X. (1996). A density-based algorithm for discovering clusters in large spatial databases with noise. In *Proceedings of the 2nd International Conference on Knowledge Discovery and Data Mining* (pp. 226–231). Portland, Oregon. AAAI Press.
14. Ester, M., Kriegel, H.-P., Sander, J., Wimmer, M., & Xu, X. (1998). Incremental clustering for mining in a data warehousing environment. In *Proceedings of the 24th VLDB Conference* (pp. 323–333). New York City. Morgan Kaufmann.
15. Everitt, B. S., Landau, S., & Leese, M. (2001). *Cluster Analysis* (4th ed.). Arnold Publishers, London.

16. Fisher, D. (1996). Iterative optimization and simplification of hierarchical clusterings. *Journal of Artificial Intelligence Research, 4*, 147–179.
17. Halkidi, M., Batistakis, Y., & Vazirgiannis, M. (2002). Cluster validity methods: Part I. *SIGMOD Record (ACM Special Interest Group on Management of Data), 31*(2), 40–45.
18. Halkidi, M., Batistakis, Y., & Vazirgiannis, M. (2002). Clustering validity checking methods: Part II. *SIGMOD Record (ACM Special Interest Group on Management of Data), 31*(3), 19–27.
19. Hamerly, G., & Elkan, C. (2002). Alternatives to the k-means algorithm that find better clusterings. In *Proceedings of the 11th International Conference on Information and Knowledge Management* (pp. 600–607), McLean, Virginia. ACM Press.
20. Han, J., Kamber, M., & Tung, A. (2001). Spatial clustering methods in data mining: A review. In H. J. Miller & J. Han (Eds.), *Geographic Data Mining and Knowledge Discovery* (pp. 188–217). Taylor and Francis, London.
21. Hartigan, J. (1975). *Clustering Algorithms*. Wiley, New York.
22. Hastie, T., Tibshirani, R., & Friedman, J. H. (2001). *The Elements of Statistical Learning: Data Mining, Inference, and Prediction*. Springer, New York.
23. Jain, A. K., & Dubes, R. C. (1988). *Algorithms for Clustering Data*. Prentice Hall Advanced Reference Series. Prentice Hall. Available online at http://www.cse.msu.edu/~jain/Clustering_Jain_Dubes.pdf (accessed on 25 June 2024)..
24. Jain, A. K., Murty, M. N., & Flynn, P. J. (1999). Data clustering: A review. *ACM Computing Surveys, 31*(3), 264–323.
25. Jardine, N., & Sibson, R. (1971). *Mathematical Taxonomy*. Wiley, New York.
26. Karypis, G. (2003). CLUTO 2.1.1: Software for clustering high-dimensional datasets. Available at: www.cs.umn.edu/~karypis (accessed on 25 June 2024).
27. Karypis, G., Han, E.-H., & Kumar, V. (1999). Multilevel refinement for hierarchical clustering. Technical Report TR 99-020, University of Minnesota, Minneapolis, MN.
28. Kaufman, L., & Rousseeuw, P. J. (1990). *Finding Groups in Data: An Introduction to Cluster Analysis*. Wiley Series in Probability and Statistics. John Wiley and Sons, New York.
29. Kleinberg, J. M. (2002). An impossibility theorem for clustering. In *Proceedings of the 16th Annual Conference on Neural Information Processing Systems* (pp. 9–14).
30. Larsen, B., & Aone, C. (1999). Fast and effective text mining using linear-time document clustering. In *Proceedings of the 5th International Conference on Knowledge Discovery and Data Mining* (pp. 16–22), San Diego, California. ACM Press.
31. MacQueen, J. (1967). Some methods for classification and analysis of multivariate observations. In *Proceedings of the 5th Berkeley Symposium on Mathematical Statistics and Probability* (pp. 281–297). University of California Press.
32. Milligan, G. W. (1996). Clustering validation: Results and implications for applied analyses. In Arabie, P., Hubert, L., & Soete, G. D. (Eds.), *Clustering and Classification* (pp. 345–375). World Scientific, Singapore.

33. Mirkin, B. (1996). *Mathematical Classification and Clustering* (Vol. 11 of Nonconvex Optimization and Its Applications). Kluwer Academic Publishers.

34. Mitchell, T. (1997). *Machine Learning*. McGraw-Hill, Boston, MA.

35. Murtagh, F. (1985). *Multidimensional Clustering Algorithms*. Physica-Verlag, Heidelberg and Vienna.

36. Pelleg, D., & Moore, A. W. (2000). X-means: Extending k-means with efficient estimation of the number of clusters. In *Proceedings of the 17th International Conference on Machine Learning* (pp. 727–734). Morgan Kaufmann, San Francisco, CA.

37. Romesburg, C. (1984). *Cluster Analysis for Researchers*. Life Time Learning, Belmont, CA.

38. Sander, J., Ester, M., Kriegel, H.-P., & Xu, X. (1998). Density-based clustering in spatial databases: The algorithm GDBSCAN and its applications. *Data Mining and Knowledge Discovery, 2*(2), 169–194.

39. Savaresi, S. M., & Boley, D. (2004). A comparative analysis on the bisecting K-means and the PDDP clustering algorithms. *Intelligent Data Analysis, 8*(4), 345–362.

40. Sneath, P. H. A., & Sokal, R. R. (1971). *Numerical Taxonomy*. Freeman, San Francisco.

41. Späth, H. (1980). *Cluster Analysis Algorithms for Data Reduction and Classification of Objects* (Vol. 4 of Computers and Their Application). Ellis Horwood Publishers, Chichester.

42. Steinbach, M., Karypis, G., & Kumar, V. (2000). A comparison of document clustering techniques. In *Proceedings of KDD Workshop on Text Mining, Proceedings of the 6th International Conference on Knowledge Discovery and Data Mining*. Boston, MA.

43. Zahn, C. T. (1971). Graph-theoretical methods for detecting and describing gestalt clusters. *IEEE Transactions on Computers, C-20*(1), 68–86.

44. Zhang, B., Hsu, M., & Dayal, U. (1999). K-Harmonic means—A data clustering algorithm. Technical Report HPL-1999-124, Hewlett Packard Laboratories.

45. Zhao, Y., & Karypis, G. (2004). Empirical and theoretical comparisons of selected criterion functions for document clustering. *Machine Learning, 55*(3), 311–331.

CHAPTER 9

Cluster Analysis: Additional Issues and Algorithms

LEARNING OBJECTIVES

After studying this chapter, you will be able to:

- Explore the issues related to the characteristics of data, clusters, and clustering algorithms
- Discuss the prototype-based clustering
- Examine the density-based clustering

KEY TERMS FROM THIS CHAPTER

Psychology	Statistics
Pattern recognition	Information retrieval
Clustering algorithm	DBSCAN
K-means clustering	Data sets
Fuzzy clustering	Prototype-based clustering
Fuzzy set theory	Random initialization
Probability	Gaussian distribution
Density-based clustering	Grid-Based Clustering
Subspace Clustering	

INTRODUCTION

Data is grouped (clusters) based on whether they are meaningful, practical, or both. The natural structure of the data should be captured by the clusters if the objective is to form meaningful groups. Cluster analysis, however, is sometimes only a good place to start for other tasks, like data summarization. Cluster analysis has long been used extensively for understanding or practical purposes in many different fields, including biology, statistics, machine learning, pattern recognition, information retrieval, data mining, psychology and other social sciences, and statistics.

Numerous clustering algorithms have been created for various applications across a range of domains. There isn't an algorithm here that works for every kind of data, cluster, or application. As a matter of fact, it appears that there is always room for a new clustering algorithm that is more effective or more appropriate for a specific kind of data, application, or cluster. Rather, all we can say is that we have methods that we find to be effective in certain circumstances. The reason for this is that a good set of clusters is often ambiguous and subject to personal interpretation. Furthermore, the problem of determining the optimal clustering is frequently computationally impractical when an objective measure is used to provide a precise definition of a cluster.

This chapter examines the ideas and methods that have been developed to address significant problems in cluster analysis. We start out by going over the main points of cluster analysis, which are the properties of data, clusters, and algorithms that have a big influence on clustering. These questions are crucial for comprehending, characterizing, and contrasting clustering techniques. They also serve as the foundation for selecting the best technique for a given circumstance. For instance, many clustering algorithms are unsuitable for large data sets because they have an $O(m^2)$ time or space complexity, where m is the number of objects.

9.1. CHARACTERISTICS OF DATA, CLUSTERS, AND CLUSTERING ALGORITHMS

Concerns about data properties, clusters, and algorithms that are crucial for a thorough grasp of cluster analysis are examined in this section. Managing noise and outliers is one of the challenges that these issues represent. Other problems concern a desired algorithmic characteristic, like the algorithm's ability to generate an identical result regardless of the sequence in which the data objects are processed. Numerous "dimensions" that can be used to characterize and contrast different clustering algorithms and the clustering outcomes they yield are identified in this section along with the discussion of various clusterings and cluster types.

9.1.1. Example: Comparing K-Means and DBSCAN

In order to make the comparison easier, we'll assume that DBSCAN always assigns a border point that is connected to multiple core points to the closest core point, and that there are no distance ties for either K-means or DBSCAN.

- Both DBSCAN and K-means are partitional clustering algorithms that place each object in a single cluster; however, DBSCAN discards objects that it deems to be noise, whereas K-means usually clusters every object.
- A cluster is conceptualized using a prototype in K-means, while a density-based concept is used in DBSCAN.
- DBSCAN is not significantly impacted by noise or outliers and can handle clusters of various sizes and shapes. Non-globular clusters and clusters of varying sizes present challenges for K-means. The performance of both algorithms may be compromised in cases where cluster densities vary greatly.
- K-means can only be applied to data, like a mean or median, that have a clearly defined centroid. DBSCAN demands that its definition of density—which is predicated on the conventional Euclidean understanding of density—make sense in relation to the data.

- Document data is an example of sparse, high-dimensional data that can be used with K-means. As a result of the traditional Euclidean definition of density's poor performance with high-dimensional data, DBSCAN generally performs poorly with such data.
- Although K-means and DBSCAN were initially developed to process Euclidean data, they have both been expanded to process other kinds of data as well.
- DBSCAN does not assume anything regarding the data's distribution. A statistical clustering method (mixture models) that assumes all clusters originate from spherical Gaussian distributions with distinct means but the same covariance matrix is equivalent to the fundamental K-means algorithm.
- Both K-means and DBSCAN search for clusters using all available attributes; they do not search for clusters that might only include a portion of the attributes.
- Even if they overlap, K-means can identify poorly separated clusters, but DBSCAN combines overlapped clusters.
- Except in certain circumstances, like low-dimensional Euclidean data, the DBSCAN algorithm has an $O(m^2)$ time complexity, whereas the K-means algorithm has an O(m) time complexity.
- Different runs of DBSCAN yield different sets of clusters, whereas K-means, which is usually applied with centroids initialized randomly, does not.
- The number of clusters is automatically determined by DBSCAN; however, it must be specified as a parameter for K-means. Eps and MinPts, two additional DBSCAN parameters, need to be specified.
- One way to think of K-means clustering is as an optimization problem; i.e., reduce each point's total squared error with respect to its nearest centroid, and as an example of a statistical clustering technique (mixture models). There is no formal model that DBSCAN is based on.

9.1.2. Data Characteristics

The following are some characteristics of data that can strongly affect cluster analysis.

- *High Dimensionality*: The classic Euclidean concept of density—the number of points per unit volume—becomes meaningless in high-dimensional data sets. To understand this, keep in mind that the volume grows quickly as the number of dimensions increases and that the density tends to zero unless the number of points increases exponentially with the number of dimensions. (The number of dimensions has an exponential effect on volume. For example, the volume of a hypersphere with radius r and dimension d is proportional to r^d). Furthermore, in high-dimensional spaces, proximity tends to become more homogeneous. Another way to look at this fact is that the proximity between two points tends to be more uniform because there are more dimensions (attributes) contributing to the proximity. Since most clustering methods rely on density or proximity, high-dimensional data can frequently present challenges for them. Using dimensionality reduction techniques is one way to tackle such issues. Redefining the concepts of density and proximity is another strategy.

- **Size**: Larger data sets are too big for many clustering algorithms that perform well with small or medium-sized data sets. This is covered in more detail in the section on the properties of clustering algorithms, which covers scalable clustering algorithms. Scalability is one of these properties.
- **Sparseness**: Asymmetric attributes, in which non-zero values are more significant than zero ones, are frequently found in sparse data. As such, similarity metrics that are suitable for asymmetric attributes are frequently employed. But related problems also come up. For instance, does the clustering perform best when there are only two values, 0 and 1, or are the magnitudes of non-zero entries significant or do they distort the clustering?
- **Noise and Outliers**: Clustering algorithms, particularly prototype-based ones like K-means, can be significantly hampered by an abnormal point, or outlier. Noise, however, has the ability to cause methods, like single link, to join clusters that shouldn't be joined. Sometimes a noise and outlier removal algorithm is run first, followed by a clustering algorithm. Alternatively, during the clustering process, certain algorithms can identify points that represent noise and outliers and then remove them or otherwise mitigate their negative effects.
- **Type of Attributes and Data Set**: Aspects can be binary, discrete, continuous, or categorical (nominal or ordinal), as well as quantitative (interval or ratio). Data sets can be structured, graphed, or ordered. Various measures of density and proximity are suitable for various kinds of data. In certain circumstances, discretization or binarization of the data may be required in order to apply a preferred proximity measure or clustering algorithm. When attributes, such as continuous and nominal, are of radically different kinds, there is an additional complication. In these situations, density and proximity are more arbitrary and harder to define. Finally, in order to handle some types of data efficiently, specific data structures and algorithms might be required.
- **Scale**: Different scales may be used to measure the same attribute, such as weight and height. These variations can have a significant impact on the similarity or distance between two objects and, in turn, the outcomes of a cluster analysis. Think about grouping individuals according to their weights, expressed in kilograms, and their heights, expressed in meters. People will be grouped primarily according to the weight attribute and height will have minimal bearing if we use Euclidean distance as our proximity measure. However, because of the scale difference, we will have eliminated effects if we standardize each attribute by

deducting its mean and dividing by its standard deviation. In general, these problems are usually resolved through the use of normalization techniques.

- **Mathematical Properties of the Data Space**: Certain clustering methods use mathematical operations that are only valid in Euclidean space or other restricted data spaces, or they compute the mean of a set of points. The definition of density must make sense for the data in order for other algorithms to work.

9.1.3. Cluster Characteristics

Various cluster types, including prototype, graph, and density-based clusters. We now go over some additional significant cluster properties.

- **Data Distribution**: Certain clustering methods presuppose a specific kind of data distribution. More precisely, they frequently believe that data may be represented as coming from a combination of distributions, with each cluster representing a different distribution.
- **Shape**: Certain clusters have a regular shape, like e.g., clusters can be globular, rectangular, or any other shape in general. Clusters of any shape can be handled by methods like DBSCAN and single link, but not by prototype-based schemes or certain hierarchical methods like group average and complete link. Techniques like CURE and Chameleon were created especially to deal with this issue.
- **Differing Sizes**: Different cluster sizes cause problems for many clustering techniques, including K-means.
- **Differing Densities**: Densities that vary greatly within a cluster can be problematic for DBSCAN and K-means algorithms. This problem is addressed by the SNN density based clustering technique.
- **Poorly Separated Clusters**: Certain clustering techniques combine clusters that ought to remain apart when they touch or overlap. Points are arbitrarily assigned to different clusters even by methods that identify distinct clusters. One method for handling data that does not form well-separated clusters is fuzzy clustering.
- **Relationships among Clusters**: The majority of clustering techniques do not explicitly take into account the relationships, like relative positions, between clusters. One clustering method that takes relationships between clusters into account is called self-organizing maps, or SOM. More specifically, the definitions of neighboring clusters are impacted when a point is allocated to one cluster.
- **Subspace Clusters**: Only a subset of dimensions (attributes) may contain clusters, and clusters identified with one set of dimensions may not be at all similar to clusters identified with another set. This problem can occur in as few as two dimensions, but as dimensionality rises, it gets worse because there are exponentially more possible subsets of dimensions than there are dimensions in total. Therefore, unless there are a relatively small number of dimensions, it is not practical to simply search for clusters in all possible subsets of dimensions.

The application of feature selection is one strategy. Nevertheless, this method is predicated on the idea that the clusters are contained in a single subset of dimensions. Clusters can actually be found in a wide variety of unique subspaces, or sets of dimensions, some of which overlap.

9.1.4. General Characteristics of Clustering Algorithms

Numerous clustering algorithms exist. Here we give a broad overview of some of the key features of clustering algorithms, and we get more specific when we talk about specific methods.

- **Order Dependence**: The order in which the data is processed can have a significant impact on the quality and quantity of clusters generated by certain algorithms. Even though it would seem preferable to stay away from such algorithms, there are situations in which the order dependence is negligible or the algorithm may have other advantageous features. One example of an order-dependent algorithm is SOM.
- **Non-determinism**: Although clustering algorithms, like K-means, do not depend on the order in which they are run, they do yield distinct outcomes because they require a random choice to be made during the initialization step. It may be necessary to do multiple runs because the quality of the clusters can differ from one run to the next.
- **Scalability**: Millions of objects can often be found in a data set; therefore, the clustering algorithms applied to such data sets should have time and space complexity that is linear or nearly linear. For large data sets, algorithms with a complexity of $O(m^2)$ are impractical. Moreover, it is not always possible for clustering techniques for data sets to assume that all of the data will fit in main memory or that data elements can be accessed at random. Large data sets are unsuitable for these kinds of algorithms.
- **Parameter Selection**: The majority of clustering algorithms require the user to adjust one or more parameters. The general consensus is that "the fewer parameters, the better," as selecting the appropriate values can be challenging. Selecting parameter values becomes even more difficult if the clustering results are significantly altered by a small change in the parameters. Finally, a user of the algorithm is limited to utilizing trial and error to find appropriate parameter values unless a procedure (which may involve user input) is provided for determining parameter values.

  For partitional clustering algorithms like K-means, the problem of "selecting the right number of clusters" is arguably the most well-known parameter selection challenge.
- **Transforming the Clustering Problem to Another Domain**: Certain clustering techniques map the clustering problem to a problem in another domain as one of their methods. For example, the task of finding clusters is mapped to the task of dividing a proximity graph into connected components using graph-based clustering.
- **Treating Clustering as an Optimization Problem**: A user-specified objective function is used

to measure the goodness of the final set of clusters, and clustering is often thought of as an optimization problem where the points are divided into clusters in a way that maximizes this goodness. The K-means clustering algorithm, for instance, seeks to identify the collection of clusters that minimizes the total squared distance between each point and the closest cluster centroid. Theoretically, these kinds of issues can be resolved by counting all potential cluster sets and choosing the cluster with the highest value of the objective function; however, this exhaustive method is not computationally feasible. Because of this, a lot of clustering methods rely on heuristic strategies that result in decent but not ideal clusterings. Using greedy or local objective functions is an additional strategy. Specifically, at every stage of the clustering process, the hierarchical clustering techniques move forward by making locally optimal (greedy) decisions.

9.2. PROTOTYPE-BASED CLUSTERING

Within the framework of prototype-based clustering, a cluster is any collection of objects that are more closely aligned with the cluster's defining prototype than with any other cluster's prototype. an easy-to-use clustering algorithm that bases its cluster prototype on the centroid of its member objects. Clustering techniques that build upon prototype-based clustering in one or more ways are covered in this section and are covered in the following sections:

- Objects are allowed to belong to more than one cluster. More specifically, an object belongs to every cluster with some weight. Such an approach addresses the fact that some objects are equally close to several cluster prototypes.
- A cluster is modeled as a statistical distribution, i.e., objects are generated by a random process from a statistical distribution that is characterized by a number of statistical parameters, such as the mean and variance. This viewpoint generalizes the notion of a prototype and enables the use of well-established statistical techniques.
- Clusters are constrained to have fixed relationships. Most commonly, these relationships are constraints that specify neighborhood relationships; i.e., the degree to which two clusters are neighbors of each other. Constraining the relationships among clusters can simplify the interpretation and visualization of the data.

These extensions of prototype-based clustering are demonstrated by looking at three distinct clustering algorithms. Fuzzy c-means is a clustering scheme that is similar to K-means but does not require a hard assignment of a point to only one cluster. It does this by utilizing ideas from fuzzy logic and fuzzy set theory. A set of clusters can be modeled as a mixture of distributions, one for each cluster, according to the theory behind mixture model clustering. The Self-Organizing Maps (SOM)-based clustering scheme operates within a framework that necessitates that clusters have a predetermined relationship to one another, e.g., an arrangement of two-dimensional grids.

9.2.1. Fuzzy Clustering

A clean classification of the data objects into disjoint clusters appears to be the best course of action if the objects are dispersed into well-defined groups. Nevertheless, there will typically be some arbitraryness involved in allocating an object to a specific cluster because the objects in a data set cannot be divided into clearly defined clusters. Think about an item that is marginally closer to one of two clusters but lies close to their boundaries. In a lot of these situations, it might be more appropriate to give each object and cluster a weight that represents the extent to which the object is a member of the cluster. In mathematics, object xi's weight within cluster C_j is represented by w_{ij}.

Probabilistic methods can also yield such weights, as will be demonstrated in the following section. Even though probabilistic methods are helpful in many circumstances, choosing the right statistical model can be challenging at times. Non-probabilistic clustering techniques are required in these situations in order to offer comparable capabilities. Based on fuzzy set theory, fuzzy clustering techniques offer a natural way to create a clustering where membership weights (the w_{ij}) have a natural interpretation that is not probabilistic. This section gives a detailed explanation of fuzzy clustering's general methodology along with a fuzzy c-means (fuzzy K-means) example.

9.2.1.1. Fuzzy Sets

In 1965, Lotfi Zadeh introduced fuzzy logic and fuzzy set theory as methods for handling ambiguity and imprecision. In summary, fuzzy logic permits a statement to be true with a degree of certainty between 0 and 1, while fuzzy set theory permits an object to belong to a set with a degree of membership between 0 and 1. Conventional logic and set theory are special cases of fuzzy counterparts, which limit the degree of certainty or set membership to either 0 or 1. Numerous fields have benefited from the application of fuzzy concepts, such as data analysis (classification and clustering), pattern recognition, and control systems.

Take a look at this fuzzy logic example. The percentage of clouds in the sky can be used to determine the degree of truth of a statement like "It is cloudy." For example, if 50% of the sky is cloud covered, the degree of truth for the statement would be 0.5. We can also assign a degree of membership to each day in the two sets, "cloudy days" and "non-cloudy days," if we have two sets. A day would therefore have a 25% degree of membership in "cloudy days" and a 75% degree of membership in "non-cloudy days" if it had a 25% cloudiness percentage."

9.2.1.2. Fuzzy Clusters

Assume that we have a set of data points $X = \{x_1, \ldots, x_m\}$, where each point, x_i, is an n-dimensional point, i.e., $x_i = (x_{i1}, \ldots, x_{in})$. A collection of fuzzy clusters, $C_1, C_2, \ldots, C_k$ is a subset of all possible fuzzy subsets of X. (This simply means that the membership weights (degrees), w_{ij}, have been assigned values between 0 and 1 for each point, xi, and each cluster, C_j) However, we also want to impose the following reasonable conditions on the clusters in order to ensure that the clusters form what is called a fuzzy psuedo-partition.

1. All the weights for a given point, xi, add up to 1.

$$\sum_{j=1}^{k} w_{ij} = 1$$

2. Each cluster, C_j, contains, with non-zero weight, at least one point, but does not contain, with a weight of one, all of the points.

$$0 < \sum_{i=1}^{m} w_{ij} < m$$

9.2.1.3. Fuzzy c-Means

Although there are numerous forms of fuzzy clustering—in fact, a wide range of data analysis algorithms can be "fuzzified"—we solely take into account fuzzy c-means, which is essentially K-means' fuzzy variant. The fuzzy community coined the term "c-means" to refer to the fuzzy version of K-means, which is sometimes used in the clustering literature when it does not employ incremental updates of cluster centroids. Algorithm 9.1 provides the fuzzy c-means algorithm, sometimes referred to as FCM.

Algorithm 9.1. Basic fuzzy c-means algorithm.

1: Select an initial fuzzy pseudo-partition, i.e., assign values to all the w_{ij}.
2: **repeat**
3: Compute the centroid of each cluster using the fuzzy pseudo-partition.
4: Recompute the fuzzy pseudo-partition, i.e., the w_{ij}.
5: **until** The centroids don't change.
(Alternative stopping conditions are "if the change in the error is below a specified threshold" or "if the absolute change in any w_{ij} is below a given threshold.")

Following initialization, until the partition remains unchanged, FCM computes the fuzzy pseudo-partition and the centroids of each cluster repeatedly. The structure of FCM is comparable to that of the K-means algorithm, which, following initialization, alternates between updating the centroids and allocating each object to the closest centroid. More specifically, the assignment step is equivalent to computing a fuzzy pseudopartition. Similar to K-means, FCM is based on a fuzzy version of the sum of squared errors (SSE), but it can also be understood as an attempt to minimize SSE. In fact, K-means and FCM behave very similarly, making them suitable for consideration as a special case of each other. The information about FCM is explained below.

- **Computing SSE**: The definition of the sum of the squared error (SSE) is modified as follows:

$$\text{SSE}(C_1, C_2, \ldots, C_k) = \sum_{j=1}^{k}\sum_{i=1}^{m} w_{ij}^{p}\, dist(\mathbf{x}_i, \mathbf{c}_j)^2 \tag{9.1}$$

where c_j is the centroid of the jth cluster and p, which is the exponent that determines the influence of the weights, has a value between 1 and ∞. Note that this SSE is just a weighted version of the traditional K-means SSE.

- **Initialization**: A common practice is random initialization. Specifically, weights are assigned at random, with the requirement that the total of all weights assigned to an object be one. Similar to K-means, random initialization is easy to use and frequently yields a clustering that, in terms of the SSE, represents a local minimum.

- **Computing Centroids**: The definition of the centroid given in Eqn. 9.2 can be derived by finding the centroid that minimizes the fuzzy SSE as given by Eqn. 9.1. For a cluster, C_j, the corresponding centroid, c_j, is defined by the following equation:

$$c_j = \sum_{i=1}^{m} w_{ij}^{p} \mathbf{x}_i / \sum_{i=1}^{m} w_{ij}^{p} \tag{9.2}$$

The fuzzy centroid definition is similar to the traditional definition except that all points are considered (any point can belong to any cluster, at least somewhat) and the contribution of each point to the centroid is weighted by its membership degree. In the case of traditional crisp sets, where all w_{ij} are either 0 or 1, this definition reduces to the traditional definition of a centroid.

There are a few considerations when choosing the value of p. Choosing p = 2 simplifies the weight update formula—see Eqn. 9.4. However, if p is chosen to be near 1, then fuzzy c-means behaves like traditional K-means. Going in the other direction, as p gets larger, all the cluster centroids approach the global centroid of all the data points. In other words, the partition becomes fuzzier as p increases.

- **Updating the Fuzzy Pseudo-partition**: Since the fuzzy pseudo-partition is defined by the weight, this step involves updating the weights w_{ij} associated with the ith point and jth cluster. The weight update formula given in Eqn. 9.3 can be derived by minimizing the SSE of Eqn. 9.1 subject to the constraint that the weights sum to 1.

$$w_{ij} = (1/dist(\mathbf{x}_i, \mathbf{c}_j)^2)^{\frac{1}{p-1}} \Big/ \sum_{q=1}^{k} (1/dist(\mathbf{x}_i, \mathbf{c}_q)^2)^{\frac{1}{p-1}} \tag{9.3}$$

This formula may appear a bit mysterious. However, note that if p = 2, then we obtain Eqn. 9.4, which is somewhat simpler. We provide an intuitive explanation of Eqn. 9.4, which, with a slight modification, also applies to Eqn. 9.3.

$$w_{ij} = 1/dist(\mathbf{x}_i, \mathbf{c}_j)^2 \Big/ \sum_{q=1}^{k} 1/dist(\mathbf{x}_i, \mathbf{c}_q)^2 \tag{9.4}$$

Intuitively, the weight w_{ij}, which indicates the degree of membership of point $\mathbf{x}_i$ in cluster C_j, should be relatively high if $\mathbf{x}_i$ is close to centroid c_j (if dist($\mathbf{x}_i$, c_j) is low) and relatively low if $\mathbf{x}_i$ is far from centroid c_j (if dist($\mathbf{x}_i$, c_j) is high). If $w_{ij} = 1/\text{dist}(\mathbf{x}_i, c_j)^2$, which is the numerator of Equation 9.4, then this will indeed be the case. However, the membership weights for a point will not sum to one unless they are normalized; i.e., divided by the sum of all the weights as in Eqn. 9.4. To summarize, the membership weight of a point in a cluster is just the reciprocal of the square of the distance between the point and the cluster centroid divided by the sum of all the membership weights of the point.

Now consider how Eqn. 9.3 is affected by the exponent $1/(p - 1)$. The weight given to clusters near the point is decreased by this exponent if $p > 2$. In fact, weights tend to $1/k$ and the exponent tends to 0 as p approaches infinity. Conversely, when p gets closer to 1, the exponent raises the membership weights of the points that are near the cluster. The closest cluster's membership weight increases to 1 as p approaches 1, while all other clusters' membership weights decrease to 0. K-means is in line with this.

Example 9.1 (Fuzzy c-means on Three Circular Clusters)

The outcome of using fuzzy c-means to identify three clusters from a two-dimensional data set of 100 points is displayed in Figure 9.1. The cluster with the highest membership weight was allocated each point. Different marker shapes indicate the points that belong to each cluster, and the shading indicates the cluster's degree of membership. Their membership in the cluster to which they have been assigned is stronger for darker points. A cluster's membership is greatest in its center and lowest at the locations where clusters are not connected.

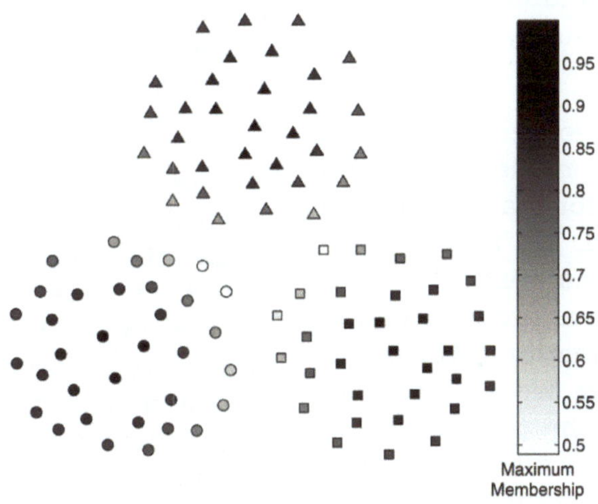

Figure 9.1. *Fuzzy c-means clustering of a two-dimensional point set.*

Source: Pang-Ning Tan, Michael Steinbach, and Vipin Kumar. Introduction to Data Mining. Pearson. https://www.ceom.ou.edu/media/docs/upload/Pang-Ning_Tan_Michael_Steinbach_Vipin_Kumar_-_Introduction_to_Data_Mining-Pe_NRDK4fi.pdf.

9.2.1.4. Strengths and Limitations

One advantage of FCM is that it generates a clustering that shows how much a point belongs to a particular cluster. Other than that, it is slightly more computationally demanding than K-means but otherwise has many of the same advantages and disadvantages.

9.2.2. Clustering Using Mixture Models

Statistical model-based clustering is discussed in this section. Assuming that data has been produced by a statistical process and describing the data using the statistical model that best fits the data—a statistical model that is defined in terms of a distribution and a set of parameters for that distribution—is frequently convenient and effective. Choosing a statistical model for the data and deriving the model's parameters from the data are the main steps in this process. This section discusses mixture models, a specific type of statistical model that uses multiple statistical distributions to model the data. Every distribution has a corresponding cluster, and each distribution's parameters give an explanation of the corresponding cluster—usually in terms of its spread and center.

This section's discussion goes like this. We first describe mixture models and then look at how parameters for statistical data models can be estimated. We first explain how parameters for simple statistical models can be estimated using a process called maximum likelihood estimation (MLE), and then we talk about how we can extend this method to estimate the parameters of mixture models. We specifically discuss the widely used Expectation-Maximization (EM) algorithm, which estimates the parameters first and then refines them iteratively. We describe the advantages and disadvantages of the EM algorithm and provide examples of how it can be applied to cluster data by estimating the parameters of a mixture model.

To fully comprehend this section, one must have a solid understanding of probability and statistics. Additionally, we refer to both probability and probability density by the term "probability" for convenience in the discussion that follows.

9.2.2.1. Mixture Models

According to mixture models, the data are a collection of observations drawn from various probability distributions. Although there is no restriction on the probability distributions, multivariate normal distributions are commonly assumed because they are well-understood, straightforward to manipulate mathematically, and have a track record of yielding accurate results. Ellipsoidal clusters can be modeled by these kinds of distributions.

Mixture models conceptually match the subsequent data generation process. Choose a random distribution from a set of distributions, usually of the same type but with different parameters, and use it to create an object. When m is the number of objects, repeat the procedure m times.

More formally, assume that there are K distributions and m objects, $X = \{\mathbf{x}_1, \ldots, \mathbf{x}_m\}$. Let the jth distribution have parameters θ_j, and let Θ be the set of all parameters, i.e., $\Theta = \{\theta_1, \ldots, \theta_K\}$. Then, $prob(\mathbf{x}_i|\theta_j)$ is the probability of the ith object if it comes from the jth distribution. The probability that the jth distribution is chosen to generate an object is given by the weight w_j, $1 \leq j \leq K$, where these weights (probabilities) are subject to the constraint that they sum to one, i.e., $\sum_{j=1}^{K} w_j = 1$. Then, the probability of an object x is given by Equation 9.5.

$$prob(\mathbf{x}|\Theta) = \sum_{j=1}^{K} w_j p_j(\mathbf{x}|\theta_j) \tag{9.5}$$

If the objects are generated in an independent manner, then the probability of the entire set of objects is just the product of the probabilities of each individual $\mathbf{x}_i$.

$$prob(\mathcal{X}|\Theta) = \prod_{i=1}^{m} prob(\mathbf{x}_i|\Theta) = \prod_{i=1}^{m}\sum_{j=1}^{K} w_j p_j(\mathbf{x}_i|\theta_j) \tag{9.6}$$

Each distribution for mixture models describes a distinct group, i.e., an alternative cluster. We can characterize these distributions (clusters) by estimating the parameters of these distributions from the data using statistical techniques. We are also able to determine which objects are a part of which clusters. However, mixture modeling provides the probability that a given object belongs to a specific cluster rather than a clean assignment of objects to clusters.

Example 9.2 (Univariate Gaussian Mixture):

We give a specific example of a mixture model expressed in terms of Gaussian distributions. At any given point x, the probability density function of a one-dimensional Gaussian distribution is.

$$prob(x_i|\Theta) = \frac{1}{\sqrt{2\pi}\sigma} e^{-\frac{(x-\mu)^2}{2\sigma^2}}. \tag{9.7}$$

The Gaussian distribution parameters are represented by the formula $\theta = (\mu, \sigma)$, where σ represents the standard deviation and μ denotes the distribution mean. Assume that there are two Gaussian distributions, with a common standard deviation of 2 and means of –4 and 4, respectively. Additionally, suppose that there is an equal chance of selection for each of the two distributions, i.e., we have $w_1 = w_2 = 0.5$. Equation 9.5 then becomes as follows:

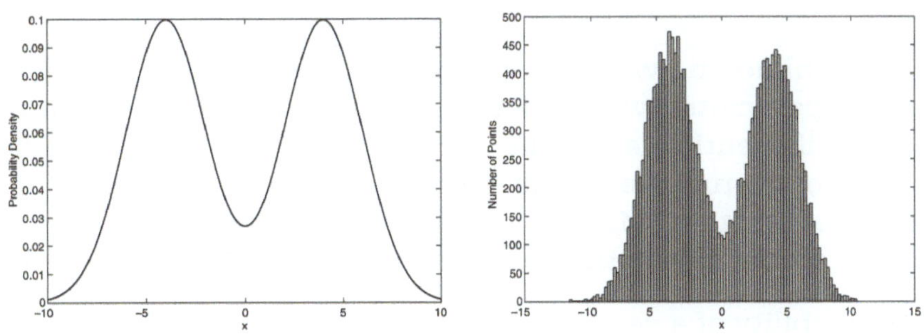

(a) Probability density function for the mixture model.

(b) 20,000 points generated from the mixture model.

Figure 9.2. *Mixture model consisting of two normal distributions with means of -4 and 4, respectively. Both distributions have a standard deviation of 2.*

Source: Pang-Ning Tan, Michael Steinbach, and Vipin Kumar. Introduction to Data Mining. Pearson. https://www.ceom.ou.edu/media/docs/upload/Pang-Ning_Tan_Michael_Steinbach_Vipin_Kumar_-_Introduction_to_Data_Mining-Pe_NRDK4fi.pdf.

$$prob(x|\Theta) = \frac{1}{2\sqrt{2\pi}}\, e^{-\frac{(x+4)^2}{8}} + \frac{1}{2\sqrt{2\pi}}\, e^{-\frac{(x-4)^2}{8}}. \tag{9.8}$$

The probability density function of this mixture model is plotted in Figure 9.2(a), and the histogram for 20,000 points produced by this mixture model is displayed in Figure 9.2(b).

9.2.2.2. Estimating Model Parameters Using Maximum Likelihood

Estimating the model's parameters is required given a statistical model for the data. We now go over maximum likelihood estimation, a common strategy for this kind of work.

First, let's take a look at a set of m points that come from a Gaussian distribution with one dimension. The probability of these points is simply the sum of the individual probabilities, assuming that each point is generated independently. (Once more, we're working with probability densities, but we'll just refer to them as probabilities to keep things simple). Eqn. 9.7 allows us to express this probability as Eqn. 9.9 does. Equation 9.10 illustrates how we usually use the log probability when dealing with such a small probability.

$$prob(\mathcal{X}|\Theta) = \prod_{i=1}^{m} \frac{1}{\sqrt{2\pi}\sigma}\, e^{-\frac{(x_i-u)^2}{2\sigma^2}} \tag{9.9}$$

$$log\ prob(\mathcal{X}|\Theta) = -\sum_{i=1}^{m} \frac{(x_i-u)^2}{2\sigma^2} - 0.5m\log 2\pi - m\log\sigma \tag{9.10}$$

If u and σ are unknown, we would like to determine a method for estimating them. Selecting the parameter values for which the data is most probable (likely) is one method. Stated differently, select the values of μ and σ that optimize Equation 9.9. The maximum likelihood principle is the name given to this strategy in statistics, and maximum likelihood estimation (MLE) is the process of using this principle to determine the parameters of a statistical distribution based on the data.

Because the probability of a set of data, when viewed as a function of the parameters, is referred to as a likelihood function, the principle is also known as the maximum likelihood principle. To highlight that we see the statistical parameters μ and σ as our variables and that the data is treated as a constant, we rewrite Equation 9.9 as Equation 9.11. It is more common to use the log likelihood for pragmatic reasons. Equation 9.12 displays the log likelihood function that was obtained from the log probability of Equation 9.10. Take note that since log is a function that increases monotonically, the parameter values that maximize log likelihood also maximize likelihood.

$$likelihood(\Theta|\mathcal{X}) = L(\Theta|\mathcal{X}) = \prod_{i=1}^{m} \frac{1}{\sqrt{2\pi}\sigma} e^{-\frac{(x_i-\mu)^2}{2\sigma^2}} \tag{9.11}$$

$$log\ likelihood(\Theta|\mathcal{X}) = \ell(\Theta|\mathcal{X}) = -\sum_{i=1}^{m} \frac{(x_i-\mu)^2}{2\sigma^2} - 0.5m\log 2\pi - m\log\sigma \tag{9.12}$$

Example 9.3 (Maximum Likelihood Parameter Estimation):

We offer a practical example of how to find parameter values using MLE. Assume that the 200 points in our set are represented by the histogram in Figure 9.3(a). The maximum log likelihood plot for the 200 points under consideration is displayed in Figure 9.3(b). Close to the parameter values of the underlying Gaussian distribution, $\mu = -4.0$ and $\sigma = 2.0$, are the values of the parameters for which the log probability is a maximum: $\mu = -4.1$ and $\sigma = 2.1$.

If there are more than two parameters, graphing the likelihood of the data for various parameter values is not feasible. Therefore, taking the derivative of the likelihood function with respect to a statistical parameter, setting the result equal to 0, and solving are the standard statistical procedures for determining the maximum likelihood estimates of a statistical parameter. Specifically, it can be demonstrated that the sample points' mean and standard deviation, for a Gaussian distribution, represent the maximum likelihood estimates of the corresponding parameters of the underlying distribution. Specifically, the mean and standard deviation of the 200 points, or $u = -4.1$ and $\sigma = 2.1$, were the parameter values that maximized the log likelihood for the 200 points in our example.

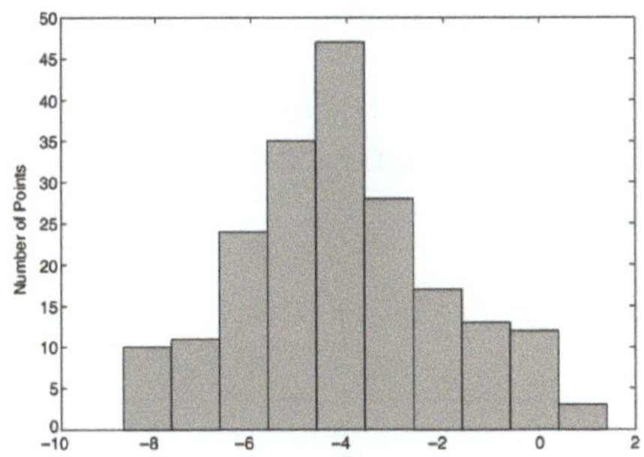

(a) Histogram of 200 points from a Gaussian distribution.

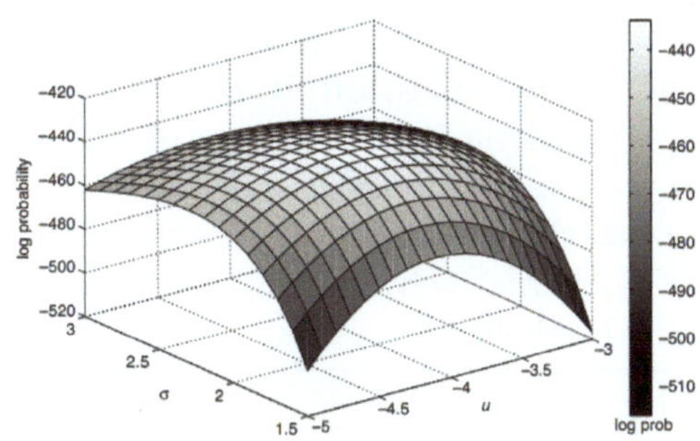

(b) Log likelihood plot of the 200 points for different values of the mean and standard deviation.

Figure 9.3. *200 points from a Gaussian distribution and their log probability for different parameter values.*

Source: Pang-Ning Tan, Michael Steinbach, and Vipin Kumar. Introduction to Data Mining. Pearson. https://www.ceom.ou.edu/media/docs/upload/Pang-Ning_Tan_Michael_Steinbach_Vipin_Kumar_-_Introduction_to_Data_Mining-Pe_NRDK4fi.pdf.

9.2.2.3. Estimating Mixture Model Parameters Using Maximum Likelihood: The EM Algorithm

The maximum likelihood method can also be used to estimate the model parameters for a mixture model. In the most basic scenario, the problem reduces to estimating the parameters of a single distribution given data from that distribution since we are aware of which data objects originate from which distributions. The maximum likelihood estimates of the parameters for the majority of common distributions are determined using straightforward formulas involving the data.

In a broader (and more practical) context, we are unsure of which distribution produced which points. Because of this, it appears that we are unable to use the maximum likelihood principle to estimate parameters because we are unable to directly calculate the probability of each data point. The EM algorithm, which is demonstrated in Algorithm 9.2, provides a solution to this issue. In summary, the EM algorithm estimates the probabilities that each point belongs to each distribution given a guess for the parameter values. It then uses these probabilities to compute a new estimate for the parameters. These are the parameters that optimize the probability. Until the parameter estimates either barely change or remain unchanged, this iteration is carried out. Therefore, we continue to use maximum likelihood estimation, but through an iterative process.

Algorithm 9.2. EM algorithm.

```
1: Select an initial set of model parameters.
   (As with K-means, this can be done randomly or in a variety of ways.)
2: repeat
3:    Expectation Step For each object, calculate the probability
      that each object belongs to each distribution, i.e., calculate
      prob(distribution j|x_i, Θ).
4:    Maximization Step Given the probabilities from the expectation step,
      find the new estimates of the parameters that maximize the expected
      likelihood.
5: until The parameters do not change.
   (Alternatively, stop if the change in the parameters is below a specified
   threshold.)
```

The K-means algorithm and the EM algorithm are comparable. In fact, the EM algorithm for spherical Gaussian distributions with equal covariance matrices but different means is a special case of the K-means algorithm for Euclidean data. The K-means step of grouping each object into a cluster and the expectation step are equivalent. Rather, every object has a probability assigned to it within each cluster (distribution). The cluster centroids are computed in the maximizing step. Rather, the likelihood is maximized through the selection of all distributional parameters, including the weight parameters. Since the parameters are usually calculated using formulas derived from maximum likelihood estimation, this process is frequently simple. The mean of the distribution's objects, for example, is the MLE estimate of the mean for a single Gaussian distribution. Every object belongs to a distribution with a certain probability, which is taken into account in the computation of the mean when using mixture models and the EM algorithm. This is further demonstrated in the example that follows.

Example 9.4 (Simple Example of EM Algorithm)

Using the data in Figure 9.2, this example shows how EM functions. In order to maintain the example's simplicity, we'll assume that we are aware of the fact that both distributions' standard deviations are 2.0 and that points were produced from each distribution with an equal probability. The left and right distributions will be referred to as distributions 1 and 2, respectively.

We begin the EM algorithm by making initial guesses for μ_1 and μ_2, say, $\mu_1 = -2$ and $\mu_2 = 3$. Thus, the initial parameters, $\theta = (\mu, \sigma)$, for the two distributions are, respectively, $\theta_1 = (-2, 2)$ and $\theta_2 = (3, 2)$. The set of parameters for the entire mixture model is $\Theta = \{\theta_1, \theta_2\}$. For the expectation step of EM, we want to compute the probability that a point came from a particular distribution; i.e., we want to compute prob(distribution $1|x_i$, Θ) and prob(distribution $2|x_i$, Θ). These values can be expressed by the following equation, which is a straightforward application of Bayes rule:

$$prob(distribution\ j|x_i, \theta) = \frac{0.5\ prob(x_i|\theta_j)}{0.5\ prob(x_i|\theta_1) + 0.5\ prob(x_i|\theta_2)}, \tag{9.13}$$

Where; 0.5 is the probability (weight) of each distribution and j is 1 or 2.

For instance, assume one of the points is 0. Using the Gaussian density function given in Equation 9.7, we compute that prob($0|\theta_1$) = 0.12 and prob($0|\theta_2$) = 0.06. (Again, we are really computing probability densities.) Using these values and Equation 9.13, we find that prob(distribution $1|0$, Θ) = 0.12/(0.12 + 0.06) = 0.66 and prob(distribution $2|0$, Θ) = 0.06/(0.12 + 0.06) = 0.33. This means that the point 0 is twice as likely to belong to distribution 1 as distribution 2 based on the current assumptions for the parameter values.

In the maximization step of the EM algorithm, we compute new estimates for μ_1 and μ_2 (using Equations 9.14 and 9.15) after computing the cluster membership probabilities for all 20,000 points. Notice that the new estimate for the mean of a distribution is just a weighted average of the points, where the weights are the probabilities that the points belong to the distribution, i.e., the prob(distribution $j|x_i$) values.

$$\mu_1 = \sum_{i=1}^{20,000} x_i \frac{prob(distribution\ 1|x_i, \Theta)}{\sum_{i=1}^{20,000} prob(distribution\ 1|x_i, \Theta)} \tag{9.14}$$

$$\mu_2 = \sum_{i=1}^{20,000} x_i \frac{prob(distribution\ 2|x_i, \Theta)}{\sum_{i=1}^{20,000} prob(distribution\ 2|x_i, \Theta)} \tag{9.15}$$

Table 9.1. First Few Iterations of the EM Algorithm for the Simple Example

Iteration	μ_1	μ_2
0	−2.00	3.00
1	−3.74	4.10
2	−3.94	4.07
3	−3.97	4.04
4	−3.98	4.03
5	−3.98	4.03

Source: Pang-Ning Tan, Michael Steinbach, and Vipin Kumar. Introduction to Data Mining. Pearson. https://www.ceom.ou.edu/media/docs/upload/Pang-Ning_Tan_Michael_Steinbach_Vipin_Kumar_-_Introduction_to_Data_Mining-Pe_NRDK4fi.pdf.

Until the estimates of μ_1 and μ_2 either remain unchanged or change significantly, we repeat these two steps. The initial iterations of the EM algorithm applied to the set of 20,000 points are provided in Table 9.1. We can also calculate the mean of the points from each distribution because we know which distribution produced which point for this set of data. $\mu_1 = -3.98$ and $\mu_2 = 4.03$ are the means.

Example 9.5 (The EM Algorithm on Sample Data Sets):

We present three examples that demonstrate how to find clusters using mixture models and the EM algorithm. The data set utilized to demonstrate the fuzzy c-means algorithm is the basis for the first example (refer to Figure 9.1). This data was modeled as a mixture of three Gaussian distributions in two dimensions, each having a distinct mean and an identical covariance matrix.

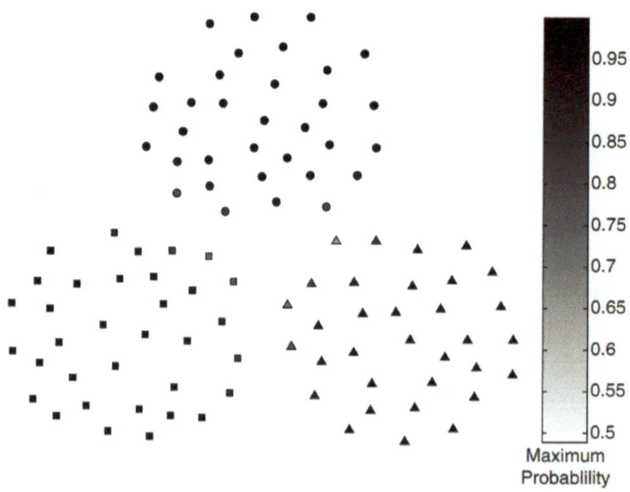

Figure 9.4. *EM clustering of a two-dimensional point set with three clusters.*

Source: Pang-Ning Tan, Michael Steinbach, and Vipin Kumar. Introduction to Data Mining. Pearson. https://www.ceom.ou.edu/media/docs/upload/Pang-Ning_Tan_Michael_Steinbach_Vipin_Kumar_-_Introduction_to_Data_Mining-Pe_NRDK4fi.pdf.

The EM algorithm was then used to cluster the data. Figure 9.4 displays the findings. The cluster with the highest membership weight for each point was designated as its home. The shading indicates the degree of membership in the cluster, while the various marker shapes indicate the points that belong to each cluster. Points that are on the edge of two clusters have relatively weak membership, but strong membership exists in other places. A comparison of the membership weights and probabilities between Figures 9.4 and 9.1 is intriguing.

In the second example, we use mixture model clustering on data that has varying densities of clusters. There are two naturally occurring clusters in the data, each with about 500 points. Two sets of Gaussian data, one with a center at (−4,1) and a standard deviation of 2, and the other with a center at (0,0) and a standard deviation of 0.5, were combined to create this data. The clustering that the EM algorithm produced is displayed in Figure 9.5. The EM algorithm is fairly successful in identifying the original clusters despite the variations in density.

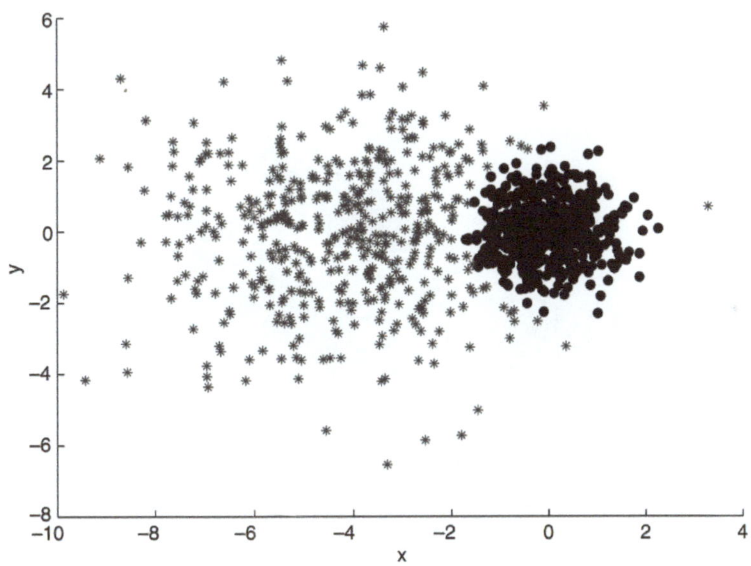

Figure 9.5. *EM clustering of a two-dimensional point set with two clusters of differing density.*

Source: Pang-Ning Tan, Michael Steinbach, and Vipin Kumar. Introduction to Data Mining. Pearson. https://www.ceom.ou.edu/media/docs/upload/Pang-Ning_Tan_Michael_Steinbach_Vipin_Kumar_-_Introduction_to_Data_Mining-Pe_NRDK4fi.pdf.

In the third example, we employ mixture model clustering on a set of data that is too large for K-means to handle. Figure 9.6(b) displays the K-means clustering of the same set of 1000 points, while Figure 9.6(a) displays the clustering generated by a mixture model algorithm. Each point has been allocated to the cluster for which it has the highest probability in the mixture model clustering process. Different markers are used to identify distinct clusters in both figures. The "+" and "x" markers in Figure 9.6(a) should not be confused.

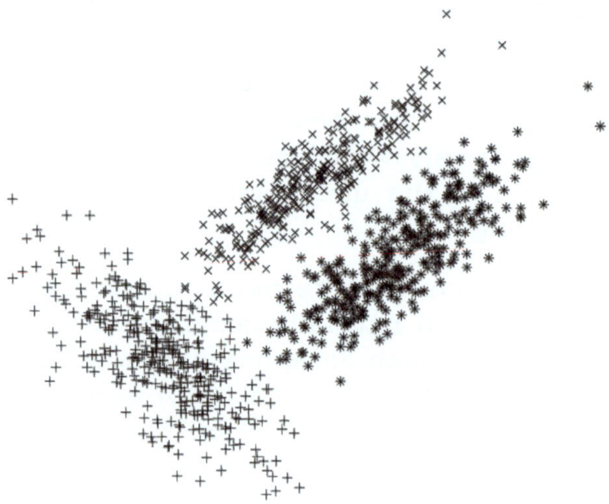

(a) Clusters produced by mixture model clustering.

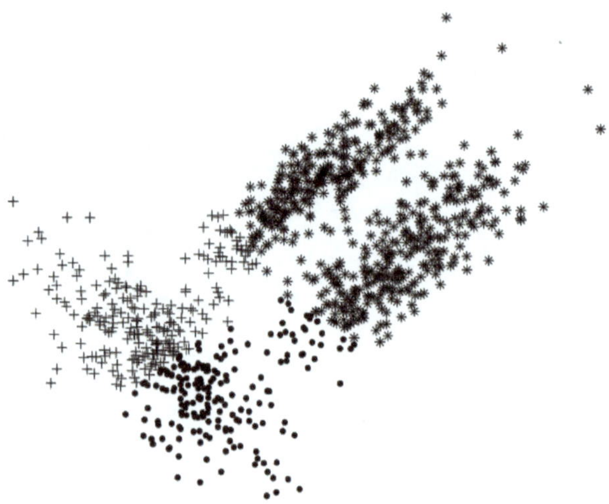

(b) Clusters produced by K-means clustering.

Figure 9.6. *Mixture model and K-means clustering of a set of two-dimensional points.*

Source: Pang-Ning Tan, Michael Steinbach, and Vipin Kumar. Introduction to Data Mining. Pearson. https://www.ceom.ou.edu/media/docs/upload/Pang-Ning_Tan_Michael_Steinbach_Vipin_Kumar_-_Introduction_to_Data_Mining-Pe_NRDK4fi.pdf.

9.2.2.4. Advantages and Limitations of Mixture Model Clustering Using the EM Algorithm

There are a number of benefits and drawbacks to modeling the data using mixture models to identify clusters and using the EM algorithm to estimate the parameters of those models. The EM algorithm's drawbacks include its potential for slowness, impracticality for models with many components, and poor performance in clusters with few or nearly co-linear data points. Additionally, there is an issue with determining the precise model form to be used or, more broadly, with estimating the number of clusters. Traditionally, a Bayesian approach has been used to tackle this problem. In general, this approach provides an estimate based on the data that indicates the likelihood of one model versus another. While efforts have been made to address this issue, mixture models may also struggle with noise and outliers.

Positively, because mixture models can use different types of distributions, they are more general than K-means or fuzzy c-means. Mixture models (which rely on Gaussian distributions) can thus identify clusters with a variety of sizes and elliptical shapes. Furthermore, a model-based strategy offers a methodical means of removing some of the intricacy related to data. When data needs to be made simpler in order to reveal patterns, fitting the data to a model—assuming the model fits the data well—is a useful method of doing so. Furthermore, because the generated clusters can be defined by a limited set of parameters, characterizing them is simple. Ultimately, a large number of data sets do, in fact, originate from random processes, and as such, they ought to meet the statistical presumptions of these models.

9.2.3. Self-Organizing Maps (SOM)

A clustering and data visualization method based on a neural network perspective is called the Kohonen Self-Organizing Feature Map (SOFM or SOM). Even though SOM originated in neural networks, it is easier to explain as a variant of prototype-based clustering. The objective of SOM, like other centroid-based clustering techniques, is to identify a set of centroids (referred to as reference vectors) and allocate each object in the data set to the centroid that best approximates that object. In the language of neural networks, every centroid is linked to a single neuron.

The closest centroid is updated when each data object is processed individually, just like in incremental K-means. In contrast to K-means, SOM updates neighboring centroids and places a topographic ordering on the centroids. Moreover, SOM does not record an object's present cluster membership, and unlike K-means, it does not update the previous cluster centroid explicitly when an object moves clusters. It goes without saying that the old cluster might have been updated because it was close to the new cluster. Points are processed until a predefined threshold is reached or the centroids show little variation. The set of centroids that implicitly define clusters is the final result of the SOM technique. The points in each cluster are those that are closest to a specific centroid. The specifics of this procedure are examined in the section that follows.

9.2.3.1. The SOM Algorithm

One characteristic of SOM that sets it apart is that it gives the centroids (neurons) a topographic (spatial) organization. An example of a two-dimensional SOM with nodes arranged in a rectangular lattice as the centroids is shown in Figure 9.7. The coordinates (i, j) of each centroid are assigned. Such a network is sometimes depicted with links between neighboring nodes, but that can be deceptive as one centroid's influence over another occurs through a neighborhood that is defined by coordinates, not by links. We limit our discussion to two-dimensional SOMs with a rectangular or hexagonal organization of the centroids, though there are many different kinds of SOM neural networks.

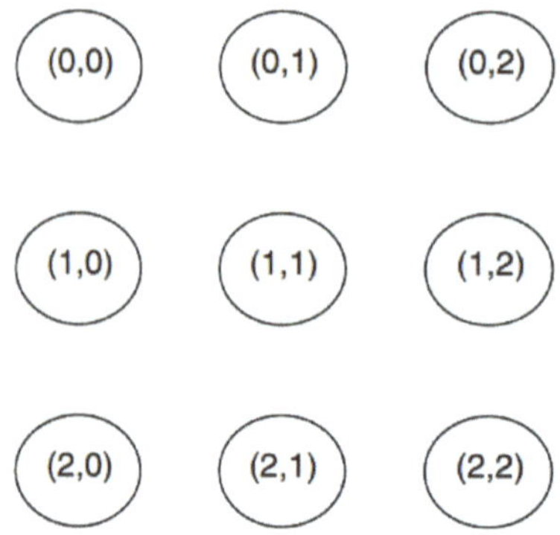

Figure 9.7. *Two-dimensional 3-by-3 rectangular SOM neural network.*

Source: Pang-Ning Tan, Michael Steinbach, and Vipin Kumar. Introduction to Data Mining. Pearson. https://www.ceom.ou.edu/media/docs/upload/Pang-Ning_Tan_Michael_Steinbach_Vipin_Kumar_-_Introduction_to_Data_Mining-Pe_NRDK4fi.pdf.

SOM differs fundamentally from K-means and other prototype-based approaches, despite their similarities. There is a preset topographic ordering relationship for centroids used in SOM. SOM updates the closest centroid and neighboring centroids in the topographic ordering with each data point during the training process. SOM generates an ordered set of centroids in this manner for any given set of data. Stated differently, the SOM grid's nearby centroids have a stronger relationship with one another than do the farther-off centroids. The centroids of a two-dimensional SOM can be thought of as lying on a two-dimensional surface that attempts to fit the n-dimensional data as closely as possible due to this constraint. An alternative way to conceptualize the SOM centroids is as the outcome of a nonlinear regression with respect to the data points.

The general steps involved in clustering using the SOM technique are outlined in Algorithm 9.3.

Algorithm 9.3. Basic SOM Algorithm

1: Initialize the centroids.
2: **repeat**
3: Select the next object.
4: Determine the closest centroid to the object.
5: Update this centroid and the centroids that are close, i.e., in a specified neighborhood.
6: **until** The centroids don't change much or a threshold is exceeded.
7: Assign each object to its closest centroid and return the centroids and clusters.

- **Initialization:** There are several ways to carry out this step (line 1). One method is to randomly select each component of a centroid from the data's observed range of values for that component. Although effective, this strategy isn't always the best one, particularly when it comes to achieving quick convergence. Choosing the initial centroids at random from the available data points is an additional strategy. This is akin to choosing the centroids of a K-means cluster at random.

- **Selection of an Object:** The selection of the subsequent object is the first action in the loop (line 3). Although it's not too complicated, there are a few challenges. Each data object may be used more than once since convergence may take several steps, particularly if there are few objects. That being said, not all of the objects must be used if there are a lot of them. Increasing the frequency of a particular group of objects in the training set can also increase its influence.
- **Assignment:** It is also simple to find the nearest centroid (line 4), though it does necessitate defining a distance metric. Both the dot product metric and the Euclidean distance metric are frequently employed. The reference vectors are normally normalized at each step and the data vectors are normally normalized prior to using the dot product distance. In these situations, applying the cosine measure is equal to applying the dot product metric.
- **Update:** The update step (line 5) is the most complicated. Let m_1, . . ., m_k be the centroids. (For a rectangular grid, note that k is the product of the number of rows and the number of columns.) For time step t, let p(t) be the current object (point) and assume that the closest centroid to p(t) is m_j. Then, for time t + 1, the jth centroid is updated by using the following equation. (We will see shortly that the update is really restricted to centroids whose neurons are in a small neighborhood of m_j.)

$$\mathbf{m}_j(t+1) = \mathbf{m}_j(t) + h_j(t)(\mathbf{p}(t) - \mathbf{m}_j(t)) \quad (9.16)$$

Thus, at time t, a centroid $m_j(t)$ is updated by adding a term, $h_j(t)(p(t) - m_j(t))$, which is proportional to the difference, $p(t) - m_j(t)$, between the centroid, $m_j(t)$, and the current object, p(t). $h_j(t)$ determines the effect that the difference, $p(t) - m_j(t)$, will have and is chosen so that (1) it diminishes with time and (2) it enforces a neighborhood effect, i.e., the effect of an object is strongest on the centroids closest to the centroid m_j. Here we are referring to the distance in the grid, not the distance in the data space. Typically, $h_j(t)$ is chosen to be one of the following two functions:

$$\begin{aligned} h_j(t) &= \alpha(t) exp(-dist(\mathbf{r}_j, \mathbf{r}_k)^2/(2\sigma^2(t))) && \text{(Gaussian function)} \\ h_j(t) &= \alpha(t) \text{ if } dist(\mathbf{r}_j, \mathbf{r}_k) \leq threshold, \text{ 0 otherwise} && \text{(step function)} \end{aligned}$$

These functions require more explanation. $\alpha(t)$ is a learning rate parameter, $0 < \alpha(t) < 1$, which decreases monotonically with time and controls the rate of convergence. $r_k = (x_k, y_k)$ is the two-dimensional point that gives the grid coordinates of the kth centroid. $dist(r_j, r_k)$ is the Euclidean distance between the grid location of the two centroids, i.e., $\sqrt{(x_j - x_k)^2 + (y_j - y_k)^2}$. Consequently, for centroids whose grid locations are far from the grid location of centroid m_j, the influence of object p(t) will be either greatly diminished or non-existent. Finally, note that σ is the typical Gaussian variance parameter and controls the width of the neighborhood, i.e., a small σ will yield a small neighborhood, while a large σ will yield a wide neighborhood. The threshold used for the step function also controls the neighborhood size.

Remember, it is the neighborhood updating technique that enforces a relationship (ordering) between centroids associated with neighboring neurons.

- **Termination:** An important question is when we are close enough to a stable set of centroids. Iteration should ideally go on until convergence, or until the reference vectors either barely change or do not change at all. There are several factors that will influence the rate of convergence, including the data and α(t). We won't go into more detail about these problems other than to say that convergence isn't always guaranteed and can happen slowly.

Example 9.6 (Document Data):

We offer two instances. In the first scenario, we document data using SOM using a 4-by-4 hexagonal grid. 3204 articles from 6 different sections of the Los Angeles Times newspaper—Entertainment, Financial, Foreign, Metro, National, and Sports—were clustered. The SOM grid is displayed in Figure 9.8. Since we're using a hexagonal grid, each centroid can have six immediate neighbors as opposed to four. All SOM grid cells, or clusters, have been labeled with the associated points' majority class label. Each category's clusters form contiguous groups, and we can learn more about each category by examining how its clusters relate to other cluster categories, for example, that all stories in the Metro section are connected to those in the other sections.

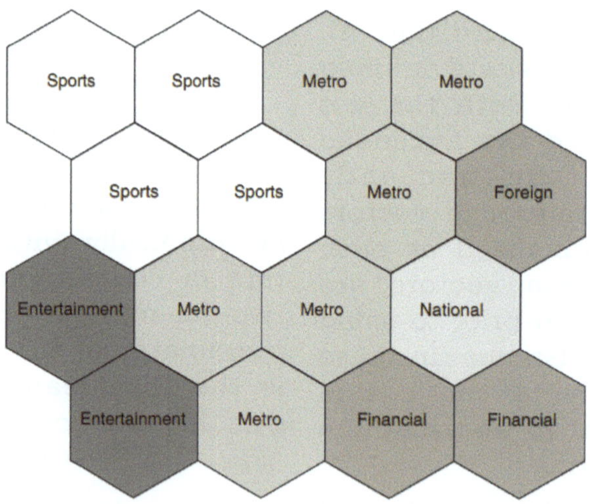

Figure 9.8. *Visualization of the relationships between SOM cluster for Los Angeles times document data set.*

Source: Pang-Ning Tan, Michael Steinbach, and Vipin Kumar. Introduction to Data Mining. Pearson. https://www.ceom.ou.edu/media/docs/upload/Pang-Ning_Tan_Michael_Steinbach_Vipin_Kumar_-_Introduction_to_Data_Mining-Pe_NRDK4fi.pdf.

Example 9.7 (Two-Dimensional Points):

In the second scenario, a set of two-dimensional data points and a rectangular SOM are used. The points and locations of the 36 reference vectors (represented as x's) generated by SOM are displayed in Figure 9.9(a). The five classes of points are hexagons (stars), squares, triangles, circles, and diamonds. The points are arranged in a checkerboard pattern. With random initialization, a six-by-six two-dimensional rectangular grid of centroids was employed. The centroids tend to disperse to the dense areas, as Figure 9.9(a) illustrates. The majority class of the points connected to that centroid is shown in Figure 9.9(b). Both the centroids linked to the four other types of points and the clusters associated with triangle points are contained within a single contiguous region. This is the outcome of the SOM-enforced neighborhood restrictions. Observe that the centroids are not distributed uniformly, even though each of the five groups has the same number of points. This is caused by both the general point distribution and the artifact of grouping every centroid into a single cluster.

(a) Distribution of SOM reference vectors (**X**'s) for a two-dimensional point set.

diamond	diamond	diamond	hexagon	hexagon	hexagon
diamond	diamond	diamond	circle	hexagon	hexagon
diamond	diamond	circle	circle	circle	hexagon
square	square	circle	circle	triangle	triangle
square	square	circle	circle	triangle	triangle
square	square	square	triangle	triangle	triangle

(b) Classes of the SOM centroids.

Figure 9.9. *SOM applied to two-dimensional data points.*

Source: Pang-Ning Tan, Michael Steinbach, and Vipin Kumar. Introduction to Data Mining. Pearson. https://www.ceom.ou.edu/media/docs/upload/Pang-Ning_Tan_Michael_Steinbach_Vipin_Kumar_-_Introduction_to_Data_Mining-Pe_NRDK4fi.pdf.

- **Applications:** Once the SOM vectors are identified, clustering is not the only use for them. For instance, using a two-dimensional SOM, one can visualize the results using different kinds of plots and associate different quantities with the grid points connected to each centroid (cluster). Plotting the quantity of points connected to every cluster, for instance, produces a plot that shows how points are distributed among clusters. A non-linear projection of the original probability distribution function into two dimensions is known as a two-dimensional SOM. It has been said that employing SOM to capture the structure of the data is like "pressing a flower" because this projection aims to preserve topological features.

- **Strengths and Limitations:** SOM is a clustering method that makes the cluster centroids it produces adhere to neighborhood relationships. As a result, clusters that share a neighbor have a higher degree of relatedness than those that do not. These connections make it easier to understand and see the clustering results. In fact, a lot of applications have made use of this feature of SOM, including the visualization of gene array data and Web documents.

  Additionally, SOM has several drawbacks, which are mentioned below. Certain limitations are applicable solely if SOM is regarded as a conventional clustering method that seeks to identify the real clusters within the data, instead of a method that employs clustering to assist in identifying the data's structure. Additionally, some of these restrictions have been overcome by either SOM extensions or SOM-inspired clustering algorithms.

- The user must choose the settings of parameters, the neighborhood function, the grid type, and the number of centroids.
- Frequently, a SOM cluster does not match a single natural cluster. A single natural cluster may occasionally be divided into multiple SOM clusters, or a SOM cluster may occasionally include multiple natural clusters. The use of a grid of centroids and the tendency of SOM, like other prototype-based clustering techniques, to split or combine natural clusters when they vary in size, shape, and density are two contributing factors to this issue.
- SOM is devoid of a clear goal function. SOM looks for a set of centroids that, given the topographic constraints among the centroids, best approximates the data; however, the degree to which SOM is successful in this endeavor cannot be quantified. This can make comparing various SOM clustering results challenging.
- SOM is not guaranteed to converge, although, in practice, it typically does.

9.3. DENSITY-BASED CLUSTERING

Clusters in density-based clustering are areas with a higher density than the rest of the data set (Kriegel, Hans-Peter et al., 2011). Typically, objects in sparse areas—which are necessary to divide clusters—are regarded as border points and noise (Ester, Martin et al., 1996).

Regions of high density that are divided from one another by regions of low density are located using density-based clustering. Further density-based clustering methods that tackle efficiency, subspace clustering, and more realistic density modeling are covered in this section. Firstly, we take a look at grid-based clustering, which divides the data space into grid cells and then groups together sufficiently dense cells. This kind of approach, at least with low-dimensional data, can be productive and efficient. Subspace clustering, which searches subsets of all dimensions for clusters (dense regions), is the next topic we will discuss. In a data space with n dimensions, it may be necessary to search through up to 2^n–1 subspaces, so an effective method is required. Based on the insight that dense areas in a high-dimensional space imply the existence of dense areas in a lower-dimensional space, the grid-based clustering algorithm CLIQUE offers an effective method for subspace clustering. Lastly, we present DENCLUE, a clustering method that models density as the total of the influences of individual data objects by using kernel density functions. Although DENCLUE is not inherently a grid-based method, it does use a grid-based strategy to increase productivity.

9.3.1. Grid-Based Clustering

At least when it comes to low dimensions, a grid is an effective tool for data organization. To create a set of grid cells, the possible values of each attribute are divided into a number of contiguous intervals. (For the purposes of this discussion and the rest of the section, we will assume that our attributes are continuous, interval, or ordinal). Every object is contained in a grid cell whose associated attribute intervals hold the object's values. In a single pass through the data, objects can be assigned to grid cells, and at the same time, details about each cell, like its point count, can be obtained.

There are many ways to use a grid for clustering, but the majority of methods are, at least partially, based on density. For this reason, we will refer to density-based clustering using a grid as "grid-based clustering" in this section. A fundamental method of grid-based clustering is explained by Algorithm 9.4. Next, several facets of this strategy are examined.

Algorithm 9.4. Basic Grid-Based Clustering Algorithm

1: Define a set of grid cells.
2: Assign objects to the appropriate cells and compute the density of each cell.
3: Eliminate cells having a density below a specified threshold, τ.
4: Form clusters from contiguous (adjacent) groups of dense cells.

9.3.1.1. Defining Grid Cells

Since there are numerous ways to divide the range of values for each attribute into a number of consecutive intervals, this is a crucial but also the least defined step in the process. Dividing the values into equal width intervals is a common method for continuous attributes. The number of points in a cell is a convenient way to define its density. If this method is used for every attribute, the resulting grid cells will all have the same volume.

But more advanced methods can also be applied. Specifically, for continuous attributes, one can apply any of the widely used discretization techniques. This involves (1) discretizing the values of an attribute into intervals such that each interval contains an equal number of points, i.e., equal frequency discretization, or (2) using clustering in addition to the equal width approach previously discussed. The subspace clustering algorithm MAFIA employs an alternative method that involves first dividing the set of values for an attribute into a large number of intervals with equal widths, and then combining intervals with comparable densities.

Whichever strategy is used, the clustering results are significantly influenced by the grid's definition. We'll talk about particular facets of this later.

9.3.1.2. The Density of Grid Cells

The density of a grid cell, or a region with a more general shape, can be naturally defined as the number of points divided by the region's volume. Stated differently, density is the number of points per unit of space, independent of the space's dimensionality. The number of road signs per mile (one dimension), the number of eagles per square kilometer of habitat (two dimensions), and the number of gas molecules per cubic centimeter (three dimensions) are specific, low-dimensional examples of density. However, as previously indicated, a typical strategy is to use uniformly sized grid cells so that the density of each cell can be directly determined by counting the number of points within it.

Example 9.8 (Grid-Based Density):

Two sets of two-dimensional points are shown in Figure 9.10, separated into 49 cells by a 7-by-7 grid.

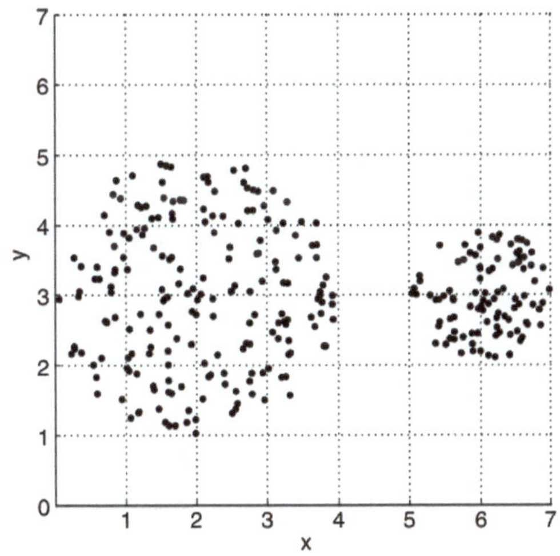

Figure 9.10. *Grid-based density.*

Source: Pang-Ning Tan, Michael Steinbach, and Vipin Kumar. Introduction to Data Mining. Pearson. https://www.ceom.ou.edu/media/docs/upload/Pang-Ning_Tan_Michael_Steinbach_Vipin_Kumar_-_Introduction_to_Data_Mining-Pe_NRDK4fi.pdf.

200 points were produced from a uniform distribution over a circle with a radius of two in the first set, and 100 points were produced from a uniform distribution over a circle with a radius of one in the second. Table 9.2 shows the counts for the grid cells. We can take these values to be the cell densities because each cell has the same volume (area).

Table 9.2. Point Counts for Grid Cells

0	0	0	0	0	0	0
0	0	0	0	0	0	0
4	**17**	**18**	**6**	0	0	0
14	**14**	**13**	**13**	0	**18**	**27**
11	**18**	**10**	**21**	0	**24**	**31**
3	**20**	**14**	**4**	0	0	0
0	0	0	0	0	0	0

Source: Pang-Ning Tan, Michael Steinbach, and Vipin Kumar. Introduction to Data Mining. Pearson. https://www.ceom.ou.edu/media/docs/upload/Pang-Ning_Tan_Michael_Steinbach_Vipin_Kumar_-_Introduction_to_Data_Mining-Pe_NRDK4fi.pdf.

9.3.1.3. Forming Clusters from Dense Grid Cells

Cluster formation from nearby dense cell groups is comparatively simple. (For instance, it is evident that there would be two clusters in Figure 9.10). But there are a few problems. We must clarify what is meant to be meant by adjacent cells. In particular, when only occupied cells are stored, we need an efficient method to find the adjacent cells. For instance, does a two-dimensional grid cell have four or eight adjacent cells?

Some of the limitations of the clustering approach described by Algorithm 9.4 could be addressed by slightly increasing the algorithm's sophistication. For instance, the edge of a cluster is likely to have some partially empty cells. These cells are frequently not dense. In that case, a portion of a cluster will be lost and they will be thrown away. Four portions of the larger cluster would be lost if the density threshold was set at nine, as demonstrated by Figure 9.10 and Table 9.2. Though more processing would be needed, the clustering procedure could be changed to prevent discarding such cells.

Enhancing basic grid-based clustering can be achieved by incorporating more than just density information. In many instances, data includes both spatial and non-spatial features. Some attributes may pertain to the objects' locations in time or space, while others may describe different aspects of the objects. For example, houses have both a location and various characteristics like price or square footage. Due to spatial or temporal autocorrelation, objects within a specific cell often exhibit similar values for their other attributes. In such scenarios, it is feasible to screen the cells based on the statistical properties of one or more non-spatial attributes (e.g., average house price) and subsequently create clusters based on the density of the remaining points.

9.3.1.4. Strengths and Limitations

Positively, grid-based clustering has the potential to be highly productive and successful. Every object's grid cell and each grid's count can be found in a single pass through the data, provided that each attribute has been partitioned. Additionally, only non-empty cells require the creation of grid cells, despite the possibility of a large number of potential grid cells. As a result, O(m), where m is the number of points, is the only time and space complexity required to define the grid, assign each object to a cell, and calculate the density of each cell.

The whole clustering process will be extremely effective, for example, with a time complexity of O(m log m), if nearby, occupied cells can be accessed effectively, for example, by using a search tree. For this reason, many clustering algorithms, including STING, GRIDCLUS, WaveCluster, Bang-Clustering, CLIQUE, and MAFIA, are based on the grid-based approach to density clustering.

The selection of the density threshold τ is a critical factor in grid-based clustering, as it affects most density-based clustering schemes. This is a drawback. Clusters will be lost if τ is too high. Two clusters that ought to be apart might get joined if τ is too low. Moreover, finding a single τ value that is effective across the entire data space might not be feasible if there are clusters and noise with varying densities.

In addition, there are several problems with the grid-based method. For instance, the density of the circular boundary areas is not adequately captured by the rectangular grid cells in Figure 9.10. We could try to solve this issue by fine-tuning the grid, but since the points in the cluster are not distributed uniformly, the number of points in the grid cells associated with a cluster would probably exhibit more fluctuation. In fact, there's a chance that some grid cells—including those inside the cluster—are empty.

Another problem is that a group of points can appear in a single cell or be divided among multiple cells, contingent on the arrangement or dimension of the cells. In the first scenario, a set of points may belong to a cluster, but in the second, it may be discarded. Ultimately, the number of possible grid cells grows exponentially in the number of dimensions as dimensionality increases. It is possible for the majority of grid cells to contain a single object, even though empty grid cells do not always need to be taken into account. Put differently, grid-based clustering typically performs poorly when dealing with high-dimensional data.

9.3.2. Subspace Clustering

Using all of the attributes, the clustering methods that have been considered up to this point have found clusters. But if only certain subsets of the features are taken into account, i.e., subspaces of the data, the clusters we discover may differ significantly between subspaces. Subspace clusters might be intriguing for two reasons. Initially, the data could be randomly distributed with regard to the remaining attributes, but clustered with regard to a select few attributes. Second, there are instances where distinct clusters can be found in various sets of dimensions. Examine a dataset that documents the sales of different products at different points in time. The items are the objects, and the times are the dimensions. Certain items may behave similarly (cluster together) during specific sets of months, such as summer, but distinct clusters are probably characterized by distinct months (dimensions) (Parsons, Lance et al. (2004).

Example 9.9 (Subspace Clusters):

A collection of points is displayed in three dimensions in Figure 9.11(a). The entire space is divided into three point clusters, each symbolized by a square, a diamond, or a triangle. Furthermore, in three-dimensional space, there is one set of points (represented by circles) that are not clusters. The example data set's dimensions (attributes) are divided into a fixed number (η) of equal width intervals. Each interval in $\eta = 20$ has a size of 0.1. The data space is divided into rectangular cells with equal volumes as a result, and the fraction of points in each unit determines its density. Contiguous collections of dense cells make up clusters. As an example, Figure 9.12, which displays a histogram of the data points of Figure 9.11(a) for the x attribute, can be used to identify three one-dimensional clusters if the threshold for a dense cell is $\xi = 0.06$, or 6% of the points.

Plotting the points in the xy plane is shown in Figure 9.11(b). (The z attribute doesn't matter. Additionally, the distribution of the points with respect to their x and y coordinates is displayed by the histograms along the x and y axes in this figure. (Inversely, a higher bar denotes a corresponding interval with relatively more points. Three clusters are visible when we look at the y axis. One is made up of square points, one is made up of diamond and triangle points, and the other is made up of circle points that do not form a cluster in the entire space. The three clusters in the x dimension are also three; they match the three clusters in the entire space, which are squares, triangles, and diamonds. In the xy plane, these points also create unique clusters. Plotting the points in the xz plane is shown in Figure 9.11(c). If we solely take the z attribute into account, we find two clusters. The points denoted by circles make up one cluster, and the points represented by diamonds, triangles, and squares make up the other.

In the xz plane, these points also form unique clusters. Taking into account both the y and z coordinates, Figure 9.11(d) shows three clusters. The points denoted by squares make up one of these clusters, while the circles make up another. In the yz plane, the triangles and diamonds combine to form a single cluster.

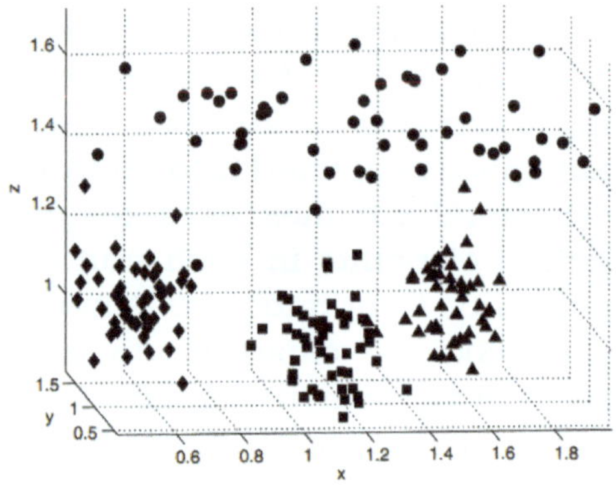

(a) Four clusters in three dimensions.

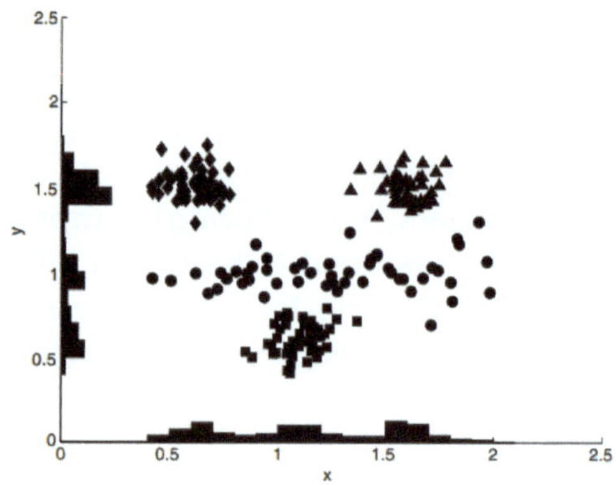

(b) View in the xy plane.

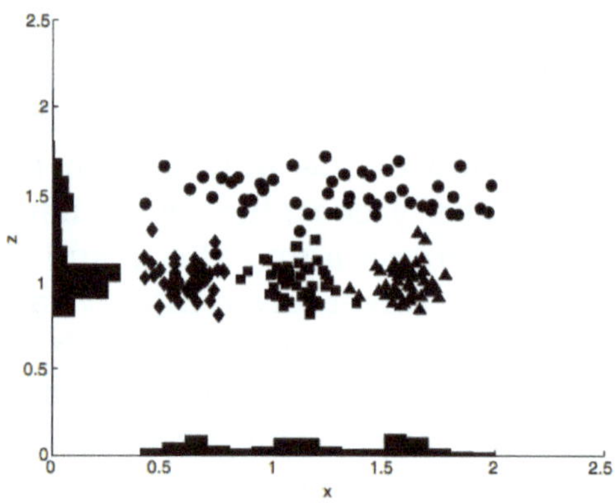

(c) View in the xy plane.

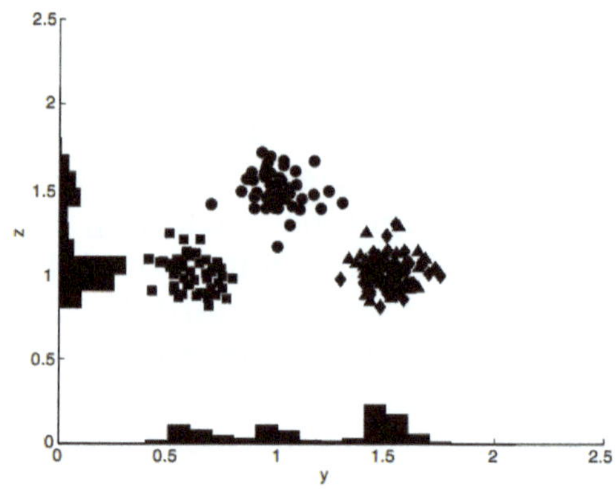

(d) View in the xy plane.

Figure 9.11. *Example figures for subspace clustering.*

Source: Pang-Ning Tan, Michael Steinbach, and Vipin Kumar. Introduction to Data Mining. Pearson. https://www.ceom.ou.edu/media/docs/upload/Pang-Ning_Tan_Michael_Steinbach_Vipin_Kumar_-_Introduction_to_Data_Mining-Pe_NRDK4fi.pdf.

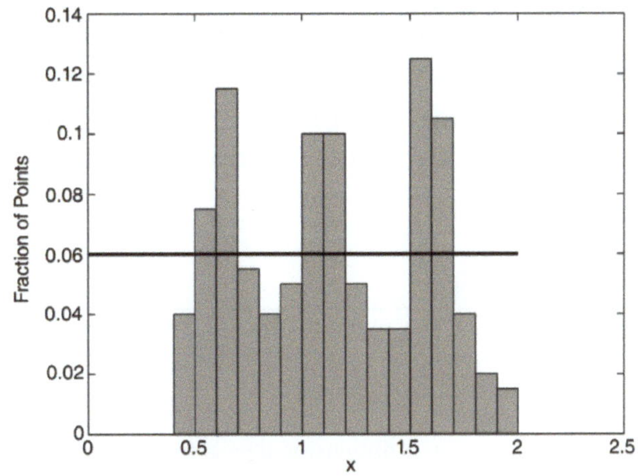

Figure 9.12. *Histogram showing the distribution of points for the x attribute.*

Source: Pang-Ning Tan, Michael Steinbach, and Vipin Kumar. Introduction to Data Mining. Pearson. https://www.ceom.ou.edu/media/docs/upload/Pang-Ning_Tan_Michael_Steinbach_Vipin_Kumar_-_Introduction_to_Data_Mining-Pe_NRDK4fi.pdf.

A few key facts are illustrated by these figures. First, a collection of points, represented by the circles, might form a cluster in a subspace rather than the full data space. Second, in lower-dimensional spaces, clusters that are present throughout the entire data space (or even a subspace) manifest as clusters. While many of the clusters we find in subspaces may only be "shadows" (projections) of higher-dimensional clusters, the first fact suggests that we might need to search in subsets of dimensions in order to find clusters. Finding the clusters and the dimensions in which they reside is the aim, however clusters that are projections of higher-dimensional clusters usually don't pique our interest as much.

9.3.2.1. Clique

A grid-based clustering algorithm called CLIQUE (CLustering In QUEst) systematically locates subspace clusters. Since the number of such subspaces is exponential in the number of dimensions, it is not practical to check every subspace for clusters. Rather, CLIQUE depends on the following attribute:

- **Monotonicity Property of Density-Based Clusters:** A collection of points is included in a density-based cluster in all conceivable subsets of k dimensions (attributes) if it forms one in those k dimensions.

  Suppose you have a cluster of k-dimensional adjacent cells, i.e., a group of nearby cells with densities higher than the designated threshold ⊠ are present. Eliminating one of the k dimensions (attributes) yields a corresponding set of cells in k – 1. Each low-dimensional cell contains all the points of the corresponding high-dimensional cell, and the lower-dimensional cells are still adjacent to one another. It might also include extra points. For this reason, the density of a low-dimensional cell is larger than or equal to that of the corresponding high-dimensional cell. The low-dimensional cells thus group together to form a cluster; i.e., the points group together according to the fewer attributes.

The steps involved in CLIQUE are simplified in Algorithm 9.5. From a conceptual standpoint, the CLIQUE algorithm and the Apriori algorithm for identifying frequent itemsets are similar.

Algorithm 9.5. CLIQUE

Find all the dense areas in the one-dimensional spaces corresponding to each attribute. This is the set of dense one-dimensional cells.
$k \leftarrow 2$
repeat
    Generate all candidate dense k-dimensional cells from dense $(k-1)$-dimensional cells.
    Eliminate cells that have fewer than ξ points.
    $k \leftarrow k + 1$
until There are no candidate dense k-dimensional cells.
Find clusters by taking the union of all adjacent, high-density cells.
Summarize each cluster using a small set of inequalities that describe the attribute ranges of the cells in the cluster.

9.3.2.2. Strengths and Limitations of CLIQUE

The most practical aspect of CLIQUE is that it offers a productive method for looking for clusters within subspaces. This approach's properties are well known because it is based on the well-known Apriori principle from association analysis. The capacity of CLIQUE to condense, using a limited set of inequalities, the list of cells that make up a cluster is another helpful feature.

Numerous constraints of CLIQUE are the same as the constraints of other grid-based density schemes that were previously discussed. There are additional restrictions that resemble those of the Apriori algorithm. To be more precise, CLIQUE can identify clusters that share objects, just as frequent itemsets can share items. Permitting clusters to merge can result in a significantly higher number of clusters and complicate interpretation. An additional concern is the possibility of exponential time complexity with Apriori and CLIQUE. Specifically, CLIQUE will struggle if an excessive number of dense cells are produced at lower values of k. This issue can be resolved by raising the density threshold ξ.

9.3.3. DENCLUE: A Kernel-Based Scheme for Density-Based Clustering

The overall density of a set of points is modeled by the density-based clustering technique known as DENCLUE (Density Clustering) as the sum of the influence functions connected to each point. There will be local peaks in the overall density function that results, i.e., local density maxima, and these local peaks can be naturally employed to delineate clusters. In other words, a hill-climbing process locates the closest peak to each data point, and the collection of all data points connected to a specific peak—referred to as a local density attractor—becomes a cluster. However, the points in the related cluster are categorized as noise and eliminated if the density at a local peak is excessively low. Additionally, the clusters linked to these local peaks merge if a path of data points connecting one local peak to another has a density at each point above the minimum density threshold. As a result, any shape of cluster can be found.

Example 9.10 (DENCLUE Density):

Figure 9.13, which depicts a potential density function for a one-dimensional data set, serves as an example to highlight these ideas. The local density attractors are represented by the peaks of this density function, which are points A–E. The local density attractors' spheres of influence are indicated by the .ted vertical lines. These regions' points will form center-defined clusters. The horizontal dashed line represents the density threshold, ξ. Points connected to a local density attractor with a density smaller than ξ, like those connected to C, will all be eliminated. Every other cluster is retained. Keep in mind that as long as they are connected to local density attractors that have densities higher than ξ, this can include points with densities lower than ξ. Clusters linked by a path of points with a density greater than ξ are finally combined. Clusters D and E would be combined, but clusters A and B would stay apart.

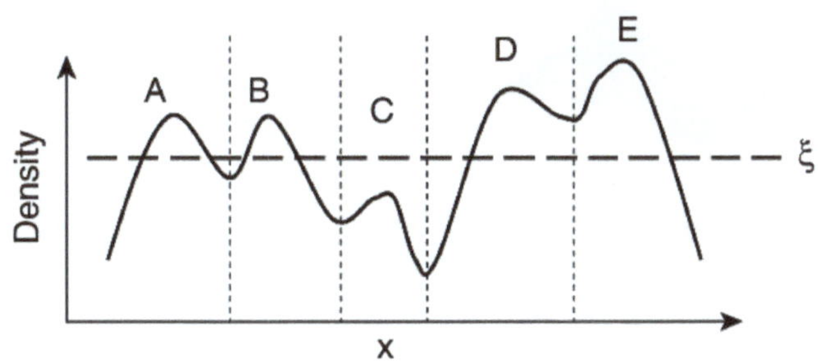

Figure 9.13. *Illustration of DENCLUE density concepts in one dimension.*

Source: Pang-Ning Tan, Michael Steinbach, and Vipin Kumar. Introduction to Data Mining. Pearson. https://www.ceom.ou.edu/media/docs/upload/Pang-Ning_Tan_Michael_Steinbach_Vipin_Kumar_-_Introduction_to_Data_Mining-Pe_NRDK4fi.pdf.

Algorithm 9.6 provides a summary of the DENCLUE algorithm's high-level details. Subsequently, we delve deeper into several DENCLUE features. After giving a quick introduction to kernel density estimation, we show the grid-based method that DENCLUE employs to approximate the density.

Algorithm 9.6. DENCLUE algorithm.

1: Derive a density function for the space occupied by the data points.
2: Identify the points that are local maxima.
(These are the density attractors.)
3: Associate each point with a density attractor by moving in the direction of maximum increase in density.
4: Define clusters consisting of points associated with a particular density attractor.
5: Discard clusters whose density attractor has a density less than a user-specified threshold of ξ.
6: Combine clusters that are connected by a path of points that all have a density of ξ or higher.

9.3.3.1. Kernel Density Estimation

Kernel density estimation is a robust field in pattern recognition and statistics that forms the foundation of DENCLUE. Determining the function that best describes the data's distribution is the aim of this set of techniques (as well as many other statistical techniques). An influence or kernel function is used to express each point's contribution to the overall density function in kernel density estimation. The total of the influence functions connected to every point is the overall density function.

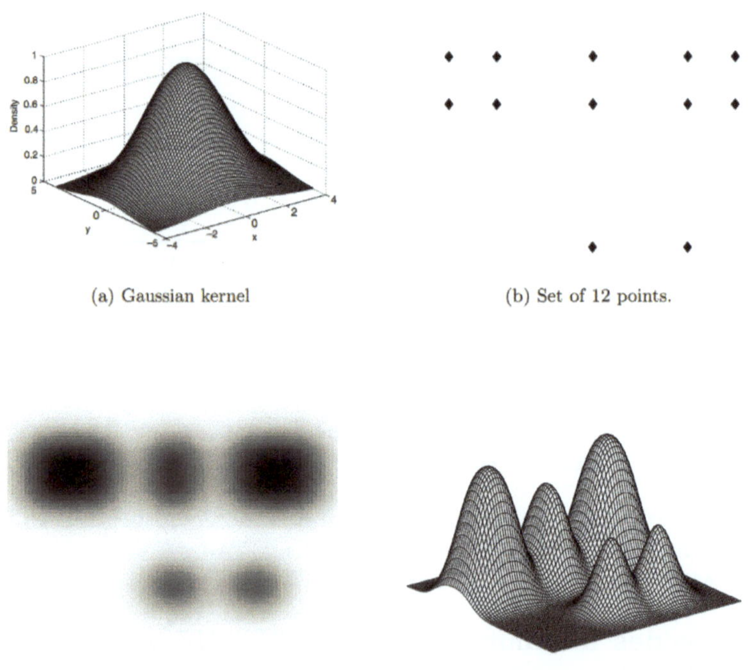

(a) Gaussian kernel

(b) Set of 12 points.

(c) Overall density—gray scale plot.

(d) Overall density—surface plot.

Figure 9.14. *Example of the Gaussian influence (kernel) function and an overall density function.*

Source: Pang-Ning Tan, Michael Steinbach, and Vipin Kumar. Introduction to Data Mining. Pearson. https://www.ceom.ou.edu/media/docs/upload/Pang-Ning_Tan_Michael_Steinbach_Vipin_Kumar_-_Introduction_to_Data_Mining-Pe_NRDK4fi.pdf.

The influence or kernel function is usually symmetric, meaning that it is the same in all directions. Its value, or contribution, diminishes with increasing distance from the point. For instance, the Gaussian function, $K(y) = e^{-distance(x,y)2/2\sigma 2}$, is frequently employed as a kernel function for a given point, x.

The parameter σ, which is comparable to the standard deviation, determines the rate at which a point's influence diminishes. Figures 9.14(c) and 9.14(d) depict the overall density function that is obtained by applying the Gaussian influence function to the set of points shown in Figure 9.14(b), while Figure 9.14(a) depicts what a Gaussian density function would look like for a single point in two dimensions.

9.3.3.2. Implementation Issues

The cost of computing kernel density can be high, and DENCLUE implements its fundamental strategy in an efficient manner by utilizing several approximations. Firstly, density is only explicitly computed at data points. Since the density at each point is a function of the density contributed by each point, this would still result in an $O(m^2)$ time complexity. DENCLUE employs a grid-based implementation to effectively define neighborhoods and, as a result, reduce the number of points that must be taken into consideration in order to define the density at a point, thereby reducing the time complexity. A set of grid cells is first created during a preprocessing step. Only occupied cells are generated, and a search tree makes it easy to retrieve both these cells and the data they contain. Then, DENCLUE only takes into account the nearby points when calculating a point's density and locating its nearest density attractor; i.e., points both within the same cell and in cells that are linked to the cell with the points. Although density estimation accuracy may be somewhat compromised using this method, computational complexity is significantly decreased.

9.3.3.3. Strengths and Limitations of DENCLUE

Because it is based on kernel density functions and the idea of kernel density estimation, which is a well-established field of statistics, DENCLUE has a strong theoretical foundation. Because of this, DENCLUE offers a potentially more accurate and flexible method of computing density than DBSCAN and other grid-based clustering techniques. (DBSCAN is DENCLUE's specific instance. DENCLUE uses grid-based techniques to overcome the computationally expensive nature of an approach based on kernel density functions. However, DENCLUE may incur higher computational costs compared to alternative density-based clustering methods. Additionally, using a grid can have a negative impact on density estimation accuracy and expose DENCLUE to issues that are typical of grid-based techniques; e.g., the challenge of selecting the appropriate grid size. Broadly speaking, DENCLUE has many of the advantages and disadvantages of other density-based strategies. For example, DENCLUE finds clusters of various sizes and shapes and performs well when dealing with noise and outliers. However, it struggles when dealing with high-dimensional data and data that contains clusters of widely disparate densities.

ROLE MODEL

MARTIN ESTER

Martin Ester FRSC (born November 5, 1958) is a Canadian-German Full Professor of Computing Science at Simon Fraser University. His research focuses on researcher data mining and machine learning.

Career

After earning his MSc., Ester worked for Swissair before earning a position at the University of Munich as an Assistant Professor in 1993. Three years later, in 1996, Ester, Hans-Peter Kriegel, Jörg Sander and Xiaowei Xu proposed a data clustering algorithm called "Density-based spatial clustering of applications with noise" (DBSCAN). Their proposal won the 2014 KDD Test of Time Award for "outstanding papers from past KDD Conferences beyond the last decade that have had an important impact on the data mining research community."

A few years later, Ester moved to Vancouver and accepted a position at Simon Fraser University. In 2009, Ester was selected to become an Associate Editor of the IEEE Transactions on Knowledge and Data Engineering.

Between 2010 and 2015, Ester served as the SFU School of Computing Science director, before being succeeded by Greg Mori. In 2016, Arnetminer listed Ester as the world's most influential scholar in data mining. At the time, Arnetminer recorded that Ester authored 169 papers, which gained more than 21,000 citations, and hitting 50 on the h-index. Besides working as a Full Professor at SFU, Ester is also heading research at British Columbia Children's Hospital regarding genetic influence in drug reception and reactions in patients. His research team received a $9.9 million grant from Genome Canada for their research through Genome Canada's 2017 Large-Scale Applied Research Project Competition: Genomics and Precision Health.

As a result of his research, Ester was elected a Fellow of the Royal Society of Canada in 2019.

CLASS ACTIVITY

Students consider a set of documents. Assume that all documents have been normalized to have unit length of 1. What is the "shape" of a cluster that consists of all documents whose cosine similarity to a centroid is greater than some specified constant? In other words, $\cos(d, c) \geq \delta$, where $0 < \delta \leq 1$.

SUMMARY

- Cluster analysis divides data into groups (clusters) that are meaningful, useful, or both. If meaningful groups are the goal, then the clusters should capture the natural structure of the data. In some cases, however, cluster analysis is only a useful starting point for other purposes, such as data summarization
- A large number of clustering algorithms have been developed in a variety of domains for different types of applications. None of these algorithms is suitable for all types of data, clusters, and applications.
- Both DBSCAN and K-means are partitional clustering algorithms that assign each object to a single cluster, but K-means typically clusters all the objects, while DBSCAN discards objects that it classifies as noise.
- Clustering algorithms, such as K-means, are not order-dependent, but they produce different results for each run since they rely on an initialization step that requires a random choice. Because the quality of the clusters can vary from one run to another, multiple runs can be necessary.
- In prototype-based clustering, a cluster is a set of objects in which any object is closer to the prototype that defines the cluster than to the prototype of any other cluster. A simple prototype-based clustering algorithm that uses the centroid of the objects in a cluster as the prototype of the cluster.
- The Kohonen Self-Organizing Feature Map (SOFM or SOM) is a clustering and data visualization technique based on a neural network viewpoint. Despite the neural network origins of SOM, it is more easily presented—as a variation of prototype-based clustering.
- Density-based clustering locates regions of high density that are separated from one another by regions of low density.
- A grid is an efficient way to organize a set of data, at least in low dimensions. The idea is to split the possible values of each attribute into a number of contiguous intervals, creating a set of grid cells.
- CLIQUE (CLustering In QUEst) is a grid-based clustering algorithm that methodically finds subspace clusters. It is impractical to check each subspace for clusters since the number of such subspaces is exponential in the number of dimensions.
- DENCLUE (DENsity CLUstEring) is a density-based clustering approach that models the overall density of a set of points as the sum of influence functions associated with each point. The resulting overall density function will have local peaks, i.e., local density maxima, and these local peaks can be used to define clusters in a natural way.

REVIEW QUESTIONS

1. Explain the difference between K-means and DBSCAN
2. Name the different types of datasets?

3. Name the types of clusters.
4. What is Density-based clustering?
5. What is DENCLUE in data mining?

REFERENCES

1. Barbara, D. (2002). Requirements for clustering data streams. *SIGKDD Explorations Newsletter, 3*(2), 23–27.
2. Bilmes, J. (1997). A gentle tutorial on the EM algorithm and its application to parameter estimation for Gaussian mixture and hidden Markov models (Technical Report ICSITR-97-021). University of California at Berkeley.
3. Bradley, P. S., Fayyad, U. M., & Reina, C. (1999). Scaling EM (Expectation Maximization) clustering to large databases (Technical Report MSR-TR-98-35). Microsoft Research.
4. Ertoz, L., Steinbach, M., & Kumar, V. (2001). A new shared nearest neighbor clustering algorithm and its applications. In *Workshop on Clustering High Dimensional Data and its Applications, Proc. of Text Mine'01, First SIAM Intl. Conf. on Data Mining*, Chicago, IL, USA.
5. Ertoz, L., Steinbach, M., & Kumar, V. (2003). Finding clusters of different sizes, shapes, and densities in noisy, high dimensional data. In *Proc. of the 2003 SIAM Intl. Conf. on Data Mining*, San Francisco. SIAM.
6. Ester, M., Kriegel, H.-P., Sander, J., & Xu, X. (1996). A density-based algorithm for discovering clusters in large spatial databases with noise. In E. Simoudis, J. Han, & U. M. Fayyad (Eds.), *Proceedings of the Second International Conference on Knowledge Discovery and Data Mining (KDD-96)* (pp. 226–231). AAAI Press.
7. Ganti, V., Gehrke, J., & Ramakrishnan, R. (1999). CACTUS–Clustering categorical data using summaries. In *Proc. of the 5th Intl. Conf. on Knowledge Discovery and Data Mining* (pp. 73–83). ACM Press.
8. Gersho, A., & Gray, R. M. (1992). *Vector Quantization and Signal Compression* (Vol. 159). Kluwer Academic Publishers.
9. Gibson, D., Kleinberg, J. M., & Raghavan, P. (2000). Clustering categorical data: An approach based on dynamical systems. *VLDB Journal, 8*(3–4), 222–236.
10. Gowda, K. C., & Krishna, G. (1978). Agglomerative clustering using the concept of mutual nearest neighborhood. *Pattern Recognition, 10*(2), 105–112.
11. Guha, S., Meyerson, A., Mishra, N., Motwani, R., & O'Callaghan, L. (2003). Clustering data streams: Theory and practice. *IEEE Transactions on Knowledge and Data Engineering, 15*(3), 515–528.
12. Han, E.-H., Karypis, G., Kumar, V., & Mobasher, B. (1998). Hypergraph based clustering in high-dimensional data sets: A summary of results. *IEEE Data Eng. Bulletin, 21*(1), 15–22.
13. Hoppner, F., Klawonn, F., Kruse, R., & Runkler, T. (1999). *Fuzzy Cluster Analysis: Methods for Classification, Data Analysis and Image Recognition*. John Wiley & Sons.

14. Jarvis, R. A., & Patrick, E. A. (1973). Clustering using a similarity measure based on shared nearest neighbors. *IEEE Transactions on Computers, C-22*(11), 1025–1034.

15. Jonyer, I., Cook, D. J., & Holder, L. B. (2002). Graph-based hierarchical conceptual clustering. *Journal of Machine Learning Research, 2*, 19–43.

16. Karypis, G., & Kumar, V. (1998). Multilevel k-way partitioning scheme for irregular graphs. *Journal of Parallel and Distributed Computing, 48*(1), 96–129.

17. Karypis, G., Han, E.-H., & Kumar, V. (1999). CHAMELEON: A hierarchical clustering algorithm using dynamic modeling. *IEEE Computer, 32*(8), 68–75.

18. Kohonen, T., Huang, T. S., & Schroeder, M. R. (2000). *Self-Organizing Maps*. Springer-Verlag.

19. Kriegel, H.-P., Kröger, P., Sander, J., & Zimek, A. (2011). Density-based clustering. *WIREs Data Mining and Knowledge Discovery, 1*(3), 231–240.

20. Michalski, R. S., & Stepp, R. E. (1983). Automated construction of classifications: Conceptual clustering versus numerical taxonomy. *IEEE Transactions on Pattern Analysis and Machine Intelligence, 5*(4), 396–409.

21. Mishra, N., Ron, D., & Swaminathan, R. (2004). A new conceptual clustering framework. *Machine Learning Journal, 56*(1–3), 115–151.

22. Murtagh, F. (2000). Clustering massive data sets. In J. Abello, P. M. Pardalos, & M. G. C. Reisende (Eds.), *Handbook of Massive Data Sets*. Kluwer.

23. Ng, R. T., & Han, J. (2002). CLARANS: A method for clustering objects for spatial data mining. *IEEE Transactions on Knowledge and Data Engineering, 14*(5), 1003–1016.

24. Parsons, L., Haque, E., & Liu, H. (2004). Subspace clustering for high dimensional data: A review. *ACM SIGKDD Explorations Newsletter, 6*(1), 90–105.

25. Peters, M., & Zaki, M. J. (2005). CLICKS: Clustering categorical data using K-partite maximal cliques. In *Proc. of the 21st Intl. Conf. on Data Engineering*, Tokyo, Japan.

26. Sheikholeslami, G., Chatterjee, S., & Zhang, A. (1998). Wavecluster: A multi-resolution clustering approach for very large spatial databases. In *Proc. of the 24th VLDB Conf.* (pp. 428–439). Morgan Kaufmann.

27. Stepp, R. E., & Michalski, R. S. (1986). Conceptual clustering of structured objects: A goal-oriented approach. *Artificial Intelligence, 28*(1), 43–69.

CHAPTER 10

Anomaly Detection

LEARNING OBJECTIVES

After studying this chapter, you will be able to:

- Discuss on overview of anomalies
- Understand the preliminaries
- Focus on statistical approaches of anomaly detection
- Describe the proximity-based outlier detection
- Explain the density-based outlier detection
- Define the clustering-based techniques

KEY TERMS FROM THIS CHAPTER

Anomaly detection
Ecosystem Disturbances
Intrusion Detection
Outlier detection
Public Health
Density-Based Techniques
Fraud Detection
Multivariate Normal Distribution
Proximity-based approaches

INTRODUCTION

The aim of anomaly detection is to identify objects that are not like most other objects. Anomalies are frequently referred to as outliers because they are located far from other data points on a scatter plot of the data. Since anomalous objects have attribute values that differ noticeably from typical or expected values, anomaly detection is also known as exception mining or deviation detection. Alternatively, anomaly mining is known as anomaly mining since anomalies are unique in some way. The terms anomaly and outlier will be mostly used. Numerous methods from various fields, such as statistics, machine learning, and data mining, are available for anomaly detection. All attempt to convey the notion that an anomalous data object is distinct from other objects or inconsistent in some other way. Unusual things or events are by definition relatively rare, but that doesn't mean they don't happen frequently enough. An event that is "one in a thousand," for instance, may happen millions of times when billions of events are taken into account.

Most events and objects in the natural world, human society, or data sets are by definition commonplace or ordinary. We are cognizant of the possibility of strange or extraordinary objects, though. This includes seasons that are unusually rainy or dry, well-known sportsmen, or an attribute value that differs greatly from the others. Because anomalous events and objects are frequently of unusual importance—a drought can threaten crops, an athlete's extraordinary skill can propel them to victory, and anomalous values in experiment results can point to either an issue with the experiment or a new phenomenon that needs to be looked into—we are interested in them.

The following examples illustrate applications for which anomalies are of considerable interest.

- **Fraud Detection:** A credit card thief's purchasing habits are most likely not the same as those of the card's original owner. Credit card companies look for purchasing patterns that indicate theft or notice deviations from normal behavior in an effort to identify instances of theft. Comparable methods are applied to other forms of fraud.
- **Intrusion Detection**: Attacks against computer networks and systems are regrettably frequent. Although certain attacks, like those intended to take down or overwhelm computers and networks, are easily recognized, others, like those meant to surreptitiously collect data, are more challenging to identify. Monitoring systems and networks for anomalous activity is the only way to find many of these intrusions.
- **Ecosystem Disturbances**: There are unusual occurrences in the natural world that can profoundly impact people. Hurricanes, floods, droughts, heat waves, and fires are a few examples. Predicting these events' likelihood and their causes is frequently the aim.
- **Public Health**: Hospitals and clinics in many nations submit different statistics to national organizations for additional examination. Let's say that every child

in a city has received the vaccination against a specific disease, for instance., measles, then the emergence of a few cases dispersed throughout different hospitals in a city is an unusual occurrence that might point to a problem with the city's vaccination programs.

- **Medicine**: Unusual test results or symptoms for a specific patient could point to possible health issues. However, other factors about the patient, like age and sex, may determine whether a specific test result is abnormal. In addition, classifying a result as anomalous or not comes at a cost, as there may be harm to the patient if a condition goes undiagnosed and untreated, as well as needless additional testing if the patient is healthy.

While applications focusing on anomalies have fueled much of the recent interest in anomaly detection, anomaly detection (and removal) has traditionally been seen as a method to enhance the analysis of typical data objects. For example, the mean and standard deviation of a set of values or the set of clusters that a clustering algorithm produces can be distorted by a relatively small number of outliers. As a result, data preprocessing frequently includes anomaly detection and elimination.

10.1. OVERVIEW OF ANOMALIES

Data patterns that deviate from a well-defined concept of normal behavior are called anomalies. Anomalies in a basic 2-dimensional data set are shown in Figure 10.1. Since the majority of observations are located in these two regions, the data has two normal regions, N_1 and N_2. Points that are sufficiently far away from the regions, e.g., anomalies are points in region O_3, points o_1 and o_2, and points.

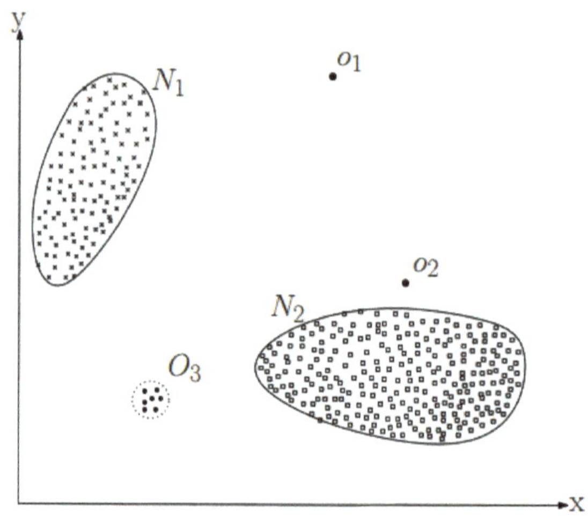

Figure 10.1. *A simple example of anomalies in a 2-dimensional data set.*

Source: http://cucis.ece.northwestern.edu/projects/DMS/publications/AnomalyDetection.pdf.

Anomalies can occur in data for a number of reasons, such as malicious activity like credit card fraud, cyber-intrusion, terrorist activity, or system breakdown. However, regardless of the cause, all anomalies share the common trait of being intriguing to analysts. The "interestingness" and real-world significance of anomalies are essential aspects of anomaly detection. Although different from noise removal, anomaly detection is connected to it (Teng et al., 1990) and noise accommodation (Rousseeuw & Leroy, 1987), which address undesired noise present in the information. One way to characterize noise in data is as a phenomenon that causes problems for data analysis even though the analyst is not interested in it. Prior to performing any data analysis on the data, the need to eliminate any undesired objects motivates noise removal. The term "noise accommodation" describes how to protect a statistical model estimate from unusual observations (Huber, 1974).

10.1.1. Challenges

A pattern that deviates from expected normal behavior is the definition of an anomaly at the abstract level. Therefore, defining a region that represents normal behavior and classifying any observation in the data that does not fall into this normal region as an anomaly is a simple method for detecting anomalies. But several factors make this apparently simple approach very challenging:

- It is very challenging to define a normal region that includes all possible normal behavior. Furthermore, the line separating typical behavior from abnormal behavior is frequently ill-defined. Consequently, an anomalous observation near the boundary may in fact be normal, and vice versa.
- When malicious adversaries cause anomalies, they frequently modify their behavior to make the anomalous observations seem normal, which makes it more challenging to define normal behavior.
- Normal behavior is constantly changing in many domains, so a definition of normal behavior today might not be adequate in the future.
- The precise definition of an anomaly varies depending on the application domain. For instance, a slight departure from normal in the medical field (such as variations in body temperature) might be regarded as abnormal, but a similar deviation in the stock market field (such as variations in a stock's value) might be accepted as normal. It is therefore difficult to transfer a technique developed in one domain to another.
- Typically, a significant problem is the lack of labeled data available for the training or validation of models utilized by anomaly detection methods.
- Often the data contains noise which tends to be similar to the actual anomalies and hence is difficult to distinguish and remove.

The anomaly detection problem is difficult to solve in its most general form because of the aforementioned difficulties. Actually, the majority of anomaly detection methods now in use address a particular way that the problem is formulated. Many factors, including the type of anomalies to be detected, the availability of labeled data, and the nature of the data, influence the formulation. These variables are frequently dictated by the application domain where anomalies must be found. Concepts from a variety of fields, including information theory, statistics, machine learning, data mining, and spectral theory, have been adapted by researchers and applied to particular problem formulations. Figure 10.2 illustrates the essential elements linked to any anomaly detection method.

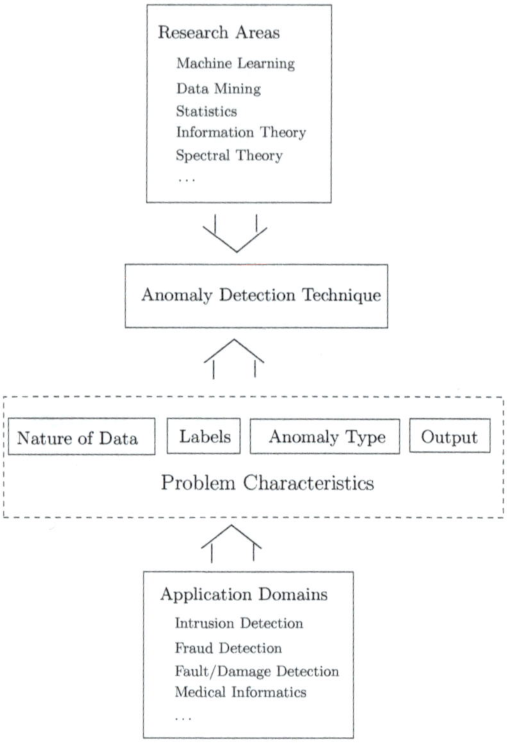

Figure 10.2. *Key components associated with an anomaly detection technique.*

Source: http://cucis.ece.northwestern.edu/projects/DMS/publications/AnomalyDetection.pdf.

10.1.2. Related Work

Anomaly detection is a critical area in data analysis that focuses on identifying patterns in data that do not conform to expected behavior. It is widely used in various domains, such as fraud detection in finance, network security, healthcare, and industrial monitoring. The process begins with understanding the dataset, including its structure and the distribution of its features. Techniques like visualization using histograms, scatter plots, and box plots help in the initial identification of outliers or anomalies. Basic statistical methods such as Z-score and Interquartile Range (IQR) are often employed to detect anomalies by measuring how far a data point deviates from the mean or the central range of the data. More advanced methods involve machine learning algorithms like Isolation Forest and One-Class SVM, which are designed to identify anomalies by learning patterns from the data. Isolation Forest works by randomly selecting features and then splitting the data to isolate anomalies, while One-Class SVM tries to separate the normal data from outliers by finding a decision boundary in the feature space. These techniques are implemented using Python libraries such as Pandas for data manipulation, Matplotlib and Seaborn for visualization, and Scikit-Learn for machine learning.

Hodge and Austin (2004) provide an extensive survey of anomaly detection techniques developed in machine learning and statistical domains. A broad review of anomaly detection techniques for numeric as well as symbolic data is presented by Agyemang et al. (2006). An extensive review of novelty detection techniques using neural networks and statistical approaches has been presented in Markou and Singh (2003a) and Markou and Singh (2003b), respectively. Patcha and Park (2007) and Snyder (2001) present a survey of anomaly detection techniques used specifically for cyber-intrusion detection. A substantial amount of research on outlier detection has been done in statistics and has been reviewed in several books (Rousseeuw & Leroy, 1987; Barnett & Lewis, 1994; Hawkins, 1980) as well as other survey articles (Beckman & Cook, 1983; Bakar et al., 2006).

10.1.3. Different Aspects of an Anomaly Detection Problem

The process of anomaly detection entails locating observations, events, or data points that substantially differ from the bulk of the data. An anomaly detection problem's main components are the kind of data, the kind of anomalies, and the application's context. Anomaly detection techniques differ depending on the type of data, which can include images, unstructured text, time series, and spatial data. Anomalies can take three different forms: point anomalies, which are outlier individual data points; contextual anomalies, which are anomalous data points in particular contexts; or collective anomalies, which are abnormalities in which a collection of related data points deviates from the norm. In order to prevent false positives, anomalies must be interpreted in light of domain-specific knowledge, which is where context comes into play. There are several ways to identify anomalies: from statistical techniques like hypothesis testing and Z-scores to machine learning strategies like neural networks, clustering, and classification. To evaluate the effectiveness of anomaly detection systems, evaluation metrics such as area under the ROC curve, precision, and recall are crucial. Developing strong and trustworthy anomaly detection solutions also requires addressing important issues with handling unbalanced data, algorithm scalability, and result interpretability.

10.1.3.1. Nature of Input Data

Any anomaly detection method's foundational element is the type of input data used. Typically, input consists of a collection of data examples. A single attribute (univariate) or several attributes (multivariate) may be present in each data instance. When dealing with multivariate data instances, each attribute may consist of a single type or a combination of various data types. The suitability of anomaly detection methods depends on the characteristics. For instance, distinct statistical models must be applied for continuous and categorical data when using statistical techniques. Similar to this, the type of attributes would dictate the distance measure to be used in nearest neighbor based techniques. The pairwise distance between instances is frequently given in the form of a distance (or similarity) matrix rather than the actual data. Techniques such as many statistical and classification-based methods, which call for original data instances, are not applicable in these situations. The relationship between data instances can also be used to categorize input data (Tan et al., 2005). The majority of anomaly detection methods currently in use work with record data, also known as point data, where no relationship between the data instances is presumptive.

Data instances can generally be connected to one another. Graph, spatial, and sequence data are a few examples. Sequence data, such as genome sequences, protein sequences, and time-series data, are arranged linearly. Each instance of data in spatial data—such as data on traffic in vehicles or ecological data—is connected to its neighboring instances. Sporocotemporal data, such as climate data, is defined as spatial data with a temporal (sequential) component. Data instances in graph data are shown as vertices in a graph, joined to other vertices by edges.

10.1.4. Type of Anomaly

An important aspect of an anomaly detection technique is the nature of the desired anomaly. Anomalies can be classified into following three categories:

10.1.4.1. Point Anomalies

A single data instance is referred to as a point anomaly if it can be deemed anomalous in relation to the remaining data. The bulk of anomaly detection research focuses on this kind of anomaly since it is the most basic kind. Points o_1 and o_2, as well as points in region O_3, for instance, in Figure 10.1, lie outside the borders of the normal regions and are, therefore, point anomalies because they differ from normal data points. Take credit card fraud detection as an actual-world illustration. Assign the data set to a specific person's credit card transactions. Let's assume for simplicity's sake that the data is defined by just one feature, the amount spent. A transaction will be considered point anomalous if the total amount spent is significantly more than the average for that individual.

10.1.4.2. Contextual Anomalies

If a data instance is anomalous in a specific context (but not otherwise), then it is termed as a contextual anomaly (also referred to as conditional anomaly (Song et al., 2007). The structure of the data set creates the idea of a context, which needs to be defined as part of the problem formulation process ach data instance is defined using following two sets of attributes:

- **Contextual Attributes:** The context (or neighborhood) for that instance is ascertained using the contextual attributes. Contextual attributes in spatial data sets include, for instance, a location's latitude and longitude. Time is a contextual feature in time series data that establishes where an instance falls within the sequence as a whole.
- **Behavioral Attributes:** An instance's non-contextual characteristics are defined by its behavioral attributes. For instance, the quantity of rainfall at any given place is a behavioral attribute in a spatial data set that describes the average rainfall across the entire planet.

The values for the behavioral attributes in a particular context are used to identify the anomalous behavior. In one context, a data instance might be a contextual anomaly; however, in another context, the same data instance—in terms of behavioral attributes—might be regarded as normal. This characteristic is essential for determining behavioral and contextual characteristics for a contextual anomaly detection method.

Contextual anomalies have been most commonly explored in time-series data (Weigend et al., 1995; Salvador & Chan, 2003) and spatial data (Kou et al. 2006; Shekhar et al., 2001). Figure 10.3 shows one such example for a temperature time series which shows the monthly temperature of an area over last few years. A temperature of 35F might be normal during the winter (at time t_1) at that place, but the same value during summer (at time t_2) would be an anomaly. The field of credit card fraud detection has an analogous example. The moment of purchase may be a contextual attribute in the credit card domain. Assume that a person's weekly shopping bill is \$100 on average, but it rises to \$1,000 during Christmas week. While spending the same amount during Christmas week will be regarded as normal, a new purchase of \$1,000 in a week in July will be regarded as a contextual anomaly because it deviates from the person's typical behavior within the time frame. The significance of the contextual anomalies in the intended application domain dictates whether or not to use a contextual anomaly detection technique. Contextual attributes' accessibility is another important component. It makes sense to use a contextual anomaly detection technique in certain situations where defining a context is simple. In other situations, it can be challenging to define a context, which makes applying these techniques challenging.

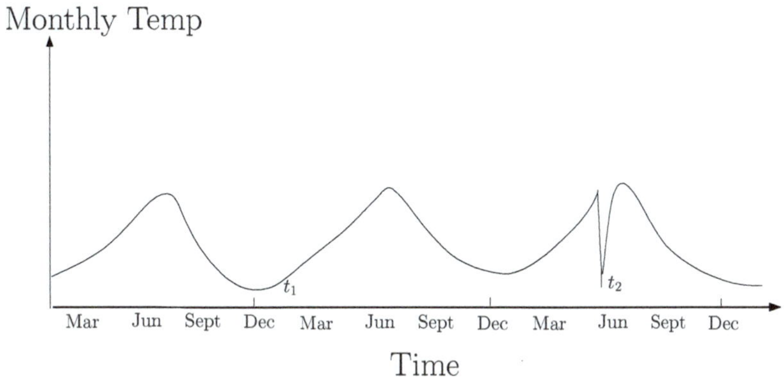

Figure 10.3. *Contextual anomaly t_2 in a temperature time series. Note that the temperature at time t_1 is same as that at time t_2 but occurs in a different context and hence is not considered as an anomaly.*

Source: http://cucis.ece.northwestern.edu/projects/DMS/publications/AnomalyDetection.pdf.

10.1.4.3. Collective Anomalies

A group of related data instances is referred to as a collective anomaly if they are anomalous for the entire data set. The occurrence of the individual data instances in a collective anomaly as a collection is anomalous, even though they might not be anomalies on their own. Figure 10.4 illustrates an example which shows a human electrocardiogram output (Goldberger et al., 2000). Because the same low value persists for an unusually long period of time (corresponding to an atrial premature contraction), the highlighted region indicates an anomaly. Keep in mind that the low value is not unusual in and of itself.

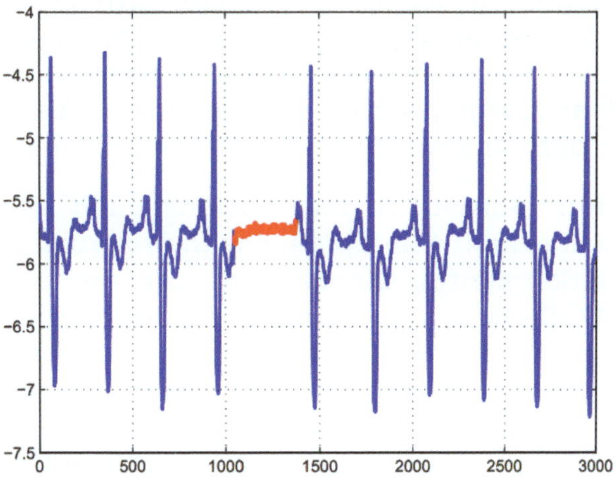

Figure 10.4. *Collective anomaly corresponding to an atrial premature contraction in a human electrocardiogram output.*

Source: http://cucis.ece.northwestern.edu/projects/DMS/publications/AnomalyDetection.pdf.

10.2. PRELIMINARIES

We give some additional background before delving into a discussion of particular anomaly detection algorithms. To be more precise, we (1) investigate the reasons behind anomalies, (2) examine different anomaly detection strategies, (3) differentiate approaches based on whether they employ class label data, and (4) outline problems that are typical of anomaly detection methods. A collection of attributes (also known as a variable, characteristic, feature, field, or dimension) can be used to characterize each instance of data. Different types of attributes, like binary, categorical, or continuous, are possible.

10.2.1. Causes of Anomalies

Anomalies can often be caused by the following: errors in data measurement or collection, data from different classes, and natural variation.

10.2.1.1. Data from Different Classes

Anomalies arise when an object belongs to a different type or class than other objects. For example, a person who uses a credit card fraudulently is not a member of the same class as someone who uses a credit card lawfully. Anomalies are instances of something other than objects, as evidenced by the majority of the examples given at the beginning of the chapter, which include fraud, intrusion, disease outbreaks, and abnormal test results. These anomalies are the subject of anomaly detection in the data mining industry since they are frequently of great interest. The statistician Douglas Hawkins's definition of an outlier, which is frequently cited, states that anomalous objects originate from a different source (class) than most data objects.

- **Natural Variation:** Statistical distributions such as the normal (Gaussian) distribution, which exhibit a sharp decline in probability with increasing distance from the distribution center, can be used to model a wide range of data sets. Stated differently, there is a small chance that an object will differ significantly from the average object, since most objects are located near this center. For instance, a person who is unusually tall is abnormal only in the sense that they have an extreme value for a characteristic (height) that all objects have, not in the sense that they belong to a different class of objects. Often, anomalies that signify extreme or improbable variations are fascinating.
- **Data Measurement and Collection Errors:** Anomalies can also originate from mistakes made during the measurement or data collection processes. For instance, noise, malfunctioning of the measuring equipment, or human error could all lead to inaccurate measurements. Such anomalies are to be removed because they

don't offer any valuable information and only serve to lower the caliber of the data and any subsequent data analysis. In fact, the goal of data preprocessing, more especially data cleaning, is to eliminate this kind of anomaly.

An anomaly could result from any of the previously listed causes or from additional causes that we overlooked. It is true that anomalies in a data set can originate from a variety of sources, and the underlying reason for any given anomaly is frequently unclear. In actual use, anomaly detection methods concentrate on identifying objects that deviate significantly from the majority of other objects; the methods remain unaffected by the anomaly's cause. As a result, the anomaly's underlying cause only matters in relation to the intended use.

10.2.2. Approaches to Anomaly Detection

An essential component of data analysis and machine learning is anomaly detection, sometimes referred to as outlier detection. It entails locating uncommon objects, occurrences, or observations that raise questions because they materially deviate from the bulk of the data. Here are some common approaches to anomaly detection:

- **Model-Based Techniques**: Many methods for detecting anomalies begin with creating a model of the data. Things that don't quite fit the model are called anomalies. For instance, by estimating the parameters of a probability distribution using the data, a model of the distribution of the data can be produced. Something doesn't quite fit the model; that is to say. If it is not very likely under the distribution, it is an anomaly. An object that does not strongly belong to any cluster, if the model is a collection of clusters, is called an anomaly. An object that deviates significantly from its expected value is referred to as an anomaly in regression modeling. Models of these two classes can be created using classification techniques, since anomalous and normal objects can be seen as defining two different classes. Naturally, in order to create a training set, classification techniques can only be applied in the event that class labels are available for a portion of the objects. Additionally, it is important to consider the relative rarity of anomalies when selecting a classification method and the evaluation metrics. In some cases, it is difficult to build a model; e.g., because the statistical distribution of the data is unknown or no training data is available. In these situations, techniques that do not require a model.
- **Proximity-Based Techniques**: Many methods for detecting anomalies are predicated on proximities, which can be used to define a proximity measure between objects. Objects that are far away from the majority of other objects are considered abnormal. Known as distance-based outlier detection techniques, a large number of methods in this field are based on distances. By examining points that are separated from the majority of other points, one can visually identify distance-based outliers in data that can be shown as a two- or three-dimensional scatter plot.

- **Density-Based Techniques:** Calculating object density estimates is not too difficult, especially if one knows a measure of how close the objects are to one another. Low density objects are relatively far away from their neighbors and may be regarded as anomalous. A more advanced method recognizes that data sets may contain regions with substantially different densities and only labels a point as an outlier if its local density is noticeably lower than that of the majority of its neighbors.

10.2.3. The Use of Class Labels

The three fundamental methods for detecting anomalies are semi-supervised, supervised, and unsupervised. The main difference is the extent to which at least some of the data have class labels (normal or anomalous).

- **Supervised Anomaly Detection**: The existence of a training set containing both abnormal and normal objects is necessary for the application of supervised anomaly detection techniques. (Take note that there might be more than one class that is normal or abnormal. Since anomalies are comparatively uncommon in comparison to normal objects, classification strategies that tackle the so-called rare class problem are especially pertinent, as was previously mentioned.
- **Unsupervised Anomaly Detection**: There are numerous real-world scenarios where class labels are unavailable. Under these circumstances, the goal is to give each instance a score (or label) that indicates how unusual it is. It should be noted that if there are numerous anomalies that are comparable to one another, they may all be classified as normal or receive a low outlier score. Consequently, anomalies need to be unique from normal objects in order for unsupervised anomaly detection to be effective.
- **Semi-Supervised Anomaly Detection**: There are situations when training data has labeled normal data but lacks information about anomalous objects. Finding an anomaly label or score for a set of given objects using data from labeled normal objects is the goal in the semi-supervised setting. The existence of numerous related outliers in the set of objects to be scored in this instance has no bearing on the outlier evaluation, it should be noted. Finding a small set of representative normal objects can be challenging in many real-world scenarios, though.

10.2.4. Issues

There are a variety of important issues that need to be addressed when dealing with anomalies.

- **Number of Attributes Used to Define an Anomaly**: If an object has only one attribute, then the question of whether its value for that attribute is anomalous determines whether the object is anomalous. An object may, however, have anomalous values for some attributes and ordinary values for other attributes because it may have many attributes. Furthermore, even if none of an object's attribute values are abnormal on their own, an object may still be abnormal. For instance, it is typical to see people who are 300 pounds or two feet tall (children), but it is unusual to see someone who is both of those things. How the values of various attributes are used to determine whether an object is an anomaly or not needs to be specified in a general definition of an anomaly. When the dimensionality of the data is high, this becomes an especially significant issue.

- **Global versus Local Perspective**: When compared to all other objects, an object might appear unusual, but not when compared to objects in its immediate neighborhood. For instance, a person who stands six feet five inches tall is considered exceptionally tall by the general public, but not by professional basketball players.
- **Degree to Which a Point Is an Anomaly**: Certain techniques report the assessment of an object's anomaly status in a binary manner—that is, an object is either an anomaly or it is not. This often fails to acknowledge the fundamental fact that certain objects are more extreme anomalies than others. Therefore, having an evaluation of how anomalous an object is desirable. The anomaly or outlier score is the name given to this evaluation.
- **Identifying One Anomaly at a Time versus Many Anomalies at Once**: Certain techniques eliminate anomalies one by one; that is, they start with the most anomalous instance and work their way down. For other methods, a group of anomalies is recognized collectively. Masking is a common issue with techniques that try to identify one anomaly at a time, where the presence of multiple anomalies hides the presence of all of them. However, methods that identify many outliers simultaneously may encounter a phenomenon known as swamping, in which ordinary objects are mistakenly identified as outliers. These effects can occur in model-based approaches because the anomalies cause the data model to be distorted.
- **Evaluation**: Measures of classification performance can be used to assess an anomaly detection scheme's efficacy if class labels for distinguishing anomalies from normal data are available. However, measures like accuracy are less appropriate than precision, recall, and false positive rate because the anomalous class is typically much smaller than the normal class. Evaluation becomes challenging in the event that class labels are unavailable. For model-based methods, on the other hand, the measure of outlier detection efficacy can be determined by looking at how much the model improves after anomalies are removed.
- **Efficiency**: The computational cost of different anomaly detection schemes varies significantly. While the creation of the classification model for classification-based schemes can involve substantial resources, their implementation is typically low cost. Similarly, statistical methods can classify an object in constant time after developing a statistical model. Since

proximity-based methods typically require the computation of the proximity matrix to obtain the necessary information, their time complexity is naturally $O(m^2)$, where m is the number of objects. In certain situations, like low-dimensional data, this time complexity can be decreased by using specific data structures and algorithms.

10.3. STATISTICAL APPROACHES

Models are the foundation of statistical approaches, i.e., objects are assessed based on how well they fit the model after a model is developed for the data. The majority of statistical methods for detecting outliers rely on creating a probability distribution model and evaluating an object's likelihood under it. The parameters of a user-specified distribution are estimated from the data to create a probability distribution model. In the event that a Gaussian distribution is assumed for the data, the data's mean and standard deviation can be used to estimate the mean and standard deviation of the underlying distribution. Next, it is possible to estimate the probability of each object under the distribution.

Among the important issues facing this approach to outlier detection are the following:

- **Identifying the Specific Distribution of a Data Set**: While a few common distributions, like the Poisson, binomial, or Gaussian, can describe a wide range of data types, non-standard distributions are relatively common in data sets. Of course, it is possible to mistakenly identify an object as an outlier if the incorrect model is selected. For instance, even though the data is modeled as coming from a Gaussian distribution, it might actually originate from a distribution with a higher likelihood of having values that deviate from the mean than the Gaussian distribution. In practice, statistical distributions that exhibit this kind of behavior are frequently referred to as heavy-tailed distributions.
- **The Number of Attributes Used**: Most statistical outlier detection techniques apply to a single attribute, but some techniques have been defined for multivariate data.
- **Mixtures of Distributions**: The data can be modeled as a mixture of distributions, and outlier detection schemes can be developed based on such models. Although potentially more powerful, such models are more complicated, both to understand and to use. For example, the distributions need to be identified before objects can be classified as outliers.

10.3.1. Detecting Outliers in a Univariate Normal Distribution

We will use one of the most widely used distributions in statistics, the Gaussian (normal) distribution, to explain a straightforward method for statistical outlier detection. The notation $N(\mu, \sigma)$ is used to represent this distribution, which has two parameters: σ and μ, which stand for the standard deviation and mean, respectively. Figure 10.5 displays $N(0, 1)$'s density function.

There is little chance that an object (value) from a N(0, 1) distribution will occur in the tails of the distribution. For instance, there is only a probability of 0.0027 that an object lies beyond the central area between ±3 standard deviations. More generally, if c is a constant and x is the attribute value of an object, then the probability that |x| ≥ c decreases rapidly as c increases. Let α = prob(|x| ≥ c).

When the distribution is N(0, 1), here are some sample values for c and the matching values for α. A value that deviates more than four standard deviations from the mean is considered to be an anomaly occurring once every 10,000 times (Table 10.1),

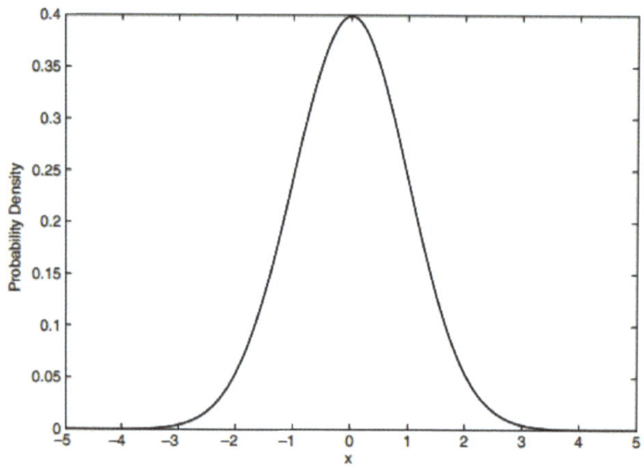

Figure 10.5. *Probability density function of a Gaussian distribution with a mean of 0 and a standard deviation of 1.*

Source: https://www.ceom.ou.edu/media/docs/upload/Pang-Ning_Tan_Michael_Steinbach_Vipin_Kumar_-_Introduction_to_Data_Mining-Pe_NRDK4fi.pdf.

Table 10.1. Sample Pairs (c, α), α = prob(|x| ≥ c) for a Gaussian Distribution with Mean 0 and Standard Deviation 1

c	α for $N(0,1)$
1.00	0.3173
1.50	0.1336
2.00	0.0455
2.50	0.0124
3.00	0.0027
3.50	0.0005
4.00	0.0001

Source: https://www.ceom.ou.edu/media/docs/upload/Pang-Ning_Tan_Michael_Steinbach_Vipin_Kumar_-_Introduction_to_Data_Mining-Pe_NRDK4fi.pdf.

A test to determine whether an object (value) is an outlier as indicated can be based on a value's distance c from the center of the N(0, 1) distribution, which is directly related to the value's probability.

(Outlier for a Single N(0,1) Gaussian Attribute). An object with attribute value x from a Gaussian distribution with mean of 0 and standard deviation 1 is an outlier if:

$$|x| \geq c, \tag{1}$$

where; c is a constant chosen so that prob(|x|) ≥ c = α.

In order to apply this definition, α must have a value specified. α represents the likelihood that we will incorrectly identify a value from the provided distribution as an outlier based on the theory that unusual values (objects) indicate a value from a different distribution. When considering an outlier as a rare value within a N(0, 1) distribution, the value of α indicates the extent of its rarity.

If the distribution of an attribute of interest (for the normal objects) has a Gaussian distribution with mean µ and a standard deviation σ, i.e., a N(µ, σ) distribution, then to use. We need to transform the attribute x to a new attribute z, which has a N(0, 1) distribution. In particular, the approach is to set z = (x – µ)/σ. (z is typically called a z score.) However, µ and σ are typically unknown and are estimated using the sample mean x and sample standard deviation s_x. In practice, this works well when the number of observations is large. However, we note that the distribution of z is not actually N(0, 1).

10.3.2. Outliers in a Multivariate Normal Distribution

We would like to use a method similar to that described for a univariate Gaussian distribution for multivariate Gaussian observations. Specifically, if a point has a low probability in relation to the data's estimated distribution, we want to categorize it as an outlier. Additionally, it would be nice to be able to assess this using a straightforward test, like measuring a point's separation from the distribution's center. However, a multivariate normal distribution is not symmetrical with respect to its center due to the correlation between the various variables (attributes). However, a multivariate normal distribution is not symmetrical with respect to its center due to the correlation between the various variables (attributes). The probability density of a two-dimensional multivariate Gaussian distribution with mean of (0,0) and a covariance matrix of:

$$\Sigma = \begin{pmatrix} 1.00 & 0.75 \\ 0.75 & 3.00 \end{pmatrix}$$

We will require a distance measure that considers the shape of the data distribution if we are to employ a straightforward threshold to determine whether an object is an outlier. One such distance is the Mahalanobis distance. Equation 2 displays the Mahalanobis distance between a point x and the mean of the data x.

$$mahalanobis(\mathbf{x}, \overline{\mathbf{x}}) = (\mathbf{x} - \overline{\mathbf{x}})\mathbf{S}^{-1}(\mathbf{x} - \overline{\mathbf{x}})^T, \tag{2}$$

Where; S is the covariance matrix of the data.

It is simple to demonstrate that the probability of a point is directly related to its Mahalanobis distance from the underlying distribution mean. Specifically, the log of the point's probability density plus a constant equals the Mahalanobis distance.

10.3.3. A Mixture Model Approach for Anomaly Detection

A mixture model based anomaly detection technique. It is assumed by the mixture model approach that each cluster can be uniquely identified by one of a variety of probability distributions from which the data originates. The data is modeled as a mixture of two distributions—one for regular data and another for outliers—for anomaly detection procedures. The aim is to maximize the overall likelihood (probability) of the data for both clustering and anomaly detection by estimating the parameters of the distributions. Each probability distribution's parameters are estimated for clustering using the EM algorithm. However, this method of anomaly detection is more straightforward. When the set of anomalous objects is first created, it contains nothing and all of the objects are placed in the set of normal objects. Next, if moving items from the regular set to the anomalous set increases the likelihood of the data overall, an iterative process does so.

Let us assume that the data set D comprises items from two probability distributions mixed together: M, which represents the distribution of most (normal) objects, and A, which represents the distribution of anomalous objects.

The overall probability distribution of the data can be written as:

$$D(\mathbf{x}) = (1-\lambda)M(\mathbf{x}) + \lambda A(\mathbf{x}) \tag{3}$$

Where; ⊠ is a number between 0 and 1 that indicates the expected fraction of outliers, and x is an object. While the distribution A is frequently assumed to be uniform, the distribution M is estimated from the data. Let M_t and A_t represent the normal and anomalous object sets at t, respectively. A_t the beginning, M_0 = D and A_0 is empty at time t = 0. At an arbitrary time t, the likelihood and log likelihood of the entire data set D are given by the following two equations, respectively:

$$L_t(D) = \prod_{\mathbf{x}_i \in D} P_D(\mathbf{x}_i) = \left((1-\lambda)^{|M_t|} \prod_{\mathbf{x}_i \in M_t} P_{M_t}(\mathbf{x}_i) \right) \left(\lambda^{|A_t|} \prod_{\mathbf{x}_i \in A_t} P_{A_t}(\mathbf{x}_i) \right) \tag{4}$$

$$LL_t(D) = |M_t| \log(1-\lambda) + \sum_{\mathbf{x}_i \in M_t} \log P_{M_t}(\mathbf{x}_i) + |A_t| \log \lambda + \sum_{\mathbf{x}_i \in A_t} \log P_{A_t}(\mathbf{x}_i) \tag{5}$$

Where; P_D, PM_t, and PA_t are the probability distribution functions for D, M_t and A_t, respectively.

To do so, it is necessary to make the simplifying assumption that the probability is 0 for both of the following situations: (1) an object in A is a normal object, and (2) an object in M is an outlier. Algorithm 1 gives the details.

The distribution of normal objects may not change significantly when an object is moved to the set of anomalies because there are a lot more normal objects than anomalies. Then, each normal object's contribution to the total likelihood of the normal objects will stay largely unchanged. Additionally, every object added to the set of anomalies increases the likelihood of the anomalies by a fixed amount if a uniform distribution is assumed for the anomalies. Thus, the probability of the object under a uniform distribution (weighted by λ) minus the probability of the object under the distribution of the normal data points (weighted by 1−λ) roughly equals the overall change in the total likelihood of the data when an object is moved to the set of anomalies. As a result, rather than falling under the distribution of the normal objects, the set of anomalies will typically comprise those objects that have a noticeably higher probability under a uniform distribution.

Algorithm 1. Likelihood-Based Outlier Detection

1: Initialization: At time $t = 0$, let M_t contain all the objects, while A_t is empty. Let $LL_t(D) = LL(M_t) + LL(A_t)$ be the log likelihood of all the data.
2: **for** each point $\mathbf{x}$ that belongs to M_t **do**
3: Move $\mathbf{x}$ from M_t to A_t to produce the new data sets A_{t+1} and M_{t+1}.
4: Compute the new log likelihood of D, $LL_{t+1}(D) = LL(M_{t+1}) + LL(A_{t+1})$
5: Compute the difference, $\Delta = LL_t(D) - LL_{t+1}(D)$
6: **if** $\Delta > c$, where c is some threshold **then**
7: $\mathbf{x}$ is classified as an anomaly, i.e., M_{t+1} and A_{t+1} are left unchanged and become the current normal and anomaly sets.
8: **end if**
9: **end for**

Classifying objects with a low probability under the distribution of normal objects as outliers is roughly equivalent to the method outlined by Algorithm 1. This method would identify points A and B as outliers, along with other points that deviate significantly from the mean. Nevertheless, the outcomes of this method will differ from those obtained by simply labeling low-probability objects as outliers if the distribution of the normal objects changes considerably as anomalies are eliminated or if the distribution of the anomalies can be more intricately modeled. This strategy is also applicable in cases where there are multiple modes of object distribution.

10.3.4. Strengths and Weaknesses

Outlier detection statistical methods are based on well-established statistical methods, like estimating a distribution's parameters. These tests can be highly successful when the data and the appropriate test type are sufficiently understood. Numerous statistical outliers tests are available for individual attributes. Fewer options are available for multivariate data, and these tests can perform poorly for high-dimensional data.

10.4. PROXIMITY-BASED OUTLIER DETECTION

A key strategy in data mining is the use of proximity-based approaches. By searching documents for specific keywords and phrases, they are used to identify patterns in huge databases. Because they don't need a lot of storage space or expensive hardware and can scale up effectively to accommodate larger databases, they are extremely common.

- **Advantages of Proximity-Based Methods:**
  1. Proximity-based methods make use of machine learning techniques, in which algorithms are trained to respond to certain patterns.
  2. Using a random sample of documents, the machine learning algorithm analyzes the keywords and phrases used in them and makes predictions about the probability that these words appear together across all documents.
  3. Proximity can be calculated by calculating a similarity score between two collections of training data and then comparing these scores. The algorithm then tries to compute the maximum similarity score for two distinct sets of training items.
- **Disadvantages of Proximity-Based Methods:**
  1. Important words may not be as close in proximity as we expected.
  2. Over-segmentation of documents into phrases. To counter these problems, a lexical chain-based algorithm has been proposed.

When determining collections of documents containing specific words based on prior knowledge, proximity-based techniques work incredibly well. Nevertheless, when the background knowledge is not already divided into categories, performance is constrained. Assigning categorical values to each document and using these documents as training data to run proximity-based methods in the hopes of obtaining accurate representations of the categories is how sets of documents containing particular categories are found. Density-based outlier detection is one method of locating outliers by figuring out how far they are from the rest of the data set.

10.4.1. Types of Proximity-Based Outlier Detection Methods

- **Distance-Based Outlier Detection Methods:** A statistical method is a distance-based outlier detection technique. These techniques usually calculate the separations between individual data points and the other members of their respective groups. A programmable error threshold is another feature of many methods that helps identify when a point is an outlier. There are a lot of distance-based outliers techniques available. The techniques compute the distances between individual points and look for outliers using distance statistics like the Euclidean, Manhattan, or Mahalanobis distance. The following three outlier detection methods have been selected based on their performance:

- WLSMV (Weighted Least Squares Minimization) method
- SVM (Support Vector Machines) method,
- RMSProp method.

- **Density-Based Outlier Detection Methods:** The density of an entity object and the objects that are closest to it are examined using a density-based outlier detection technique. Numerous applications, such as malware detection, awareness, behavior analysis, and network intrusion detection, use this method in important ways. Density-based outlier detection techniques have certain limitations until it is established that the outliers being detected are simply a small portion of a much larger distribution of data rather than true outliers. Using density-based outlier detection techniques has the drawback that, in order to be implemented and have the right value set, the density function needs to be defined and understood.

10.4.2. Strengths and Weaknesses

The distance-based outlier detection method discussed earlier, as well as similar methods, are straightforward but have limitations. Proximity-based techniques usually require $O(m^2)$ time, which can be costly for large datasets. While specialized algorithms can help with lower dimensional data, the method is still dependent on parameter selection. Additionally, it struggles with datasets that have varying densities across different regions as it employs global thresholds unable to adapt to such variations.

10.5. DENSITY-BASED OUTLIER DETECTION

Items in low-density areas are considered outliers from a density-based perspective. The inverse of the density surrounding an object is its outlier score. Since density is typically defined in terms of proximity, density-based outlier detection and proximity-based outlier detection are closely related. Determining density by taking the reciprocal of the average distance to the k nearest neighbors is a popular method. The density is high if this distance is small, and vice versa.

$$density(\mathbf{x}, k) = \left(\frac{\sum_{\mathbf{y} \in N(\mathbf{x},k)} distance(\mathbf{x}, \mathbf{y})}{|N(\mathbf{x}, k)|} \right)^{-1} \qquad (6)$$

Where; N(x, k) is the set containing the k-nearest neighbors of x, |N(x, k)| is the size of that set, and y is a nearest neighbor.

Another definition of density is the one used by the DBSCAN clustering algorithm.

- **Count of Points within a Given Radius:** The number of objects that are within a given distance d of an object is its surrounding density. It is important to choose the parameter d carefully. Many normal points may have low density and a high outlier score if d is too small. Many outliers may have densities (and outlier scores) that are comparable to normal points if d is selected to be large. The features and constraints of proximity-based outlier schemes are similar to those of outlier detection using any of the density definitions.

Another method is to compute the relative density as the ratio of the density of a point x and the average density of its nearest neighbors y as follows:

$$average\ relative\ density(\mathbf{x}, k) = \frac{density(\mathbf{x}, k)}{\sum_{\mathbf{y} \in N(\mathbf{x},k)} density(y, k)/|N(\mathbf{x}, k)|} \qquad (7)$$

10.5.1. Detection of Outliers Using Relative Density

We present a method based on the concept of relative density. Algorithm 2 describes this technique, which is a condensed version of the Local Outlier Factor (LOF) technique. We first determine the density of an object density(x, k) based on its closest neighbors before calculating the outlier score for each object for a given number of neighbors (k). Equation 7 shows how to compute the average relative density of a point by first calculating the average density of the point's neighbors. This number is interpreted as x's outlier score and indicates whether x is located in a denser or sparser area of the neighborhood than its neighbors.

Algorithm 2. Relative Density Outlier Score Algorithm

{k is the number of nearest neighbors}
for all objects $\mathbf{x}$ **do**
  Determine $N(\mathbf{x}, k)$, the k-nearest neighbors of $\mathbf{x}$.
  Determine $density(\mathbf{x}, k)$, the density of $\mathbf{x}$ using its nearest neighbors, i.e., the objects in $N(\mathbf{x}, k)$.
end for
for all objects $\mathbf{x}$ **do**
  Set the $outlier\ score(\mathbf{x}, k) = average\ relative\ density(\mathbf{x}, k)$ from Equation 10.7.
end for

10.5.2. Strengths and Weaknesses

Relative density-based outlier detection provides a quantitative assessment of an object's outlier status and can function effectively even in the presence of densities that vary across data regions. Similar to distance-based techniques, these methods' time complexity is naturally $O(m^2)$ (where m is the number of objects); however, by employing specific data structures, this can be lowered to O(m log m) for low-dimensional data. Although the standard LOF algorithm takes care of this by looking at a range of values for k and then taking the maximum outlier scores, parameter selection can still be challenging. The upper and lower bounds of these values must still be determined, though.

10.6. CLUSTERING-BASED TECHNIQUES

While anomaly detection finds objects that are not strongly related to other objects, cluster analysis finds groups of objects that are. Thus, it should come as no surprise that outlier detection can be accomplished using clustering. Eliminating tiny clusters that are isolated from other clusters is one method of applying clustering for outlier detection. This method works with any clustering technique; however, it needs thresholds set for the minimum size of a cluster and the separation between a small cluster and neighboring clusters. The procedure is frequently made simpler by eliminating any clusters that are smaller than a certain size. The number of clusters selected has a significant influence on this scheme. Additionally, this scheme makes it difficult to associate an outlier score with an object. It should be noted that while this broadens the definition of outliers from individual objects to groups of objects, it makes no fundamental changes.

A more methodical approach would be to group all of the objects first, and then determine the extent to which each object is a member of a cluster. The distance between an object and its cluster center in prototype-based clustering can be used to determine how much of an object is part of a cluster. Broader still, we can use the objective function to evaluate an object's degree of membership in any cluster when using clustering techniques that are based on it. To be more specific, we would label an object as an outlier if its removal leads to a significant improvement in the goal. As an example, in K-means, removing an object that is distant from the center of its corresponding cluster can significantly enhance the cluster's sum of squared errors (SSE).

- **Clustering-Based Outlier:** A cluster-based outlier is any object that does not exhibit strong cluster membership. This definition is a specific instance of the definition of a model-based anomaly when applied to clustering schemes with an objective function. It is a natural fit for prototype-based or objective-functioning schemes, and it can also include density- and connectivity-based clustering techniques for outlier detection. Specifically, if an object's density is too low for density-based clustering, it does not strongly belong to any cluster; conversely, if an object has weak connectivity, it does not strongly belong to any cluster.

10.6.1. Assessing the Extent to Which an Object Belongs to a Cluster

There are multiple approaches to determine how much an object belongs to a prototype-based cluster. One approach is to calculate the object's distance from the cluster prototype and use that distance to determine the object's outlier score. On the other hand, if the densities of the clusters vary, we can create an outlier score that calculates an object's relative distance from the cluster prototype in relation to the distances of the other objects in the cluster. Using the Mahalanobis distance is an additional option if the clusters can be precisely represented in terms of Gaussian distributions. When using clustering techniques with an objective function, we can give an object an outlier score that indicates how the objective function improves after the object is removed. On the other hand, determining how much a point deviates from the norm using the objective function can require a lot of computation.

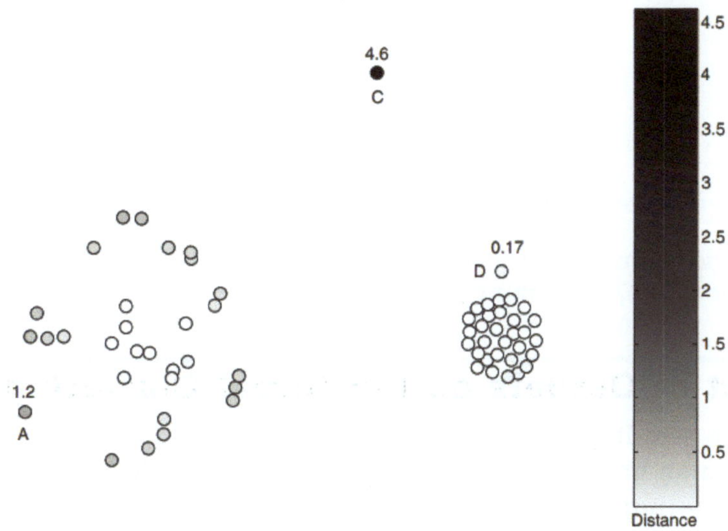

Figure 10.6. *Distance of points from closest centroid.*

Source: https://www.ceom.ou.edu/media/docs/upload/Pang-Ning_Tan_Michael_Steinbach_Vipin_Kumar_-_Introduction_to_Data_Mining-Pe_NRDK4fi.pdf.

- **Clustering-Based Example:** The outlier score of a point is calculated using two different methods in prototype-based clustering, which employs the K-means algorithm. The first method uses the point's distance from its closest centroid, and the second uses the point's relative distance from its closest centroid, which is the ratio of the point's distance from the centroid to the median distance of all the points in the cluster from the centroid. In order to account for the significant density difference between the compact and loose clusters, the latter method is employed. Outlier scores that resulted are displayed in Figures 10.6 and 10.7. As before, the shading indicates the outlier score, which is in this case determined by the distance or relative distance. In every instance, two clusters are used. The approach based on raw distance encounters issues because the clusters have different densities, for example. D is regarded as not being an outlier. The points (A, C, and D) that were previously identified as outliers using LOF also appear as outliers for the relative distances approach.

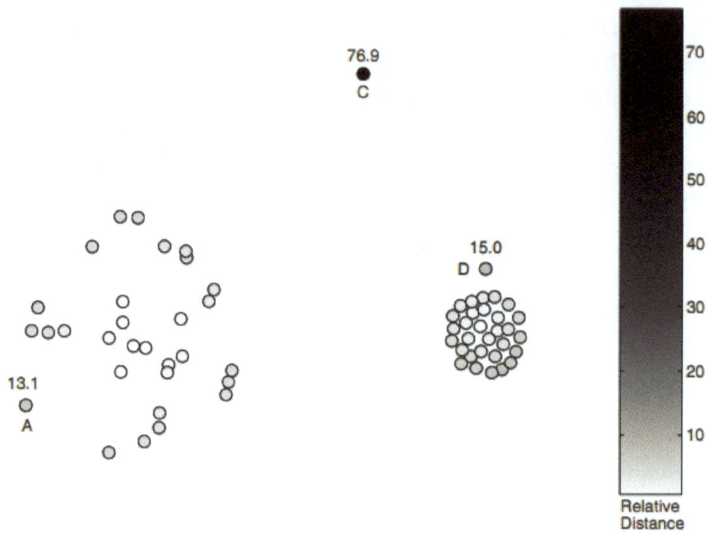

Figure 10.7. *Relative distance of points from closest centroid.*

Source: https://www.ceom.ou.edu/media/docs/upload/Pang-Ning_Tan_Michael_Steinbach_Vipin_Kumar_-_Introduction_to_Data_Mining-Pe_NRDK4fi.pdf.

10.6.2. Impact of Outliers on the Initial Clustering

The validity of the results is called into question if outliers are found through clustering, since outliers have an impact on the clustering. This problem can be solved by clustering the objects, eliminating the outliers, and then clustering the objects once more. This method is simple to apply, even though there is no assurance that it will produce the best outcomes. Creating a special group for objects that don't currently fit well in any cluster is a more advanced strategy. Potential outliers are represented by this group. Clusters evolve during the clustering process. The set of potential outliers is expanded by adding objects that no longer strongly belong to any cluster, and it is reduced by testing objects that are already in the set to see if they can be eliminated from the list of potential outliers because they no longer strongly belong to any cluster. Outliers are those objects that are still part of the set after the clustering process. Once more, there is no assurance that this method will be more effective than the earlier, simpler one, or even that there will be an ideal solution. A cluster of noise points, for instance, might appear to be a genuine cluster devoid of outliers. If the relative distance is used to calculate the outlier score, this issue becomes even more problematic.

10.6.3. The Number of Clusters to Use

The number of clusters is not always determined automatically by clustering techniques like K-means. This is an issue because the number of clusters can affect whether an object is classified as an outlier or not when using clustering for outlier detection. For example, if only a few large clusters are found, a group of ten objects may be relatively close to each other, but they may also be included as part of a larger cluster. In that scenario, even though ten points would have formed a cluster if a sufficient number of clusters had been specified, each point could be considered an outlier.

This problem has no easy solution, just like some of the others. Rerunning the analysis with varying numbers of clusters is one tactic. Finding a lot of tiny clusters is another strategy. Here, the idea is that: (1) objects that are an outlier even in the presence of a large number of small clusters are probably true outliers; and (2) smaller clusters are generally more cohesive. The drawback is that outliers can cluster together to form tiny clusters that evade detection.

10.6.4. Strengths and Weaknesses

An outlier detection method based on clustering techniques like K-means can be very effective because these algorithms have linear or nearly linear time and space complexity. Additionally, it is typically possible to find both clusters and outliers at the same time because the definitions of the two terms are complementary. The number of clusters used and the existence of outliers in the data can have a negative impact on the set of outliers generated and their scores. For instance, outliers have the potential to distort clusters generated by prototype-based algorithms. The quality of clusters generated by a clustering algorithm has a significant influence on the quality of outliers generated by the algorithm. Because each clustering algorithm is only appropriate for a specific kind of data, it is important to select the clustering algorithm carefully.

CASE STUDY

DATA ANOMALY DETECTION

A Large Comprehensive E-commerce solutions & Competitive intelligence provider our customer is a Global E-commerce solutions provider who offers MAP Violations Monitoring, Buy Box Intelligence and Competitive Pricing Monitoring to their end customers such as product owners and sellers with registered brands across multiple online marketplaces. Our client approached Mobius to enhance their platform capabilities by collecting related attributes to increase revenue, reduce cost, and check the quality of E-Commerce product listings. As an overall solution, they wanted to enhance their price monitoring solution by incorporating advanced analytical models to detect price anomalies and delivering proactive outcomes.

- **The Business Need:** A custom solution developed for our business owner can detect anomalies or extreme outliers or polar values that tend to deviate from an ideal data distribution. The primary objective of the requirement was to monitor the product price ranges with respect to multiple SKUs and retail marketplaces. Also, they required the visibility to validate the normal values against the anomalies and appropriately label them for an insightful analysis. Our solution helped the client to automate the quality management process, effective tracking of the product prices and retail SKUs in real time.
- **Challenges:** E-commerce companies similar to our customer deal with vast amounts of data, and manually monitoring prices for anomalies can be time-consuming and error-prone. A few prominent challenges include Pricing errors, inconsistencies/insufficiency in the data, whether it's due to human error, technical glitches, or other issues, anomalies in price data can cause potential revenue loss or customer dissatisfaction.

- **Solutions**: Mobius has developed a customized model that proactively identifies the anomalies, reduces the manual efforts and avoids potential errors with the application of machine learning techniques and provided the respective solution using the below steps
  - Exploratory analysis & Input data ingestion
  - Data pre-processing & Anomaly detection model creation
  - Testing and validation of predicted outputs
  - Feedback-based monitoring & Accuracy check
- **Highlights**: Generally, brands can monitor the pricing listed by sellers on the platforms to ensure that the minimum levels are not breached. However, in case of rare occurrences of price variations/fluctuations due to market demand might lead to outlier values that need to be monitored on a real-time basis. With our in-house anomaly detection process, these extremities are flagged and reported periodically to the customer for a sustained flow of price monitoring.
  - **Competitive Pricing Analysis:** Anomaly detection allows e-commerce companies to monitor the prices of their SKUs in real time.
  - **Price Optimization:** By detecting unusual pricing patterns and outliers, anomaly detection can provide valuable insights into potential opportunities for price optimization.
  - **Fraud Detection:** Anomalies in price data may indicate fraudulent activities, such as price manipulation or unauthorized changes to product prices.
  - **Improved Customer Experience:** Accurate and consistent pricing enhances customer trust and satisfaction.
  - **Demand and Supply Forecasting:** Unusual price fluctuations can be indicative of changes in demand or supply for certain products.
  - **Data-Driven Decision-Making:** By leveraging anomaly detection insights, e-commerce companies can make data-driven decisions on pricing, inventory management, and marketing strategies, leading to better overall performance and competitiveness.
  - **Early Warning S**ystem: Anomaly detection serves as an early warning system, alerting the company to potential issues in price data before they escalate into larger problems.

CLASS ACTIVITY

CHALLENGES FACED IN DETECTING AN ANOMALY

Anomaly detection, while highly beneficial, also presents several challenges that can impact its effectiveness. Understanding these challenges is essential for organizations aiming to implement or improve their anomaly detection systems. Some of the key challenges include:

- High false positive rates
- Data quality and availability
- Dynamic data and changing patterns
- Defining anomaly
- Scalability and performance
- Domain-specific challenges
- Integration with existing systems
- Cost and resource constraints
- Interpretation of results

SUMMARY

- Anomaly detection is the process of analyzing company data to find data points that don't align with a company's standard data pattern. Companies use anomalous activity detection to define system baselines, identify deviations from that baseline, and investigate inconsistent data.
- A data anomaly is any data point or suspicious event that stands out from the baseline pattern. When data unexpectedly deviates from the established dataset, it can show an early sign of system malfunctions, breaches, or newly-discovered security gaps.
- Anomaly detection models can track the ongoing success of security controls and ensure data is stored, accessed, and moved securely. Plus, these types of anomaly detection tools use logs and offer reporting capabilities to demonstrate data anomalies during security audits.
- Anomaly detection in data science is only valuable if it can identify true outliers, which means teams must train the system before it can be useful. Otherwise, the system can relay an excessive number of alerts beyond what a team could feasibly investigate.

- Supervised anomaly detection involves training a model with pre-labeled data. These datasets contain predefined normal data and clearly labeled examples of anomalies.
- With modern anomaly detection capabilities, cutting-edge business analytics and insights are now available to much smaller teams. With an enterprise-grade decision making platform like Enrich, organizations can easily build decision-making products that solve various anomaly detection use cases without depending on DevOps, software engineers, or a big-tech sized Data Science/ ML Engineering team.
- Clustering is one of the most widely used techniques in the field of unsupervised learning. Clustering-based anomaly detection operates upon the assumption that data points that are similar belong to similar clusters, as is determined by how far away they are from local centroids.One of the most popular clustering algorithms is 'K-Means.'
- Hierarchical anomaly detection uses the standard approaches to flagging anomalies but treats sub-groups of the data as independent dimensions. For instance, consider a dataset containing sale volume and visitor volume to an e-commerce website.
- Due to the massive risks posed by malicious entities and data breaches, many experts argue that modern-day cybersecurity standards are impossible to achieve without a robust, algorithmic anomaly detection system.

REVIEW QUESTIONS

1. What are the common types of fraud that anomaly detection techniques can identify?
2. Discuss the role of anomaly detection in intrusion detection systems (IDS).
3. How do the nature and type of anomalies influence the choice of detection methods?
4. Why is it important to distinguish between different types of anomalies?
5. Describe the approaches to anomaly detection.
6. Explain the concept of leverage points in the context of multivariate outliers.
7. What is a Gaussian Mixture Model (GMM) and how is it used for anomaly detection?
8. Compare and contrast the k-nearest neighbors (k-NN) method and the Local Outlier Factor (LOF) method for outlier detection.

REFERENCES

1. Abraham, B., & Chuang, A. (1989). Outlier detection and time series modeling. *Technometrics, 31*(2), 241–248.
2. Aggarwal, C. C., & Yu, P. S. (2001). Outlier detection for high dimensional data.

In *Proc. of 2001 ACM-SIGMOD Intl. Conf. on Management of Data* (pp. 37–46). ACM Press.

3. Barnett, V. (1978). The study of outliers: Purpose and model. *Applied Statistics, 27*(3), 242–250.
4. Barnett, V., & Lewis, T. (1994). *Outliers in Statistical Data*. Wiley Series in Probability and Statistics. John Wiley & Sons, 3rd edition.
5. Breunig, M. M., Kriegel, H.-P., Ng, R. T., & Sander, J. (1999). OPTICS-OF: Identifying local outliers. In *Proceedings of the Third European Conference on Principles of Data Mining and Knowledge Discovery* (pp. 262–270). Springer-Verlag.
6. Chawla, N. V., Japkowicz, N., & Kolcz, A. (Eds.). (2004). *SIGKDD Explorations Newsletter, Special Issue on Learning from Imbalanced Datasets, Volume 6*(1). ACM Press.
7. Dunagan, J., & Vempala, S. (2004). Optimal outlier removal in high-dimensional spaces. *Journal of Computer and System Sciences, 68*(2), 335–373.
8. Hawkins, D. M. (1980). *Identification of Outliers*. Monographs on Applied Probability and Statistics. Chapman & Hall.
9. Huber, P. (1974). *Robust Statistics*. Wiley.
10. Joshi, M. V., Kumar, V., & Agarwal, R. C. (2001). Evaluating boosting algorithms to classify rare classes: Comparison and improvements. In *Proc. of the 2001 IEEE Intl. Conf. on Data Mining* (pp. 257–264).
11. Knorr, E. M., & Ng, R. T. (1998). Algorithms for mining distance-based outliers in large datasets. In *Proc. of the 24th VLDB Conf.* (pp. 392–403).
12. Lane, T., & Brodley, C. E. (1997). An application of machine learning to anomaly detection. In *Proc. 20th NIST-NCSC National Information Systems Security Conf.* (pp. 366–380).
13. Lazarevic, A., Ertöz, L., Kumar, V., Ozgur, A., & Srivastava, J. (2003). A comparative study of anomaly detection schemes in network intrusion detection. In *Proc. of the 2003 SIAM Intl. Conf. on Data Mining*.
14. Lazarevic, A., Kumar, V., & Srivastava, J. (2005). Intrusion detection: A survey. In P. Dasgupta & S. N. M. Vishwanathan (Eds.), *Managing Cyber Threats: Issues, Approaches and Challenges* (pp. 19–80). Kluwer Academic Publisher.
15. Markou, M., & Singh, S. (2003a). Novelty detection: A review—Part 1: Statistical approaches. *Signal Processing, 83*(12), 2481–2497.
16. Markou, M., & Singh, S. (2003b). Novelty detection: A review—Part 2: Neural network-based approaches. *Signal Processing, 83*(12), 2499–2521.
17. Rousseeuw, P. J., & Leroy, A. M. (1987). *Robust Regression and Outlier Detection*. John Wiley & Sons, Inc.
18. Teng, H., Chen, K., & Lu, S. (1990). Adaptive real-time anomaly detection using inductively generated sequential patterns. In *Proceedings of IEEE Computer Society Symposium on Research in Security and Privacy* (pp. 278–284). IEEE Computer Society Press.

19. Weigend, A. S., Mangeas, M., & Srivastava, A. N. (1995). Nonlinear gated experts for time-series – Discovering regimes and avoiding overfitting. *International Journal of Neural Systems, 6*(4), 373–399.

Index

D

FSC
www.fsc.org
MIX
Papier | Fördert
gute Waldnutzung
FSC® C083411

Kolibri 360 GmbH
Ferdinand-Jühlke-Straße 7
99095 Erfurt, Deutschland
produktsicherheit@kolibri360.de